RICHARD STRAUSS

SERIES EDITED BY STANLEY SADIE

The Master Musicians Series

Titles available from Schirmer Books

Brahms	*Malcolm MacDonald*
Elgar	*Robert Anderson*
Handel	*Donald Burrows*
Liszt	*Derek Watson*
Mahler	*Michael Kennedy*
Rachmaninoff	*Geoffrey Norris*
Sibelius	*Robert Layton*
Richard Strauss	*Michael Kennedy*
Stravinsky	*Paul Griffiths*
Vivaldi	*Michael Talbot*

RICHARD STRAUSS

MICHAEL KENNEDY

SCHIRMER BOOKS
An Imprint of Simon & Schuster Macmillan
New York

Prentice Hall International
London Mexico City New Delhi Singapore Sydney Toronto

Schirmer Books
An Imprint of Simon & Schuster Macmillan
866 Third Avenue
New York, NY 10022

First published in Great Britain by J. M. Dent & Sons Ltd.
This edition published in Great Britain by
Oxford University Press
Walton Street
Oxford OX2 6DP

Library of Congress Catalog Card Card Number: 95-22574

ISBN: 0-02-864517-0

PRINTED IN GREAT BRITAIN

Printing number
1 2 3 4 5 6 7 8 9 10

Library of Congress Cataloging-in-Publication Data
Kennedy, Michael, 1926–
    Richard Strauss / Michael Kennedy.—1st American ed.
      p.   cm.—(The master musicians)
    Includes bibliographical references and index.
    ISBN 0–02–864517—0 (hard cover)
    1. Strauss, Richard, 1864–1949. 2. Composers—Germany—Biography.
I. Title. II. Series: Master musicians series.
ML410.S93K45 1996
780'.92—dc20   95–22574
    [B]   CIP
                                                         MN

Typeset by Hope Services (Abingdon) Ltd.
Printed in Great Britain
on acid-free paper by
Butler & Tanner Ltd.
Frome, Somerset

Preface

Richard Strauss's music is more popular with the public than it has ever been, but it still divides critical opinion into friendly and hostile camps. It always will; it is that kind of music. You can take it or leave it, but if you leave it you will miss a great deal of pleasure. Strauss himself summed it up in his reply to a young man who confessed that, try as he might, he could not bring himself to like *Der Rosenkavalier*. 'What a shame for you', said Strauss. Now that Elgar and Mahler have been rehabilitated, Richard Strauss remains the most misunderstood and misrepresented great composer of the last hundred years, Schoenberg included.

Nobody writing about Strauss in English can fail to acknowledge the debt owed to Norman Del Mar's masterly three-volume survey of the works and to William Mann's critical study of the operas. They were able to go into detail inappropriate to this series, and I unreservedly recommend readers who seek more information on the works to consult these fine books. Certain of Strauss's works which Norman Del Mar and William Mann felt unsure about I happen to admire, so I have allowed my enthusiasm to rise above the 'received opinions'.

Strauss the man is equally controversial. He was the subject, or object, of a grossly distorted television film by Ken Russell, and he has been pilloried in a book by George R. Marek because he did not involve himself in the realms of higher statesmanship during two world wars. The facts speak for themselves, and I have tried to present these facts without bias so that Strauss's position may be judged fairly.

In assembling illustrations for the first edition I was aided by Boosey & Hawkes, the Mansell Collection, the *Radio Times* Hulton Picture Library, the late Dr Franz Strauss and the Richard Strauss Archive at Garmisch.

I gratefully acknowledge permission to reprint extracts from Strauss's correspondence with Hofmannsthal, thanks to the courtesy of William

Collins, Sons & Co. Music examples are reproduced by kind permission of the publishers: Universal Edition (London) Ltd (Ex. 1); Steingräber Verlag (U.K. agents: Bosworth & Co. Ltd) (Ex. 2.); Peters Edition London, New York and Frankfurt (Exx. 3–8); Musikverlag S.E.C. Leuckart (U.K. agents: Novello & Co. Ltd) (Ex. 9), and Boosey & Hawkes, Music Publishers Ltd (Exx. 10–28).

NOTE ON THE SECOND EDITION

For this new edition, I have enlarged and revised the text and appendices. I am grateful to those kind people who have pointed out errors and omissions, especially to Mr K. A. Pollak. I owe a particular debt of gratitude to Dr Stephan Kohler, director of the Richard Strauss Institute in Munich, for his advice and practical help. In particular I acknowledge the Institute's kindness in providing me with the entry from Strauss's private diary quoted on pp. 107–8. I am grateful to Thames & Hudson for permission to quote from Kurt Wilhelm's *Richard Strauss: an Intimate Portrait*, translated by Mary Whittall.

M.K.
1995

For Harold and Hannelore,
with my love,
remembering Salzburg 1969

Mein Herz und Seel' wird bei Ihr bleiben
wo Sie geht und steht, bis in alle Ewigkeit.
26th September 1974

This revised and enlarged edition is dedicated, without permission and
with affection, to Felicity Lott, 1995.

Contents

Preface   *v*
Illustrations   *xi*

 1   Munich childhood   1
 2   'Richard the Third'   7
 3   Tone-poet   14
 4   Weimar and Munich   20
 5   A hero's life   32
 6   Vulcan's labours   40
 7   Comedy for music   47
 8   Airy-fairy   51
 9   The crisis   58
10   Vienna   64
11   Helen and Arabella   77
12   Under the Nazis   85
13   Gregor and Krauss   95
14   Greeting to the world   106
15   Early works   114
16   The tone-poems   120
17   The operas (1)   132
18   The operas (2)   162
19   Ballets and other orchestral works   175
20   Songs and choral music   184

     Appendices
     A   Calendar   197
     B   List of works   212
     C   Personalia   221
     D   Select bibliography   225
     E   The self-quotations in *Ein Heldenleben*   229

     Index   231

Illustrations

Between pages 116 and 117

1 Strauss in London, 1903 (*The Mansell Collection. Photo: E. O. Hoppé*)
2 Autographed photo given to Elgar, 1904 (*by kind permission of the Trustees of the Elgar Foundation*)
3 With his wife, Pauline, in 1914 (*The Mansell Collection*)
4 Part of the autograph MS. of the quartet 'Eine Störrische zu trösten' from *Ariadne auf Naxos*, 1912 (*Strauss Bild-Archiv, Garmisch*)
5 A signed photograph of Strauss in 1925
6 Conducting the *Alpine Symphony* in Munich, 1941 (*Strauss Bild-Archiv, Garmisch*)
7 With Hugo von Hofmannsthal at Garmisch, 1911 (*Strauss Bild-Archiv, Garmisch*)
8 With Pauline and their elder grandchild, Richard, 1929 (*Strauss Bild-Archiv, Garmisch*)
9 Arriving at Northolt Airport, 4 October 1947 (*The Associated Press*)
10 In Berlin, 1939, with Heinz Tietjen and Herbert von Karajan (*Strauss Bild-Archiv, Garmisch*)
11 With Clemens Krauss in London, 1947 (*Popperfoto*)
12 Rehearsing the Philharmonia Orchestra in London, 1947 (*Press Illustrations*)

'Haven't I the right, after all, to write what music I please? I cannot bear the tragedy of the present time. I want to create joy. I need it.'

Richard Strauss, in 1924.

'I wish you well, better than most people have done in your life. You have not looked for many friends, and have not had many.'

Hugo von Hofmannsthal to Strauss, in 1918.

Munich childhood

The long lifetime of Richard Strauss, from 1864 to 1949, spanned almost a century of an unparalleled period in the history of mankind. Music, no less than science, progressed through major developments and cataclysms. Strauss grew up beneath the giant shadow thrown across European art by Wagner; a glow from the fading rays of the Wagnerian sunset was still warming him in his own long twilight. Not for him Stravinsky's indefatigable self-renewal nor Schoenberg's impassioned intellectual theorizing: he remained consistently within his own capabilities, which he knew exactly, their extent and their limitations. 'I'm the only composer nowadays', he wrote in 1916, 'with some real humour and a sense of fun and marked gift for parody.' If his music lacks mystical and spiritual depth—and it does, except in one late work—it has worldly, human rapture and insight, realism, and humour. From first to last he put his trust in tonality, melody, dramatic instinct, and a vein of fantasy which belongs to all the greatest story-tellers. In his young manhood he was regarded by many as the very arch-fiend of modernism and cacophony; in his old age he was debunked as an irrelevant survivor of a vanished epoch. Yet uninterruptedly since the first decade of the twentieth century several of his operas have held the stage of the world's leading opera-houses, and no symphony orchestra can plan rewarding programmes without his symphonic poems in its repertory. To adapt a saying by Benjamin Jowett, you must believe in Strauss whatever the pundits may tell you.

Richard Georg Strauss was born in Munich at 2 Altheimer Eck, on 11 June 1864. He was the first-born of Franz Joseph Strauss (1822–1905), principal horn-player in the Munich Court Orchestra, and his second wife, Josephine Pschorr (1837–1910), a member of the wealthy family of brewers. Franz was a great instrumentalist and a cantankerous man, embittered by a hard childhood. His first wife and their two children died in a cholera epidemic. A humble musician, he was regarded by the Pschorr family as a poor match for one of their daughters. He courted Josephine for seven years before their marriage in Munich Cathedral in August 1863. Musically Franz was intensely conservative, worshipping Haydn, Mozart, and Beethoven, and detesting the later works of 'Mephisto Richard Wagner', as he called him, marvellously as he played the horn solos in

Tristan, Die Meistersinger and *Der Ring des Nibelungen*. Because of his financial independence, Franz Strauss was able to treat conductors and composers with boorish rudeness and get away with it. The conductor Hans Richter once said: 'Strauss's son may be happy that he has not his father in his orchestra'.[1] Richard said that his father 'would have considered it dishonest ever to revise a judgment on an artistic subject once he had arrived at it'.[2] The worst of him is shown by his refusal—honest, in his own lights—to join the rest of the orchestra in standing in silent tribute to Wagner on the morrow of his death;[3] the best by his solemn dedication to his work, for he would spend weeks preparing for difficult solos in Weber, Beethoven, Mendelssohn—and Wagner—and would arrive at rehearsal an hour before the rest of the orchestra to practise his part.

Temperamental and tyrannical though Franz was at home, his marriage was happy, and Richard's childhood was untroubled. Religion played no part in his upbringing. At four and a half Richard had pianoforte lessons from August Tombo, his father's harpist colleague, and later from Carl Niest, and at eight Benno Walter, his father's cousin, taught him the violin. He saw his first operas (*Der Freischütz* and *Die Zauberflöte*) when he was six and, at the same age, had written his first compositions, a Christmas carol and the *Schneiderpolka* for pianoforte. Alongside his musical training he received a classical education. After elementary schooling from 1870 to 1874 he entered the Ludwigsgymnasium, Munich. 'I was always fonder of composing than studying,' he wrote,[4] 'but I managed to pass my matriculation examination without discredit at the age of eighteen.' He never went to an academy of music but, from the age of eleven, had a thorough education in musical theory, harmony and instrumentation from one of the court conductors, Friedrich Meyer. His father insisted on a firm grounding in the old masters. Strauss said (inaccurately) that he heard nothing but classical music until he was sixteen. Thereafter, despite Franz's disapproval and discouragement, he came to know the Wagner operas in score and performance. His childhood was musically blessed by taking place within the influence of the Munich Opera 'and its wonderful orchestra'. But his first experiences of Wagner on the stage left him puzzled. 'The prejudices inculcated by upbringing may have influenced me strongly', he wrote.[5] 'It was not until, against my father's orders, I studied the score of *Tristan* that I entered into this magic work, and later into *Der Ring*.'

We receive a vivid account of the teenage Strauss's musical tastes from

[1] C. Fifield, *True Artist and True Friend: a Biography of Hans Richter* (Oxford, 1993), p. 27.

[2] R. Strauss, 'Reminiscences of my Father' in *Recollections and Reflections* (Zürich, 1949; London, 1953).

[3] E. Newman, *The Life of Richard Wagner*, vol. iii (New York, 1941), p. 378.

[4] R. Strauss, 'Letter on the *Humanistische Gymnasium*' in *Recollections and Reflections*, op. cit.

[5] R. Strauss, 'Reminiscences of my Father', op. cit.

his letters[6] to his friend Ludwig Thuille (1861–1907), an orphan whom Richard first met in 1872. Thuille was regarded as virtually a member of the Strauss family. He became professor of music at the Munich Conservatory and composed three operas, symphonic, choral, and chamber works. In their boyhood Strauss told him what he was composing, they exchanged views on technicalities, and they ribbed each other about their enthusiasms. Thus, Strauss writing from Munich on 6 February 1878, when he was thirteen, says:

> I find your criticism not entirely correct, for the *Leonore* Overture [No. 3], as wonderfully beautiful as it is, is never greater than the *Jupiter* Symphony. For me Beethoven is *never* greater than Mozart, the two of them are at the exact same level in their own way; Mozart is even more many-sided than Beethoven . . . My trio has been performed several times already at my uncle's, Anton Knözinger, royal chief auditor and prosecutor, to whom I dedicated the piece as cellist . . .

On 1 March 1878:

> A good musician must also be educated! . . . Recently we had a Greek exam, a Greek quiz, a Latin and maths exam, of which I passed the first with a one/two, the second with a one, the third with a two; we haven't had the fourth back yet. We have geography and history exams next . . .

Later the same month:

> Your criticism I more or less agree with, I am only surprised that you don't mention anything about the splendid Samson aria and its composition and you shouldn't call Saint-Saëns a dolt or an ass; on the contrary, he is a genius . . . I have heard very nice things by him, for example a very pretty piano quartet, and a G minor piano concerto that he performed here himself this winter was very much praised *by my father*, which says a great deal in the case of a new composer . . .

In June 1878 Strauss went to a performance of *Siegfried*. He reported to Thuille:

> I was bored stiff, I was quite frightfully bored, so horribly that I cannot even tell you. But it was beautiful, incredibly beautiful, this wealth of melodies, this dramatic intensity, this fine instrumentation, and it was clever, eminently beautiful! You will think 'he's lost his senses', well I will make it all right again and tell you it was dreadful . . .

He then described the opera, with musical examples, unflatteringly but conceded that 'the only thing that at least *made sense* was the song of the wild bird'. He was much more impressed by Auber's *La Muette de Portici*, a composer for whom he retained affection.

---

[6] F. Trenner (ed.), *Richard Strauss–Ludwig Thuille: Ein Briefwechsel* (Tutzing: Schneider, 1980), trans. by Susan Gillespie in *Richard Strauss and his World*, B. Gilliam (ed.) (Princeton, 1992), pp. 193–226.

The boy's literary tastes also emerge from this correspondence. He wrote to Thuille:

That you advise me to give up Shakespeare surprises me very much; perhaps you think I don't understand the half of it; but there I can tell you without lying that up to now (I have read *King John*, *Richard II* and *Henry IV parts 1 and 2*) not a speck has been unclear to me and I like him enormously, especially in *Henry IV* the great scene between Henry IV and the Prince of Wales in the fifth act of the second part. I have now also got *Ivanhoe* by the splendid Walter Scott and I am looking forward to it very much . . . I went to *La Dame Blanche*, opera by Boieldieu which I liked a great deal. Such noble melodies, such magnificence and drama and such beautiful instrumentation!

In October 1878 he heard *Die Walküre* and wrote a sarcastic letter to Thuille pretending to compare Mozart adversely with Wagner and adding: 'At a couple of points in the third act, for example Wotan's Farewell and the Magic Fire, one can still tell what key one is in—I can never forgive Wagner for this outrage against his own music . . .' In December 1878 he heard Clara Schumann play Beethoven's G major piano concerto

with a technique, an attack and an artistic interpretation the likes of which I never heard before. Every note she struck was pure, every phrase she played corresponded to the overall artistic quality of the composition . . . Here there is none of the fakery with which piano players of both sexes try to rouse the audience to enthusiasm and of which even Herr von Bülow cannot claim to be entirely free, as Papa said, although he plays delightfully (I have heard him myself); here the sole concern is for art itself . . .

Schoolboy fun pervades these letters. Strauss to Thuille on 22 February 1879:

O thou infatuated Schumann fan! A Schumann *adagio* comparable to a Beethoven *adagio*! ha! ha! ha! ha! ha! ha! That is terrible. What are you thinking! That is the limit! That makes one want to run and hide. Schumann may have beautiful things, but comparable to Beethoven! ha! ha! ha! ha! ha! ha! . . . As far as his things for piano are concerned, I find the *Kinderszenen* and some of the *Fantasiestücke* the most beautiful, although once he has a rhythm he rides it so to death that one often can't stand listening to him . . . I promised to send you my critique of *Lohenyellow (Lohengreen)*; the introduction consists of an A major rustling of the violins in the highest register, which sounds terribly sweet and sickly like the whole opera; there are beautiful moments in it but then again such boring stuff . . . the orchestration is rough, the whole opera has terribly much in common with *Euryanthe* (i.e. plagiarised), only the plot is beautiful . . .

On 22 July 1879 Strauss wrote:

I have composed a romance in E flat major for clarinet and orchestra [Wo061] . . . which turned out quite well . . . I have finally finished the A minor overture [Wo062]; I tell you, it makes a hellish noise, but I believe it would be effective . . . I am now playing Mozart piano concertos diligently from our Mozart edition, and I tell you it is splendid, for me it is the greatest enjoyment. This wealth of ideas, this richness of harmonies and yet moderation in everything, the splendid, graceful, tender, delicious thoughts themselves, this fine accompaniment! But to play anything like this is not possible any more! Now nothing but smarminess will do—either sweet rustlings or harsh booming and thundering or uninteresting musical nonsense! While Mozart, using few means, says everything that can refresh and truly please and improve a listener, those others, applying all the means, say nothing at all or practically nothing. This is precisely the world turned upside down! Enough to make you want to run away! But what I have sworn is that when some day I perform in a larger concert, and can be accompanied well, in a fine manner, then I will play a Mozart concerto.

He kept his word, at Meiningen in 1885.

In another letter to Thuille, dated Tuesday, 26 August 1879, Strauss describes graphically the events which were to lead over thirty years later to *Eine Alpensinfonie*:

Recently we made a great hiking party to the top of the Heimgarten, on which day we walked for twelve hours. At two in the morning we rode on a handcart to the village, which lies at the foot of the mountain. Then we climbed by the light of lanterns in pitch-dark night and arrived at the peak after a five-hour march. There one has a splendid view. Lake Stafelsee (Murnau), Riegsee, Ammersee, Würnsee, Kochelsee, Walchensee. Then the Isar valley with mountains, Ötz and Stubeir glaciers. Innsbruck mountains, *Zugspitze*, and so on. Then we hiked down the other side to get to Lake Walchensee, but we took a wrong trail and had to climb around in the midday heat for three hours with no path. Lake Walchensee is a beautiful lake but makes a melancholy impression, since it is enclosed by forests and high mountains . . . Then we took a boat across the lake to Uhrfelden [Urfelden]. It lies at the foot of Mount Herzogstand, which is next to the Heimgarten. From there an hour over Mount Kössel [Kessel], an hour to Lake Kochelsee (Kösselberg Inn). On the way there a terrible thunder storm had overtaken us, which uprooted trees and threw stones in our faces. We hardly had time to find a dry spot before the storm broke. Lake Kochelsee, a very romantic beautiful lake, made huge waves so that it was impossible even to think about crossing it. After the storm had passed, we had to settle for walking all the way around the lake, whether we wanted to or not. On the way the rain came again and that is how we arrived in Schlehdorf, after a breakneck march (we did not rest for a single moment)— tired, soaked to the skin—and spent the night, then the next morning we rode as calm as could be in the hay wagon on to Murnau. The hike was interesting, unusual and original in the highest degree. The next day I described the whole hike on the piano. Naturally huge tone paintings and smarminess à la Wagner . . .

These are writings and thoughts of an exceptionally intelligent boy who was already an experienced composer. A musical prodigy, he was also well balanced and normal in his daily life. A school report when he was eleven, written by his form-master, glows with praise:

5

His enthusiasm is huge, he enjoys learning, and it comes easily to him. Pleasure in each new accomplishment spurs him on to work yet harder. He pays close attention in class, nothing escapes him. And yet he is incapable of sitting still for a moment, his bench is a torment to him. Unclouded merriment and high spirits sparkle in his blue eyes day after day; candour and good nature are written on his face. His work is good, very good . . .[7]

Franz Strauss conducted a semi-professional orchestra known as 'Wilde Gung'l'. At its weekly rehearsals Richard learned much of the practical side of orchestration. When he was a few days short of his sixteenth birthday a gavotte he had written was played at one of its concerts. In 1881 he composed a setting of a chorus from Sophocles' *Electra* which was performed at the Gymnasium. A string quartet in A major which he wrote in 1879–80 was played in Munich on 14 March 1881 by a quartet led by Benno Walter. A *Festmarsch* in E flat major, composed in 1876, was played by 'Wilde Gung'l' on 26 March 1881 and was published as his Op. 1 later that year.[8] Four days later Hermann Levi conducted the Court Orchestra in the sixteen-year-old's Symphony in D minor. There is no sign in this work (now recorded) of the real Strauss, but it is attractive in its Mendelssohnian way and is gracefully scored. Other works dating from this time included the *Five Piano Pieces*, Op. 3, and the piano sonata in B minor, Op. 5.

For the winter and spring terms of 1882–3 Strauss attended Munich University to read philosophy, aesthetics and the history of art, but left to concentrate on music. At the age of eighteen he stood on the threshold of a meteoric ascent to national and international fame. No tale here of an unhappy, poverty-haunted childhood; no serious strife between parents and son; no struggle to adopt a career in the face of opposition. Strauss's sister Johanna, three years his junior, wrote of their childhood holidays: 'Excursions to lonely valleys among the peaks, then coffee with whipped cream and little cakes . . . There were innumerable joys and freedom which ever remained in Richard's heart.' Nevertheless, Franz Strauss was short-tempered and tyrannical, often quarrelling with Richard while music-making. The mediator was Strauss's mother, on whom the strain was eventually to tell.

[7] K. Wilhelm, *Richard Strauss personlich* (Munich, 1984), trans. by Mary Whittall as *Richard Strauss, an Intimate Portrait* (London, 1989), p. 22.

[8] The publishers were Breitkopf & Härtel, but the cost was underwritten by Strauss's uncle, Georg Pschorr.

2

'Richard the Third'

While he was at university, Richard Strauss made his first public appearance in Vienna, in the Bösendorfersaal, as pianist with the violinist Benno Walter in his own Violin Concerto, which he had composed while at school. He described himself as 'never technically efficient'[1] as a pianist because he did not enjoy practising. That performance was on 5 December 1882, and the critic Eduard Hanslick noted 'unusual talent'. A week earlier, on 27 November, his *Serenade* in E flat major for thirteen wind instruments had been performed in Dresden by the court orchestra under Franz Wüllner, the first Strauss first-performance in a city which was to hear many of them. A year later, on 28 November 1883, Hermann Levi conducted Strauss's Concert Overture in C minor in Munich. One can imagine how the news must have travelled on the German musical grapevine that the son of that old curmudgeon Strauss the hornplayer had genuine talent as a composer. Levi and Wüllner were celebrated conductors of their day. Levi was forty-four and had been court conductor at Munich since 1872. He conducted the first *Parsifal* at Bayreuth in July 1882. (Franz Strauss played in the orchestra and took Richard to hear the new work.) Wüllner, at this date aged fifty, was in Munich from 1864 to 1877. He then went to Dresden. These musicians recognized something extraordinary in the work of the eighteen-year-old Strauss.

In December 1883, Strauss visited Dresden as guest of his father's friend Ferdinand Böckmann, principal cellist of the opera orchestra. Together they gave the second performance of Strauss's Cello Sonata. Just before Christmas Strauss moved on to Berlin. There he went to the opera, met painters, sculptors and poets, and completed his Symphony in F minor, which had its first performance in December 1884 not in Germany, nor indeed in Europe, but in New York where that astonishing talent-spotter Theodore Thomas conducted it for the Philharmonic Society, having been shown the manuscript by his old friend Franz Strauss while on a visit to Europe.

---

[1] R. Strauss, 'Recollections of my Youth and Years of Apprenticeship' in *Recollections and Reflections*, op. cit.

In Berlin, Richard was given a free pass to all performances at the opera and playhouse. Thus he saw Sardou's play *Fedora* which excited him 'enormously', he wrote to his sister. 'I was still trembling in every fibre three hours later.' He continued to report his musical experiences to Thuille. The Joachim Quartet was 'the finest in existence. The sheer beauty of the sound, the purity, the ensemble, the wonderful nuances, everything you could possibly ask for is there.' He thought the woodwind and horns of the Berlin Philharmonic were 'wretched' compared with those of the Dresden court orchestra. He heard several performances of Brahms's Third Symphony. At first, as he told his father, he could not understand it, but after a third hearing he found it 'really very beautiful' and told Thuille that it was 'probably the most important symphony that has ever been written . . . I'm beginning to get very attached to Brahms as a whole'.

His own Concert Overture in C minor was performed in Berlin while he was there, as was his Cello Sonata, and there were several performances of the *Serenade* for thirteen wind instruments. Four of these were by the orchestra of the Konzerthaus conducted by Benjamin Bilse. Strauss found Bilse's interpretation much too slow. 'I thought they were all going to sleep and the players' intonation was completely out.' On 27 February the *Serenade* was played by the Meiningen Orchestra conducted by Franz Mannstädt. While in Berlin, too, Strauss visited art galleries and exhibitions—as he always did in every city he visited throughout his life—and went to many balls ('I seldom get to bed before 1.30', he told Thuille, 'very often it's 3 or 4 and it was 7 after the Artists' Ball'), and indulged in several flirtations, one with the wife of a sculptor. And in the house of Hermann Klose, a coffee dealer and former Munich resident, he learned to play the card game Skat which became a lifelong passion.

The most significant factor in the Berlin visit, however, was Strauss's first meeting with the great conductor and pianist, Hans von Bülow, who had been court conductor at Munich from 1864 to 1869 and was now at Meiningen where, within a few months of his appointment in 1880, he had made the orchestra into a superb instrument, the first virtuoso orchestra of modern times even though it contained only forty-eight players compared with the Vienna Philharmonic's ninety. The Meiningen's strength was in the marvellous precision of its ensemble playing rather than in its beauty of tone. There was no opera at the Meiningen court, so Bülow was free to rehearse the symphonic repertory with a thoroughness undreamed of elsewhere.

Strauss's first publisher, Eugen Spitzweg, a friend of Bülow, sent the wind *Serenade*—which Strauss later in life described as 'nothing more than the respectable work of a music student'[2]—to Bülow, who included

[2] R. Strauss, 'Reminiscences of Hans von Bülow' in *Recollections and Reflections*, op. cit.

it in his orchestra's touring repertoire. 'An uncommonly gifted young man', Bülow wrote to the impresario Hermann Wolff. 'By far the most striking personality since Brahms.' Even though he himself had not conducted the *Serenade* (except at rehearsal), Bülow commissioned Strauss to write a similar piece. That summer he composed the four-movement *Suite* in B flat major, also for thirteen wind instruments. 'Happy days of my youth,' he reflected, 'when I could still work to order'—but this was a cynical jest. Strauss could always, and did always work, to order or not. His industry compels admiration. He was not a composer who waited for the spark from heaven to fall; he worked and worked, in the hope that something good would sometimes be the result. From 1878 onwards his list of compositions grew at an amazing rate. He was particularly prolific from 1881 to 1885. In addition to works already mentioned, he had composed within this period the Cello Sonata, First Horn Concerto, the Pianoforte Quartet, many songs, including the Nine Lieder to words by Gilm which contained his first masterpieces in this genre, *Zueignung*, *Die Nacht* and *Allerseelen*, and the Brahmsian *Wandrers Sturmlied*, a setting of Goethe for a six-part chorus and orchestra. 'Work is a constant and never tiring source of enjoyment to which I have completely dedicated myself', he wrote at this time.

Bülow's percipience in detecting Strauss's potential greatness was all the more to his credit in view of his reaction to the first music by Strauss which he encountered. Spitzweg in 1881 had sent him the *Five Piano Pieces*. Bülow replied that he disliked them profoundly—'unripe and precocious. . . . I miss the spirit of youthful invention. . . . We have here to deal not with genius but with the kind of talent that comes ten a penny'. But by 1884, when Spitzweg was losing money on the several Strauss works which his little firm of Joseph Aibl had published, Bülow bolstered his resolve by this advice: 'Stay with him. In five years you will make money.' Jestingly he called his protégé 'Richard the Third', because after Richard the First (Wagner) there could be no Second; but the jest was apposite, and Bülow knew it. Bülow accepted the new *Suite*, rehearsed it in Meiningen and, showing thoughtfulness, decided to give the first performance when the orchestra visited Munich. Moreover, he invited the composer to conduct it. Strauss was overjoyed but pointed out that he had never had a baton in his hand before, so when could he rehearse? Bülow replied that the orchestra had no time for rehearsals on tour. On the day of the concert, 18 November 1884, Strauss went to Bülow's hotel where he found the great man 'in a dreadful mood', raving against Munich, which had driven out Wagner and himself. Bülow did not attend the performance. Chain-smoking, he paced furiously up and down the conductor's room. When Strauss returned, his father looked in to thank Bülow.

> Like a furious lion he pounced upon my father: 'You have nothing to thank me for,' he shouted, 'I have not forgotten what you have done to me in this

damned city of Munich. What I did today I did because your son has talent and not for you.' Without saying a word my father left. . . . This scene had, of course, completely spoiled my début for me. Only Bülow was suddenly in the best of spirits.[3]

In the first quarter of 1885 Wüllner conducted (in Cologne) the first European performance of Strauss's F minor Symphony, and at Meiningen Bülow conducted the first performance of the Horn Concerto. At this time also, Bülow's assistant conductor, Franz Mannstädt, was appointed conductor of the Berlin Philharmonic. Through Spitzweg, Bülow—having rejected Felix Weingartner—offered Strauss the vacant post—'the most joyous surprise imaginable', Strauss wrote to Bülow on 26 May. Perhaps, he suggested, he could occasionally conduct preliminary rehearsals, but the big attraction was to be able to attend all Bülow's rehearsals and 'to study closely your interpretation of our symphonic masterpieces'. In preparation, he went in July to the Raff Conservatoire in Frankfurt to attend Bülow's lectures on Beethoven's pianoforte works.

On 1 October 1885, three months after his twenty-first birthday, Strauss took up his new post—assistant to the greatest conductor of the day, with a virtuoso orchestra on which to learn. Every morning he attended Bülow's rehearsals:

Ever since that time the memory of the works he then conducted, all of them by heart, has never been effaced from my mind. In particular, I found the way in which he brought out the poetic content of Beethoven's and Wagner's works absolutely convincing. . . . Everything was of compelling necessity, born of the form and content of the work itself.[4]

For a fortnight this apprenticeship continued, 'a good grounding in conducting, at least in theory', Strauss wrote. Bülow conducted both performances and rehearsals by heart; at the latter he gave Strauss the scores, frequently asking him searching questions. Practical work began on 15 October when, for Strauss's public début, Bülow invited him to play the solo part in Mozart's C minor pianoforte concerto (K491) and then to conduct his own F minor Symphony. In the audience was Brahms, who was in Meiningen for rehearsals of the Fourth Symphony, which was to have its first performance on 25 October. He commented: 'Quite pretty, young man.' He added what Strauss called a 'memorable piece of advice':

'Take a good look at Schubert's dances, and try your luck at inventing simple eight-bar melodies.' . . . I also remember clearly a further criticism made by the great master: 'Your symphony is too full of thematic irrelevances. There is no point in this piling up of many themes which are only contrasted rhythmically

[3] R. Strauss, 'Reminiscences of Hans von Bülow', op. cit.
[4] For a less adulatory view, see Weingartner's *Über das Dirigieren* (Leipzig, 1898; 3rd edn 1905; Eng. trans. New York, 1969).

on a single triad.' It was then that I realized that counterpoint is only justified when poetic necessity compels a temporary union of two or several themes contrasted as sharply as possible.[5]

The performance of the Brahms symphony was to be a turning-point for Strauss. He noted the contrast between Bülow's enthusiasm and conscientiousness and the composer's indifference towards the dynamics and presentation of his work. Nevertheless the second performance of the symphony a few days later at Frankfurt led to a bitter quarrel between Bülow and Brahms because Brahms elected to conduct it himself. Bülow, who was naturally impulsive and was becoming a little tired of Meiningen, where players he had trained kept leaving for posts elsewhere, resigned. Strauss, after a month's training and very little practical experience, became his successor on 1 November 1885. Yet conductors are born, not made, and Strauss was a born conductor. He was immediately at ease and in command on the rostrum—just as Gustav Mahler was, with even less training and preparation for the task. As Felix Mottl said: 'One stands up and can do it.'

The Duke of Sachsen-Meiningen, Georg II, made every effort to persuade Bülow to return. He failed, and began to lose interest in the orchestra now that he had no star conductor. He proposed to reduce the number of players, but offered Strauss an extension of his contract. Strauss at this juncture received the offer of the post of third conductor at Munich. Rather half-heartedly, he signed a three-year contract to run from 1 August 1886 and left Meiningen during April.

The six months at Meiningen were potent in several ways in their influence on Strauss. First, there was Bülow, whose magic was such that working with him for only a month left an indelible impression. There was a memorable evening together in his home when Bülow played Johann Strauss waltzes—'the most endearing of all God-gifted dispensers of joy', Strauss called his namesake.[6] How could he have written the *Rosenkavalier* waltzes without the example of 'this wonderful phenomenon'? Then there was the theatre at Meiningen. Not only did the Duke make history with his court orchestra, he was equally enlightened about plays. With a small company of gifted players, he staged productions in which every role was carefully studied, cast and rehearsed. Close attention was paid to details of production. Strauss attended as many performances as he could: his profound sense of theatre was developed there. When he left Meiningen a member of the ducal entourage told him that they were sorry to be losing 'the best cheer leader we've had in our theatre for a long time'.

Yet the most far-reaching influence came not from Bülow but from one of the violinists in the orchestra, Alexander Ritter. He was fifty-two

---

[5] R. Strauss, 'Reminiscences of Hans von Bülow', op. cit.
[6] R. Strauss, 'On Johann Strauss' in *Recollections and Reflections*, op. cit.

in 1885 and had been at school with Bülow. He was the son of Julie Ritter, a generous patron of Wagner, and became a conductor and composer of minor rank. He married Wagner's niece Franziska, came to know Wagner well and was a member of Liszt's circle at Weimar. With his enthusiasm for the music of Berlioz, Liszt and Wagner and his dislike of the music of Brahms, he was firmly entrenched in the avant-garde camp of *Zukunftsmusik* (the music of the future), but he struck hard times and ran a music shop. It was from this that Bülow rescued him to play at Meiningen. When Strauss arrived in Meiningen, Ritter's interest in his benefactor's protégé was aroused, especially when he discovered that Strauss's upbringing had been thoroughly conservative. He invited the young man to his home. Strauss described the effect in these words: 'His influence on me was in the nature of the storm-wind':

> I scarcely knew Richard Wagner's writings at all. Ritter, with patient explanations, introduced me to them and to Schopenhauer; he made me familiar with them and proved to me that the road led from the 'musical expressionist' Beethoven . . . via Liszt who, with Wagner, had realized correctly that Beethoven had expanded the sonata form to its utmost limits . . . and that in Beethoven's epigones and especially in Brahms, sonata form had become an empty shell. . . . New ideas must search for new forms—this basic principle of Liszt's symphonic works, in which the poetic idea was really the formative element, became henceforward the guiding principle for my own symphonic work.[7]

Ritter's anti-Semitism was particularly strong, but Strauss did not need instruction from this teacher in this field. His father was at one with Wagner on this subject alone, and Richard grew up listening to Franz inveighing against Hermann Levi's choice of tempi and shouting at Richard, when he erred similarly, 'Why this Jewish haste?' This was the conventional, thoughtless anti-Semitism typical of the German *petite bourgeoisie*. It may be compared with some Englishmen's 'hatred' of 'those damned foreigners'. Yet Englishmen who speak like that often have strong personal liking and admiration for individual foreigners, just as Strauss had strong liking and admiration for individual Jews. Some would say that the gas-chambers were the logical result of even such casual racial prejudice, but only a fanatic would press the charge against Strauss. It should be remembered, too, that many opera houses and orchestras were controlled by Jews: to label a rival 'anti-Semitic' was sometimes a device intended to harm a career or forestall an engagement.

In 1855 Strauss was deeply distressed by his mother's mental illness which necessitated her removal to a nursing-home then and at frequent intervals between 1894 and 1909. His own cultivation of a phlegmatic temperament—'diverting and dispersing the dark thoughts', in his

---

[7] R. Strauss, 'Recollections of my Youth and Years of Apprenticeship', op. cit.

words—was undoubtedly the psychological result of this family crisis. It seems that Josephine Strauss's illness, at the significant age of forty-seven, was caused by the strain of maintaining some kind of tranquillity in her relationship with her choleric husband. Richard has said that making music with his father was pleasure mixed with apprehension, for Franz at home was 'very vehement, short-tempered, tyrannical . . . How much suffering this may have caused my mother with her very sensitive nerves is impossible for me to judge.' Josephine also had to intervene in the many heated disputes over music between father and son. Eventually she came to believe that her family were persecuting her; given an over-dose of morphine to calm her, she became ravingly insane until taken to a nursing-home. Johanna Strauss was away from home at the time of her mother's first attack and Richard wrote to her:

> She is often fully lucid now for half an hour at a time, she's read your card, we take her sweets and flowers . . . When I pull myself together as best I can and comfort Papa, it's a waste of time trying to distract him—that's the sad thing—he's becoming more and more unsociable, I think he feels that he's doing dear Mama a moral wrong of some kind if he allows himself to be dis-tracted and doesn't sit all day brooding on our misfortune . . . I do the best I can to work off some part of the immense debt I owe him in these circum-stances, and I hope my resolution will hold out until you come home.

Ten days later he wrote that Josephine was 'very happy and contented, perfectly lucid and rational, only a little excited and restless . . . She knows full well that all the dark thoughts she had were pure nonsense and she remembers all of them in minutest detail.'

During the months at Meiningen, Strauss had little time for composi-tion. While he was there he played the pianoforte part in his already completed Pianoforte Quartet and dedicated it to the Duke when he heard that it had been awarded first prize in a competition organized by the Berlin Tonkünstlerverein. He composed a Scherzo for piano and orchestra for Bülow to perform, but Bülow said it was unplayable. A few weeks later Strauss himself tried out the piece, thought it was 'pure nonsense', and laid it aside. Four years later he looked it out and re-titled it *Burleske*. It contains passages which show that the mature Strauss was on the brink of emerging in 1885, acquaintance with Liszt and Wagner notwithstanding.

3

Tone-poet

Strauss said that his 'first hesitant attempt' at a new 'expressionist' style of composition was in the suite *Aus Italien*. He had long wished to visit Italy and, spurred by a suggestion from Brahms, went there in the three summer months of 1886 between the end of his Meiningen engagement and the start of his Munich contract. Financed by his father and his uncle Georg Pschorr, he visited Verona, Bologna, Rome, Naples and Florence. He saw the great sculptures and pictures—Raphael's St Cecilia moved him to tears—he saw the ancient ruins on the Campagna, he heard Verdi's *Aida* ('*Indianermusik*') and *Requiem* ('pretty and original') and Rossini's *Il barbiere di Siviglia*. (He wrote to his father: 'I will never be converted to Italian music.') The shopkeepers overcharged him, he said; but, like so many composers before (and after) him, he fell under Italy's spell and the impressions he formed he put down in sketches for a 'symphonic fantasy' which he completed and orchestrated during the autumn and winter of 1886. On his way home to Munich he stayed in Bayreuth and attended performances of *Tristan und Isolde* and *Parsifal*.

The next three years were to be crucial in Strauss's life. Within their span he emerged as the composer we know, his fame spread, his name was surrounded by controversy, and he learned to reconcile the conflicting demands of a career as conductor and composer. His experiences as third conductor of the Munich Opera were far from pleasing, however. Wagner's King Ludwig of Bavaria died in June 1886 and with his removal the opera house lost much of its prestige. Hermann Levi was a sick man much of the time and the second conductor, Franz Fischer, was described by Strauss as 'a real criminal on the rostrum'.[1] In addition the Intendant since 1867, Karl von Perfall, now sixty-two years of age, was hostile to Strauss's music. Understandably, the third conductor was given only what were considered to be the least interesting operas. Under the Munich régime of 1886 these included not only works by Boieldieu, Marschner and Cherubini, but Verdi's *Un ballo in maschera*, Bizet's *Carmen* and Mozart's *Così fan tutte*. Conducting Verdi compelled Strauss to revise his opinion of Italian music; the Mozart became one of

---

[1] R. Strauss, 'Reminiscences of my Father', op. cit.

his greatest interpretations and the credit for its revival in modern times is largely his. He understood its unique place among Mozart's dramatic works through its psychological exploitation of a hypothetically ridiculous situation.

The first opera Strauss conducted was Boieldieu's *Jean de Paris*, which he liked sufficiently to conduct it in Vienna nearly forty years later. In the three years he conducted only forty-three performances. He might, perhaps, have had more if he had not been absent frequently as guest conductor of his compositions. The impetus for these invitations stemmed from the excitement aroused by the first performance of *Aus Italien* in Munich on 2 March 1887, conducted by Strauss. It is difficult today to understand, òr to have much sympathy with, the controversy that raged in the last quarter of the nineteenth century over the relative merits of 'absolute' classical music (Brahms) and avant-garde programmatic music with its literary, poetic and pictorial associations (Liszt and Wagner). Munich on the whole was reactionary and thought that young Strauss, to judge from his early works, was a Brahmsian. *Aus Italien* seemed to prove otherwise, and there was uproar. Franz Strauss, distressed, went to the artists' room where he found his son sitting on a table swinging his legs gleefully. Richard then wrote to a girl friend, Lotti Speyer: 'Some people applauded lustily, others hissed loudly, but finally the applause won the day . . . I was immensely proud. This is the first work of mine to have met with opposition from the mob, so it must be of some importance.' He asked his hero, Bülow, to accept the dedication of 'this symphonic fantasy embellished by local opposition'. Bülow agreed. It is likely that even then he perceived what, with hindsight, we now know: that Strauss was not the prologue to a new era but the epilogue of an old. The opposition to Strauss would appeal to Bülow, who knew from experience that the 'revolutionary' young man is attacked by the entrenched vested interests not because they genuinely believe he is a bad artist but because they are frightened by him and by the threat he represents to the established order. But Bülow's percipience was not attributable to any special sympathy on his part for the avant-garde. He regarded Mahler's music, for example, with horror, and he was lukewarm at first about Strauss's *Macbeth* and *Don Juan*; but *Aus Italien* is a transitional work, 'the connecting link between the old and the new methods', as Strauss said. Conductors were eager to perform it; its first and third movements were performed in London on 28 November 1889 under Henschel, the first orchestral music by Strauss to be played in England.

His conducting engagements during 1887 took him to Frankfurt, Hamburg and Cologne. From Leipzig, where he conducted his F minor symphony in October, he wrote to Bülow: 'I made a new and very attractive acquaintance in Herr Mahler [aged twenty-seven at this time], who seemed to me a highly intelligent musician and conductor—one of

15

the few modern conductors who know about tempo rubato.' So began his generally friendly relationship with his great contemporary, whose music he consistently championed.

Even more significant was the beginning of the most important relationship of his life. He took a holiday in late August of 1887 at the village of Feldafing, where his Pschorr relatives had a villa. Living nearby were General de Ahna and his two daughters. Ahna was a music-lover and an amateur singer good enough to give recitals locally at which he sang Wagner extracts. His elder daughter, Pauline, who was twenty-five, two years older than Strauss, had studied singing as a soprano at Munich University but had not made any progress professionally. This family were thrilled to meet the much-talked-about young conductor-composer; he was interested in Pauline and agreed to give her lessons. He realized the potentialities of her voice and told her she had the talent to become a star—and he was to be proved right. Strauss, an ardent spirit, was by no means unsusceptible to women and his boyish love affairs had caused his parents some concern. But he did not fall in love with Pauline until 1892, by which time she had been his singing pupil for five years.

The first important relationship in Strauss's life had begun in 1885 before he went to Meiningen. He fell passionately in love with Dora Wihan, wife of the Czech cellist Hanuš (Hans) Wihan who became a member of the Munich court orchestra in 1880. Wihan was the dedicatee of Strauss's Cello Sonata, of which he gave the first performance in 1883. Dora, from a Dresden family named Weis, was a good enough musician to play the piano part in the sonata in private performances. She was five years younger than her husband and four years older than Strauss. Her marriage was soon on the rocks. Strauss's sister Johanna, who remained a close friend of Dora's until the latter's death in 1938, described her as 'rather coquettish' and Wihan as 'insanely jealous . . . I often witnessed scenes. For instance, she often asked me to spend the night with her when her husband came in later from the opera and sometimes had had a drop to drink, so that she wasn't alone all evening. And when Richard was with us, we used to make music.'[2]

The Wihans legally separated in 1885. When Strauss was in Rome in April 1886, his sister wrote to say that Dora was there too. Strauss replied that he had not seen her. Whether this was true or exercise of discretion, nobody knows. Dora left Munich for good in 1887 after her divorce. She went to America and then took a job in one of the Greek islands. Strauss and she corresponded regularly. She kept his letters all her life, asking for them to be destroyed after her death, and on her

[2] W. Schuh, *Richard Strauss: Jugend und Frühe Meisterjahre. Lebenschronik 1864–1898* (Zürich, 1986), trans. by Mary Whittall as *Richard Strauss, a Chronicle of the Early Years, 1864–1898* (Cambridge, 1982), pp. 84–5.

piano always stood his photograph, inscribed 'To his beloved and only one, R.'. Strauss, who kept all letters addressed to him, destroyed Dora's. But one of his to her and three of hers survived. His letter, written on 9 April 1889, complains of their long separation and includes the phrase 'You really mustn't leave me alone for so long—my God, I have hoped for two years, only to close the book of my hopes at the end of that period with the words "It just isn't possible" . . . Farewell, now, stay fond of me . . .'

It would seem that the relationship cooled, as far as any prospective marriage was concerned, in 1889–90. The second surviving letter from Dora dates from April 1890 and she addresses him with the formal 'Sie' in place of the intimate 'Du' of an 1889 letter. She was in Dresden in 1890 and returned permanently from Greece in 1891. Strauss obtained a ticket for her at Bayreuth that summer, but whether she went is not known. Johanna, who undoubtedly would have preferred her to Pauline as a sister-in-law, continued to see her. Dora's last meeting with Strauss was in Dresden in January 1911 during the early performances of *Der Rosenkavalier*. Johanna tactlessly invited her to join her, Richard and Pauline on several occasions. This brought a written rebuke to his sister from Strauss a few weeks later: 'Since you obviously had no consideration for her, you have no reason to be surprised that Pauline, who is very sensitive in these matters, proved somewhat withdrawn. At all events, it was not her intention that you should notice her mood, but it is very difficult for her to disguise her feelings when something has upset her.'[3]

During 1887 Strauss composed several songs, including the justly famous *Ständchen*, and a Violin Sonata. But the work which principally occupied him was a symphonic poem, *Macbeth*. He was convinced, as we have seen, that his future lay in programme music, notwithstanding the disapproval which this genre had incurred from purist and academic musical opinion since the days of Vivaldi's *The Four Seasons*. In the 1880s the symphonic poem was at its peak. The term itself was Liszt's invention for the twelve he wrote, but Mendelssohn's and Berlioz's large-scale overtures had been symphonic poems. Liszt's example was followed by Smetana, Saint-Saëns, Tchaikovsky, Dvořák, Franck and many others. Strauss took the form at the flood, as it were, devised his own name for it—tone-poem—and imparted to it new life and urgency. His approach to programme music can be summed up in words he wrote in 1896: 'I am a musician first and last, for whom all "programmes" are merely the stimulus to the creation of new forms, and nothing more.'

Strauss completed *Macbeth* in 1888 and sent the score to Bülow,

³ W. Schuh, *Richard Strauss, a Chronicle of the Early Years*, op. cit., pp. 173–4.

describing it as the 'most independent and purposeful work' he had so far composed. He drew attention to its 'violent and gruesome content'. Bülow was not impressed. To the publisher Spitzweg he called it 'Macbethian soup from the witches' kitchen', but to the composer he helpfully suggested revisions. Meanwhile, inspired by his love for Dora, Strauss had begun another tone-poem dealing with the perennially fascinating figure of Don Juan. He wrote to Bülow in 1888: '*Macbeth* rests peacefully in its grave in my desk where, no doubt, *Don Juan* will shortly keep it company.' He told Ritter that he was dissatisfied with the scoring: 'There are too many inner parts . . . the principal themes do not stand out as clearly as I intended.'

During the early part of the summer of 1888 he again went to Italy. In Bologna he heard *Tristan und Isolde* and for the first time became fully aware that 'it is a most beautiful *bel canto* opera'. He longed to conduct it, and this longing no doubt deepened the depression he was experiencing in his Munich Opera post where Perfall frustrated and Levi antagonized him. It was obvious that an explosion would occur and it is remarkable that it did not come earlier than the winter of 1888–9, when Perfall allocated him the revival of Wagner's *Die Feen*. Just before the final dress rehearsal Perfall ruled that Fischer would now take over because such an important revival could not be entrusted to the third conductor. On Bülow's recommendation Strauss saw Hans von Bronsart, Intendant of Weimar Opera, and the conductor there, Eduard Lassen, men of integrity and musical idealism. They appointed Strauss as assistant conductor from 1 October 1889. In addition, Bülow obtained him a post during the summer of 1889 as a musical assistant at Bayreuth. There he heard performances conducted by Mottl and Richter and, most important of all, was shown favour by Cosima Wagner and invited to Wahnfried. Pauline de Ahna was with him, and Cosima gave advice to Strauss and his pupil on the interpretation of *Lohengrin* and *Tannhäuser*. He was overjoyed to have put the Munich experience behind him.

A first-hand account of Richard's outlook at this time is in the letter he wrote to Dora Wihan on 9 April 1889. It is also a useful guide to the dating of progress on certain works:

> Just think! I have joined the ranks of the Lisztians! In short, it is hard to imagine a more progressive viewpoint than the one I now hold. I feel wonderful; a new clarity has overcome me. . . . I am employed in Bayreuth as 'assistant', piano rehearsals, etc. Recently I made the acquaintance of Frau Wagner, who is quite interested in me. . . . Where am I going? . . . to Weimar. . . . What a splendid change from Munich! To the city of the future, Weimar, to the post where Liszt worked so long! I have great hopes. . . . Lassen is old and tired [he was fifty-nine] and looks forward to relief from his labours. . . . As to the libretto of my opera, I have the first act and part of the second act, to the end of the big love scene, tentatively ready. (That means until I revise it again.)

Ritter likes it very much. In addition I have sketched out a new tone-poem, to be called (probably) *Tod und Verklärung*.[4]

Ritter's hold, it can be seen, was still strong; in 1887 he gave Strauss a newspaper article about Austrian medieval secret societies. Strauss was attracted to the subject and promptly invented the name of his hero, Guntram. So during these Munich years he had on the stocks, simultaneously, three tone-poems and an opera libretto. This was the energetic young man who set out hopefully for Weimar. A photograph taken at this time shows him smartly dressed, sitting with arms folded. His hair is bushy and naturally curly. The first traces of a moustache cover his long top lip. The mouth is firm, the chin slightly weak. One has to look long and hard to see that this face will become that of the noble old man of sixty years later. But in the eyes is a look of arrogant self-confidence, the look of the man who had written, in *Don Juan*, a work of genius.

[4] Text published in *Richard Strauss Jahrbuch 1959–60*.

4

Weimar and Munich

When he arrived in Weimar, Strauss played *Don Juan* on the pianoforte to Bronsart and Lassen. They were so impressed that they urged him to include it in the season of concerts which was about to begin. His letters to his father describing the rehearsals capture the excitement and apprehension with which the orchestra tackled this difficult and ardent work, the fruit of his passion for Dora (and for Lotti Speyer, perhaps). In its demands on their technique, it was revolutionary. Strauss himself knew that the lessons he had learned at the conductor's desk were standing him in good stead. He wrote to old Franz:

> The sound was wonderful, immensely glowing and exuberant. It will make a tremendous stir here. . . . The orchestra huffed and puffed but did its job famously. One of the horn players sat there out of breath, sweat pouring from his brow, asking 'Good God, in what way have we sinned that you should have sent us this scourge!' We laughed till we cried! Certainly the horns blew without fear of death. . . . I was really sorry for the wretched brass. They were quite blue in the face, the whole affair was so strenuous.

The first performance on 11 November 1889 was a triumph. Strauss overnight became nationally recognized as the most important German composer since Wagner. 'The piece sounded magical, dear Papa,' he wrote. Bülow was present; it is ironical that this great work should have become the cause of a rift between him and Strauss. Or perhaps the real cause was Cosima Wagner, whose influence on Strauss was intensifying. Bülow conducted the first Berlin Philharmonic performance of *Don Juan* on 30 January 1890 with immense success, but Strauss was dissatisfied with his mentor's interpretation. He wrote to his father that Bülow was mixing now with an 'ugly Jewish circle'. He had presented to Berlin 'merely an interesting piece of music, not my *Don Juan*. He no longer understands poetic music, he has lost the touch.'

Strauss conducted three other first performances of his works in 1890, two of them in one concert at Eisenach on 21 June. He had recently become friendly with the pianist-composer Eugen d'Albert, to whom he had shown the *Scherzo* for pianoforte and orchestra written for Bülow in 1885. D'Albert persuaded him to release the piece and, under the new title of *Burleske*, played it at Eisenach. Strauss was still doubtful about its merit and rejected a substantial sum offered by a publisher. After the *Burleske* he conducted *Tod und Verklärung* (Death and Transfiguration). Then, at Weimar on 13 October, he conducted his revised *Macbeth*. He had provided a new ending, as Bülow had wished, and had considerably revised the scoring. But after the first performance, he revised it yet again. There was no further performance for fifteen months until, on 29 February 1892, Strauss conducted the definitive version in Berlin at Bülow's invitation, an occasion which brought them closer again. The rehearsal was also the occasion for one of Bülow's most celebrated witticisms, attributed to various conductors but here authenticated by Strauss:

> I had not looked at the piece for a long time and (always a little careless in that respect, since I used to rely on my reasonable skill in reading scores) had not looked at the score even before the rehearsal, so that the members of the Philharmonic Orchestra witnessed the spectacle of a composer glued to the notes of his score. This annoyed the conscientious Bülow, and afterwards he reproached me bitterly: 'You should have the score in your head and not your head in the score' (anticipating my rejoinder) 'even if you have composed the thing yourself.'[1]

Macbeth was enthusiastically received. Bülow told Strauss: 'It's quite a good piece after all.' To Spitzweg he used the phrase 'a work of genius'. Strauss, it seemed, could not put a foot wrong. Yet there were voices of dissent from the chorus of adulation, loudest among them that of the critic Hanslick, not surprisingly. He attended the first Vienna performance of *Don Juan*, conducted by Richter on 10 January 1892, and his notice included these phrases: 'Colour is everything, musical thought nothing. . . . This is no "tone painting" but rather a tumult of brilliant daubs.' A year later, *Tod und Verklärung* provoked him to call Strauss 'a brilliant virtuoso of the orchestra, lacking only musical ideas'.

But what of Strauss's conducting at Weimar? The company contained no 'star' names and the orchestra was small, but one of the young singers, who was to become a very great star—Marie Gutheil-Schoder—said in her reminiscences that Strauss made Weimar 'the centre of the musical life of Germany'. He conducted operas by Bellini, Lortzing, Marschner, Weber, Nicolai, Mozart (*Die Zauberflöte*) and Wagner (*Lohengrin, Tannhäuser, Rienzi, Der fliegende Holländer*). Pauline joined the company and, under his tutelage, was good enough to sing the roles of Pamina (*Zauberflöte*), Elvira (*Don Giovanni*), Elsa (*Lohengrin*) and Elisabeth (*Tannhäuser*). Another of his singing pupils in the company was the *Heldentenor* Heinrich Zeller. This suggests that Strauss's extraordinary understanding of the voice, particularly the

---

[1] R. Strauss, 'Reminiscences of Hans von Bülow', op. cit.

female voice, was instinctive; no doubt he was helped and advised by Pauline, but there is also no doubt that he 'made' her career.

Strauss also championed contemporary German opera while at Weimar. He conducted a double bill of Ritter's *Der Faule Hans* and *Wem die Krone?* He conducted the first performances of Eugen Lindner's *Der Meisterdieb*, Hans Sommer's *Loreley*, Mottl's *Fürst und Sänger*, Richard Metzdorf's *Hagbart und Signe*, and Humperdinck's *Hänsel und Gretel*. When he first read the score of the last-named, Strauss wrote to his friend: 'It's a masterpiece of the highest quality . . . You are a great master and have given the Germans a work they hardly deserve, but let us hope all the same that they will soon learn how to appreciate it fully.'

In his staging of Wagner at Weimar, Strauss worked directly under the influence of Cosima. This alarmed Bronsart, the Intendant, who did not fancy his opera house becoming a subsidiary of Bayreuth. He left Strauss in no doubt of his opinion: 'Some modification of your ultra-radical views would be altogether desirable . . . Ever since you assumed your office I have seen you advance further along that path.' Other musicians, he warned his young conductor, had 'a better and more reliable knowledge' of Wagner's works than 'the Meister's unmusical widow'. He then told Strauss some home truths:

> You must learn to control yourself at least enough, even when you are excited, to stop using at every moment turns of phrases which you would condemn severely in the mouth of another person. You *must* learn to respect individualities in your dealings with *your* artists at least enough, even though they are working under your general direction, to acknowledge their entitlement to a certain degree of artistic judgment, and you must not call it 'style-less' every time somebody feels differently from you about a matter . . . If you will take to heart what I am here saying to you truly from the heart and in fatherly sincerity, you will . . . forestall bitter experiences which might otherwise have a crippling and destructive effect on all your activities, wearing you out spiritually and physically before your time, while you will also preserve for the good of us all an artistic ability more promising than any I have ever dared to dream of . . .[2]

In May 1891 Strauss had pneumonia. For a time he was dangerously ill. Convalescing at the Pschorr villa in Feldafing he wrote to the critic Arthur Seidl: 'Dying may not be so bad, but I should first like to conduct *Tristan*.' His passion for this opera was unabated to his last day. (In 1933 he wrote to Fritz Busch: 'Even if only *one* person pays for a seat at *Tristan* it must be performed for him, because he must be the last surviving German.') To his joy, he was allocated *Tristan* for the 1891–2 season in Weimar and spent Christmas with Cosima discussing its every aspect. The first performance, uncut, was on 17 January 1892; he wrote to Cosima afterwards describing it as the most wonderful day of his life.

[2] W. Schuh, *Richard Strauss, a Chronicle of the Early Years*, op. cit., pp. 201–2.

At the revival in 1894 Pauline sang Isolde—'too early, of course', Strauss wrote,[3] 'but somehow because of her youth and great acting a particularly charming performance'.

His appetite for work was as great as ever. In one week of March 1892 his engagements were: Tuesday night, *Tristan*; 11.30 p.m. to Leipzig. Wednesday, 10 to 2.30, first rehearsal for a Liszt concert. Evening back to Weimar. Thursday, conducted *Lohengrin* in Eisenach. Return to Leipzig 1 a.m. Friday, rehearsals 10 to 1 and 3 to 6. Saturday, rehearsal and concert. Not surprisingly, the list of his own compositions shrinks during these Weimar years: it was not only Mahler who was a 'summer-composer'. Strauss's chief occupation was conducting, and in his youth he did not set aside several months of the summer, as Mahler did, exclusively for creative work. Later he followed Mahler's routine. He told several correspondents that he could only work in the summer, because the winter 'froze his brain'. He usually revised and orchestrated during winter. Between 1889 and 1893 his only compositions, once *Macbeth* and *Tod und Verklärung* were completed, were a march for the twenty-fifth anniversary of his father's 'Wilde Gung'l' orchestra, some occasional music for the golden wedding of the Grand Duke and Duchess of Weimar performed on 8 October 1892, and two songs for Heinrich Zeller. 'The theatre and cards, as well as my fiancée, claimed almost all my attention,' Strauss wrote, although Pauline and he were not yet engaged. In September 1890 he had completed his adaptation of Gluck's *Iphigenia in Tauris*. He told the publisher Adolph Fürstner that he had taken Wagner's version of *Iphigenia in Aulis* as his model. 'My revision consists of a completely new translation, actually a new text in parts (with some elements taken from Goethe's play), especially in the first act, in which the order of the scenes has been entirely changed, the last act, for which I have composed a new ending, as well as changes in the scoring to bring it into line with modern requirements at least to some extent . . .' (This version was published in 1895 but not performed at Weimar until 1900, long after Strauss had left.) He had also devoted much time to revising the libretto of his opera, *Guntram*, and began to sketch the music in the spring of 1892. But in June he had a severe attack of pleurisy and bronchitis and his life was again in danger. His Uncle Georg insisted that he should spend the winter in the sun and gave him 5,000 marks to enable him to visit Egypt.

He sailed in November 1892, making Greece his first call. 'From the moment when, coming from Brindisi, I saw from the deck of the Italian steamer the island of Corfu and the blue mountains of Albania, I have always been a German Greek.'[4] Falling in love with Greece and its ancient civilization stimulated his creative impulses, and he worked

---

[3] R. Strauss, 'Recollections of my Youth and Years of Apprenticeship', op. cit.
[4] R. Strauss, 'Letter on the *Humanistische Gymnasium*', op. cit.

steadily at his opera, revising the libretto of the third act before leaving Athens. During his convalescence and on the voyage he had read Nietzsche's works and had been particularly attracted by 'his polemic against Christianity'. Strauss's objection was to any religion which relieved its followers of responsibility for their actions by means of confession. This was relevant to Guntram's situation in Act III. The opera's 'spiritual godfather', Ritter, who had followed every move Strauss made while writing the libretto, was a Roman Catholic and saw the work as a study in religious morals and ethics. Strauss re-wrote his last act so that Guntram renounced society (symbolizing a religious order) and went his own way. Ritter was horrified, and pleaded with Strauss to throw the new third act into the fire because it was 'an immoral mockery of every ethical creed. . . . Go and read with inner enlightenment a chapter of the gospels.' Strauss was unmoved. He tried to reason with Ritter, but Ritter never forgave him and their relationship became much cooler. Yet all that Strauss had done, in essence, was to give Guntram a creed summed up in his line: 'My God speaks to me through myself.'

Working six hours a day on the short score, Strauss completed *Guntram* in Cairo on Christmas Eve, writing on the manuscript 'Deo gratia! Und dem heiligen Wagner'. He then began the orchestration while staying in Luxor. This task was completed at Marquartstein in September.

At the time of his illness in the summer of 1892 Strauss was already disenchanted with his work at Weimar. In later life he wrote: 'People were very nice to me, but I recklessly squandered some of the goodwill they bore me by my youthful energy and love of exaggeration.'[5] Writing to Bülow on 30 June 1892 he said that Bronsart, the Intendant, was blocking his advancement and did not agree with the way he conducted Beethoven. Bronsart also thought that Strauss's orchestral concerts included too much Liszt, Berlioz, Wagner and Strauss—and they were eventually to include Mahler's First Symphony, which the composer conducted, at Strauss's invitation, in June 1894. 'I am going to move on', Strauss told Bülow. While he was in Egypt he received a long letter from his father containing the extraordinary news that Hermann Levi, still the chief conductor at Munich, had sought a meeting with Franz Strauss to inquire if Richard would be friendly enough to him to accept the post of associate conductor. Richard naturally hesitated: he had been glad enough to escape from Munich, why return? He applied instead to Mottl at Karlsruhe, but no position was available. While he still hesitated, Cosima advised him to accept Levi's offer. There were several good reasons to do so: he was tired of an orchestra at Weimar which had a string section of twenty-one players; Perfall was nearly seventy and Levi, with his increasingly uncertain health, might retire at any time; his proposed

[5] R. Strauss, 'Recollections of my Youth and Years of Apprenticeship', op. cit.

salary at Munich was nearly double what Weimar paid him; he would conduct major works; and, last but certainly not least, there was a chance that *Guntram* would be performed there. He agreed to accept, but negotiations were so protracted that he stayed for Weimar's 1893–4 season, which was to prove memorable for several reasons.

On 23 December 1893 he conducted the first performance of Humperdinck's *Hänsel und Gretel*. It was accidental, because the world première had been planned for Munich under Levi but had to be postponed when one of the principals became ill. So the Weimar production became the first, and it, too, was accident-prone. The dress rehearsal, Strauss reported to the composer, was 'truly dreadful'. The Gretel had had to learn the part of Hänsel in three days because Pauline de Ahna, the intended Hänsel, had hurt her foot and was in bed. She found the part too low 'but did all that was humanly possible' while the substitute Gretel was 'very good as far as her little voice allowed'. Eight of the orchestra had influenza. Pauline returned to the cast in January.

In the new year Strauss decided to stage *Guntram*, come what may. He had already had warning of the difficulties he could expect: Mottl, whom Strauss admired, had been anxious to give the first performance and he put the opera into rehearsal at Karlsruhe, but abandoned it when the tenor said the role of Guntram was impossible. Mahler, recently installed at the Hamburg Opera, also had to abandon the project. Strauss hoped for an easier time, for in the leading roles of Guntram and Freihild he cast two of his pupils, Zeller and Pauline. Here is his own account written in 1942:

> Zeller suffered torments with the insanely taxing vocal part . . . became hoarser with each rehearsal and only finished the first performance with difficulty. . . . In the course of one of the last rehearsals, when I had to interrupt Zeller time and time again, we at last came to Pauline's scene in Act III, which she obviously knew. In spite of this she did not feel sure of herself and apparently envied Zeller because he had been given so many chances of 'repeating'. Suddenly she stopped singing and asked me, 'Why don't you interrupt me?' I replied, 'Because you know your part.' With the words 'I want to be interrupted' she threw the piano score . . . at my head but, to the delight of the orchestra, it landed on the desk of the second violinist, Gutheil.[6]

Pauline ran to her dressing-room, followed by an angry Strauss. Raised voices were heard, then silence. Eventually the orchestra's leader knocked on the door and told Strauss, who opened it, that the players were shocked by Pauline's behaviour and refused to play in any opera in which she sang. To which Strauss replied: 'That pains me very much, for I have just become engaged to Fräulein de Ahna.'[7] Two days after

---

[6] R. Strauss: 'Reminiscences of the First Performances of my Operas' in *Recollections and Reflections*, op. cit.

[7] Lotte Lehmann, in *My Many Lives*, ascribes this incident to a *Tannhäuser* rehearsal, but in view of the date of the official engagement it was obviously during *Guntram*.

the first performance on 10 May 1894, the betrothal was officially announced, although they had been secretly engaged since March.

The opera was mildly successful, though how its instrumentation for ninety-two players sounded on the Weimar orchestra of barely half that number can scarcely be imagined. The score was published early in 1895 and Strauss sent a copy to Verdi, as a token of his admiration for *Falstaff* (1893). He kept Verdi's courteous acknowledgement—'I perceive that your *Guntram* is a work fashioned by a knowing hand'—all his life. One to whom he could not send a score was Bülow, who had died in February 1894. Strauss last saw him the previous month. He took over Bülow's Berlin Philharmonic concerts but was not yet ready for such a post: 'Precocious though I was, I was slow in becoming a conductor and was unable to hold my own after this great man. In 1895 H. Wolff put the magnificent Nikisch in charge of the concerts and I had to be content with my 7,000 marks in Munich.'[8]

Nevertheless the outstanding event of 1894 for Strauss was his marriage to Pauline in Marquartstein on 10 September. Richard was phlegmatic and 'unflappable', Pauline temperamental, fiery, tactless, rude and beguiling. Lotte Lehmann described them in their home, after twenty-five years of marriage, in these significant words:

> I often caught a glance or a smile passing between her and her husband, touching in its love and happiness, and I began to sense something of the profound affection between those two human beings, a tie so elemental in strength that none of Pauline's shrewish truculence could ever trouble it seriously. In fact, I rather suspect that they were always putting on a kind of act for their own benefit as well as for that of outsiders.[9]

Everything about Pauline Maria de Ahna was in primary colours. She expressed her views on anyone and anything without any conditional clauses. Her volatile nature was the opposite of her husband's, and the chemistry between them was such that their relationship intensified through the years. Before there was any romantic attachment, while Strauss was her teacher, sparks had flown. Strauss on more than one occasion terminated their friendship. In 1892 intervention by Franz Strauss, colluding with General de Ahna, had brought them together again. 'A man of good breeding can always allow some latitude to a lady of that kind without lowering himself', Franz wrote to his son. 'Also I am sure she is the singer who will come closest to realising your intentions.'[10] After their marriage, it was Richard who had to arbitrate between parents-in-law and daughter-in-law. In a letter to them he referred to Pauline's 'small and in part really quite harmless faults (which she and I know better than anyone else)' and to her 'unthinking,

---

[8] R. Strauss, 'Recollections of my Youth and Years of Apprenticeship', op. cit.

[9] L. Lehmann, *Singing with Richard Strauss* (London, 1964).

[10] W. Schuh, *Richard Strauss: a Chronicle of the Early Years*, op. cit., pp. 352–7.

excited, over-boisterous, but essentially good-hearted, childlike and naive manner'. He had chosen her as his wife, he reminded them, 'after very mature deliberation'; he loved and honoured her 'in spite of her faults'.

Pauline in later years liked to tell people that her parents opposed her marriage because she, a general's daughter, was marrying a horn-player's son. This was one of her jokes and is the reverse of the truth. Her parents helped to patch up pre-engagement quarrels and if anyone had misgivings about the forthcoming marriage, it was Pauline herself, and not for any snobbish reasons. Writing to Strauss as late as 24 March 1894, when they were engaged, and addressing him as 'Mein lieber Herr Strauss', she betrayed that she was worried about giving up her career, especially as she had had an offer of an engagement with Hamburg Opera (where Mahler was conductor and Pollini the Intendant). 'I am sometimes terribly afraid', she wrote. 'Will I be capable of being what you want and what you deserve? May I not first fulfil my guest engagement in Hamburg, so that I shall at least have a triumph to show off proudly to my respected teacher . . .? My dear friend, we don't need to marry so soon; if each of us could first get accustomed to finding all the happiness we can in our careers . . . Forgive this letter, but the two feelings—my happiness and my fear of a new life—weigh on me so that I am only half capable of reasoning . . . the greatest happiness is our art, dear friend, do not forget that.' And she ended with a postscript asking him to modify a passage in the role of Freihild. At this same time her father wrote to convey the joy he and his wife felt about the forthcoming marriage. 'I can only rejoice with my whole heart that your destiny has taken this course . . . Picture yourself on the one hand as an artist more or less at the mercy of the directorial whims and tyranny of Pollini, and on the other as the wife of a respected man who, although he has known all your good and less good aspects for years, none the less loves you with his whole heart and is devoted to you, living in Munich and no longer far from home and perhaps even you yourself also admired and respected as an artist . . .'[11]

The possibility of Pauline turning down Strauss at this stage angered her sister Mädi, who reminded her that Strauss had said she could continue her operatic career or give it up, whichever she chose. 'Everyone's patience gradually wears out in the end', Mädi wrote, 'and it might happen with Strauss too if you keep him in suspense for eternity. People get tired of that sort of thing, my dear Pauline, you love him so don't go on playing this purely superficial role . . .'[12] Strauss appears to have remained unflappable throughout all this havering and showed characteristic humour when he told Pauline's father that if she came 'under an unfamiliar director in Hamburg', it would make her properly appreciate

[11] W. Schuh, *Richard Strauss: a Chronicle of the Early Years*, op. cit., p. 354.
[12] Ibid., p. 355.

being conducted by him at last. Pauline then produced a new red herring: would she be engaged at Munich Opera when Strauss went there? Mädi returned to the fray:

> Give up this eternal struggling with your fiancé, in the long run it's bound to annoy him seriously if he sees that all the love and respect he has for you never gets any other response than your *rather dull* refrain: being an opera singer is the most important thing for me! You can continue the two so easily . . . All it needs from you is a little more self-control—for when the boorish words are out you always regret them at once—and the two of you will make a very happy and contented musical couple. It will be all right if you have a little row now and again—I think Strauss quite enjoys *some* variety—as long as you don't do it in front of a third person . . . If Johanna comes, promise us that you will be calm and equable, of course it wouldn't do if you exaggerate things, don't ever let her hear of a serious disagreement with Strauss, his family think the world of him, quite rightly, and from other quarters too we hear nothing but praise for his talent and for his artistic reputation in the world at large . . .[13]

Pauline's father added his final exasperated comment on 9 April 1894: 'Take heed that I am tired of having my old age soured by you. At your age . . . one ought to know what one wants and not promise *today* to be a good and loyal wife and suddenly declare tomorrow that one has changed one's mind . . . If you want to make yourself unhappy and cast a shadow over whole families, then do so, but thereafter I wash my hands of you.'[14]

No sign of parental opposition there, nor of any belief that Pauline was marrying 'beneath her'. On their wedding day Strauss gave four songs, his Op. 27, to her, dedicated 'to my beloved Pauline'. They were *Ruhe, meine Seele!, Cäcilie, Heimliche Aufforderung* and *Morgen!*, four of his greatest Lieder. As a gift from composer to wife, they merit comparison with Wagner's *Siegfried Idyll*.

In the month before his marriage Strauss conducted for the first time at Bayreuth, with Pauline singing Elisabeth in *Tannhäuser*. He took up his post at Munich on 1 October 1894. It was to prove no happier an experience than his first period there, although there were better artistic compensations. Perfall remained hostile, but Strauss liked his assistant, Ernst von Possart, brilliant as a producer and himself a popular actor. Levi was frequently absent through illness, so Strauss at last had the satisfaction of conducting *Tristan* and *Die Meistersinger* in the city where they had first been produced. With Possart as producer, he conducted revivals of three Mozart operas—*Die Entführung aus dem Serail, Così fan tutte*, and *Don Giovanni*—at a Mozart festival at the Residenztheater. 'Shining memories in my life', he called these occasions, writing in 1928.[15]

---

[13] W. Schuh, *Richard Strauss: a Chronicle of the Early Years*, op. cit., pp. 356–7.
[14] Ibid., p. 357.
[15] R. Strauss: 'On the Munich Opera' in *Recollections and Reflections*, op. cit.

Less happy was his second attempt to establish *Guntram*, which had one unfortunate performance at Munich on 16 November 1895. Pauline again sang Freihild, but two of the other leading singers, Milka Ternina and the tenor Heinrich Vogl, had refused to take part, the orchestra led by his cousin and former teacher Benno Walter had sent a deputation to the Intendant asking him to spare them 'this scourge of God', and the tenor Mikorey said after the performance that he would only sing another if his pension were to be increased. There was no second performance. Strauss was deeply hurt, and bitterly resented those who had harmed the opera. To Seidl he wrote: 'It is incredible what enemies *Guntram* has made for me. I shall shortly be tried as a dangerous criminal.' Years later in Garmisch he dug a grave in his garden and erected a stone inscribed: 'Here rests the honourable and virtuous young man Guntram . . . who was horribly slain by the symphony orchestra of his own father.' Throughout his life, Strauss never fully reconciled himself to the failure of his first opera.

Yet this was to be a rich period for Strauss the composer. On his way home from Egypt in 1894 he had begun to think of the opera he would write after *Guntram*. He had settled on the subject of the medieval folk hero, the rascally Till Eulenspiegel. He began to write a libretto, but abandoned it, realizing that he had no talent for poetry and being by this time thoroughly discouraged about opera. In the winter of 1894–5 he wrote a rondo for orchestra on the subject, completing it on 6 May 1895. Because of Levi's illness and rehearsals for *Guntram*, he entrusted the first performance of *Till Eulenspiegels lustige Streiche* to one of his earliest champions, Franz Wüllner, at a Gürzenich concert in Cologne on 5 November 1895. It was an immediate success, its brilliance and humour endearing it to audiences then and ever since. Within four months it had had its first Viennese, American and English performances. Bruckner went to a repeat performance in Vienna because he had found the work 'extraordinarily interesting' and had not fully understood it on a first hearing; Hanslick called it a box of tricks. Perhaps the gaiety of the music reflects the happiness Strauss found in his first year of marriage. The working sketches have comments in Pauline's writing—'mad', 'dreadful mess', 'rotten composing'—which suggest lighthearted marital backchat around the piano.

More Lieder poured from Strauss at this time, and he began work on another tone-poem. This bore the name of Friedrich Nietzsche's famous poem *Also sprach Zarathustra* and embodied Strauss's homage to the genius of its author. It was completed on 24 August 1896 and Strauss conducted the first performance in Frankfurt-am-Main on 27 November. The first Berlin performance, under Nikisch, followed three days later. This work, too, was well received, but with rather more solemnity. He was then deep into composition of another large-scale orchestral work, his third within four years. This, completed on 29 December 1897, was

29

Don Quixote, 'fantastic variations on a theme of knightly character'. He again gave the first performance to Wüllner at Cologne, on 8 March 1898, because he himself was fulfilling engagements in Madrid. He conducted the work's second performance, on 18 March in Frankfurt.

Within this period, Perfall had handed over to Possart at the Munich Opera and, in 1896, Levi retired and Strauss became chief conductor on 1 October. But already he was disillusioned by Munich. In February 1896 he had sought the opera directorship at Mannheim at a lower salary than he was receiving in Munich. Later he made approaches to Karlsruhe. A week before his appointment came into effect he had a violent quarrel with Possart over annulment of a contract for Pauline to make twenty guest appearances. 'Dirty, rotten trickery', he wrote in his diary. Another crisis arose in August 1897 when he was offered the directorship of Hamburg Opera in succession to Mahler, who had gone to Vienna. But the Hamburg Intendant, Pollini, refused to engage Pauline. Strauss wrote to her: 'If Pollini will engage you, I shall go to him, if he won't have you any more than Possart will, then I'll stay in Munich. Oh, this eternal theatrical chicanery, how it disgusts me!'; Pauline implored him to 'give no consideration at all to *my* engagement, but if *you* will be happier and better off in Hamburg, go there . . . Let us both take care to earn a lot of money so that you can soon live *your own life* . . . For now a good, good night, my Richard! I hug you with the utmost love! Paula.' Strauss decided to stay in Munich for the time being when he was awarded an immediate salary increase.

The success of his works, especially *Don Juan* and *Till*, meant that he was much in demand as a guest conductor: he visited Russia, he conducted at the Lower Rhine Festival in Düsseldorf; in 1897 he toured in Germany as pianist with Possart, for whom he had written the melodrama *Enoch Arden*, and he undertook conducting engagements in Holland and Spain. He visited London for the first time, conducting the first English performance of *Tod und Verklärung* at Queen's Hall on 7 December, and he conducted in Paris in November.

It was while he was in Stuttgart performing *Enoch Arden* that his son was born on 12 April 1897. Pauline was thirty-five and had had a difficult pregnancy and delivery. Both parents were thrilled about their child, who was named Franz Alexander (the second name after Ritter, who had died on 12 April 1897) but usually known as Bubi. On his son's birthday Strauss dedicated six new songs, Op. 37, including *Meinem Kinde*, 'to my beloved wife'. Pauline accompanied him on his first Paris conducting engagement in November 1897 and was soloist in several of his songs, including *Morgen!* which was encored. She had fully resumed her career and in January 1898 sang seven Strauss songs in Zürich and went to Bayreuth to sing St Elisabeth in Liszt's oratorio. It was on this occasion that she remarked to Cosima Wagner while having tea at

Wahnfried, 'Oh, my Richard is just too bourgeois for words', to which Cosima retorted, 'Be glad of it, dear girl!'

Early in 1898 Strauss received two offers of new posts. Felix Weingartner had vacated the position of chief conductor of the Royal Court Opera in Berlin. Hochberg, the Intendant, and Pierson, his lieutenant, offered the post to Strauss at a high salary, on a ten-year contract, summer and winter holidays, a life pension and a widow's pension—a pointer to the high regard in which he was held. At the same time the Metropolitan Opera, New York, offered him their conductorship at over double the Berlin salary but on a short-term contract. Strauss had little hesitation in accepting Berlin. He wrote to his mother on 10 April 1898: 'I shall still be able to graze in American pastures ten years from now, while at the moment it's more important to make myself still better known in Europe . . . Ah, the joy of being able at last to throw the big stick back at the feet of that crew in Munich, who have treated me really shamefully . . . I shall breathe more easily, away from the atmospheric pressure in Munich.' Two months later he wrote from Munich to his Belgian admirer Georges Khnopff: 'They've made the most marvellous attempts to keep me here, I'm beginning to be extremely popular here now—*too late!*' Strauss was generous to Munich. Although his contract finally expired on 30 September, he conducted three opera performances there in October and another at short notice in December. At what had been expected to be his last performance, on 18 October (*Fidelio*), he was crowned with six laurel wreaths. He wrote to Pauline, who was already in Berlin: '*Fidelio* for the last time! Then *finis!* Off and away—into your arms!'

So the future looked rosy for the Strauss family when they went to their Marquartstein villa in the summer of 1898. Richard had the sketches of a new orchestral work with him, his biggest to date. 'Beethoven's *Eroica* is so little beloved of our conductors, and is on this account now only rarely performed,' he wrote ironically, 'that to fulfil a pressing need I am composing a largeish tone-poem entitled *Heldenleben* [Hero's Life], admittedly without a funeral march, yet in E flat, with lots of horns, which are always a yardstick of heroism.'

5

A hero's life

'I had no reason ever to regret my association with Berlin; on the whole, my stay there was pure joy, and I found much appreciation and hospitality.' Thus Strauss wrote[1] in old age. Berlin between 1900 and 1914 was a contrast with the Vienna of the same period, a contrast that is curiously epitomized in the music of Strauss, Berlin Opera's conductor from 1898 to 1910, and of Mahler, Vienna Opera's conductor from 1897 to 1907. Much that was exciting, new and glorious in the arts occurred in Vienna at this period, yet the atmosphere of Austrian twilight, as Emperor Franz Joseph grew older, was everywhere, and not only twilight but corruption and decay. In Berlin, where Bismarck died in 1898, Kaiser Wilhelm ruled over a strong, buoyant, militaristic and proud nation. It was a rich city, mixing the grandiose and the sentimental in its architecture, literature and music. The prosperous middle class prospered still more, largely oblivious of the seamy streak inseparable from the social conditions of a country 'on the make'.

Critics of Strauss maintain that he was the very man for this atmosphere. But he was much too complex both as man and artist to be conveniently fitted into any one category. He had little interest in, or knowledge of, politics and was—as will be seen—pitifully naïve when they encroached upon him. First and last he was a court musician and he understood musical politics and mastered them. One has only to read Weingartner's disagreeable autobiography[2] to gain a strong impression of the intrigues and skulduggery rampant in European musical life and of the power exercised by the opera intendants and their henchmen. If only half of what he recounts was true, it still leaves a scarifying picture (nor, of course, is it a thing of the past). In Strauss we see constantly at work the conflicts and tensions which stemmed from his personality: the instinctive musician, overwhelmingly brilliant and intelligent—'in music one can say everything', he said, 'people won't understand you'—and the bourgeois, non-intellectual and down to earth.

Penetrating analysis and description of Strauss at this point in his

---

[1] R. Strauss, 'Recollections of my Youth and Years of Apprenticeship', op. cit.
[2] F. Weingartner, *Buffets and Rewards* (Eng. trans. by Marguerite Wolff, London, 1937).

career may be found in the writings of the French author Romain Rolland, who had first met him casually in 1891 when they were fellow lunch guests of Cosima at Bayreuth, but came to know him well in Berlin and Paris from 1898. He described him in his fourth-floor flat at No. 30, Knesebeckstrasse, Charlottenburg:

> Very young face; dark hair receding, very little hair on the forehead, which is rounded, full and rather handsome; very pale eyes; the moustache so fair as to be almost white. . . . Tall, but holds himself with extreme lassitude. Childish and involuntary shyness in his smile and gestures; but one feels underneath a pride which is cold, self-willed, indifferent or contemptuous of the majority of things and people.[3]

To Rolland, Strauss described Berlin's opera audience as 'nothing but bankers and shopkeepers'. But Rolland wrote in his diary, 'when the word "people" is mentioned, this disciple of Nietzsche understands— rabble. . . . The tradition and the conventionalism of the Schauspielhaus . . . disgust him'. Rolland quickly noticed the two faces of Strauss. He saw him as 'the typical artist of the new German empire, the powerful reflection of that heroic pride, which is on the verge of becoming delirious, of that contemptuous Nietzscheism, of that egotistical and practical idealism, which makes a cult of power and disdains weakness'. But: 'He has certain dispositions which I had not seen clearly before, and which strictly speaking belong more to the people of Munich, the South Germans: an elemental vein of the clownish humour, paradoxical and satirical, of a spoilt child, or of Till Eulenspiegel.'

In his memoirs,[4] Rolland gives a penetrating personal estimate of Strauss who, he said,

> never stopped working, *nulla dies sine linea*, and always retained his respect for his noble calling. But somehow in a flash another man would appear at his elbow, who was possessed by a demon of lassitude, limpness, irony and indifference. Strauss was on his guard, however. He knew the dangers of his own nature better than anyone, and while he would stroke the demon affectionately, he always kept it on a tight leash . . . He played the jesting cynic in order to pull the wool over the philistines' eyes . . . but *tête à tête* with a friend whom he respected (*rara avis!*) he revealed his true self: very judicious and moderate . . . His tone and manner altered completely according to the person he was speaking to.

Yet this 'typical artist of the new German empire' made it plain to Rolland that he was uneasy with the strictness and moral hypocrisy of Berlin, that it had been predicted that because of his outspokenness he would lose his head, and that he had something less than an adulatory

---

[3] Quoted from R. Myers (ed.), *Richard Strauss and Romain Rolland: Correspondence, diary and essays* (London, 1968).
[4] R. Rolland, *In My Life: Memories of Childhood and Youth* (Amsterdam, 1949).

opinion of the Kaiser, who had described Strauss as 'a serpent I've harboured in my bosom'. Strauss's account of his first interview with the Kaiser, recorded in Rolland's diary for 1 March 1900,[5] is often quoted, and deservedly:

> The Emperor . . . frowns as he looks at him: 'You're yet another of these modern musicians?' He [Strauss] bows. 'I have heard Schillings's *Ingwelde*; it's execrable, there's no melody.' 'Forgive me, Your Majesty, there is melody but it is hidden beneath the polyphony.' He looks at him with a stern eye: 'You are one of the worst.' Another bow. 'The whole of modern music is worth nothing, there's no melody.' Same game. 'I like *Freischütz* better.' 'Your Majesty, I too like *Freischütz* better'.

Rolland wrote: 'He seems to live in a rather isolated way in Berlin. . . . He does not like society, nor does his wife. They always vie with one another in not accepting invitations. . . . In Berlin he is the enemy of the conservatives' camp, of which the Mendelssohns are the patrons and Joachim the god.' What particularly worried Strauss in Berlin was the increasing puritanical attitude to art and its reflection in extended powers of censorship. Although he conducted several new operas, he felt frustrated because he had no direction of artistic policy: he was chief conductor, but the Intendant was the director. His rose-coloured recollection of 'pure joy' must be interpreted within this context.

Another criticism of Strauss—especially by English puritans—is that he knew the value of money and especially his own value in money. He was, after all, the scion of a business family, and he saw no virtue in starving in garrets. His money-consciousness was not selfish. In 1898 he sought the aid of two friends, Friedrich Rösch, a lawyer, and the much older H. F. A. Zincke, physicist-turned-composer (under the name Hans Sommer) in founding a society with the aims of improving German copyright law, obtaining higher royalties, determining a minimum fee, and establishing an agency for the collection of royalties and fees. The society was named *Genossenschaft deutscher Tonsetzer* (Fellowship of German Composers). It took seven years, against opposition from publishers, politicians, and composers, before the struggle was won and a performing-rights society was established. In all this, Strauss was the principal champion of his colleagues' dues.

His contract at the Berlin Opera began on 1 November 1898 and he chose *Tristan* for his first appearance. After a few weeks he wrote to his father:

> I like Berlin with its splendid transport facilities, my apartment in its wonderful position, every domestic convenience, the servant problem solved satisfactorily . . . My work to date has been very agreeable. I have conducted to date,

---

[5] Norman Del Mar ascribes this conversation to November 1904, but it must have been in 1898 or 1899.

without rehearsal in every case, *Carmen, Hänsel, Fidelio, Die lustigen Weiber von Windsor, Rienzi* and, with one orchestral rehearsal, *La Muette de Portici* . . . The orchestra has excellent discipline. I am treated with the greatest respect. A real blessing after Munich.

In his first eight months in Berlin he conducted twenty-five different operas in a total of seventy-one performances (including a *Ring* cycle) and in his second season he was at the desk for ninety performances of thirty works. His chief assistant was Karl Mück. His international fame (and notoriety) continued to spread. Just before he began his work in Berlin he went again to 'staid and solid Amsterdam' for 'the greatest triumph of my career' (as he wrote to his father). In 1895 the twenty-four year old Willem Mengelberg had become conductor of the Concertgebouw Orchestra and rapidly made it a superb instrument. In October 1898, Strauss conducted it in *Also sprach Zarathustra*, 'the most beautiful performance . . . I have ever experienced; it had been rehearsed in sectional rehearsals for three weeks'. In gratitude, Strauss dedicated *Ein Heldenleben* to Mengelberg and the Concertgebouw Orchestra, but the dedicatees did not give the first performance, which Strauss conducted at Frankfurt on 3 March 1899.

The new tone-poem had a mixed reception. Because it was easily identifiable as musical autobiography and there was a long section of quotations from some of Strauss's other works, the work was labelled by some commentators as 'megalomaniac'. (Why literary autobiography and pictorial self-portraiture should be considered respectable but musical autobiography be 'tasteless' is an aesthetic mystery that defies rational solution.) Also, there was the section about the 'adversaries', in other words the critics, who are depicted as spiteful, whining and pompous. Franz Strauss thought that it was 'beneath one's dignity to notice' the adversaries his son depicted, and many people still agree with him. It has also been pointed out that, apart from *Guntram*, Strauss's career had been unhindered by failures attributable to the critics. But his successes had been with the public and other conductors rather than with the critics. Hostility to the new was general, and was often venomously expressed. In writing the adversaries section, Strauss was probably thinking not only of himself but of Wagner, Liszt and Berlioz and even of some of his contemporaries, such as Mahler. The adversaries also include the philistine elements in German life which he had detested in Munich and was to find also in Berlin.

If Strauss was less than magnanimous in his attitude to criticism, he did not lack the more important virtue of helpfulness to colleagues. In the opera house he was always willing to conduct a new contemporary work provided he could persuade the Intendant to risk it. At his concerts he several times conducted works by Mahler (though not the first performances with which he has often been credited, and credited himself); he recommended Reger to his own publisher; and England must never forget that on 20 May 1902, the day after a Düsseldorf performance of *The Dream of Gerontius*, Strauss proposed a toast to 'the first English progressivist, Meister Edward Elgar', and thereafter remained a friend and admirer of Elgar.[6] He championed the music of the French composers Dukas and Chabrier: on 14 January 1899 he conducted a staged performance of the only completed act of Chabrier's *Brisëis*. 'Very free, highly seasoned', he described it to his parents. As an Edinburgh Festival performance in 1994 showed, *Brisëis* is highly erotic and seductively scored music which Strauss may well have remembered when he came to compose *Salome*. From October 1901 until the summer of 1903 he was conductor of the Berlin Tonkünstler Orchestra 'in concerts of exclusively new works', thereby often giving himself in the winter a working day of six hours' orchestral rehearsals for works like *Don Juan* and Bruckner's Third Symphony, followed by *Tristan* at the opera in the evening.

Strauss wrote the last notes of *Ein Heldenleben* on 27 December 1898. It was to be his last orchestral work for over three years. Since *Guntram* he had, on his own admission, 'lost the courage to write for the stage'. Maybe. The fact remains that he was continually considering libretti. He progressed some distance with an elaborate three-act ballet scenario called *Die Insel Kythere*, based on Watteau's painting *Embarquement pour Cythère*. This occupied him for much of 1900, a year in which his published output was confined to a fine crop of songs. It was laid aside, but the music survives and is found to contain themes which he used in later works.

In 1898 he met Ernst von Wolzogen, nine years his senior, a writer who founded the *Überbrettl* movement, a rather superior kind of barbed cabaret-song satire. Still seething at the way he had been treated in Munich, Strauss told Wolzogen that he wanted to 'wreak some vengeance' by composing an opera in which Munich's philistinism towards Wagner and himself could be lampooned. Both men agreed to look for a suitable subject, and Strauss discovered the Flemish legend *The Extinguished Fires of Audenaarde*, in which a spurned suitor is publicly humiliated by his girl and has revenge aided by a magician, who puts out all the fires in the town and makes it known that they can only be re-lit one at a time from the flame which will spring from the girl's anus when she is exhibited naked in the market-place. Wolzogen changed the location to medieval Munich and made the hero a sorcerer's apprentice. He introduced topical allusions by aligning the sorcerer with Strauss and his master with Wagner. The libretto contains puns on the names Wagner, Strauss and Wolzogen, the music quotes Wagner, and the revised plot, set on midsummer's eve, is obviously inspired by *Die*

---

[6] Elgar and Strauss first met in August 1897 when Elgar heard him conduct *Tristan und Isolde* in Munich. Strauss conducted *Cockaigne* in Berlin early in 1902 and Elgar sent him some notes about tempi.

Meistersinger, especially the hero Kunrad's long monologue on the nature of art and inspiration, ending with the assertion that warmth and light spring only from women and from love.

Wolzogen called the poem *Feuersnot* (*Trial by Fire*). It was finished in October 1900. Strauss then began to sketch the music. He worked fast—it would be 'pure Lortzing', he told old Franz, 'supremely popular and melodious'—and finished the sketches by Christmas. Orchestration took from 1 January until 22 May 1901, which was Wagner's birthday. 'Completed on the birthday and to the greater glory of the "Almighty",' he wrote on the last page—blasphemy enough to damn *Feuersnot* in the eyes and ears of those at whom its barbs were aimed. '. . . Kunrad's sermon was the most important issue to me', Strauss wrote in his memoirs in 1945, 'and the rest merely a jolly background, and anyway people should at least acknowledge the courage that it took for an at that date still unsuccessful operatic composer to read his own compatriots a little lecture for their behaviour towards Richard Wagner.'

Two opera houses applied to Strauss for the first performance, Mahler's Vienna and Ernst von Schuch's Dresden. He awarded it to Schuch, who at this time was fifty-five and had been in full charge at Dresden since 1882. Strauss had been profoundly impressed by Schuch's conducting of *Till* in December 1895. He knew that Vienna would cause trouble over the licentious parts of the libretto, and when Dresden surprised him by doing likewise he refused to accept their suggested alterations. The first performance on 21 November 1901 was highly successful. 'Schuch is a marvel,' Strauss told his father. 'He has let me see my work as it really is.' In consequence there were to be eight more Dresden premières of Strauss operas over the next thirty-seven years.

The Vienna première of *Feuersnot*, two months later under Mahler, was also a success. It has been fancifully described by Alma Mahler.[7] She states, wrongly, that Mahler did not conduct 'because he had a horror of the work'. Not only did he conduct the first but also several later performances—he liked the opera. Alma describes Pauline as 'raging the whole time. Nobody, she said, could possibly like that shoddy work . . . there wasn't an original note in it, all stolen from Wagner and many others.' Strauss commented on this: 'My wife always particularly liked *Feuersnot*.' Later Pauline and Strauss had one of their famous rows, which Richard explained to Alma thus: 'My wife's dreadfully rude sometimes, but that's what I need, you know.'

This seems the appropriate moment at which to outline Strauss's relationship with one of the giants of twentieth-century music, Arnold Schoenberg. Just married, the twenty-seven-year-old Schoenberg had gone to Berlin in December 1901 to work with Wolzogen in the *Überbrettl*. Perhaps encouraged by Wolzogen, he wrote to Strauss seeking a

[7] A. Mahler, *Gustav Mahler: Memories and Letters* (Eng. trans. by B. Creighton, ed. D. Mitchell, London, 1968).

meeting in April 1902. Strauss was composing his big choral work *Taillefer* and arranged for Schoenberg to copy the parts. He also tried to obtain a teaching post for him at the Stern Conservatory, offered to help him financially in his capacity as president of the German Musical Society and wrote to Max von Schillings in Munich to ask him to 'write a splendid testimonial' for 'a man who lives in the most dire poverty and is *very* talented'. Strauss and Schillings were trustees of a scholarship which was part of the Liszt Foundation, and Schoenberg was twice awarded the scholarship of 1,000 marks a year. Strauss also introduced Schoenberg to Maeterlinck's *Pelléas et Mélisande*, not knowing about Debussy's opera, and Schoenberg immediately began to compose his tone-poem, completing it in 1903. When Schoenberg left Berlin later that year to work in Vienna, he wrote to Strauss to thank him 'for all the help you have given me at a sacrifice to yourself . . . I will not forget this for the whole of my life and will always be grateful to you for it'.

Over the next few years Schoenberg wrote several times asking Strauss to include some of his works in his orchestral concerts. Strauss showed polite interest but did nothing. Eventually Schoenberg sent him the *Five Orchestral Pieces*, Op. 16. Strauss returned the score with a friendly letter but no hope of a performance: 'You know I am glad to help people and I also have courage. But your pieces are such daring experiments in content and sound that for the moment I dare not introduce them to the more than conservative Berlin public.'

In Vienna Schoenberg became an adherent of Mahler and said later that 'since I have understood Mahler, I have inwardly rejected Strauss'. When Mahler died in 1911, a foundation bearing his name was set up with Strauss as one of the trustees. Mahler's widow Alma suggested a payment to Schoenberg, to which Strauss agreed, although by now he was totally out of sympathy with Schoenberg's method of composition. But he wrote in a letter to her: 'I believe that it would be better for him to be shovelling snow than scrawling on music paper.' Alma had no more tact or sense than to show this to Schoenberg, who was mortified. Asked in 1914 to write a tribute to Strauss on his fiftieth birthday, he refused and told the editor of the journal concerned: 'As an artist he does not interest me at all nowadays, and as for what I may have learned from him in the past, thank God that I misunderstood it.' The personal rift was never healed, but Schoenberg never denied what he had learned from Strauss and was one of the few musicians who recognized that the opera *Intermezzo* was a masterpiece when it appeared in 1924. Strauss for his part, when he was dismissed from the Vienna Opera in 1924, wrote to a critic that 'I would also have performed Schoenberg and Krenek, for I do not subscribe to the point of view that the novelties which I perform should be personally pleasing to me'.

But this is to look ahead. Although he did not know it at the time, the most significant event in Strauss's operatic career had occurred before he began to compose *Feuersnot*. In the first days of March 1900, while he was conducting in Paris, he met the twenty-six-year-old Austrian poet and playwright Hugo von Hofmannsthal, who went to him with a suggestion for collaboration in a ballet. Strauss showed interest. In mid-November Hofmannsthal sent him the almost-completed scenario. Strauss replied from Charlottenburg on 14 December, in a letter which shows how accurately he planned his work schedule:

> I shall not set it to music, much as I like it. . . . My own ballet [*Kythere*], which I pieced together last summer, though probably inferior to your work, is nevertheless so much nearer to me that I shall certainly tackle it first, as soon as a little opera of mine is finished [*Feuersnot*]. And *after* this ballet (i.e. in about three years' time) the symphonic composer who has lain entirely dormant for the past two years will no doubt break through violently.[8]

This was the unpromising prelude to one of the most fruitful collaborations in the history of music.

[8] *Correspondence between R. Strauss and H. von Hofmannsthal* (Eng. trans. by H. Hammelmann and E. Osers, London, 1961).

6
Vulcan's labours

During the first years of the twentieth century Strauss was a regular visitor to Britain, conducting his works in London, Birmingham and Glasgow (he directed the Scottish Orchestra in the first complete British performance of *Aus Italien*). In June 1903 there was a Strauss Festival in London at the St James's Hall, at which he and Mengelberg conducted the Concertgebouw Orchestra. A still valid summing-up of the enlightened British attitude to Strauss was written on 17 October 1902 by one of England's most brilliant music critics, Arthur Johnstone of the *Manchester Guardian*, who died in 1904 at the age of forty-three:

> Of course the upholders of a turnip-headed orthodoxy will not hear of him, any more than they would hear of Richard I a quarter of a century ago, and he seems to have an irritating effect on all critics, except a certain very small minority. . . . He is enigmatic, Sphinx-like, a complex personality not to be conveniently catalogued. . . . Those who assert that Strauss is a mere eccentric will sooner or later find themselves in the wrong. He has in a few cases played tricks on the public, but he is nevertheless a master-composer, in the full and simple sense of those words—a master-composer just as Mozart was.[1]

The 'mere eccentric' was on the verge of upsetting the turnip heads more than ever. In April 1902—ironically, the month before Pauline threatened him with divorce over a misunderstanding which later formed the plot of the opera *Intermezzo* (see Chapter 17)—he began work on a large-scale symphonic poem. Progress was slow, by Strauss standards, and the draft sketch of what he was to call by a Latin title, *Symphonia Domestica*, was not completed until July 1903 when he was staying in the Isle of Wight. The full score was finished on New Year's Eve 1903 and dedicated 'to my dear wife and our son'. It was scored for an orchestra of nearly 110 players, including five clarinets, eight horns and four (optional) saxophones. 'In the home one can't make so much noise!' old Franz Strauss protested.

Strauss reserved the first performance for his and Pauline's first visit to the United States. He was enticed to the New World at very high fees by an expatriate German musician, Hermann Hans Wetzler, who had

[1] A. Johnstone, *Musical Criticisms* (Manchester, 1905).

40

founded his own orchestra in New York. With this short-lived orchestra Strauss made his American conducting début in Carnegie Hall on 27 February 1904. The new work was to be performed on 21 March, and Strauss told the Press that it represented 'a day in the life of my family, part lyrical, part humorous'. Nothing could have been better calculated to concentrate people's ears on extra-musical matters, and Strauss was naïve to expect otherwise.

Since that day the *Symphonia Domestica* has been the butt of heavy humour; worse, there was real hostility because Strauss had 'exploited' his private life in his music. People who contentedly read novels or attended plays and operas in which broken lives and adulterous passions were romanticized were 'shocked' or 'embarrassed' by Strauss's depiction of his blameless Bavarian home life. Also there was still so much fatuous controversy about the relative aesthetic values of programme and absolute music that Strauss, who was as sensitive and irritated about it as Mahler was, tried to cover his tracks by deleting from the printed score his numerous original headings for the various incidents, but some remained accidentally (for example the uncles' and aunts' comments on the baby: 'Just like his father', 'Just like his mother') and gave the game away. The work was politely received by the public and most impolitely by the American critics. Meanwhile the German Press denounced him for conducting two afternoon concerts in a New York department store, Wanamaker's, when the new work was repeated. Such conduct was 'a prostitution of art'. Strauss replied that the concerts had been given in artistic conditions and, anyway, it was no disgrace to earn money.

The furore over the new tone-poem was a nine-day wonder, to be totally overshadowed by the response to Strauss's next work, the one-act opera *Salome*. With unerring artistic (and business) instinct he perceived that here was the perfect subject; it symbolized the decadence of late-Romantic literature and painting and mixed lust and religion against the fashionable background of orientalism. A winner, surely! Oscar Wilde's play, written in French for Sarah Bernhardt, had been published in Paris in 1893. He interpreted the character of Salome in a new way: erotic desire, he decided, was at the root of her behaviour. Bernhardt acted the role in Paris in 1896.

The first German production of the play was in Breslau in 1901. The following year *Salomé* was staged in Berlin by a twenty-nine-year-old producer, Max Reinhardt, and ran for 200 performances. Strauss first read the play when it was sent to him in 1902 by the Austrian poet Anton Lindner,[2] who offered to convert it into a libretto and, after Strauss showed interest, sent 'a cleverly versified' opening scene as a sample. Strauss did not like Lindner's contribution. He saw that Wilde's

---

[2] Strauss had set Lindner's poem 'Hochzeitlich Lied' in 1897–8 as No. 6 of the *Sechs Lieder*, Op. 37.

text, in Hedwig Lachmann's German translation—particularly the opening line 'How beautiful the Princess Salome is tonight'—had distinct musical possibilities, and he began sketches. His copy of the play reveals that against various crucial lines he scribbled musical ideas which must have occurred to him while he read. In November 1902 he attended the Reinhardt production, with Gertrud Eysoldt in the title-role. Afterwards a friend said to him: 'Surely you could make an opera of this?' He replied: 'I am already composing it.'

The bulk of the composing was done after his return from America. The full sketch was completed during his 1904 summer holiday, and the score was fully orchestrated by 20 June 1905. He played some of it to his father, who commented: 'It's like having ants in your pants.' It was the last new music by his son that Franz heard. He died, aged eighty-three, on 31 May 1905. A few days before that, Strauss was in Strasbourg with Mahler and his wife, Alma, and played *Salome* to them in a pianoforte showroom. The score was then complete except for the Dance of the Seven Veils. Mahler asked if it was not risky to write it later 'when you're not in the same mood'. Strauss replied light-heartedly: 'I'll soon fix that.'

In truth, Strauss was still very much in the mood. On 5 July, a fortnight after completing the opera, he told his publisher Adolph Fürstner that he would make a French version of *Salome* in which the orchestration would be retained but the vocal line altered to accommodate Wilde's original French text. He sought the help of Romain Rolland, who urged him to study Debussy's *Pelléas et Mélisande*. Strauss found inconsistencies, what he termed an 'undisciplined approach', in Debussy's accenting of French words and refused to make amendments in Wilde's text which Rolland pointed out were bad French. 'I should like to achieve a quite special French edition of my opera', he told Rolland, 'which does not give the impression of being a translation but of being a real setting of the original. It must become a real French opera, not a translation!!!'

Strauss composed the Dance of the Seven Veils on 30 August while working on the French version, which he finished on 13 September. After Rolland had made many suggestions, Strauss sent this version to Fürstner in November, and it was published in piano score during 1906. It is probable that it was used for the Paris première, a private performance in March 1907 at the Petit-Théâtre. In the same month it was performed in Brussels at the Théâtre de la Monnaie. Strauss conducted the German version at the Théâtre du Châtelet in May 1906. No doubt the existence of two versions, involving singers in learning them both, was impracticable. At any rate, nothing further was heard of the French *Salomé*; and in 1909 Strauss agreed to a free French translation of Lachmann's German libretto which fitted the vocal line of the original score. Strauss's French version was totally forgotten, its existence unknown, until it was rediscovered in the 1980s by the Richard Strauss Institute in Munich. A semi-staged performance was given at Montpellier in July 1989 and a staged performance at the Opéra de Lyon in May 1990. A recording followed which allows a wide public to appreciate how subtly Strauss altered his score to achieve his aim of 'a real French opera'. There are two Strauss operas, *Salome* and *Salomé*.

Strauss offered the first performance of his German version to Schuch at Dresden. At the first read-through in the summer of 1905 the soloists returned their parts to the conductor except for Karel Burrian (Herod), who already knew his by heart. The Salome, Marie Wittich, caused the most trouble. 'I won't do it, I'm a decent woman,' she kept saying. She was excessively fat, but had the voice for a part which Strauss had described as 'the sixteen-year-old princess with the voice of Isolde'. However, her procrastination caused the projected November première to be postponed. Strauss warned Schuch that 9 December was the last date for which he could guarantee Dresden the first performance and this deadline was met. At the dress rehearsal Strauss sat in the front row behind Schuch. After the last chord, there was silence. Strauss turned to the invited audience and said 'Well, I enjoyed that'. Then the applause began. It was a roaring success, and this news spread to all major opera houses, fifty of which staged several performances within two years. By the end of 1907 there had been fifty Berlin performances, but only after an initial ban by the Kaiser (who never saw the opera) had been overcome by the Intendant, Georg von Hülsen, who arranged for the Star of Bethlehem to appear at the end! *Salome* encountered its worst censorship trouble in Vienna, as Mahler had warned Strauss that it would. Mahler offered his resignation but to no avail; this work was not performed in Vienna's great opera house until 1918. The rest of Austria was more amenable and Mahler saw *Salome* at Graz on 16 May 1906. He saw it again twice in Berlin in January 1907 with Emmy Destinn as Salome. His opinions are fascinating: 'It is emphatically a work of genius, very powerful, and decidedly one of the most important works of our day. A Vulcan lives and labours under a heap of slag, a subterranean fire—not merely a firework! It is exactly the same with Strauss's whole personality. . . . It is one of the greatest masterpieces of our time.'[3]

Toscanini conducted the first Italian performance. Strauss, who was in Italy to conduct *Salome* in Turin, wrote to Pauline: 'In Milan, Toscanini, with the aid of a mercilessly raging orchestra, simply butchered the singers and the drama (à la Mottl). It is a miracle it was nevertheless a success . . . The conductor played a symphony without singers.' In New York in 1907 there was such an outcry, led by the daughter of the influential financier J. Pierpont Morgan, after the first

---

[3] A. Mahler, *Gustav Mahler: Memories and Letters*, op. cit.

Metropolitan performance—'moral stench . . . loathsome . . . abhor-
rent'—that further performances were cancelled and the work disappeared from that theatre until 1934. At Covent Garden in 1910, when
Beecham conducted, some alterations were made in the text to appease
the Lord Chamberlain and were ignored in performance without
anyone noticing. The total effect was that Strauss became unquestion-
ably the most famous living composer, notwithstanding Puccini. And
not only famous. The Kaiser commented: 'I really like this fellow
Strauss, but *Salome* will do him a lot of damage.' Strauss drily comments in his reminiscences: 'The damage enabled me to build the villa
in Garmisch.'

In the winter of 1903–4 Max Reinhardt followed Wilde's *Salomé* with
'a new version' of Sophocles' *Electra* by Hugo von Hofmannsthal.
Strauss sounded the playwright on the possibility of his adapting it as a
libretto. Hofmannsthal completed the task in 1905. Three months after
Salome had been launched, he wrote from his home at Rodaun, near
Vienna, to ask if Strauss had made any progress. Strauss was by now
having doubts whether he could tackle so similar a subject so soon after
Salome. Perhaps they could do something else first. He added these
remarkable words: 'I would ask you urgently to give me first refusal of
anything composable that you write. Your manner has so much in common with mine; we were born for one another and are certain to do fine
things together if you remain faithful to me.'

Hofmannsthal persisted that *Elektra* ought to be their first collaboration and a contract was signed whereby he received 25 per cent of the
royalties on their joint work. They never quarrelled over their business
arrangements. Strauss's 'mercenary' nature is often pilloried, but in a letter to his collaborator on 5 June 1906 he set out his views in a manner
that commands respect:

> One does not need to be a businessman to wish to derive decent remuneration
> after sitting up with a long opera score night after night for two or three years.
> Once the pleasure of creation has passed, then the annoyance of performances
> and those blessed criticisms begin, and only a good stipend can compensate one
> for that. . . . I merely say out loud what other 'idealists' think to themselves.

By mid-June of 1906 Strauss had begun to compose *Elektra*, 'making
rather heavy weather'. Work on it stretched over the next two years,
being completed on 22 September 1908. 'You are the born librettist', he
told Hofmannsthal after receiving the Recognition Scene. 'The end is
juicy', he wrote to Schuch at Dresden. 'The principal role must now
undoubtedly be given to the most dramatic soprano you have.' They
chose Annie Krull. Strauss found Schuch's treatment of the teeming
orchestral score too subdued and colourless during rehearsals but admitted that the first performance was perfectly balanced. (Otto Klemperer
said that Strauss himself made *Elektra* sound 'like an opera by

Lortzing'.[4]) The first performance, in Dresden on 25 January 1909, was no more than a *succès d'estime*. It was part of a 'Strauss Week' and, according to the playwright and critic Hermann Bahr,

all Europe is in Dresden, my hotel porter proudly confided to me . . . The splendid thing about [Strauss] is that he is not at all like his admirers. A durable, weather-proof, remarkably collected man, calm and good-tempered. Gardeners look like this, and people who spend a lot of time looking through microscopes . . . He is still quite young, but doesn't even look his 44 years, the eyes are not yet twenty, so trusting and unclouded is the gaze with which they view the world in innocence, romantic Wanderlust and confidence . . . His is a unique case: an artist who frightens the cognoscenti with his audacity, but wins the crowd at first hearing.[5]

But many people who heard *Elektra* echoed the opinions of Ernestine Schumann-Heink, the first Klytämnestra, who declared in New York that the opera was 'a horrible din'. Nevertheless, being by Strauss it was eagerly sought by other opera houses. Vienna staged it on 24 March, and Milan shortly afterwards; Beecham conducted it in London in February 1910, with Edyth Walker as Elektra.

The Covent Garden performances, played to excited full houses, led to a famous controversy. Ernest Newman, reviewing *Elektra* in *The Nation* on 26 February 1910, allowed that Strauss was 'the greatest living musician' but that 'much of the music is as abominably ugly as it is noisy. . . . One still clings to the hope that the future has in store for us a purified Strauss, clothed and in his right mind, who will help us to forget the present Strauss—a saddening mixture of genius, ranter, child and charlatan.' Newman was answered by Bernard Shaw, who described these remarks as 'ridiculous and idiotic'. He added that the power of 'the passion that detests and must and finally can destroy that evil' was what made the work great 'and makes us rejoice in its horror'.[6]

Strauss himself conducted two of the first nine London performances, on 12 and 15 March 1910. The critic of the *Daily Mail*, probably Richard Capell, described him brilliantly: 'His thin long hand held the tapering baton like a pen. His head was immobile; only his eagle eyes flashed from time to time. . . . His elbows seemed riveted to his body. . . . The baton did not cleave the air with fantastic arabesques; he seemed a mathematician writing a formula on an imaginary blackboard, neatly and with supreme knowledge.' Shaw, in one of his letters rebutting Newman's strictures, mentioned the performances: 'It was interesting to compare our conductor, the gallant Beecham, bringing out the points in Strauss's orchestration until sometimes the music sounded like a concerto for six drums, with Strauss himself, bringing out the meaning

[4] P. Heyworth, *Conversations with Klemperer* (London, 1973), p. 44.
[5] Quoted in K. Wilhelm, *Richard Strauss, An Intimate Portrait*, op. cit., pp. 122–3.
[6] G. B. Shaw (ed. D. H. Laurence), *How to Become a Musical Critic* (London, 1960), pp. 257–67.

and achieving the purpose of his score so that we forgot that there was an orchestra there at all and could hear nothing but the conflict and storm of passion.' When Strauss conducted *Elektra* in Vienna in June 1909 it was his first appearance at the Court Opera there. Vienna was to be the scene of his next and most famous opera. He had had enough of horror and tragedy. 'Next time I'll write a Mozart opera.'

In later years Strauss sometimes affected to be bored with his early 'green horror'. But the conductor Karl Böhm had a touching memory of the old composer at a rehearsal of *Elektra*: 'Strauss was sitting in the stalls with my wife; about fifteen minutes from the end he grabbed her hand and wouldn't let go. When we had finished she asked him what was wrong, and he simply said: "Did I write that music? I'd almost forgotten it." ' In his old age, when a younger generation upbraided him for not embracing atonality, he remarked: 'Me, a renegade? Is that what they say? And yet I was one of the first in that business with *Elektra*.'

7

Comedy for music

In thinking about providing Strauss with a comedy, Hofmannsthal re-read Beaumarchais's *Le Mariage de Figaro* and other French novels and plays, notably Louvet de Couvray's *Les Amours du Chevalier de Faublas*. He wanted to give Strauss characters with the psychological interest of Figaro, Susanna, Cherubino and the Countess. In February 1909 he stayed in Weimar with Count Harry Kessler, diplomat and journalist. They worked out the action of a comedy, taking some of the names and situations from Couvray's novel. Hofmannsthal outlined a scenario which owed more than is often acknowledged to Kessler's ideas. It contained these points:

> Sophie, with the pretty Faublas, tells of her forthcoming marriage. She is astonished that he is troubled by it. . . . The Intriguers. . . . Bedroom of the Marquise. Night of love. Pourceaugnac announced. Faublas remains in disguise. . . . Hairdresser, servants etc. . . . While the Marquise has her coiffure dressed, P. invites the chambermaid to supper . . . Room at the inn. . . . The Marquise appears. . . . The disguised Faublas reveals himself.

Hofmannsthal wrote to Strauss from Weimar on 11 February: 'I find the scenario enchanting. . . . It contains two big parts, one for baritone and another for a graceful girl dressed up as a man, *à la* Farrar, or Mary Garden. Period: the old Vienna under the Empress Maria Theresa.' Strauss replied: 'We'll go ahead with this. . . . You go straight home and send Act I as soon as you can.' So began what the world knows as *Der Rosenkavalier*, although its authors did not give it that title until it was almost completed. Faublas became Oktavian, Pourceaugnac the Baron Ochs and the Marquise the Feldmarschallin. Both men worked enthusiastically at astonishing speed, as extracts from their marvellous correspondence show:

Strauss (in Garmisch), 21 April 1909: 'Am impatiently waiting for the next instalment. The opening scene is delightful: it'll set itself to music like oil and melted butter; I'm hatching it out already. You're da Ponte and Scribe rolled into one. . . .'

Hofmannsthal (in Rodaun), 24 April: 'Do try and think of an old-fashioned Viennese waltz, sweet and yet saucy, which must pervade the whole of the last act.'

S. 4 May: 'The final scene [Act I] is magnificent: I've already done a bit of exper-
imenting with it today. I wish I'd got there already. But since, for the sake
of symphonic unity, I must compose the music from the beginning to the end
I'll just have to be patient. . . . I'll need very good actors again; ordinary
operatic singers won't do.'
  16 May: 'My work is flowing along like the Loisach: I am composing everything—neck and crop.[1] I am starting on the Levée tomorrow.'
H. 12 June: 'Everything you played to me from the first act of the opera is most
beautiful, and has given me great and lasting pleasure. I have now re-read
Act II and am absolutely determined to make drastic changes in the last five
minutes. . . . I know already how to do it.'

On 9 July Strauss wrote a long letter critizing Act II severely and suggesting in considerable detail a complete revision of the action. From
Ochs's return after signing the marriage contract to the end of the act is
entirely in accordance with Strauss's new ideas. Reconstruction of this
act occupied most of the remainder of 1909, and Hofmannsthal decided
to put completion of Act III aside for some months to 'mature and
enrich' it. During the winter of 1909–10 it was decided that Alfred
Roller, the great stage designer whose work with Mahler in Vienna had
revolutionized opera presentation, should provide the settings and costumes. On 23 April 1910 Strauss wrote: 'I am in Garmisch and am in
agonies waiting for Act III! The full score of Act II is already with the
printer! . . . Roller's costume sketches are magnificent!' Strauss began
composing Act III in May. At this stage he still favoured the title *Ochs
auf Lerchenau*.

On 6 June Hofmannsthal wrote to say that he had completed the act.
Significantly he added: 'The Marschallin is the central figure for the public, for the women above all, the figure with whom they feel and *move*.'
Strauss was conducting *Elektra* in various cities, including Vienna, and
at Strauss Weeks in his native Munich and Frankfurt.[2] It was not until
1 July that he briefly wrote 'Received end of *Rosenkavalier*: seems perfect to me.' This is the first indication that the opera's title had been
decided. (Strauss always spelt it *Rosencavalier*.) On 30 August
Hofmannsthal had sudden misgivings about the end, after Ochs's exit—
'a definite falling-off in interest'. He sent Strauss some cuts. Strauss's
reply was masterly: 'That it sounds a bit flat in reading is obvious. But
it is at the conclusion that a musician, if he has any ideas at all, can
achieve his best and supreme effects—so you may safely leave this for
me to judge. . . . From the Baron's exit onwards, I'll *guarantee* that, provided you undertake to guarantee the rest of the work.'

On 26 September Strauss completed the full score of what, recogniz-

---

[1] He was not exaggerating. In one scene he 'composed' one of Hofmannsthal's stage
directions.
[2] In Munich he conducted *Feuersnot*, *Salome* and *Elektra* and several of his orchestral
works. A plaque was fixed to his birthplace.

ing the supreme quality of the libretto, he insisted that the publisher should describe as a 'Comedy for Music in three acts by Hugo von Hofmannsthal: music by Richard Strauss'. He had begun negotiations for its production at Dresden when he saw Count von Seebach, Intendant of the Court Theatre there, earlier in 1910. Seebach objected to certain passages. The curtain could not rise on the Marschallin in bed; Ochs could not refer to tumbling girls in the hay; a Neapolitan general became a Russian general, etc. Strauss and Hofmannsthal devised a series of alternatives which appeared either in libretto, vocal score or full score but never in all three.

When Strauss went to an early rehearsal he was dismayed by the inadequacy of Georg Toller's production. So he asked Max Reinhardt to supervise the carrying out of his own ideas, but told nobody he had done so. Toller was furious. 'I couldn't possibly have foreseen that so intelligent a man as Toller would not have been simply delighted to have been helped by a Reinhardt,' Strauss wrote to Schuch with surpassing naïveté, 'just as even today I would be ready to learn like a schoolboy from you or Mahler or anybody else without a thought of being knocked off my pedestal.' Seebach insisted that Reinhardt should give his advice from the stalls, but later relented and allowed him on the stage. But only Toller's name was printed in the programme.

Even more important was the casting. For Ochs, Strauss always had in mind the great Vienna Opera bass, Richard Mayr, but he could not be released from his commitments there. The alternatives were Paul Bender, of Munich, or Dresden's Carl Perron, who was fifty-three and had created the roles of Jokanaan in *Salome* and Orestes in *Elektra*. Perron was chosen, but Strauss authorized cancellation of the première if Reinhardt and Hofmannsthal could not groom him for the part. The first performance, on 26 January 1911, was a dazzling success, and Strauss and Hofmannsthal gave Reinhardt principal credit for realization of the work as a true 'comedy for music'. Fifty performances were given in Dresden within a year, all sold out. Special trains were run from Berlin. So great had been the work's advance publicity that other opera houses were ready with their productions as soon as Dresden's right to the première had been fulfilled. It was produced in Nuremberg on 27 January and Mottl conducted it in Munich a few days later. In Hamburg, under Gustav Brecher, Edyth Walker sang Oktavian and the Sophie was Elisabeth Schumann, whose understudy in the role was Lotte Lehmann, eventually to be the greatest of Marschallins and, before that, to sing both Sophie and Oktavian. In Milan, where Tullio Serafin conducted, hisses and whistles greeted the second act because waltzes were tolerated only in ballet by the Scala audience—a turmoil renewed in the third act.

On 8 April 1911 Franz Schalk conducted the Vienna première, with Mayr as Ochs, Gertrud Förstel as Sophie, Marie Gutheil-Schoder as Oktavian and Lucie Weidt as the Marschallin. The audience acclaimed it; the Viennese critics gave a display of stupidity well in keeping with their long tradition in this respect (only rivalled over the years by New York critics): 'A joke against the public . . . banal tunes . . . will not retain a place for long in the repertoire of our Court Opera . . . cheap, low-class wit . . . morbid and unnatural.' Nevertheless, in the remaining eight months of 1911, *Der Rosenkavalier* was performed thirty-seven times in Vienna. In the carnival in Munich in 1911, nineteen Knights of the Rose, dressed in silver silk, rode in the procession. Cigarettes and champagne were named Rosenkavalier. Still today a train of that name crosses part of Europe daily. London and New York first heard the opera in 1913. Its popularity has never waned and there is no sign that it will.

Strauss first conducted *Der Rosenkavalier* in Cologne on 17 June 1911. He discovered that, as soon as he had left Dresden, Schuch had begun to make 'infamous cuts'. Strauss therefore infuriated him by pointing out that he had overlooked a good long cut in Act III where the action was held up for several minutes. He was referring to the greatest music in the opera, the Trio! In one of his angry letters to Schuch insisting on restoration of the excisions and the use only of the cuts he himself had sanctioned, Strauss wrote: 'I declare solemnly that the form in which you have performed *Rosenkavalier* for the last twenty-two times is a mutilation and bungled, and my objection to this is so strong that I tell you that if you do not put the matter right as I wish, then I will take legal action to ensure that you do.' In puritanical Berlin—where Strauss had resigned as court opera conductor in 1910 and was now principal guest conductor—the opera was not produced until 14 November 1911. When a friend from Dresden remarked that it had seemed shorter in Berlin, Strauss replied: 'Because there were fewer cuts.'

8

Airy-fairy

As early as 1906 Strauss and Hofmannsthal had discussed an opera on the subject of *Semiramis*, from a play by the seventeenth-century Spanish poet Pedro Calderón de la Barca. Strauss was greatly interested by this subject. On 20 February 1908 he asked for 'something tangible' by 1 June. 'Don't forget plenty of ballet, martial music and victory marching: these, apart from the erotic elements, are my strong suit.' No doubt he saw the opportunity for another *Aida*, having noted the success of that opera with the Berlin public in 1907 in a spectacular production. On 8 October 1910, when *Der Rosenkavalier* was finished, he wrote: 'The time has now almost come to think of *Semiramis*!' Hofmannsthal replied: 'No intellectual or material inducements could extract from me a play on this subject, not even a most determined effort of will.' It is possible that those dismissive words were fatefully crucial in their effect on Strauss's musical development.

Hofmannsthal then settled on *Das steinerne Herz*, based on a fairy-story by Wilhelm Hauff. 'Cheers for *Das steinerne Herz*!' Strauss wrote on 5 January 1911. 'Plenty of native atmosphere, please: German forest. Thunderstorm as Holländermichel fells his trees: this is how the thing might start.' Henceforward can be seen ever more plainly the conflict between Hofmannsthal the intellectual and Strauss the practical man of the theatre. To put it crudely, 'airy-fairy' versus 'down-to-earth'. 'What a confounded fool I was to tell you the title and the subject,' the poet replied. His idea of an adaptation was to be 'real and symbolical'. No *Freischütz* forest, peasants or scenic effects.

Hofmannsthal's first thoughts of *Die Frau ohne Schatten* were written in his notebook on 25 February 1911: '*Die Frau ohne Schatten* (first idea); Fantasy-comedy opera in the style of Gozzi. The central point a bizarre figure like Strauss's wife. The wife has sacrificed her children so as to remain beautiful (and to retain her voice) . . . Elements of *Zauberflöte* . . .' His next letter to Strauss, on 20 March, contained the germ of two operas:

> If we were to work together once more on something (and by this I mean something important, not the thirty-minute opera for small chamber orchestra which is as good as complete in my head; it is called *Ariadne auf Naxos* and is made

up of a combination of heroic mythological figures in 18th-century costume . . . and, interwoven in it, characters from the *commedia dell'arte* . . . representing the buffo element which is throughout interwoven with the heroic) . . . it would have to possess colourful and clear-cut action. I have something definite in mind. . . . It is a magic fairy-tale with two men confronting two women, and for one of the women your wife might well, in all discretion, be taken as a model. . . . Anyway she is a bizarre woman with a very beautiful soul, *au fond*, strange, moody, domineering and yet at the same time likeable.

Strauss was so anxious for work that he had even been in touch with Gabriele d'Annunzio about possible collaboration 'on an entirely modern subject'. Hofmannsthal put the damper on *Die Frau ohne Schatten*: he could not hurry such a subject. But he had a new idea for Molière, having seen *Le Bourgeois Gentilhomme* while in Paris. He planned a mixture of play and opera, the first part to be his adaptation of *Le Bourgeois Gentilhomme* (*Der Bürger als Edelmann*) with some incidental music for the dances, then a linking scene to the second part, *Ariadne auf Naxos*, with Strauss's music. He sent an outline on 19 May 1911. Strauss replied next day. Upset by Mahler's death two days earlier, he was offhand: 'The first half is very nice . . . the second half is thin. . . . For the dances of the Dancing Master, tailors and scullions, one could write some pleasant salon music.'

This novel entertainment was designed by Hofmannsthal as a challenge to the genius of Max Reinhardt. He was horrified when Strauss fixed on the *commedia* character of Zerbinetta, in the *Ariadne* half, as a star role for a coloratura soprano like Selma Kurz or Tetrazzini—he did not visualize a role for fat women, he wanted exquisite young voices, nothing remotely 'grand opera'. Yes, replied Strauss, you could get away with that while Reinhardt is in charge, but what about other theatres? They will need some star singing parts to make their profit,

> for the plot as such holds no interest and interesting costumes won't turn the scale either. Personally I am not particularly interested by the whole thing: that was why I asked you to spur your Pegasus a bit, so that the ring of the verses should stimulate me a little. You probably know my predilection for hymns in Schiller's manner and flourishes *à la* Rückert. Things like that excite me to formal orgies, and these must do the trick where the action itself leaves me cold. Soaring oratory can drug me sufficiently to keep on writing music through a passage of no interest.

Such blatant honesty offended Hofmannsthal, who wrote the first of a series of long letters explaining the psychological motives of his characters. 'When two men like us set out to produce a "trifle" like this, it has to become a very serious trifle,' he wrote portentously. In a further letter he explained 'the underlying meaning', with references to 'Death and Life at once' and 'the monologue of a lonely soul'. Strauss's reply was a delicious mixture of syrup and aloes:

Your letter . . . is so beautiful and explains the meaning of the action so w
derfully that a superficial musician like myself could not, of course, have t
bled to it. But isn't this a little dangerous? . . . If even I couldn't see it, j
think of the audiences and—the critics. . . . Surely the symbolism must leap c
alive from the action?

The plan at first was for the new work to be produced at Reinhardt's
Deutsches Theater in Berlin. But Pauline scotched it. 'Your things
demand the best, the very best, people at every level, an elegant theatre
with room to breathe in it, and good resources for sets and costumes',
she wrote to her husband. 'Producing this little opera in his place is mad.
It's good enough for a Busoni, but not for a Richard Strauss. Please listen to me, you will be grateful. I have always given you good advice!'
Strauss, pulling all available strings in Berlin, obtained permission for
the entire personnel of the Kleines Deutsches Theater to work in
Stuttgart under Reinhardt, and he would himself select the orchestra of
thirty-seven players. The Stuttgart theatre was new and well equipped.
Rehearsals began in June, and Strauss began to be enthusiastic. 'The
score is going to signpost a new road for comic opera. . . . It is a real
masterpiece of a score: you won't find another like it in a hurry.' Further
rehearsals were in October; Strauss, nurtured in drama at Meiningen,
now saw the real possibilities. 'Tremendously effective. Molière is
unspeakably funny,' he reported to Hofmannsthal. What he did not
report was that all was not well at Stuttgart, where neither the resident
actors and singers nor the theatrical management and staff welcomed the
arrival of Reinhardt's Berlin company. Since they had undertaken all the
preliminary rehearsals (which had convinced Strauss of the work's
worth) and were to take over after the first performance, they had some
cause for annoyance and Strauss did not help by telling the resident producer, who queried a technical point, 'Reinhardt will settle all that.' At
the dress rehearsal, vital members of the stage staff went to work on
another production in another theatre, leaving *Ariadne* in 'a mess', to
quote Strauss, who lost his temper and insulted various people.

There had also been difficulties over casting. Strauss had been anxious
that Emmy Destinn, an outstanding Salome, should sing Ariadne and
wrote to her in January 1912: 'Unforgettable, unsurpassable Salome! I
have written a new little opera, *Ariadne auf Naxos* . . . Will you create
Ariadne for us? A short, beautiful, lyrical role, only one big scene and
aria, plus a beautiful, purely lyrical love-duet . . . It is for you to command what fee you will! May I count on you? I will not use flattery, but
perhaps you already know that you've never had a greater admirer of
your art than me.' This best butter was to no avail and the part went to
the Czech soprano of great physical beauty whom he had heard sing in
Offenbach in Munich, Mizzi Jeritza. As Maria Jeritza she was to become
one of the immortal Strauss and Vienna singers. Writing in 1916 Strauss
described her Ariadne as 'splendid' but added 'Unfortunately the woman

has too beautiful a voice and too much talent. She hadn't the technique for the part, either musically or vocally or in the phrasing.'

The première on 25 October was a disaster. For one thing, as Strauss said, 'the playgoing public had no wish to listen to opera, and vice versa. The proper cultural soil for this pretty hybrid was lacking.' The evening was protracted to six hours because the King of Württemberg held receptions lasting fifty minutes each in the intervals during and after the play. By the time the opera was reached, the audience not surprisingly 'was somewhat tired and ill-tempered'. Strauss conducted, the only one of his operas except *Guntram* for which he took the baton at the première.

So Strauss and Hofmannsthal tasted failure. This, we may be sure, was not unwelcome to their enemies. There was in Germany and elsewhere immense envy, amounting to hatred, of Strauss's success. (England, in the 1950s, provided an exact parallel in the widespread hostility to Benjamin Britten.) His devotees, like Wagner's and Britten's, made the situation worse by their exaggerated language, but there was a malignant note in much of the written criticism. Though neither man could know it, *Der Rosenkavalier* had marked their high noon. Never glad confident morning again for Richard Strauss, only qualified, relative success and the implication that he was living off his artistic capital.

Strauss and Hofmannsthal broached the question of revisions of *Ariadne* during a meeting in Berlin. It soon emerged that Hofmannsthal was considering jettisoning the Molière play and turning the evening into a complete opera, with Prologue. On 9 January 1913 he wrote:

> This Vorspiel [Prologue] then, with the established characters (Composer, Dancing Master, singer, tenor, Zerbinetta and others) is to take place not *on* the *Ariadne* stage, but behind it, in a hall where the dressing rooms have been improvised. The scene of the action to be described as: the big country-house of a rich gentleman and patron of the arts. The Maecaenas (Jourdain) himself remains unnamed, allegorical, in the background. . . . More strongly even than before, the focal point will be the musician's destiny, exemplified by the young Composer.

On 12 June, Hofmannsthal sent Strauss the 'new definitive Vorspiel' in which the figure of the Composer had been developed as 'tragic and comic at the same time, like the musician's lot in the world. . . . Please take to it kindly.'

This was what Strauss did not do. He did not like the new Prologue. The part of the Composer was 'downright distasteful. . . . I have an innate antipathy to all artists treated in plays and novels, and especially composers, poets and painters. Besides, I now cling so obstinately to our original work. . . . To me its original version is still the right one and the second no more than a makeshift.' This was somewhat ingenuous, since the idea of the *Vorspiel* had been first suggested by Hofmannsthal in July 1911 as a prose scene preparing the ground for Ariadne. 'That's excellent,' Strauss had then said. 'It can become a hit provided you develop the parts of Composer and Dancing Master. . . . It could become a companion piece to *Meistersinger*: fifty years after . . . Zerbinetta might have an affair with the Composer, so long as he is not too close a portrait of me.' But that was written before failure. On 2 January 1914 Hofmannsthal saw *Ariadne* in Munich. 'It was an enchanting evening for me,' he wrote next day. 'You are quite right: we shall change nothing, not one thing.' And there, for a time, the matter rested.

Part of Strauss's disinclination to interest himself further in *Ariadne* arose from his desire for something large-scale. He kept asking about the progress of *Die Frau ohne Schatten*. Hofmannsthal still would not be hurried; on 8 March 1912 he produced another red herring. He had a fit of conscience that the subjects he had offered Strauss since *Elektra* had neglected to cater for the composer's 'mastery over the dark, savage side of life', and he suggested a thirty-five minute 'tragic symphony' on the subject *Orestes and the Furies* as a ballet for Nijinsky. (This was the heyday of the Diaghilev Ballet, for which Ravel and Stravinsky, among others, had composed scores.) Strauss was not interested, but Hofmannsthal believed that 'such a symphonic piece . . . might not be wholly unwelcome to you as an interim work. . . . Together with Kessler . . . I have produced a short ballet for the Russians, *Joseph in Egypt*, the episode with Potiphar's wife; the boyish part of Joseph of course for Nijinsky.'

Strauss rose to this bait, having been delighted by the Russian Ballet in Berlin. But on 11 September he wrote:

> The chaste Joseph himself isn't at all up my street, and if a thing bores me I find it difficult to set it to music. This God-seeker Joseph—he's going to be a hell of an effort. Well, maybe there's a pious tune for good boy Joseph lying about in some atavistic recess of my appendix.

Hofmannsthal, prig that he was, was offended. He thought Strauss would need to look for Joseph's music 'in the purest region of your brain'. He sent him a long lecture on Joseph's 'meaning' in mystical terms. It is extraordinary that he should have believed that Strauss could be fully inspired by a religious theme: perhaps *Salome* misled him, though he must have known that Jokanaan was widely regarded as the weak point in that opera. When Strauss played him some of the Joseph themes on 12 December 1912, he wrote arrogantly next day:

> In every task before us the final criterion can only be sensitivity in the matter of style, and of this I must consider myself guardian and keeper for the two of us. . . . There may be something absolutely right in these themes for *Joseph* . . . but as they stand they are, or strike one as, dressed up, dolled up, pastoral, *impossible* for this atmosphere, and they put one off fatally.

Strauss, as always, took this in good part and promised to do better. The subject then vanished from their correspondence until July 1913 when Strauss wrote that he had 'at last' completed the sketch of Joseph's dance. In September he reported that he was 'now at this job without interruption and shall do my best to get it ready for Paris in June: 100 pages are already scored, but it's a big and laborious job'. In fact he completed the score—for 112 players—on 2 February 1914 and the first performance of *Josephslegende* was given at the Paris Opéra on 14 May, with Strauss conducting. The rehearsals were a nightmare because of the French players' system of sending substitutes if they were giving private lessons. He admits in his memoirs that he 'became very impatient'. Stravinsky, who was there, said Strauss's manner to the orchestra was 'not admirable' but 'every corrective remark he made was exact: his ears and his musicianship were impregnable'.[1]

The roles of Joseph and Potiphar's wife were taken by Leonid Massine and Maria Kusnetzova, with choreography by Fokine and sets and costumes by Bakst, who placed the action in sixteenth-century Venice in the style of Veronese. Nijinsky's absence—the result of his rift with Diaghilev when he married—was a major blow, but the première was nevertheless an opulent occasion. Strauss went to London for the first English performance at Drury Lane, conducted by Beecham, on 23 June. 'A great success,' he wrote to Hofmannsthal, 'in spite of the fact that most of the press was angry and even the most sophisticated Englishwomen found the piece indecent. . . . Joseph's dance still inadequate and hence boring.' Beecham found the score 'heavy and plodding'; and Ernest Newman described listening to the music as 'like attending the funeral of a lost leader'. While in England, Strauss went to Oxford to receive the University's honorary degree of Doctor of Music, a tribute timed to celebrate his fiftieth birthday on 11 June. His native Munich marked this anniversary by naming a street after him.[2] Hofmannsthal reported 'decisive progress' with *Die Frau ohne Schatten* in January 1913. 'The profound meaning of this plot, the effortless symbolism of all the situations, its immensely rich humanity, never fail to fill me with delight and astonishment.' In the spring Strauss and Hofmannsthal made a car journey through Italy during which they discussed their new project. Strauss for the first time was given a real inkling of this subject which Hofmannsthal had told him 'would be related to *Zauberflöte* as *Rosenkavalier* is to *Figaro*'. The four main characters were to be the Oriental fairy-tale Emperor and Empress (she is the woman without a shadow, i.e. childless and infertile) and the earthly dyer Barak and his wife. 'In the upper sphere,' said Hofmannsthal, 'we shall have heroic recitative throughout . . . while below there is real conversation such as only the Master of *Rosenkavalier* can compose.'

But this time the recitative and conversation were not concerned with amorous intrigues in eighteenth-century Vienna but with supernatural

[1] *Stravinsky in conversation with Robert Craft* (London, 1962), pp. 89–90.
[2] Richard Straussstrasse runs off Prinzregentenstrasse.

powers, falconry, an empress who could change her shape at will, an emperor under threat of being turned to stone by his wife's father, the magician Kaikobad; with the machinations of an evil nurse, with the symbolism of childlessness, of the trials placed upon the good Barak and his passionate but shrewish wife; with unborn children and the Golden Water of Life. Hofmannsthal sent Strauss half of the first act as a New Year gift for 1914. 'Simply wonderful,' was the composer's verdict; and he began his customary suggestions for cuts and improvements. But whereas in *Der Rosenkavalier*, as the full correspondence shows, Strauss was the dominant partner, literally calling the tune, in *Die Frau ohne Schatten* it was the poet who applied most of the pressure:

> Only one thing you must not, must never forget: the Empress is, for the spiritual meaning of the opera, the central figure and her destiny the pivot of the whole action. . . . You should never for a moment lose sight of it, for otherwise the third act will become impossible, where it can and ought to be the crowning glory of the whole work . . . it is to lead us where music and poetry, without clipping each other's wings, and truly hand in hand for once, shall float lightly over the gardens of paradise.

Strauss completed the sketch of Act I on 20 August 1914; on 8 October he told Hofmannsthal: 'You've really pulled off your masterpiece here. . . . If I succeed in getting Act II ready this October I shall leave the whole thing till next Easter and then tackle the end with fresh vigour. During the winter I'll score my *Alpensinfonie*!' On the 27th he reported the second act finished 'to schedule'. By then Europe had been at war for nearly three months.

9

The crisis

Strauss was in Italy when the Sarajevo assassination occurred. A few weeks later, at Garmisch, he learned that a considerable portion of his savings over thirty years which he had deposited in London with the financier Sir Edgar Speyer had been confiscated by the British. The sum involved is said to have been £50,000. 'For a week I was very depressed,' he wrote,[1] 'then I carried on with *Die Frau ohne Schatten*, which I had just begun, and started again from the beginning to earn money by the sweat of my brow when I had just entertained hopes of devoting myself exclusively to composition from my fiftieth year onward.' He clearly regarded the war as a nuisance, its chief effect being financial inconvenience to himself. His attitude to world affairs was uncomplicated and selfish. Rolland, for example, recorded in 1900 Strauss's 'absolute indifference' to the Boer War. About the First World War, in which his own country was involved, he was at first almost as casual.

Hofmannsthal went at once into the army. 'Really,' Strauss wrote to his librettist's wife on 31 July 1914,

> poets ought to be permitted to stay at home. There is plenty of cannon fodder available: critics, stage producers who have their own ideas, actors who act Molière, etc. I am convinced there will be no world war, that the little altercation with Serbia will soon be over, and that I will receive the third act of my *Frau ohne Schatten*. May the devil take the damned Serbs.

But when the war began in earnest he took a patriotic pride in Germany's successes. 'These are great and glorious times,' he wrote on 22 August to Gerty von Hofmannsthal, 'one feels exalted, knowing that this land and this people . . . must and will assume the leadership of Europe.' Yet he was cautious. Richard Specht, writing in the Budapest *Pester Lloyd* on 12 September, reported that when signatures were being collected for the famous manifesto of German artists and intellectuals, Richard Strauss refused to give his, explaining that 'declarations about things concerning war and politics were not fitting for an artist, who must give his attention to his creations and to his work'.

Strauss allowed himself some jingoistic outbursts in his letters to

[1] R. Strauss, 'Reminiscences of the First Performances of my Operas', op. cit.

Hofmannsthal in October 1914, complaining of Reinhardt staging Shakespeare and Frankfurt performing French opera. No need to scoff at him for such silliness: in England, Wagner was excluded from the Royal Philharmonic Society's programmes and Strauss's *Don Juan* was dropped from a Promenade Concert on 15 August 1914. Over eighty years later the State of Israel still refuses to perform the music of Richard Strauss. Strauss was revolted by hypocrisy, hence this to Hofmannsthal in February 1915, when he bemoaned the kind of people

> for whom this great epoch serves merely as a pretext for bringing their mediocre products into the open, who seize the opportunity to decry real artists as hollow aesthetes and bad patriots, who forget that I wrote my *Heldenleben*, the *Bardengesang*, battlesongs and military marches in peacetime, but am now, face to face with the present events, keeping a respectful silence.

Hofmannsthal was quickly given a diplomatic post to keep him away from the front line. On 12 January 1915 he told Strauss he had resumed work on Act III of *Die Frau ohne Schatten*. It was delivered in April. 'Magnificent,' said Strauss, 'only in its quest for brevity it has become too sketchy.' Hofmannsthal had not yet heard a note of the music: Strauss played the first two acts to him on 25 April in Vienna. 'Really wonderful,' the poet told his friend Eberhard von Bodenhausen. But Strauss was far from satisfied with the Act III libretto and raised query after query which Hofmannsthal, busy with war work, did not answer with his usual speed. Progress faltered and halted. Meanwhile Strauss had completed scoring his *Alpensinfonie*, for a mammoth orchestra, on 8 February 1915. Composition had spread over four years; during this period his great Dresden interpreter Schuch had died (May 1914) and Strauss dedicated the symphony to the Dresden Intendant, Count Seebach, and to the Dresden Court Orchestra who, under Strauss, gave the first performance—but in Berlin—on 28 October. At the final rehearsal he remarked: 'At last I have learned to orchestrate. I wanted to compose, for once, as a cow gives milk.'

With *Die Frau* at a standstill, Strauss cast around for something to do. The revision of *Ariadne*! The original version was performed in Berlin in January 1916 and Strauss and Hofmannsthal saw it. They decided to adapt the piece as an opera, dropping the Molière play and substituting the new Prologue (*Vorspiel*) Hofmannsthal had written in 1913. The first performance was planned for October 1916 in Vienna. In April Strauss lobbed a grenade at his collaborator:

> The part of the Composer (since the tenors are so terrible) I shall give to Mlle. Artot.[2] Only you'll have to consider now how we might further fill out the part for her with, say, a little vocal number; or perhaps you could write an additional pretty little solo scene for the Composer at the end. . . . I can only win Mlle. Artot for our piece if I can offer her a kind of small star part.

[2] Lola Artot de Padilla, a Franco-Spanish soprano who had been Berlin's first Oktavian.

The use of a woman singer as the Composer had been suggested to Strauss by the Berlin conductor Leo Blech. Hofmannsthal was appalled.

> Your opportunism in theatrical matters has in this case thoroughly led you up the garden path. . . . To prettify this particular character, which is to have an aura of 'spirituality' and 'greatness' about it . . . strikes me as, forgive my plain speaking, odious. . . . Oh Lord, if only I were able to bring home to you completely the essence, the spiritual meaning, of these characters.

Strauss was unimpressed. 'You almost act as if I had never understood you,' he replied.

> Do whatever you like about the ending, only do it soon, please! But as for Artot . . . I am not going to budge on this point, for artistic as well as for practical reasons. A tenor is impossible . . . a leading baritone won't sing the Composer: so what is left to me except the only genre of singer not yet represented in *Ariadne*, my Rofrano [Oktavian] . . . as a rule she is the most talented woman singer in the theatre.

He and Blech were right. As in the case of Oktavian, it would be almost impossible to find for the Composer a male singer who combined the necessary youthful looks with the histrionic and vocal experience.

Hofmannsthal found the music for the *Vorspiel* 'enchanting . . . like fireworks in a beautiful park one enchanted, all too fleeting summer night'. The first performance of the revised *Ariadne auf Naxos* was given in Vienna on 4 October 1916 conducted by Franz Schalk, who had been one of Mahler's assistants (though Mahler had a poor opinion of him). Maria Jeritza sang Ariadne, Selma Kurz was Zerbinetta and Lotte Lehmann, stepping in on Strauss's insistence during rehearsals when Marie Gutheil-Schoder fell ill, had her first major success as the Composer. Leo Blech conducted the first Berlin performance on 1 November. In neither city, nor in others, was the work a success.

There are hints here that at this period Strauss was deeply conscious that he stood at an artistic crossroads. Some explanations of the generally assumed decline in his creativity have over-simplified it by relating it to the destruction in 1918 of the German superiority symbolized by the Kaiser's pre-1914 Berlin. This is facile; and in any case some critics had been 'writing off' Strauss since 1904 and earlier. It is also too easy to say that Strauss had 'gone soft', that all he wanted was to live comfortably in his villa composing out of habit rather than from compulsion. True, he sometimes took the line of least resistance; true, he could give the impression of indolence, but there is no reason to suppose that he became a less serious, dedicated and industrious artist. He involved himself as much as ever in all matters musical; and, knowing that he was in his fifties, he looked into his heart. Always a realist, he knew—or thought he knew—what was good for him and what he was good for. This crisis he did not treat emotionally and dramatically, but factually and with wry humour. It highlights the astonishing temperamental differences between Strauss and Hofmannsthal.

What a contrast they make! The German composer easy-going, comfortable, preferring to turn away wrath with a joke, at ease with practical musicians and temperamental singers; the Austrian poet aloof, stiff, subject to fits of depression, intensely well read, more than slightly snobbish, a great propagandist for his own work, mixing in all the intellectual coteries in the arts and on the fringe of politics. Both men were wealthy, but whereas Strauss lived in comfort, Hofmannsthal allowed no up-to-date equipment to mollify the spartan régime in his small rococo castle at Rodaun—no twentieth-century bathroom and no central heating, even though, like Strauss, he detested cold weather.

Strauss tried hard to signal to him in 1916 that he wanted to change direction in their choice of subjects:

> I have two things in mind: either an entirely modern, absolutely realistic domestic and character comedy . . .—or some amusing piece of love and intrigue. . . . Say a diplomatic love intrigue in the setting of the Vienna Congress. . . . You'll probably say Kitsch! But then we musicians are known for our poor taste in aesthetic matters, and besides, if *you* were to do a thing like that it wouldn't be Kitsch.

This flattery failed. Hofmannsthal confessed to 'a good laugh' over these 'truly horrid' proposals. He added:

> You have every reason to be grateful to me for bringing you (as now once again with *Die Frau ohne Schatten*) that element which is sure to bewilder people and to provoke a certain amount of antagonism, for you have already too many followers, you are already all too obviously the hero of the day, all too universally accepted. By all means get angry with me and keep harping for a while on this 'incomprehensibility', it is a mortgage to be redeemed by the next generation.

Strauss was undeterred:

> I have a definite talent for operetta. And since my tragic vein is more or less exhausted, and since tragedy in the theatre, after this war, strikes me at present as something rather idiotic and childish [so much for the 'insensitive' Strauss], I should like to use this irrepressible talent of mine—after all, I'm the only composer nowadays with some real humour and a sense of fun and a marked gift for parody. Indeed, I feel downright called upon to become the Offenbach of the 20th century, and you will and must be my poet. . . . Our road starts from *Rosenkavalier*: its success is evidence enough, and it is also this genre (sentimentality and parody are the sensations to which my talent responds most forcefully and productively) that I happen to be keenest on.

Hofmannsthal's reply was never sent—he withheld it as being 'sullen and ill-inspired'—but it has survived. He accused Strauss of failing to enter into his ideas and of treating 'quite a few things in the wrong style'. Zerbinetta's aria, for example, he had always detested. Faninal's servants in Act III of *Der Rosenkavalier*: their chorus had been written 'to be rattled off in burlesque fashion . . . what you did was to smother it with *heavy* music and so to destroy utterly the purpose of the words. . . . The fun of this passage has simply ceased to exist, the very thing a man like Offenbach would have brought out'. The footmen at the end of Act I of this opera were 'quite terrible' (few will agree with this) and Ochs's exit in Act III 'offends no less gravely against the style of the whole work'.

That was written on 11 June 1916. On 28 July Strauss returned to his problem with Act III of *Die Frau*:

> Characters like the Emperor and Empress, and also the Nurse, can't be filled with red corpuscles in the same way as a Marschallin, an Oktavian or an Ochs. No matter how I rack my brain—and I'm toiling really hard, sifting and sifting—my heart's only half in it, and once the head has to do the major part of the work you get a breath of academic chill (what my wife very rightly calls 'note-spinning') which no bellows can ever kindle into a real fire. I have now sketched out the whole end of the opera . . . but my wife finds it cold and misses the heart-touching, flame-kindling melodic texture of the *Rosenkavalier* trio. . . . Let's make up our minds that *Frau ohne Schatten* shall be the last romantic opera.

When he completed Act III in June 1917 he confessed he was uncertain what was good and what was bad. 'That's a good thing, for at my age one gets all too easily into the rut of mere routine and that is the death of true art.' He harked back to the subject which had obsessed him all summer:

> Guided by *Ariadne* and in particular the new *Vorspiel*, I hope to move forward wholly into the realm of unWagnerian emotional and human comic opera. I now see my way clearly before me and am grateful to you for opening my eyes—but now you go ahead and make me the necessary libretti . . . peopled by human beings *à la* Hofmannsthal instead of puppets. An amusing, interesting plot . . . in any form you like! I promise you I have now definitely stripped off the Wagnerian musical armour.

Hofmannsthal could not fail to respond to such candour: 'I shall do what I can to fulfil your wishes.' Whether he could respond to the Eulenspiegel element in Strauss was to determine Strauss's artistic development in a Europe which was savagely changed from the world in which their partnership had begun.

When he wrote his memoirs during the Second World War, Strauss described *Die Frau ohne Schatten* as a 'child of sorrow, finished during the war amid cares and worries which left their mark on the score, especially towards the middle of the third act, in the form of a certain nervous over-excitedness which finally expressed itself in melodrama'. A curious reference, this, to one of the greatest passages in the opera, when the Empress speaks her refusal to sacrifice another human's life. But

Strauss's ambivalence towards Act III of *Die Frau ohne Schatten* can undoubtedly be traced to the composition of the Prologue to *Ariadne auf Naxos*. This had showed him a new path and he became bored with a libretto which still required a style he was hoping to discard, even if only temporarily.

10

Vienna

A recurrent dread for Strauss seems to have been of a summer without work: he must have something to compose, even if he laid it aside to play skat. Perhaps for this reason alone he allowed Hofmannsthal to lure him into yet another version of their adaptation of Molière's *Le Bourgeois Gentilhomme*. For his part, Hofmannsthal seems to have belatedly realized that in jettisoning the Molière play in the first revision of *Ariadne auf Naxos*, they had also jettisoned the superb incidental music Strauss had composed for it. On 24 July 1916 the librettist had written to Strauss of a meeting with Hermann Bahr, the dramatist and critic (and husband of Mahler's former mistress, the soprano Anna von Mildenburg). Hofmannsthal had mentioned Strauss's desire for a *Singspiel*, and 'if Bahr can think of anything he will submit to you a scenario or a plot'. The letter continued:

> He spoke very intelligently of you, of that mixture of the hearty, Bavarian aspect of your nature with a subtle, witty mind and in this connection described your music for the *Bourgeois* as the finest thing you had done. . . . Please, dear Dr. Strauss, do not rashly waste these pieces of music; I am sure I shall succeed in inventing a second delicate action for this comedy.

By April 1917 the first performance of the new Hofmannsthal-Molière adaptation had been fixed for a year ahead, directed by Reinhardt at the Deutsches Theater in Berlin. Hofmannsthal admitted that the adaptation had given him more trouble than he had expected. Strauss had reservations; after all, the 1912 version had had little success, and he could not see that this further elaboration would be better. He was worried by Hofmannsthal's determination to end the acts without a musical finale— he had had enough of that in the original version. 'For the love of God,' he wrote, 'not a succession of three curtains after which not a hand will stir.' Hofmannsthal's reply was gratuitously offensive: 'I undertook this whole thing solely and exclusively to create for your already existing music . . . a proper and worthy outlet. . . . This genre I shall not allow to be adulterated or bent towards operetta . . . for although you are my superior in many artistic gifts and abilities, I have the greater sense of style and more reliable taste.'

When Strauss received the full text he was markedly unenthusiastic and suggested there ought to be a fourth act. Hofmannsthal's reply, for which he later apologized, called Strauss's proposals 'beneath discussion' and asked for a decision whether he was 'free to dispose otherwise of this Molière adaptation, of which I do not intend to alter one iota'. Strauss at this point seems to have decided to shrug his shoulders. He made a few more protests and kept up a show of interest, but it is difficult to feel that he was much concerned about the work's fate. When it was produced, on 9 April 1918, it ran for only thirty-one performances. Hofmannsthal suggested that they might now try to make an opera of it and that Strauss might compose entirely new music in *Ariadne* for Zerbinetta's coloratura aria, which he still considered an 'obstacle in the way of the opera's future prospects'.

In his reply, written on 12 July 1918, Strauss put an end to the seven-year obsession with the Molière play. He was prepared to leave its future to chance in the certainty that 'a more cultured public' would one day appreciate it. 'I would suggest that we stop doctoring it. . . . I should find difficulty in applying the surgeon's knife to Zerbinetta again. Shall we write something new in the same manner and form?'

In any case Strauss was by now intent on several new projects. Hofmannsthal's mention of Bahr as a possible librettist had reminded him of Bahr's play *Das Konzert* about the marriage troubles of a musician. Strauss met Bahr in Salzburg in September 1916 and suggested an opera about the misunderstanding he and Pauline had had in the summer of 1902 when she had suspected him of adultery. Bahr sent a draft libretto, on which Strauss commented: 'I am sending you a succession of scenes I have thought out, little more than cinema pictures, in which the music says everything, the writer contributing only a few cue words.' Bahr enjoyed what Strauss had done so much that 'even if you were in agreement, I would on no account substitute my dialogue. . . . My suggestion is, therefore, that this time you must write your own text.' While he spent a week in hospital in Munich in the first week of July 1917, Strauss worked on the libretto of what was to become *Intermezzo*.

It is easy to sense Strauss's restlessness in these years, his feeling that, despite the completion at last of *Die Frau ohne Schatten*, nothing engaged his wholehearted interest. Partly this may have been caused by worry about his delicate son, Franz, who was nearing the age of call-up for military service (in May 1918 he was declared 'fit only for limited service at home stations' and was never called). But a deeper, more radical cause was Strauss's growing awareness that he and his music were becoming almost grotesquely out of tune with the times. In this respect he is a parallel with Elgar, whose letters at this time betray a despondency about the future of music, and of his own music, which resulted in his almost total silence for fifteen years after the composition of his last masterpiece, the Cello Concerto, in 1919. Strauss was a less hypersensitive and depressive case than Elgar but he felt equally keenly that the post-war world was alien to him. He had no curiosity about the music of the younger generation, little interest in Stravinsky, Berg, Bartók, Schoenberg, Hindemith, Prokofiev and others. (He said to the young Hindemith: 'Why do you compose like that? You don't need to—you have talent.' Hindemith replied: 'You make your music and I'll make mine.') He saw the end of the world in which he had risen to fame, the end of the ducal courts and kingdoms with their private opera orchestras and companies, and he saw them end not only as the result of military defeat but amid a whirlwind inflation which devalued money to the point where it had no value. What was Strauss, still a rich man and still energetic, to do? Elgar took refuge in the life of a country squire and in the practical side of music, conducting and recording his own works. So did Strauss. At Garmisch he was the squire; and when the opportunity came to escape to the exciting, scheming world-within-a-world of the Vienna Opera, he seized it.

Strauss's attitude to the political upheavals around him was illustrated in a letter to Pauline just before the Armistice in 1918. It is a letter which helps to explain his attitude in 1933: 'The war is over, definitely over!', he wrote.

> But what is to come may be worse . . . They say we shall all have to diligently learn new ways now. I shall not make the effort to do so until the whole situation has become a little clearer, otherwise there will be too much twisting and turning with every wind that blows. I am still holding my head high, in the belief that Germany is too 'diligent' to fall into such a complete decline—in spite of all the nonsense the worthy government has instituted. Bismarck's dream has suffered a rude awakening, at all events . . . Let's hope that it will be replaced by better times. I don't believe that it will, but there's nothing we can do about historical facts. Please don't upset yourself unnecessarily—it won't do any good. We are going to need all our nerve now to steer our little ship safely on its way . . . I wouldn't know what else to do, even now, other than carry on as usual for as long as possible, according to plan, for as long as theatres and concerts keep going and pay fees. If you love me then there isn't much the world can do to harm us.

In April 1918, while Hans Gregor was still director of the Vienna Court Opera, Strauss conducted *Elektra*, *Ariadne* and *Der Rosenkavalier* there. On 23 May he wrote to Hofmannsthal:

> I have pursued in my mind many recollections of my pleasant stay in Vienna, and in particular have discussed with my wife (who agreed sympathetically) the possibility that, in the event of Gregor's departure, I might share in a possible Schalk directorship, perhaps as co-director, in such a way that I would spend two or three winter months in Vienna over a number of years. . . . I should gladly make a personal sacrifice to prevent some Weingartner from trying his destructive hand again on that fine artistic institution.

This was written in the month that Strauss ended his long association with the Berlin Court Opera after a quarrel with the autocratic Intendant, Hülsen. Hofmannsthal made no comment until three months later, on 1 August, when, in a remarkable letter, he expressed his candid opposition, saying he believed Strauss would put his own operas' interests above the institution. He added: 'The great danger of your life, to which you surrender and from which you try to escape in almost periodic cycles, is a neglect of all the higher standards of intellectual existence.'

Strauss took no offence. He did not intend, he said, to try to fill the post as Mahler had. But he had resolved to devote five winter months for the next ten years or so to his work as a conductor. 'It has been my devoutest wish for the past thirty years to assume the *de facto* supreme direction of a big Court Opera House on the artistic side.'

In July 1918 Leopold von Andrian-Werburg was appointed Intendant of the Vienna Court Opera, the last such appointment made by the Austrian monarchy. By now Hofmannsthal was reconciled to Strauss's intentions and promoted them eagerly. In September he reported a conversation with Andrian in which he 'explained our ideas' to the Intendant, who wanted some assurance that Strauss would refrain from conducting predominantly his own works. Hofmannsthal believed that Strauss would work well with Franz Schalk, and was determined that they should recall Alfred Roller to work with them as stage designer. On the last day of the monarchy, 10 November 1918, Andrian appointed Schalk as Director, but it was already widely known—and was accepted by Schalk—that Strauss would be brought into the partnership. A Berlin friend of Strauss said to him 'So you're going to Vienna? Where the people are so deceitful.' Strauss replied: 'People are deceitful everywhere, but in Vienna they're so pleasant about it.' He was, perhaps, over-optimistic.

In the early months of 1919 the Court Opera became the State Opera and the Republic confirmed the contract between Andrian and Strauss. His appointment was announced on 1 March. Immediately, almost the whole staff (800 members) of the Opera, with the notable exceptions of Schalk, Maria Jeritza and Selma Kurz, signed a resolution demanding his withdrawal, on the grounds that the proposed salary was too high for 'an impoverished country like the new Austria',[1] objecting that he would favour his own works, and that he was planning to give concerts with the Philharmonic in the Opera House, thus damaging the Philharmonic's subscription series under Weingartner. Their real fear, though, was that Strauss intended to purge the company of superannuated singers. Strauss's reaction was to stay in Garmisch, aloof from the

---

[1] This was 80,000 kronen for seven months as director, plus 1,200 kronen on each night when he conducted. In view of the rate of inflation the sum was meaningless; it was much less than he earned in Germany, and several officials of the Opera were being paid a similar sum.

controversy except for an offer (which he knew would be refused) to withdraw the première of *Die Frau ohne Schatten*. A group of Viennese intellectuals sent him an open telegram urging him to come to Vienna. Signatories included Stefan Zweig, Hofmannsthal, Georg Szell, Arthur Schnitzler, Alfred Roller, Richard Specht and Alma Mahler. The affair fizzled out, and Strauss went to Vienna in May as guest conductor at a festival to celebrate the Opera House's fiftieth anniversary, when he conducted *Fidelio, Tristan, Zauberflöte, Ariadne,* and *Der Rosenkavalier.* If this seems like a golden age, it should also be remembered that the spring of 1919 in Austria was marked by strikes, political uprisings, poverty and hunger.

The first performance of *Die Frau ohne Schatten* was given in Vienna on 10 October 1919 conducted by Schalk, with Jeritza as the Empress, Lotte Lehmann as Barak the Dyer's wife, Richard Mayr as Barak, Lucie Weidt as the Nurse and Karl Aagard-Oestvig as the Emperor. In spite of such a galaxy the opera was no more than moderately successful. Strauss recounted that

> its way over the German stage was fraught with misfortune. In Vienna itself, owing to the strain imposed by the vocal parts and to the difficulties over the sets, the opera was withdrawn more often than it was performed . . . It was a serious blunder to entrust this opera, difficult as it was to cast and produce, to medium and even small theatres immediately after the war.[2]

The work was first produced satisfactorily at Dresden in 1927 but even so it remained intermittently in the German opera houses' repertories. It was not produced in New York and London until 1966. Hofmannsthal, in 1921, could not agree with his critics that the libretto was to blame. He added: 'I believe the work *will* live. But I say "I believe"—in the case of *Ariadne* I say "I know".' Strauss, contrary to what has often been said, never had any difficulty with the libretto. In November 1927, for example, he reassured Hofmannsthal that 'in spite of all idiotic reviews I still believe that *Frau ohne Schatten* is not only a fine piece of poetry but also an operatic libretto of great theatrical effectiveness. Indeed there are already some people who actually "understand it". That the present is generally a bad age for art and that the public who can afford a seat in the opera today is stupid and uneducated—surely that's not our fault?'

Strauss's Vienna appointment began on 1 December 1919, to run until 30 November 1924. He agreed to be committed to Vienna for five months of each year, from 15 December to 15 May. Eventual discord in co-direction with Schalk was guaranteed by the vagueness with which their functions were defined. Schalk was 'Head of the Opera House' and Strauss 'Artistic Supervisor'. Yet it must have been obvious that, with his fame and prestige, Strauss would be generally regarded as the major

---

[2] R. Strauss, 'Reminiscences of the First Performances of my Operas', op. cit.

partner, however unjust this might be to the long-serving Schalk. Strauss made his official début in January 1920 in an uncut *Lohengrin*, the opera with which Mahler had first conquered Vienna in 1897. But the sacerdotal fanaticism with which Mahler the martinet led the Opera was not to be Strauss's way. He was out for enjoyment, the audience's and his own, and at first he and Schalk worked well together. The singers at their disposal were among the greatest of the century. They included survivors of the Mahler era in Anna von Mildenburg, Marie Gutheil-Schoder, Selma Kurz, Erik Schmedes, Leo Slezak and Richard Mayr, and later stars, among them Maria Jeritza, Maria Ivogün, Lotte Lehmann, Elisabeth Schumann, Maria Olczewska, Lotte Schoene, Luise Helletsgruber, Alfred Piccaver, Karl Aagard-Oestvig, Richard Tauber, Hans Duhan, Alfred Jerger and Josef Manowarda.

Singers adored working with Strauss, who was extraordinarily indulgent to them in his own music. He would encourage sopranos to take liberties with the score if he liked the sound of what they did; and to Hans Hotter he said: 'Who told you I wrote my songs for beauty's sake?' He wanted the high notes to sound effortful. Otto Strasser, a member of the Vienna Philharmonic Orchestra from 1922, recalled how Jeritza cut the role of Salome 'in her own individual way . . . I was curious, therefore, to see what Strauss would say. But he conducted this semi-*Salome* with every sign of enthusiasm and all he had to say to us, as he walked through the pit on the way out, was "Devil of a woman!"' Did he mean Salome or Jeritza?

Strauss fulfilled his intention of spring-cleaning the Opera's classical repertory. He conducted re-studied performances—several in what amounted to his own productions, so closely did he supervise the stage action—of *Der Freischütz*, *Carmen* (with Jeritza), *Tannhäuser*, *Hänsel und Gretel*, *Hans Heiling*, *Fidelio*, *Don Giovanni* and *Der fliegende Holländer*. At the end of their first season, in May 1920, he and Schalk inaugurated the Vienna 'festival months of master performances'. Strauss conducted his beloved *Così fan tutte* and, of his own works, *Salome* and *Elektra*. He and Schalk restored the operas of Puccini to the Vienna stage; other contemporaries whose 'novelties' were performed were Pfitzner (*Palestrina*), Franz Schreker (*Die Gezeichneten*), Erich Korngold (*Die tote Stadt*), Julius Bittner (*Die Kohlhaymerin*), Franz Schmidt (*Fredigundis*), Zemlinsky (*Der Zwerg*), and Weingartner (*Meister Andrea* and *Die Dorfschule*). In 1922 the co-directors incorporated the beautiful Hofburg Redoutensaal with the State Opera. There they conducted performances of *Le nozze di Figaro*, *Il barbiere di Siviglia*, *Don Pasquale*, *Jean de Paris* and, as a triple bill, Mozart's *Bastien und Bastienne*, Pergolesi's *La serva padrona*, and Weber's *Abu Hassan*.

Strauss was now also involved with the Salzburg Festival. In 1918, with Max Reinhardt and Schalk, he formed an 'artistic advisory council' to establish on an annual basis what had previously been intermittent festivals. Hofmannsthal, Alfred Roller and others joined the council in 1919. After labour pains, the first festival was held in 1920, when only Hofmannsthal's mystery-play *Jedermann* was performed. In 1922 Strauss and Schalk took thirty-seven players from the Vienna Opera orchestra to the Salzburg Landestheater to perform four Mozart operas, *Die Entführung aus dem Serail, Le nozze di Figaro, Così fan tutte,* and *Don Giovanni*. Strauss conducted *Don Giovanni* and *Così*, with designs by Roller. Alfred Jerger sang Don Giovanni, with Richard Mayr as Leporello and Richard Tauber as Don Ottavio. In *Così*, Elisabeth Schumann sang Despina. From these performances of *Così* may be traced the full acceptance of this masterpiece into the world's operatic repertory[3]. Strauss also conducted a Mozart concert in the Mozarteum, with Schumann as soprano soloist and Josef Szigeti playing the D major violin concerto (κ218).

In later years at Salzburg, Strauss conducted one performance of *Ariadne auf Naxos* (second version) in 1926. In 1932 he conducted the Vienna Philharmonic in *Also sprach Zarathustra* and *Eine Alpensinfonie* and in symphonies by Beethoven and Mozart; in 1933 he conducted *Fidelio* with Elisabeth Rethberg as Leonore. He did not conduct there again until Mozart programmes in 1942 and 1943.

Of his operas, *Der Rosenkavalier* was performed at Salzburg in his lifetime in every festival from 1929 to 1939, excluding 1936, and again in 1941. It returned in 1946 and 1949. *Die Frau ohne Schatten* was performed in 1932 and 1933, *Die ägyptische Helena* (in its 1933 version) in 1933 and 1934, *Elektra* in 1934 and 1937 and *Arabella* in 1942, 1943, and 1947. In 1944, as will be recounted, there was a dress rehearsal only of *Die Liebe der Danae*.

It was at this time that Strauss created the legend of his laconic, unobtrusive conducting, sometimes regarded as cold and aloof, although this was not the impression received by those who heard his performances. Like Mahler, he greatly modified his demeanour on the rostrum after the excesses of his youth. Here is Arthur Johnstone of the *Manchester Guardian* describing Strauss conducting Liszt's *Faust Symphony* at Düsseldorf in May 1902: 'A sphinx-like person who, as his abnormally big head sways on the top of his tall and bulky figure, to the accompaniment of fantastic gestures, works up his audience into a sort of phosphorescent fever.' Twenty years later the fantastic gestures had disappeared, as is evident from Romain Rolland's description of him in 1924: 'He is tall, slim, cold, impassive, precise; he makes very few gestures; at rare moments of musical frenzy one discerns the intense nervous vibration which stirs him and which suddenly makes the orchestra flare up: it's like an electric spark applied to gunpowder.'[4]

[3] For a fascinating and detailed account of several of Strauss's interpretations see L. Wurmser's 'Richard Strauss as an Opera Conductor', *Music & Letters*, vol. xlv, 1964, pp. 4–15.

[4] R. Myers (ed.), *Richard Strauss and Romain Rolland*, op. cit., p. 162.

His obsession, at this period particularly, was his overriding desire to ensure that the audience should hear the words and understand the plot. This underlay the 'Ten Golden Rules for the Album of a Young Conductor', which he wrote in 1922, and his Preface (of 1924) to his opera *Intermezzo*. Norman Del Mar has described the Rules as cynical, facetious and lacking integrity, a rather harsh judgment which leaves out of account the clue to this cynicism provided in the Preface when Strauss castigates the tendency of German orchestras to play too loudly, encouraged by 'the many concert-hall conductors who have unfortunately nowadays taken to conducting opera'. Such rules as 'Never look encouragingly at the brass' and 'If you think the brass is not blowing hard enough, tone it down another shade or two' were the outcome of long practical experience and, indeed, only echoed his master Bülow. He advised his 'Young Conductor' to conduct *Salome* and *Elektra* as if they were fairy music by Mendelssohn and advised singers to 'sing *mezza voce* and pronounce your words clearly and the orchestra will automatically accompany you better'.

Strauss's audience in Vienna in 1920 was very different from Mahler's. There is a famous cartoon by Theo Zasche depicting an evening at the opera, with Strauss conducting, Slezak and Jeritza singing, Rosé leading the orchestra; some of the audience are standing with their backs to the stage shouting to friends, a man is drinking from a bottle, many are reading papers, couples are embracing, in two boxes the occupants are playing cards, in another they are very drunk. It is an audience of *nouveaux-riches*, of profiteers. Among the true opera-lovers at this time one would hear remarks like: 'There mustn't be a full house for *Elektra*; the real enthusiasts only half fill it.' Yet in the Press and among the *aficionados* the controversies and feuds endemic to the Vienna Opera raged as potently as ever.

In order to earn dollars to support the opera, Strauss went with Schalk and the Vienna Philharmonic to South America from August to November 1920. The tour achieved its aim of winning an invitation for the entire Vienna State Opera to visit Brazil at Brazilian expense. In the late autumn of 1921 Strauss made his second visit to the United States as accompanist to the soprano Elisabeth Schumann and as guest conductor of his own works with the New York Philharmonic and Philadelphia Orchestras. Schalk had remonstrated about Strauss's absence from Vienna and the composer wrote to him frankly':[5] 'I am not going for pleasure. After England confiscated the chief part of my capital, having no pension to look forward to from any quarter, I have only the royalties from my works to fall back on if anything happened to me that stopped me going on conducting. Even operatic successes are unreliable—if the royalties fail . . . I shall be a beggar and shall leave my

[5] K. Wilhelm, *Richard Strauss, an Intimate Portrait*, op. cit., p. 161.

family in "poverty and shame". I must free myself from this worry . . .'
During his two and a half months in America, when he took part in over
forty recitals and concerts, Strauss accompanied Elisabeth Schumann in
eighteen programmes (one of them broadcast, Strauss's first encounter
with radio) and also either accompanied or conducted (when the songs
were performed with orchestra) for Claire Dux, Elena Gerhardt and
George Meader (a Metropolitan Opera tenor). At least forty of his
Lieder were sung by the various artists. In Detroit, Madison and elsewhere, when their luggage had gone astray, Schumann and Strauss substituted Schubert for his own songs. The New York critics were not
enthusiastic about the recitals, maintaining that they often heard the
songs better performed by others. But Strauss had achieved his aim and
earned 50,000 dollars, about 10 million marks at the exchange rate of
the day.

Elisabeth Schumann kept a diary during the tour from which we gain
revealing glimpses of Strauss. On their way to Cherbourg from Munich,
they stayed in Paris and went to Prunier's: 'Strauss sates himself on oys-
ters, I feast on lobster [Strauss nicknamed her Elobsterbeth] . . . He is
wild about Paris, finds *everything* so tasteful and knows of no more
beautiful city. I congratulate him on Prunier's and the marvellous lunch
and he replies: "Yes, I'm a good courier, a moderate composer, and a
rotten theatre director." ' On the voyage, Strauss played poker with
Chaliapin. In New York he was given a civic reception. He opened the
tour in Carnegie Hall conducting the Philadelphia Orchestra in *Don
Juan*, *Till Eulenspiegel*, and the *Symphonia Domestica*. 'A storm of
applause after each item', he wrote to Pauline. 'The orchestra of the very
first rank and enthusiastic—about my short rehearsals.'

Elisabeth Schumann recorded how bad-tempered he was in Baltimore:
'takes it all out on Franz—grumbles about *everything* . . . But the morning is his bad time, I've already noticed that. By midday his mood is
brightening—then he too is sorry for his insensitivity—and in the
evening he is enchanting.' She described how he played some of his songs
by heart. Once, in *All' mein' Gedanken*, by the third bar he had forgotten the accompaniment and composed a completely new song. 'I kept up
with him, the words fitted perfectly, nobody in the audience suspected a
thing and when we reached the end safe and sound, I looked to the right
out of the corner of my eye to see his reactions. All I saw was his mouth
stretching from ear to ear in one huge grin . . . Later . . . I begged him
to write down the new version, but he said "Oh, I've already forgotten
it" .'

Strauss's first post-war visit to London was in June 1922. Any misgivings he may have had were allayed by a letter from Elgar: 'I send you
a word of warm welcome and an assurance that your return to our
country gives the greatest pleasure to myself and to very many of my
musical countrymen.' Elgar and Bernard Shaw entertained him to lunch

at the United Services Club. From June to September 1923 he was in South America with the Vienna Opera.

In Vienna itself the inevitable clash between Schalk and Strauss had first occurred in 1922. There was growing discontent with Strauss's absences and with his habit of granting leave to leading Vienna singers such as Lehmann to sing his roles in other opera houses. This caused havoc with the salary system, already complicated by the precarious state of the currency. Schalk had to try to keep the Opera's head above water and not unnaturally felt that his co-director was of little assistance. 'I am here to lose money,' was Strauss's retort when shown the budget. In addition, the Press complained that the Opera had become a Richard Strauss Theatre. During his five years' tenure he conducted thirteen performances of *Der Rosenkavalier*, sixteen of *Salome* and thirteen of *Ariadne*. *Die Frau ohne Schatten* was given twelve times, *Feuersnot* seven times and the ballet *Josephslegende* nineteen times after its Vienna première on 18 March 1922. Apart from the last, these figures do not seem excessive. He was also criticized for excluding new works, but on this point he made his views remarkably clear in an article published in the *Neues Wiener Journal* on 22 June 1922. He argued that new works should only be produced in the smaller theatres, not in Berlin and Vienna where audiences were cosmopolitan and critics all-powerful.

Strauss's downfall was to come in 1924, one of the most eventful years of his life. It began with the marriage of his son Franz to the Jewish Alice Grab on 15 January (a Viennese witticism was that at the service Strauss buried his anti-Semitism—'*zu Grab begraben*'). Alice was the daughter of an industrialist, Emanuel von Grab, who owned cloth mills in Prague and elsewhere. He had known Strauss since 1907 when they were introduced in Prague by the conductor Leo Blech. Strauss stayed at Grab's country house several times before 1914 and they played skat. It was there that Franz first met Alice in 1919 when she was fifteen.

This happy start to the year soon turned sombre. The State bureaucrats in charge of the Austrian theatres were threatening drastic economies. Strauss wrote to Schalk on 4 February to say that without funds his post was meaningless, everyone was dissatisfied, he had been criticized for going to Rome to conduct *Salome*, and there was talk of the bankruptcy of the Opera, but 'was it ever solvent?' He would make another effort to reach understanding with the officials but he was pessimistic. 'Even if I become the ex-director I'll remain in Vienna: you and I can then play piano four hands or play chess. Poor *Oper*! It is really sad.'

He knew he would stay in Vienna because his house on the Jacquingasse was nearing completion. In anticipation of his sixtieth birthday the Viennese had 'lent' him a plot of land along the eastern periphery of the Belvedere. The Austrian government leased the house and grounds to him and his heirs for sixty years, after which they would revert to the state. Strauss envisaged the house as the winter residence of the director of the Vienna Opera. Pauline had become bored by their flat in the Mozartplatz and wanted a garden. Strauss himself paid for the building of the house with dollars from his American tour and some help from Emanuel von Grab. For the lease he gave the autograph score of *Der Rosenkavalier* to the Austrian National Library and that of his new ballet *Schlagobers* to Vienna City Library. He also agreed to some extra engagements with the Philharmonic. Several years later, he was approached by Franz Schneiderhan, new Intendant of the Opera, about his terms for conducting at the Opera. Strauss agreed to 100 performances over five years at no fee. In addition he gave the autograph score of *Die ägyptische Helena* to the National Library. The government had at one point been willing to give him the site. 'While I gratefully acknowledge the generosity of this initial gesture', he wrote later, 'in the interests of truth it must be stated that in the end, with 60,000 dollars worth of manuscripts and 200,000 schillings worth of conducting, I paid handsomely for my building site, indeed I probably paid too much.' In 1946 the house became the residence of the Dutch Ambassador.

As Strauss prepared for the move from his flat in the Mozartplatz, he signed a new contract in April 1924 in which he stipulated that Schalk should be retired after the 1924–5 season. The Austrian Education Minister, Schneider, was hesitant but Strauss was convinced that the authorities would concede this point. All was set, then, for the celebrations of his birthday.

This event was a national occasion in Germany and Austria. Strauss weeks were held in Berlin, Munich, Dresden, and Breslau; he was made an honorary citizen of Vienna and Munich; a square in Dresden was named after him. Vienna also honoured him with a week's festival of his operas and orchestral works. He had also planned a gift to the Viennese: his new ballet named after the whipped cream Austrians love, *Schlagobers*, a gay confection set in a confectioner's shop. He had completed it in October 1922 and conducted the first performance on 9 May 1924. It fell flat: the Vienna of the 1924 privations was in too sour a mood for whipped cream. If one seeks social comment in music on the Vienna of this period it is to be found in Ravel's *La Valse*, not in the pages of *Schlagobers*. A vivid account of this Strauss week is contained in the diaries of Romain Rolland, who attended the festival:

> 11th May . . . Vienna: a big old provincial town. It has no inkling of new trends, of the accelerated rhythm, of the contribution of such people as Stravinsky, Honegger, etc., of this frenzy which we can no longer do without in music. . . . I feel here that I am with distinguished old people half-asleep and habit-bound.

> 12th May: I find [Strauss in his flat] surrounded by a circle of ladies and boring Society people. Strauss, serious, heavy, affectionate. Very preoccupied by nationalist follies, by our threatened European civilisation. . . . He never has a

smile on his face. No sudden bursts of gaiety, of unconscious 'ragamuffinery', as there used to be. . . . The question of money also preoccupies him. . . . His ballet *Schlagobers* has just been slated by the Viennese critics. Strauss appears affected by its failure. 'People always expect ideas from me, big things. Haven't I the right, after all, to write what music I please? I cannot bear the tragedy of the present time. I want to create joy. I need it.' He appears to be absolutely indifferent to national questions and to national quarrels.[6]

Strauss overplayed his hand in Vienna, relied too much on his fame to overcome all snags. He forgot that he was at the Opera for only five months of the year, whereas Schalk was there all the time. Schalk dealt with the Ministry officials who administered the theatres, and he won their support. During the summer of 1924 he negotiated a new contract for himself with a clause that in Strauss's absences, he should have sole responsibility for making decisions. Strauss returned to Vienna in September for the first performance on the 20th of Beethoven's *Die Ruinen von Athen*, a 'festive spectacle' also incorporating parts of Beethoven's *Prometheus* ballet music which he and Hofmannsthal had adapted, and on 1 October he conducted the first Vienna performance of *Der Bürger als Edelmann* in the ideal setting of the Redoutensaal. Neither was a success.

Strauss then went to Dresden where his *Intermezzo* was to have its first performance on 4 November with Fritz Busch conducting and Lotte Lehmann in the principal soprano role. (Lehmann sang in Dresden only on the first night; thereafter Grete Nikisch took over the role of Christine.) During the final rehearsals Ludwig Karpath, who was the Austrian Education Ministry's adviser on the national theatres, arrived from Vienna to tell Strauss the details of Schalk's new contract and to gain his agreement to the 'sole responsibility' clause. It was made quite clear that he had to agree. Strauss refused and handed Karpath his resignation, though he was under no illusion but that he had been dismissed. His only public statement was that he was 'neither angry nor bitter', but to Andrian he compared his position with Wagner's departure from Munich. ('Richard must go, the Minister stays.') To Hofmannsthal on 29 January 1925 he explained: 'The annoyance with that —— Schalk was too much, the means for achieving anything worthwhile too little, and the offer of the Minister—who only wanted me as window-dressing and as a willing drudge for when he gets the post of "Director General of the State Opera", said to have been already promised him when he resigns as Minister—unworthy of me.'

Intermezzo was based on the marital misunderstanding Strauss and Pauline had experienced in 1902. Its première was given not in Dresden's big opera house but in the smaller Schauspielhaus des Dresdener Staatstheaters which was better suited to its intimate style. The sets by

---

[6] R. Myers (ed.), *Richard Strauss and Romain Rolland*, op. cit., pp. 162–8.

Adolf Mahnke were closely based on Strauss's Garmisch villa. Lotte Lehmann has recounted saying to Pauline after the performance that the opera was really a compliment to her, to which Pauline replied: 'I don't give a damn.' But she did. Extraordinary as it may seem, she did not know what the opera was about until she attended the première. She was furious and so was the maid, Anna. She told Strauss what she thought of this public exposure of their private life when they returned to their hotel. The row continued next day in the back of the car as they drove back to Garmisch in a thunderstorm. Their chauffeur did not know which was worse: the storm raging inside or outside the car. Many years later Pauline told the producer Rudolf Hartmann that 'even at her advanced age she would scratch the eyes out of any woman who came too close to Richard. But one didn't need to write a play, let alone an opera, about that.' Strauss, who was present, said: 'But I did write a beautiful duet of reconciliation at the end.' Pauline smiled and said endearingly 'like a little girl: "Yes, that's true, you did!"'

In 1916, when he had approached Hermann Bahr about the libretto of *Intermezzo*, Strauss sent him an illuminating analysis of Pauline's character and his own. It is too long to quote in full, but salient features are the following:

> She is very pedantic in her love of order and passion for cleanliness. In her heart, too, she loves seemliness and purity and rigorously deplores moral shortcomings in others, unless mitigated by some cause of fellow-feeling . . . One of the favourite subjects the couple argue about is that she, because of her pedantry, can only ever see one way to reach a goal, whereas he will weigh all the possibilities and choose the most convenient and time-saving. She will not acknowledge the help he gives in his quiet way, because she thinks he is no use in practical matters . . . Bills and receipts always cause her enormous trouble and are only mastered after enormous expenditure of effort and with the aid of the honest serving-maid of a good memory . . . Because she has the feeling that she is always doing things for him, she longs to be left on her own, but no sooner has he gone away than she experiences great longing for him.

Christine in *Intermezzo* is a portrait drawn from life.

11

Helen and Arabella

Strauss's output, large though it was, diminished between 1916 and about 1940, with his five years in Vienna the thinnest period. Partly this may be attributed to his preoccupation with operas, some of which took several years to compose and stage, but there are grounds for belief that he himself was searching for a new means of expression, recognizing that his early fertility had gone and also that he was more self-critical. In his career he wrote 213 songs: his last very fertile year for *Lieder* was 1918 in which he composed twenty-nine. By the end of that year his total was 189; in the following thirty-one years he wrote only twenty-four. He had composed none between 1906 and 1918. This can be explained partly by a dispute with publishers but mainly by Pauline's retirement from the concert platform. Thereafter he was inspired only by the voices of Elisabeth Schumann and Viorica Ursuleac. Between 1915 and 1925 his only works for orchestra were the ballet *Schlagobers*, publication of the suite from *Le Bourgeois Gentilhomme* and (another ballet) an arrangement for small orchestra of some keyboard pieces by Couperin (1922–3). His principal work at this time was the two-act *Intermezzo*, completed in Buenos Aires on 21 August 1923.

No wonder the world of music regarded him by then as almost a fossil. To the non-specialist audience his name was known because of his early tone-poems and his earlier operas. To all intents and purposes, *Der Rosenkavalier* of 1911 was his last word. An English critic, Cecil Gray, wrote in the 1920s[1] of 'the gradual degeneration and final extinction of his creative powers . . . he has become a man of second-rate talent'. Strauss was still in the dilemma he had foreseen and outlined to Hofmannsthal in 1916. He had no more wish to be affected by the 'frenzy' Rolland mentioned than had Elgar. He knew what he did best, and that did not include writing a *Wozzeck*. Berg did that best.

But Strauss, like Puccini at this same period, was well aware of his need to do something new and different in his own line. In his correspondence with Hofmannsthal he makes continual reference to this, always suggesting something light-hearted. In his way he was as sensitive

[1] C. Gray, *A Survey of Contemporary Music* (London, 1924).

to the theatre-going public's mood in the 1920s as were the impresarios of the musical-comedy stage in New York and London who provided a decade of *Rose Marie*, *Rio Rita*, *Bitter Sweet* and the like. Even Hofmannsthal reflected something of this mood, probably unconsciously. He would certainly have been horrified if it had been pointed out to him that the Sheikh he introduced into *Die ägyptische Helena* had perhaps strayed from *The Desert Song* and the celluloid world of Rudolph Valentino; and that Arabella's 'Aber der Richtige . . . der wird einmal dastehn, da vor mir' ('But the right man . . . will stand there one day, there before me') is not far removed from Gershwin's 'Some day he'll come along, the man I love'. Significantly, both Strauss and Hofmannsthal admired Fritzi Massary and Richard Tauber. Neither Strauss nor anyone else realized at the time that the greatest operas of the 1920s were being written by Janáček.

Although there is a gap of six years—1918–24—in the operatic collaboration between Strauss and Hofmannsthal, this does not imply a breakdown in their relationship. It reflects the difficulty they had in finding a mutually acceptable subject and also their changed circumstances since the war. Early in 1920, noting Strauss's renewed interest in ballet, Hofmannsthal suggested a *divertissement* and offered a 'light-hearted, operetta-like three-act sketch which closely approaches the world of Lucian' (this was called *Danae* and was to be the basis of a Strauss opera fourteen years later). Neither suggestion was taken up. In 1922 came the collaboration on Beethoven's *Die Ruinen von Athen*. But in February of that year Hofmannsthal took Strauss an outline for an opera about Helen of Troy. Strauss assented, but progress was slow. A year later Hofmannsthal wrote of his difficulties in finding the right style for a scenario 'of a lighter kind'. He added: 'What you told me recently of the unbridgeable gulf between your music even at its lightest, and the common-or-garden operetta did not need saying at all.' Hofmannsthal had never forgotten hearing Strauss say to Pauline in a Berlin restaurant when discussing Lehár: 'In a few bars of mine there is more music than in a whole Lehár operetta.' (But towards the end of his life Strauss said: 'I was unjust to Lehár. I have always been too unconciliatory.') Returning from South America in September 1923, Strauss wrote of how he hoped to find *Helena* awaiting him 'preferably with entertaining ballet interludes; a few delightful elf or spirit choruses would also be most welcome'.

'Tell yourself that you mean to handle it as if it were to be merely an operetta,' Hofmannsthal advised him. This, and more in the same vein, perhaps deluded Strauss into the belief that he was getting the Offenbach *Belle Hélène* of the twentieth century, whereas Hofmannsthal's fatal penchant for mythological philosophizing took command, producing an extraordinary plot in which an Egyptian sorceress carries off Helen and Menelaus, after their marriage, to an oasis where a Sheikh and his son fall in love with Helen. Into this, Hofmannsthal worked magic potions, a talking sea-shell, and some obscure symbolism about death and marriage with Faustian overtones. When Strauss told Romain Rolland about it, Rolland commented in his diary: 'Why does Strauss, who so well realizes his inaptitude for great subjects of thought, let himself be caught by them again?' On the other hand, George Marek's assertion[2] that in his letters to Hofmannsthal Strauss showed little conviction is wide of the mark, at any rate at the start. 'Most of it virtually sets itself to music,' he wrote from Garmisch in October 1923 when he had received Act I. 'It's coming on unbelievably fast and is giving me no end of pleasure.' (He even composed a stage direction again.) A fortnight later: 'Everything so far is wonderful.' Hofmannsthal was delighted: it reminded him, he said, of the cheerful way Strauss had received *Der Rosenkavalier*. But Act II was a different matter. Strauss kept asking for it and Hofmannsthal kept telling him how good it would be but he could make it better still. It was the familiar pattern, but Hofmannsthal was writing under difficulties. The privations of the time greatly affected him: he told Strauss of 'sleepless nights, eternal headaches and nightmares' and badgered him about the project for a film of *Der Rosenkavalier* because of his precarious financial state. He asked for the loan of a particular book because 'at the moment I cannot afford to buy any'.

By 31 July 1924 the first draft of Act I was composed. Strauss had some of Act II by now but made little progress. He could not find the style for the Egyptian oasis, and it is significant that when Hofmannsthal had first told him the plot he said after Act I: 'Surely that's the end? What could happen in the second act?' In the last months of 1924 he wrote a work for the one-armed pianist Paul Wittgenstein in fulfilment of a request made some time before.[3] Stimulus came from the recovery of his son Franz, who had contracted typhus in Egypt just after his marriage, and Strauss called the new work *Parergon zur Symphonia Domestica*, basing it on the Child's theme from *Domestica*.

The year 1925 was comparatively uneventful for him. He took no part in the *Der Rosenkavalier* film, leaving Hofmannsthal to provide the expanded plot and sub-titles and Otto Singer and Carl Alwin, husband of Elisabeth Schumann, to arrange the music, though he composed a new march. He also left to his son the editing for publication of selections from his correspondence with Hofmannsthal.[4] In June he was still 'stuck' near the start of Act II of *Helena* where the Sheikh enters. He found it difficult to avoid 'degenerating into the so-called realism of *Salome*'. At Hofmannsthal's urgent request he conducted the first performance of the *Der Rosenkavalier* film in Dresden on 10 January 1926,

---

[2] G. Marek, *Richard Strauss: the Life of a Non-Hero* (London, 1967), p. 261.
[3] Wittgenstein also commissioned works from Ravel, Prokofiev, Britten, Franz Schmidt and others.
[4] F. Strauss (ed.), *Briefwechsel mit Hugo von Hofmannsthal* (Vienna, 1925).

and in April went to conduct it in London where he also made an electrical recording of some orchestral extracts.[5] In March, Strauss had played Act I of *Helena* to Hofmannsthal who wrote that he was 'more delighted . . . than, I believe, about any of your other compositions ever . . . Everything so light and transparent, for all its high, noble seriousness'. The singer on this occasion was Elisabeth Schumann, whom Strauss had specially asked to learn 'Ein Feuer brennt', an aria she would never have contemplated singing on stage. Strauss gave her the manuscript, inscribed 'To the first Helena'. In May the full score was finished and Strauss wrote: 'I am off to Greece tomorrow [5 May] to get a few beautiful tunes for Act II—even though my biographer, Herr Specht, considers it old-fashioned that nowadays I have *only* the ambition to "make beautiful music".'

Even so, the opera was not completed for another sixteen months. In the meantime Strauss had re-visited England in April and November 1926 and in December made his peace with the Vienna Opera when he conducted *Elektra*. He was still an active and powerful *éminence grise* in its affairs. For example, in June 1926 he had confided to Hofmannsthal: 'A re-engagement of Weingartner, even as a guest conductor, would be a bad thing. . . . The aim is still: Clemens Krauss as Director with two chief producers: Wallerstein and Turnau.' The Vienna-born conductor Krauss, thirty-three years old in 1926, had caught Strauss's eye when he was an assistant conductor at the Vienna Opera from 1922 to 1924. Since 1924 he had been director of Frankfurt Opera, where he had conducted a *Frau ohne Schatten* which Strauss had admired. Strauss was to entice him back to Vienna in 1929 as successor to Schalk. At the age of thirty-six Krauss was the youngest director since Mahler, and a year younger than Mahler had been on taking office in 1897.

On 8 October 1927 Strauss completed the full score of *Die ägyptische Helena*, saying that it had 'turned out very beautiful, brilliant yet simple'. The first performance was in Dresden on 6 June 1928, with Elisabeth Rethberg as Helen. Fritz Busch conducted. Hofmannsthal had been desperately anxious that the temperamental and beautiful Maria Jeritza ('*born* for the part') should sing Helen. But her fee was out of the question for Dresden and neither Strauss nor Hofmannsthal wanted the première to be in Vienna, where she was a member of the company. Strauss persuaded Dresden to offer her a special fee, but word of this reached the Association of German Theatres, which had imposed a ban on astronomical fees for artists, with the result that it threatened to boycott all his stage works in all German theatres. Strauss then suggested that Dresden should give the world première but Vienna would perform it next day with Jeritza. This provoked Jeritza to issue an ultimatum: 'I

---

[5] 'Selected orchestral passages' from the film version of *Der Rosenkavalier*, Augmented Tivoli Orchestra conducted by R. Strauss, HMV D 1094–7 (seven sides). Recorded 13 April 1926 in Queen's Hall.

sing the world première or not at all.' Eventually, after Strauss had pacified Jeritza, it was decided that Rethberg would sing in Dresden and Jeritza in Vienna five days later. There was a last-minute alarum when it seemed that Jeritza had not learned the role and her husband, Baron Popper, complained there had not been enough publicity for his wife's 'great-hearted decision'. Leo Wurmser was on the staff of the State Opera and has left an enlightening account of the final rehearsals.[6] Busch had been ill and had missed all the piano rehearsals. Strauss was more interested in the production than in the music (no doubt he was still worried by the sea-shell, which he had described to Hofmannsthal as 'rather like a gramophone'). Pauline sat in the front of the stalls clamouring for real horses in the desert scene and complaining that there was not enough thunder at the end of Act I. Strauss let her have more, saying *sotto voce* to the orchestra: 'Women always want to thunder.' At the first dress rehearsal Busch conducted the first act while Strauss followed the score. He then asked Busch to let him conduct. 'It was like a different opera: one big broad line from beginning to end, the right tempi and rubatos, co-operation with the singers and many of the 4/4 passages beaten in 2.'

Strauss himself conducted the Vienna première on 11 June 1928, his sixty-fourth birthday. He described it to Pauline as 'perhaps the greatest triumph of my life. After the first act the audience went wild for a full quarter-hour, at the end the enthusiasm was beyond bounds, for Jeritza, too, whose triumph was undisputed'. He described her as 'particularly thrilling in the second act, which she fills so completely by her performance that we were left breathless with excitement. Vocally and musically too, she was very good. The only place where Rethberg is vocally much her superior is in the aria at the beginning of Act II ['Zweite Brautnacht'].' The opera was later performed in Berlin, Munich, Hamburg, and New York (with Jeritza), but it was not the success its authors had expected. 'Ponderous, dreary, dated, mediocre' were among the critics' adjectives. Some years later, when it was rehearsed at Salzburg, Stefan Zweig sat with Strauss as he listened:

All at once he began to drum inaudibly and impatiently with his fingers upon the arm of the chair. Then he whispered to me: 'Bad, very bad! That spot is blank.' And again, after a few minutes: 'If I could cut that out! O Lord, Lord, that's just hollow, and too long, much too long!' A little later: 'Look, that's good!' He appraised his own work as objectively and unconcernedly as if he were hearing the music for the first time and as if it were written by a composer unknown to him.[7]

This objectivity deluded Fritz Busch into the conclusion that Strauss was not 'penetrated and possessed' by his marvellous talents like other

[6] L. Wurmser, *Richard Strauss as an Opera Conductor*, op. cit.
[7] S. Zweig, *The World of Yesterday* (London, 1943), p. 279.

great artists but 'simply wears them like a suit of clothes which can be taken off at will'. Busch should have looked at Strauss's eyes, described by Zweig as 'perhaps the most watchful eyes I have ever seen in a composer, not daemonic but somehow clearsighted, the eyes of a man who recognizes his mission down to its very fundamentals'. This clearsightedness was often mistaken for cold detachment, whereas it was the hallmark of Strauss's continual striving to realize himself to the full.

What was to be the last Strauss-Hofmannsthal opera began with a remark in a letter from Strauss on 12 September 1922: 'I feel like doing another *Rosenkavalier* just now!' A year later he dropped the same hint: 'A second *Rosenkavalier*, without its mistakes and *longueurs*! You'll just *have* to write that for me some day: I haven't spoken my last word yet in that genre.' As work on *Helena* ended, Strauss's usual restlessness set in. On 1 October 1927 Hofmannsthal wrote: 'Two years ago I occupied myself with a comedy. . . . It was called *The Cabby as Count* (*Der Fiaker als Graf*). . . . Last night it occurred to me that this comedy might perhaps be done for music, with the text in a light vein.' There was a ballroom scene[8] of 'enchanting possibilities', he said, and a touch of *Rosenkavalier* about it, with 'a most attractive woman as the central figure'.

On 13 November he told Strauss that the action of *Der Fiaker* was too flimsy for an opera, but he had combined 'features of this cabbies' world with elements from another projected comedy' to give him the scenario for a three-act opera, 'indeed almost an operetta . . . which in gaiety does not fall short of *Fledermaus*, is kindred to *Rosenkavalier*, without any self-repetition'. He had had the inspired idea of incorporating the plot of his short story *Lucidor*, written in 1909, and a week later he was still bubbling. 'The characters . . . are cutting their capers under my very nose . . . the comedy might turn out better than *Rosenkavalier*. . . . The two girls (sopranos) could develop into magnificent (singing) parts. . . . As lovers a high tenor and a baritone. This latter is the most remarkable character in the piece, from a semi-alien world (Croatia), half buffo and yet a grand fellow capable of deep feelings, wild and gentle, almost daemonic.'

On 16 December Hofmannsthal read Strauss the outline of what he had already titled *Arabella*. Here at last was the subject Strauss wanted: no Freudian symbolism, no Faustian mythology. His reaction was closely and intelligently critical. He did not want this Croatian grand fellow as the main character. 'The character which ensured final victory for *Rosenkavalier* is the Marschallin. . . . The new piece . . . lacks a genuinely interesting female character.' Don't worry, Hofmannsthal replied, this Croatian, Mandryka, sets the action going

---

[8] At the annual Vienna cabbies' festival a carnival queen was chosen. All social barriers were relaxed.

but the main character is Arabella: 'She is the queen of the big ball and of the whole piece and, as in a fairy-tale, she marries the rich stranger in the end.' He sent the libretto of the first act to Strauss at the end of April 1928.

Strauss had many criticisms to make, chiefly that Arabella was not yet a part. Hofmannsthal patiently revised it. 'We understand each other better every year,' Strauss wrote. 'A pity such good, continuous progress towards perfection must come to an end some day.' He made detailed suggestions, just as he had for Act II of *Der Rosenkavalier*—'it seems to me we've reached the same point'. By August 1928 they had made many changes, but on 1 November Strauss confessed he did not yet feel enthusiastic enough to start writing the music. They met in Vienna on 29 December and talked it over. Strauss liked Acts II and III and Hofmannsthal agreed to re-draft Act I. Progress was slow, both men being ill in the early part of 1929. 'Could a little more lyricism be fitted into *Arabella*?' Strauss pleaded. 'The *aria*, after all, is the soul of opera. . . . Separate numbers with recitatives in between. That's what opera was, is and remains.' On 2 July Hofmannsthal explained his revisions, which met all Strauss's objections. Strauss was thrilled. Just one thing more, he said; he still wanted the act to end with a long aria for Arabella. Hofmannsthal sent him the text of 'Mein Elemer' on the 10th, and on the 14th Strauss telegraphed: 'First act excellent. Many thanks and congratulations.'

Hofmannsthal never opened the telegram. On 13 July his son Franz had shot himself. The great poet was grief-stricken. For three years he had been suffering from arterio-sclerosis and as he dressed to attend Franz's funeral on 15 July he had a stroke and died a few minutes later. Strauss wrote to his widow next day from Garmisch: 'No musician ever found such a helper and supporter. No one will ever replace him for me or the world of music.' He expanded on this in a private memorandum written in July 1935:

> Attacked and maligned by the press and the profession for thirty years . . . he was a faithful genius and I obstinately stuck with him. Now, after his death, he is finally recognised as 'my true poet'. I had to resign myself to admitting that my period of creating operas had come to an end . . . I flirted and negotiated with the best German poets, but in fifty years I found only the wonderful Hofmannsthal.[9]

They had collaborated on six major operas and several lesser works. 'I believe', Hofmannsthal had written, 'that they, not all of them, but nearly all of them, with their inseparable fusion of poetry and music, will continue to live for some considerable time and will give pleasure to several generations.' Despite all their bickering, these two men understood one another. Hofmannsthal's private tribute to Strauss on the

---

[9] K. Wilhelm, *Richard Strauss, an Intimate Portrait*, op. cit., p. 224.

composer's sixtieth birthday in 1924 should not be overlooked in any assessment of their strange relationship: 'The only person who always recognized whatever there was, who received it with real joy, received it productively and translated it into higher reality, was you.'

12

Under the Nazis

With his collaborator dead and only one act of the *Arabella* libretto in its final form, Strauss eagerly began to compose the music as a dedicated tribute. Although he probably recognized that if Hofmannsthal had lived, they would have made structural revisions in Acts II and III, Strauss refused to alter the main outlines although (contrary to what is often said) he made many minor alterations to the libretto. By September 1929 Act I was almost sketched but progress became slower as he realized, when problems arose, that he was on his own. 'There's no hurry', he said to inquirers. 'Until people have got halfway to understanding *Die Frau ohne Schatten*, *Intermezzo*, and *Helena*, they don't need to hear anything else.' He willingly laid it aside when the Austrian producer Lothar Wallerstein, at Clemens Krauss's suggestion, asked him to collaborate in preparing a new version of Mozart's *Idomeneo*, then practically unknown.

The revival of *Idomeneo* was planned to mark the 150th anniversary in 1931 of its Munich first performance. In a letter to the stage director and Intendant Bruno von Niessen in 1932,[1] Strauss said that he had undertaken the task to 'win [*Idomeneo*] back for the German stage' and 'if we succeed, I will personally answer for my impiety to the divine Mozart if I ever get to heaven'. He said that 'individual numbers such as the "Zeffiretti" aria and the famous E flat quartet were favourite pieces of my early youth'. Wallerstein translated the libretto into German prose and discarded the number-scheme. The plot was altered and the character of Elettra was eliminated—one operatic Elektra was enough for Strauss, perhaps!—by converting her into Neptune's priestess Ismene, intent on preventing the future king, Idamante, from marrying a Trojan slave-girl, Ilia. Strauss made heavy cuts in what he regarded as 'the interminable recitatives'. Some were re-scored for orchestra,

---

[1] For further information on the Strauss version of *Idomeneo*, readers are referred to C. Walton's essay in *Idomeneo* by J. Rushton (Cambridge, 1993), pp. 89–94; F. Grazberger (ed.), *Der Strom der Töne trug mich fort* (Tutzing, 1967), p. 338; G. Brosche and K. Dachs (eds), *Richard Strauss: Autographen in München und Wien. Verzeichnis* (Tutzing, 1979), p. 368; and S. Kohler, *Die Idomeneo-Bearbeitung Lothar Wallerstein und Richard Strauss*, Bayerische Staatsbibliothek, p. 176.

others re-written using Mozart material. Strauss included the numbers Mozart composed for the 1786 Vienna production, but he excluded Elettra's 'Idol mio', Idamante's 'No, la morte', and Idomeneo's 'Torna la pace'. Arbace, changed from bass to baritone, was deprived of both his arias (as he often is today), and the High Priest was lowered from tenor to bass. Idamante was a soprano. Strauss added two numbers of his own, both of which used Mozart material. One was an *Interludio*, placed after the chorus 'Corriamo, fuggiamo' (or 'Auf Tiefen des Meeres', as it became). Its middle section is based on the discarded aria 'Torna la pace'. Strauss knew from Mozart's letters that a quartet had originally been planned before the final chorus and he provided one for Idamante, Idomeneo, Ilia and the High Priest, basing it on Idomeneo's recitative 'Popoli, a voi l'ultima legge' and the opening of Ilia's aria 'Se il padre perdei'.

Strauss conducted the first performance at the Vienna Opera on 16 April 1931. There was a second performance in Magdeburg a few days later and it reached the Berlin State Opera in November 1932. The public liked it but most of the critics were hostile. 'Mozart with whipped cream' was a Berlin verdict. Alfred Einstein, in his revision of Köchel's catalogue, called it 'a gross act of mutilation'. Strauss's letter to Niessen ended: 'Let the critics say what they will. I know my Mozart better than those gentlemen do, and at any rate I love him more ardently than they!' Unkind critics have interpreted his love of *Idomeneo* as more akin to rape, and his desire to win it back for the German stage as a ploy to win back the German stage for himself by linking himself with Mozart. Be that as it may—and it represents a low view of Strauss's integrity—this version of *Idomeneo* has more than curiosity value. Today, when *Idomeneo* has been fully restored to the repertory and is greatly admired, it may seem totally superfluous to requirements, but it has its place in that restoration. It has not been performed since December 1941, when Strauss conducted it in Vienna. Some extracts recorded from this performance have been issued by Koch Schwann in Volume 3 of its edition Wiener Staatsoper Live (3-1453-2). They include the *Interludio* and the quartet. The *Dresdner Nachrichten*'s 1932 opinion that 'one constantly recognizes when it is Mozart's turn to speak and when Strauss's' is indubitably true, but that in itself has a fascination which need not damn the work irrevocably. It was, in any case, Strauss's intention.

During the late summer of 1931 Anton Kippenberg, the publisher, called on Strauss and mentioned one of his authors, Stefan Zweig, who at this date was fifty and at the height of his popularity as novelist and biographer. 'Ask him if he has an opera libretto for me,' Strauss said. This led to a meeting in November when Zweig suggested a free adaptation of Ben Jonson's *Epicene, or the Silent Woman* (*Die schweigsame Frau*) on the lines of his *Volpone* adaptation, which Strauss had enjoyed.

Zweig described later[2] how delighted he was by Strauss's quick response:

> While the nature of the material was being explained to him he was already shaping it dramatically and adjusting it astonishingly to the limits of his own abilities of which he was uncannily cognisant. . . . 'I am not one to compose long melodies as did Mozart. I can't get beyond short themes. But what I can do is to utilize such a theme, paraphrase it and extract everything that is in it, and I don't think there's anybody today who can match me at that.'

In mid-June of 1932 Zweig delivered the first section of Act I of *Die schweigsame Frau*. 'It is delightful,' Strauss told him, 'the born comic opera . . . more suited to music than either *Figaro* or *The Barber of Seville*. . . . I am burning to get started on it in earnest.' But the Dresden Intendant, Alfred Reucker, and Busch urged the claims of *Arabella*. Strauss completed it on 12 October, with a dedication to them.

On 17 January 1933 the complete Zweig libretto was in Strauss's hands. Thirteen days later the German President, Hindenburg, appointed Adolf Hitler as Chancellor. Four weeks later, as a result of the Reichstag Fire, Hitler established one-party rule, the rule of his National Socialists who, since September 1930, had been the second largest party and had risen to favour because of general disillusionment, rising unemployment and their selection of a scapegoat for all Germany's woes—the Jews. Strauss who, like other artists, had regarded himself as impervious to all politicians, was slowly to find that the Nazis could not be disregarded. His conduct was often contradictory, and his name has been besmirched because of that conduct. All that follows should, however, be viewed in the context of a comment passed by the shrewd Hofmannsthal in a letter to Strauss in December 1926. He was referring to the *rapprochement* with the Vienna Opera, and added: 'I do not think you care very much about these things—or indeed about almost anything apart from your productive work.' It should also be remembered that Strauss's wealth made him unpopular. F. W. Gaisberg, of the Gramophone Company, wrote to Elgar in April 1932 describing Strauss, Lehár, Oscar Straus and Kalman as having 'usurped the position of wealth and influence formerly occupied by the great Viennese bankers. . . . They seem to be the only ones in Vienna who have any money and are the envy of the threadbare Viennese.'[3]

Strauss's world was music, mostly his own music, and he was wholly wrapped up in it, composing, conducting, planning. His career began in the old Germany of ducal courts. They had gone, he remained. He had paid them lip-service, a motet for a wedding, a military march for some dreadful parade, and they left him alone. After all, he had defeated the Kaiser over *Salome*, why should these Nazis be any different? He was

---

[2] S. Zweig, *The World of Yesterday*, op. cit.
[3] J. N. Moore, *Elgar on Record* (London, 1974), p. 167.

the man to take them on, for his own sake. As he said to his family, 'I made music under the Kaiser and under Ebert, I'll survive under this one as well'. War, hunger, currency deflation—these he regarded as personal slights, interfering with his work. He was almost naïve in his belief that nothing could touch him. But did he not see that these men were evil? What about the treatment of the Jews? Strauss was very far from being alone, in Germany and elsewhere, in viewing Hitler's 1933–9 Germany in a light quite different from that in which we, with the benefit of hindsight, see it so clearly.

Why did he not make a gesture of protest, as Toscanini did? He was not cut out for heroics, like Toscanini and Huberman. In Paris in 1900 he had said to Rolland: 'I am not a hero, I haven't the necessary strength. I prefer to withdraw.' Otto Klemperer said that Strauss remained because in Germany there were fifty-six opera houses and in America two, and the reduction of income involved in such a gesture was not to be contemplated. One might charitably describe this as an over-simplistic remark. He was also—this creator of the Marschallin and the Empress—human; and the real reasons why he stayed were, first, his German patriotism and, even more important, his beloved daughter-in-law was Jewish, his grandchildren therefore half-Jewish, he had worked for over twenty years with the half-Jew Hofmannsthal, his publisher was a Jew, and his new librettist was a Jew. Which of us, except authors like George Marek and film-makers like Ken Russell who see life in black-and-white with no blurred edges, dare make a moral judgment on Strauss? Or on Shostakovich? Schoenberg said at this period: 'There are more important things today than art.' It was not only that Strauss believed nothing was more important, than art: he simply did not recognize the conflict, a symptom of a blinkered mentality as a court composer. He kept his nose in his score and ignored the raised voices in the next room.

The cultural climate of the new regime was soon apparent. On 7 March 1933, when Busch, who was not a Jew, entered the pit to conduct *Il Trovatore* at Dresden he was received with obscene catcalls. He and Reucker were dismissed from their posts. So, in Berlin, were Klemperer and Reinhardt. At a meeting in Berlin some days later, Strauss made it clear that if Busch did not conduct and Reucker produce the *Arabella* première, then it was off. He meant it. Busch wrote later that, many years after the events, friends assured him that Strauss really tried to keep his word and withdrew the work. Nevertheless he had ultimately to give way to the claims of the contracts he had signed. Krauss conducted the first performance, at Dresden, on 1 July, with Viorica Ursuleac as Arabella and Alfred Jerger as Mandryka. Later it was performed in Berlin, Munich and Vienna (21 October, with Lehmann in the title-role). It was a success of a kind, but the inevitable (and misleading) comparisons with *Der Rosenkavalier* were to its disadvantage. The wits in Vienna called it *Der Sklerosenkavalier*. An unfortunate side-effect of the *Arabella* imbroglio was that the conductor Hans Knappertsbusch, to Strauss's regret, broke off relations with Strauss because he was refused the world première in Munich where he could not offer a cast of such quality as Dresden or Vienna. Strauss's attempts at reconciliation were rebuffed.

On 20 March 1933, also, Bruno Walter was ordered not to conduct a Berlin Philharmonic concert and was warned that if he did, the hall would be wrecked. Heavy pressure was exerted on Strauss to conduct in Walter's place, not only by the Nazis but by Jewish impresarios. He agreed and gave his fee to the orchestra, who were to have been paid by Walter. He did it, he said, for their sake. Strauss happened to be in Berlin at the time conducting *Elektra* at the Staatsoper. He did not like Walter, nor did Walter like him. This stemmed from disapproval of Strauss opera performances in Munich when Walter was conductor there from 1912 to 1922. Both Strauss and Hofmannsthal were dissatisfied with Walter's treatment of the first version of *Ariadne auf Naxos* in Munich in 1912, Hofmannsthal describing him in one letter as 'this strange man' who 'seems to be constantly in a fever, pro or contra, and never able to weigh anything calmly'. In the summer Strauss agreed to conduct *Parsifal* at Bayreuth in place of Toscanini, who had withdrawn because of 'painful events'. But what must have weighed most heavily with Strauss was that 1933 was the fiftieth anniversary of Wagner's death. His devotion to Wagner and Bayreuth far outweighed any views he then may have had about Hitler and the Nazis. The invitation had come from Winifred Wagner, the first he had had from Bayreuth for thirty-nine years since he had fallen out with Siegfried Wagner. (Once when they met in Berlin while Strauss was staying in the luxurious Hotel Adlon, Siegfried remarked: 'Is your business making such good profits, then?' Strauss snapped back: 'Yes, and it's my own business, not my father's.') Replying to Winifred's letter of thanks and for her gift of a page of autograph sketches for *Lohengrin*, Strauss wrote:

> My modest help for Bayreuth was only a respectful repayment of the great debt of gratitude stored up in my heart for all that the great master gave to the world and to me in particular. It is really I who should thank you for the opportunity, in the evening of my life, to conduct his sublime work once more, in that sacred place: it was a high honour and satisfaction for me.

He returned to conduct some of the 1934 festival performances of *Parsifal*. (His interpretation was one of the fastest recorded there.) While at Bayreuth in 1933, Strauss suggested to Hitler that the new government should levy a one per cent royalty on all Wagner performances in Germany, the proceeds going to Bayreuth. Hitler refused on the well-known grounds of 'no precedent'. When he gave a reception in Wagner's house *Wahnfried*, Alice Strauss wanted to refuse the invitation, but

Winifred Wagner persuaded her that it would be unwise. So Hitler kissed her hand on greeting her, knowing that she was a Jewess.

Not unnaturally Strauss's help to Bayreuth was interpreted as showing his approval of the regime, and this view was strengthened when, on 1 November, Joseph Goebbels, the Nazi Minister of Propaganda, established a state music bureau, the *Reichsmusikkammer*, and nominated Strauss as its president. It did not take Strauss long to discover he had been duped. Some months later he explained this 'mime' to Zweig as 'knowing where my artistic duty lies. Under any regime I would have taken on these pestiferous honorary positions, but neither Kaiser Wilhelm nor Herr Rathenau ever offered one.'[4]

Although Strauss, in a private memorandum written in 1935[5], said that Goebbels had nominated him president 'without obtaining my prior agreement', and that he was not consulted about others' membership of the presidial council, a telegram offering him the post exists. This does not mean, though, that the matter was mentioned to him beforehand. Why did he accept? 'Because I hoped that I would be able to do some good and prevent worse misfortune, if from now onwards German musical life was going to be, as it was said, "reorganized" by amateurs and ignorant place-seekers.' In his opening address to the *Reichsmusikkammer* on 15 November, Strauss expressed 'the heartfelt thanks of the whole German musical fraternity' for the opening-up of the prospects of an intimacy between music and the people such as had existed in the sixteenth century. His prime objective in accepting the post was to achieve his life's aim of improving the copyright laws. He achieved this when the Nazis signed the Berne copyright agreement in 1934. In February 1935 he persuaded the German radio authorities to agree to broadcast the work of unknown composers. Just how much he misunderstood the nature of the regime is obvious from his letter of 13 December 1935 to his vice-president, Wilhelm Furtwängler, in which he asked him to instruct an over-zealous party official in Frankfurt that 'nothing stands in the way of a performance of Debussy's *Nocturnes* any more than that of any of the symphonies of Mahler, which he has not yet ventured to include in the programmes. Perhaps you would also see to it that the cultural warden is forbidden in future to meddle in programme-making.' Some hope!

He wanted, somewhat optimistically, to improve the 'abysmal quality' of the programmes of spa orchestras by suggesting to them 'music of decent quality' such as Mozart divertimenti and waltzes by the Strausses and Lanner in place of operatic pot-pourris and performances

---

[4] Walther Rathenau (1867–1922) was an industrialist who from 1916 directed Germany's war economy and in 1918 founded a new Democratic Party. In the Weimar Republic he was first Minister of Reconstruction (1921) and later Foreign Minister. He was assassinated by anti-Semitic nationalists.

[5] K. Wilhelm, *Richard Strauss, an Intimate Portrait*, op. cit., pp. 218–19.

of Siegfried's Funeral March by bands of sixteen players. He also wanted Bayreuth's exclusive right to *Parsifal* to be restored. All hopeless causes. He also urged that state-subsidized opera houses should perform a higher proportion of German works. 'The foreign repertory should occupy a third, or perhaps once in a while, as an exception, half the scheduled programme, and that is still a considerably higher percentage than foreign countries afford to us.' One has heard similar sentiments on behalf of British works put forward by British composers.

But Strauss spent most of his time in Garmisch. He did not supervise the *Reichsmusikkammer* on a daily basis and was in no position to approve or disapprove instructions and decrees issued by lesser officials. He found himself affected by an order forbidding German musicians from attending or taking part in the 1934 Salzburg Festival (where he was to have conducted *Fidelio*) because of the inimical relations between the German and Austrian governments. Three Strauss operas were to be performed, conducted by Krauss, to mark his seventieth birthday. In the event he went to Salzburg privately, took a bow after *Elektra* and was seen talking to the Jewish Bruno Walter and Stefan Zweig. But he was beginning to understand the truth of a remark Goebbels had made to him: 'The world looks different, Dr Strauss, from the way you imagine it in your study in Garmisch!' In 1938 when he was on holiday in Italy, he returned home on hearing that his eleven-year-old grandson Richard had been threatened and beaten up by boys in his school in Garmisch. He wrote to certain influential officials and eventually to Hitler. It was decreed that Richard and his six-year-old brother Christian were to be treated as Aryans, but would not be eligible for party membership, military service or public office.

Strauss's principal creative occupation during late 1932 and early 1933 was a major revision of Act II of *Die ägyptische Helena* to try to make it dramatically intelligible. The libretto was amended by Lothar Wallerstein and the new version was performed under Krauss at the Salzburg Festival on 14 August 1933, with Ursuleac as Helen but with no more success. Strauss had by then lost interest, for he was excited by Zweig's libretto, which he set almost without alteration. *Die schweigsame Frau* was completed in short score by November 1933 and the full score was finished on 20 October 1934, after Strauss had passed his seventieth birthday. This occasion was celebrated by 'Strauss Weeks' in Berlin, Munich, Vienna and Dresden, which made him a Freeman of the city. President Hindenburg awarded him the Eagle Shield of the German Reich and Hitler sent him a photograph with the inscription 'To the great composer Richard Strauss with deepest veneration'.

Through the proscribing of non-Aryans, whereby theatres were forbidden to produce works by Jews, Zweig was obviously threatened. The news that Strauss was at work on a libretto by Zweig was announced on the radio and described as 'scandalous'. Zweig knew this meant the end of the collaboration, but Strauss was sure the law did not apply to Austrians. He approached Goebbels, who agreed that there were no political accusations against Zweig. That was in May 1934; in August, at Bayreuth, Goebbels again raised the matter and warned Strauss there might be trouble at the première. However, it was referred to Hitler, who was sent the libretto and told Strauss personally that he would allow—and attend—the performance even though it broke the laws. At this point the Nazis seemed unwilling to incense world opinion by acting against Strauss.

He was already disillusioned with the *Reichsmusikkammer*, which, without reference to him, was extending its non-Aryan policy to forbid performances of *Carmen* and was prohibiting the use by artists and musicians of 'foreign-sounding names'. Strauss wrote to a friend on 4 October 1934: 'I have no wish to take part in such embarrassing blunders . . . my extensive and serious proposals for reform were rejected by the Minister. Time is too precious for me to participate in such dilettantish rubbish.' Just before Christmas he composed the Hymn commissioned from him for the opening ceremony of the Olympic Games to be held in Berlin in August 1936. To Zweig he wrote of composing it for 'this common lot—I, of all people, who hate and despise sport!' He even vented his views on sport to the president of the National Olympic Committee, who treated him to five pages of indignation in reply.

Throughout this period Strauss was constantly imploring Zweig, who was in Zürich, to collaborate with him again; he could not believe that providence would deprive him of such a librettist. Why not work secretly, he suggested; he would lock the operas in a drawer. 'In a few years, when our works will be ready, the world will probably look very different' (24 August 1934). 'I will *not* relinquish you just because we now have an anti-Semitic government. Why now raise unnecessary questions which will have taken care of themselves in two or three years?' Zweig was more realistic. The most he would do, he said, would be to suggest subjects and to supervise their completion by others. On 17 June 1935 Strauss exploded in exasperation:

> Your letter of the 15th drives me to despair! This Jewish obstinacy! It is enough to drive one to anti-Semitism! This racial pride, this feeling of solidarity—even I feel a difference. Do you imagine I have ever been guided in any course of action by the thought that I am Germanic (perhaps, *qui le sait*)? Do you suppose that Mozart was consciously 'Aryan' in his composing? For me there are only two sorts of people: those who have talent and those who haven't, and for me 'das Volk' only begin to exist when they become the Audience. It's all the same to me if they come from China, Upper Bavaria, New Zealand or Berlin, so long as they have paid at the box office.

He went on:

Who told you that I have exposed myself politically? Because I have conducted a concert in place of the slimy rascal Bruno Walter? That I did for the orchestra's sake. Because I substituted for that other 'non-Aryan' Toscanini? That I did for the sake of Bayreuth. That has nothing to do with politics. It is none of my business how the gutter press interprets what I do, and it should not concern you either . . . The show here will be terrific. Everybody is wildly enthusiastic. And with all this you ask me to forgo you? Never ever.

Strauss posted this letter in Dresden, where he was attending rehearsals of *Die schweigsame Frau*. He was overjoyed by the work and wrote to Pauline: 'The opera is magnificent . . . I hope Rosenberg [the leading Nazi ideologist and architect of anti-Jewish policy] and a few others like him will burst. One has to provide one's own compensation for all the nonsense that goes on in the world around one.' Two days before the première Strauss sent for a proof of the programme and saw that Zweig's name had been omitted. Furious, he demanded its restoration or he would return home. Paul Adolph, the Intendant, re-inserted Zweig's credit line. He was later dismissed. The first performance, on 24 June, was a success. Karl Böhm conducted and Maria Cebotari sang the principal part. But Hitler and Goebbels did not attend, as they had promised. Bad weather had prevented their flight, it was said. Three more performances were given; after the fourth, in the second week of July, the opera was banned throughout Germany.[6] Strauss's letter to Zweig had been intercepted by the State police and sent to Hitler on 1 July by a *Gauleiter*. Five days later, on Goebbels's orders, two officials called on Strauss to demand his resignation from the presidency of the *Reichsmusikkammer* 'on the grounds of ill-health'. A week later Strauss wrote to Hitler to explain the background of his letter to Zweig, that its 'improvised sentences', dashed off 'in a moment of ill-humour', did not 'represent my view of the world nor my true conviction'. He added:

My whole life belongs to German music and to a tireless effort to elevate German culture. I have never been active politically nor even expressed myself in politics. Therefore I believe that I will find understanding from you, the great architect of German social life. . . . I will devote the few years still granted to me only to the purest and most ideal goals. . . . I beg you, my Führer, most humbly to receive me for a personal discussion.

These was no response to this letter of an old man frightened for the safety of his nearest and dearest.

During these perilous days Strauss wrote some secret memoranda, not published until after his death, in which he commented on these affairs. They are worth quotation:

These are sad times when an artist of my standing has to ask a brat of a Minister what he is permitted to compose, or perform. I belong to a nation of 'servants and waiters' and almost envy the racially persecuted Stefan Zweig. . . . I must

6 In 1936 it was performed in Graz, Milan and Zürich.

confess I do not understand this Jewish solidarity and I regret that the artist in Zweig is unable to rise above political vagaries.

But that was written before he knew the Gestapo had his letter. In a later addition he confessed his total inability to understand the Nazis' Aryan policy.

I have been slandered as a servile, selfish anti-Semite, whereas in truth I have always stressed at every opportunity to all the people that count here (much to my disadvantage) that I consider the Streicher-Goebbels Jew-baiting as a disgrace to German honour, as evidence of incompetence, the basest weapon of untalented, lazy mediocrity against a higher intelligence and greater talent.

He acknowledged the help and inspiration he had received from Jews, adding that his own most malicious enemies had been Aryans—Perfall, Schalk and Weingartner among them. At the end of that crucial year of 1935 Strauss received a State questionnaire asking whether he was Aryan and requiring the names of two witnesses to his professional ability. He wrote: 'Mozart and Richard Wagner'. He was still Till Eulenspiegel, even if the heavens were beginning to fall. 'We'll outlive them all', he said to his family.

13

Gregor and Krauss

In 1934 Strauss and Zweig had discussed their next projects. Zweig suggested a comedy by the eighteenth-century Abbé Casti called *Prima la Musica e poi le Parole*. This title, which was the germ of *Capriccio*, intrigued Strauss, but he was keen on a historical subject based on the medieval Peace of Constanz. Zweig, an earnest pacifist, leapt at the idea, and Strauss had by then read Calderón's play *El sitio de Breda* (1632), which deals with Spinola's magnanimity to the defeated Dutch army in 1625. Zweig suggested transferring the action to the Peace of Osnabrück, which ended the Thirty Years' War, and calling the one-act opera *24th October 1648*.

Writing to Strauss on 21 August, Zweig outlined his plot—a besieged fortress where the Commandant refuses to yield to pleas to surrender but, knowing he can no longer hold out, plans to blow it up, himself with it. His wife prepares to die with him. The fuse is lit, but is extinguished when a cannon shot is heard. They prepare to die in open battle, but news of peace comes. The enemy Commandant arrives and the two adversaries embrace, vowing to work for a new world.

A further indication to Strauss that he could no longer pretend that politics and art were separate worlds was given in December 1934, when Furtwängler was forced to resign from the Berlin Philharmonic and had his passport confiscated because he defended Hindemith against the condemnation of *Mathis der Maler* by the Nazis and in so doing uttered a warning against the danger of political denunciation being applied 'in the fullest measure to matters of art'. Strauss was in Amsterdam to conduct *Arabella*. Goebbels announced that he had received a telegram from Strauss congratulating him on his actions against Furtwängler. It was a forgery. Strauss did not send it, and it would have been wholly untypical of him to have done so. So he cannot have been unprepared for the intensification of pressure against his collaboration with Zweig, who suggested other librettists, among them Joseph Gregor, a Viennese theatrical archivist and historian. Gregor called on Strauss in April 1935 with a draft libretto based—at Zweig's prompting—on Hofmannsthal's *Semiramis* project which Strauss had always coveted. But Strauss sent him packing. On 2 June 1935 Strauss met Zweig at Bregenz in Austria, when it emerged that he was still devoted to the *1648* opera. Zweig said Gregor was the man for it and Strauss, grudgingly, saw him on 7 July. Gregor, who was obsequiously anxious for the distinction of becoming Hofmannsthal's successor, said he took six sketch-librettos from which Strauss selected three, the *1648* theme, an opera on the Daphne legend and another not positively identified (probably *Danae*). But of these three, the first was Zweig's idea and the last Hofmannsthal's.

In September 1935 Strauss went to Vichy in his capacity as president of the permanent council of the International Society of Composers, founded in 1934 to break down national barriers. The society's first festival, Strauss said, was 'immensely important. It is the first step towards smoothing the way abroad for those of our composers who have not yet been performed in other countries.'[1] His indifference to the policies of the Third Reich was shown by his eagerness to take part in a festival in which Jewish composers were represented. One of them, Paul Dukas, had died four months earlier and in his memory Strauss not only conducted *L'apprenti sorcier* but a performance of the opera *Ariane et Barbe-bleue*. 'Civilized France was a real rest-cure', he wrote home to Garmisch. Strauss's gesture would have been noted in Berlin; the German ambassador to France withdrew from the festival. It is noticeable that between 1935 and 1939 Strauss accepted as many conducting engagements outside Germany as he could. From the mid-1920s also, he went for 'a cure' each summer at such spas as Carlsbad, Kissingen, Bad Nauheim, Baden-Baden and Baden-bei-Zürich.

Strauss showed no pleasure in the partnership with Gregor. He was still unconvinced by Zweig's attitude and he treated Gregor in a manner that suggests he was enjoying being 'top dog' after all the years of tact and cajolery with Hofmannsthal. His reception of Gregor's libretto for *1648* was expressed thus: 'I don't think I can ever find music for it. These are not real people. . . . The dialogue of the two commandants . . . is how two schoolmasters would hold a conversation on a given subject: "30 Years' War".'

Zweig supervised the work—which in October 1935 was retitled *Friedenstag (Day of Peace)*—and revised the scene between the commandants. Strauss thanked him warmly, adding: 'I have now been busying myself for a few weeks with composing it, but it won't turn into the sort of music I must expect from myself. The material is after all a bit too everyday—soldiers, war, hunger, medieval heroism, people all dying together—it doesn't really suit me.' But he continued, with Gregor living at Garmisch. The opera was completed on 16 June 1936, but no plans were made to perform it. It remains unexplained why Strauss chose *Friedenstag* as an operatic subject. Challenged directly by Rudolf Hartmann, he equivocated: 'Military matters just don't excite me.' It is

---

[1] Letter to Siegmund von Hausegger, 31 December 1934.

an anti-war opera—Zweig wrote to him of 'a hymn to the reconciliation of all peoples and to the grace and mercy of creative action'—which makes it all the more remarkable that the Nazis did not ban it. On the other hand, the theme of unthinking obedience to a leader's order, even if it meant death, probably appealed to them. At any rate, Hitler attended the Vienna première (by the Munich company) in 1939.

Gregor also worked quickly on the second of the librettos in which Strauss had shown interest, and by October 1935 had completed a draft of *Daphne*. Strauss wrote to Zweig: 'No doubt our dear friend is very gifted, but what is lacking is strength and ideas . . . as also, which is most disturbing, any distinctive theatrical atmosphere. . . . Words upon words—schoolmaster banalities.' During the composition of *Friedenstag* he had already tried to give Gregor a lesson in the basic precepts of libretto-writing: 'Action and character! No "thoughts"! No poetry! Theatre!! The audience can only hear a third of the words and if they can't follow the action, they get bored! . . . No weighing of motives, no poetic self-indulgences. Headlines!' He began composition of *Daphne* in the summer of 1936, interrupting it for a visit to London in November to conduct the Dresden State Opera's performance of *Ariadne auf Naxos* at Covent Garden on the 6th. On the previous evening he was presented by Sir Hugh Allen with the Gold Medal of the Royal Philharmonic Society before a performance of *Also sprach Zarathustra* conducted by Boult.

Strauss pondered for the best part of a year over the finale of *Daphne*. Gregor had planned the work as a double bill with *Friedenstag*, each to end with a cantata-like chorus, but Strauss did not care for this in *Daphne*. He thought it absurd if people sang to Daphne after her metamorphosis into a tree; so did Clemens Krauss, who solved the problem for him. Strauss wrote to Gregor on 12 May 1937: 'Now, in the moonlight, but fully visible, the miracle of transformation is slowly worked upon her—*only with the orchestra alone!* . . . Right at the end, when the tree stands there complete, she should sing without words—only as a voice of nature—eight more bars of the Laurel-motif!'

Friedenstag was dedicated to Clemens Krauss and his wife Viorica Ursuleac, and Krauss put pressure on Strauss (much to Gregor's annoyance) to allow it to be given separately, preceded by Beethoven's *Prometheus* ballet, at the Munich Festival on 24 July 1938—Strauss's first operatic première in his native city. The cast included Ursuleac, Hans Hotter and Ludwig Weber. Strauss was now favourable to the Munich State Opera, for Krauss had become director in 1937, with Rudolf Hartmann as producer and Ludwig Sievert as stage designer. This famous trio made a speciality of Strauss's operas, with such singers as Ursuleac, Adèle Kern, and Julius Patzak. The two works were first presented as a double bill in Dresden on 15 October 1938 when the dedicatee of *Daphne*, Karl Böhm, conducted its first performance. Daphne was sung by Margarete Teschemacher, Apollo by Torsten Ralf, and Leukippos by Martin Kremer. A few more double performances were given, one of them at Vienna in June 1939 as part of the comprehensive celebrations of Strauss's seventy-fifth birthday not only in the Austrian capital under Krauss but in Munich, Berlin and, of course, Dresden. Since then *Daphne* has made its way separately. It was Pauline's favourite among her husband's operas.

Strauss conducted the Vienna Philharmonic in his seventy-fifth birth-day concert in the suite from *Le Bourgeois Gentilhomme* and the *Symphonia Domestica*. All his family were in a box and while conduct-ing *Domestica* he kept turning to them. Otto Strasser had a moving re-collection of the occasion. Strauss was tumultuously applauded but as he left the platform he threw his baton away, stumbled to a chair in the artists' room and began to weep. Deeply distressed, he muttered: 'Now it's all over'. A few minutes later his son Franz arrived and comforted him. It was a rare moment when he let the mask slip. Next day, cheer-ful as usual, he went to Dresden to conduct *Arabella*. But the music he had written to describe his family life thirty-six years earlier in a very different Germany had moved and disoriented him. At the Berlin cele-bration of his birthday, a performance of *Salome* was conducted by a rising young star, Herbert von Karajan. Strauss invited him to breakfast to discuss the work. At the end of their conversation he said: 'You are much closer to it than I am, for whom it's so far in the past. It will be all right as it is.'

During 1936 Willi Schuh, the critic and Straussian authority, sent from Zürich a three-year-old copy of the magazine *Corona* in which had been printed Hofmannsthal's scenario *Danae, oder die Vernunftheirat* (*Danae*, or *The Marriage of Convenience*). Hofmannsthal had sent this to Strauss in April 1920, but perhaps because he was so involved in Vienna, Strauss put it in a drawer where it lay until 1933 when he let *Corona* have it. But now he was thrilled and asked Gregor if he had read it. Gregor replied that he had prepared a draft of his own on this mythological sub-ject, but Strauss brusquely said he wanted the Hofmannsthal sketch re-worked. He began to compose the opera as a means of isolating the various problems, most of which, as the correspondence shows,[2] centred on Jupiter and Midas. The opera's title was at first *King Midas* but was changed at Viorica Ursuleac's suggestion to *Die Liebe der Danae* (*The Love of Danae*).

The third act proved especially intractable until Krauss made valuable suggestions, although this brought Strauss and Gregor near to a final breach and caused Gregor to stay away from the première of *Daphne*. But Strauss had the ending he wanted and saw the chances it offered to him. 'I can continue the farewell mood of Jupiter to the end,' he wrote

[2] R. Tenschert (ed.), *Briefwechsel mit Joseph Gregor* (Salzburg, 1955).

to Gregor in 1939. 'In the last scene . . . you need not restrict yourself for space. If it contains genuine wisdom and beautiful poetry . . . I will cope! And in a posthumous work everything is allowed!' He completed it on 28 June 1940, convinced he would never hear it. *Danae*, he told Gregor, must not be staged until at least two years after the end of hostilities—'that is to say . . . after my death. So that's how long you'll have to be patient.'

Nevertheless he was already at work on another opera. He had always been deeply concerned with the relationship between music and words and in 1933 had remarked to Krauss that he would like to write 'an opera about opera . . . I really ought to write something of this sort, no lyricism, no arias, but dry wit, intelligent dialogue—a theatrical fugue'. That was why he was drawn to Zweig's suggestion of the Casti comedy *Prima la Musica e poi le Parole*, which Salieri had set and which describes the composition of a scena by composer and librettist for their patron. Zweig wanted to re-shape it and in June 1935, when he had decided to withdraw, he passed to Gregor his idea that the setting should be a feudal castle where strolling players put on an entertainment under the direction of a caricature of Max Reinhardt—a similar situation to the *Ariadne* prologue. Strauss rejected the Gregor libretto—he was furious it was not by Zweig and it was because of this that he wrote the fatal letter which the Nazis seized—but revived it in March 1939. Another draft was rejected as 'nothing like what I had in mind'. Eventually Strauss invited Krauss to write it, though he himself contributed much.

By now the principal character had emerged as a young widowed Countess, Strauss's last great soprano stage role, and the setting was a French château just before the Revolution. There poet and composer, both in love with her, collaborate in a sonnet. She cannot decide between them, as one cannot decide between words and music. But the kernel of the work is the planning of a celebration for the Countess's forthcoming birthday. Suggestions are made by various members of the house party, particularly by the theatre director La Roche. Nothing is acceptable, but the Countess suggests an opera by her rival suitors. What subject? Her brother has a brainwave—why not an opera about the events of that day? But this poses a problem for the Countess. She has told the composer that next day, in her library, she will inform him whom she has chosen, poet or composer, words or music. So how will the opera end? The question is left unanswered. Strauss and Krauss worked well and fast together, each making suggestions in a long and interesting correspondence[3] early in 1940. The introduction and first scene were composed by July and eight months later the opera was finished in sketch. At the end of July 1941 Strauss reported that the full score would be ready that week (it was finished on 3 August) and that

---

[3] W. Schuh and G.K. Kende (eds), *Briefwechsel mit Clemens Krauss* (Munich, 1964).

he was 'concerned with making the instrumentation of the last scene especially beautiful for our dear friend [Ursuleac]'. The title, *Capriccio*, and the sub-title 'A conversation piece for music', were suggested by Krauss.

Krauss was at this time supreme in German music-making. A great conductor, he was no less great an opportunist. He made no secret of his support for the Nazis,[4] and undoubtedly this eased Strauss's position because Krauss's devotion to his music ensured its continued performance in Germany and Austria even though the composer was in disfavour. With so many of his colleagues in exile or in hiding, Krauss held several of the highest conductorships and in 1942 became director of the Salzburg Festival. To celebrate this he implored Strauss to let him give the première of *Die Liebe der Danae*, but to no avail. Strauss suggested that *Capriccio* should be staged there: 'Never forget that our *Capriccio* is no piece for the broad public, any more than it should be played in a big house.' But Krauss had, with difficulty, won Goebbels's approval for a Strauss Festival in Munich in October 1942 and it was there, on the 28th, that *Capriccio* was first performed and enthusiastically received. Ursuleac sang Countess Madeleine, Horst Taubmann was Flamand and Hans Hotter was Olivier.

A year before the première, Strauss had described *Capriccio* to Krauss as 'a dainty morsel for cultural gourmets, not very substantial musically—at all events, not so succulent that the music will compensate for it if the general public does not take a liking to the libretto . . . I have no faith in its theatrical effectiveness in the usual sense'. But as he saw it come to life on the stage he began to change his mind. At one of the rehearsals, he heard Krauss call out to the singers: 'Clarity! If they don't hear every word, the opera is meaningless!' Strauss countered: 'Well, if they hear just a little of my music from time to time, I've nothing against that either.'

In October 1942 Munich was experiencing almost nightly air raids. *Capriccio* had been planned with an interval, but Krauss suggested it should be played without a break so that the audience could be out of the theatre by about 9.30pm—the raids usually began between 10 and 11pm. (Some productions today have an interval.) Rudolf Hartmann eloquently described the atmosphere of the première:

Who among the younger generation can really imagine a great city like Munich in total darkness, or theatregoers picking their way through the blacked-out streets with the aid of small torches giving off a dim blue light through a narrow slit? All this for the experience of the *Capriccio* première. They risked being caught in a heavy air raid, yet their yearning to hear Strauss's music, their desire to be part of a festive occasion and to experience a world of beauty

---

[4] But there is proof beyond doubt that he helped very many victims of Nazi persecution to escape.

beyond the dangers of war led them to overcome all these material problems
... Afterwards it was difficult to relinquish the liberating and unifying atmosphere created by the artistic quality of the new work. But outside, the blackened city waited, and one's way homeward was fraught with potential danger ...[5]

Krauss's skill in persuading Goebbels to allow a Strauss première in Munich can only be appreciated in the context of what had occurred in Berlin earlier that year in February. Goebbels, in his diary, admitted that in the first days of the Third Reich 'unfortunately we still need him, but one day we shall have our own music and then we shall have no further need of this decadent neurotic'. In February 1942 Strauss and other composers were summoned to Goebbels's office over something that Strauss had written to them in which he had made a disparaging remark about Lehár as well as saying 'It is not for Dr Goebbels to interfere'. Werner Egk described how Strauss, then seventy-seven, was called into the office alone and the others heard Goebbels screaming at him. The rest were then called in, whereupon Goebbels read out Strauss's letter and shouted at him: 'Be quiet! You have no conception of who you are, or of who I am! You dare refer to Lehár as a street musician . . . Lehár has the masses and you haven't. Stop your claptrap about the importance of serious music, once and for all. Tomorrow's art is different from yesterday's. You, Herr Strauss, belong to yesterday!' As Strauss left, he was heard to say 'If only I'd listened to my wife and stayed in Garmisch'.

Strauss and his wife spent part of the war in Vienna, where their son and daughter-in-law lived in Strauss's Belvedere Schlösschen. Franz and Alice Strauss had at one time been detained by the Gestapo for several days and their two sons were frequently attacked at school and in the street because their mother was Jewish. So when Baldur von Schirach became governor of Vienna and announced that he would make it once again the cultural centre of Europe, Strauss offered his help provided his family were left alone. Schirach was the son of a theatre intendant who was also a composer. (Strauss had conducted one of his works at a Berlin concert before 1914 and this was not forgotten.) He also 'protected' the playwright Gerhard Hauptmann in Vienna. Pauline once told Schirach that when the war was lost, she and Richard would always give him refuge at Garmisch, 'but as for the rest of that gang. . . .' In gratitude Strauss allowed the Sextet which opens *Capriccio* to be played six months before the stage performance, in Schirach's house on 7 May 1942. In the summers of 1942 and 1943 he conducted the Vienna Philharmonic in Mozart concerts at the Salzburg Festival and heard *Arabella* conducted by Clemens Krauss, with Viorica Ursuleac in the title-role she had created.

---

[5] R. Hartmann, *Richard Strauss: the Staging of his Operas and Ballets* (Oxford, 1982), p. 261.

Strauss was in Vienna for the centenary of the Vienna Philharmonic Orchestra. He had hoped to compose them a symphonic poem about the Danube with a choral finale, but, as he explained to the orchestra in a letter on their birthday, 18 February 1942, 'emotion is not as easily turned into music as in the days of the great old masters. . . . I should like to put my words of praise today into one short sentence: "Only he who has *conducted* the Vienna Philharmonic players knows what they are!" But that will remain our very own secret!' The work was never finished, and in gratitude for their congratulations on his eighty-fifth birthday in 1949 he sent the orchestra a page of the sketches inscribed 'A few drops from the dried-up source of the Danube'.

Perhaps it was the atmosphere of Vienna, perhaps it was the knowledge that in *Capriccio* he had written the work he had long had in mind, perhaps it was that in old age his thoughts went back to his youth and shut out the appalling present—whatever the cause, the fact remains that from 1942 dates Strauss's instrumental 'Indian summer', not in my opinion an emergence from decline but an astonishing 'last period' filled with creative flair. Like his own Don Quixote, he had renounced his battles, abandoned his grandiose visions and come home to simpler harmonies. The first manifestation of this new phase was the Second Horn Concerto, hardly credible as the work of a man of seventy-eight, so young is it in heart. He knew it was good but he wrote to Willi Schuh in October 1943: 'My life's work is at an end with *Capriccio*, and the music that I go on scribbling for the benefit of my heirs, exercises for my wrists (as Hermann Bahr used to say of his daily stints of dictation), has no significance whatever from the standpoint of musical history, any more than the scores of all the other symphonists and variationists. I only do it to dispel the boredom of idle hours, since one can't spend the entire day reading Wieland and playing skat.' Although he and Pauline had recurrent illnesses in the first quarter of 1943, he began work on a sonatina for wind instruments which he sub-titled 'from an invalid's workshop'. During the summer he returned to Garmisch, and in November he completed *An den Baum Daphne*, a setting for unaccompanied chorus of a text different from the discarded choral finale of the opera. (Strauss thus salved his conscience about his summary 'sacking' of Gregor.)

On the night of 2 October 1943 bombs destroyed the Munich National Theatre. 'I am beside myself,' Strauss wrote to his sister Johanna. To Willi Schuh he elaborated what the building meant to him:

> . . . made holy by the first *Tristan* and *Meistersinger* performances; in which seventy-three years ago I heard *Freischütz* for the first time, where my good father sat for forty-nine years in the orchestra as first horn. . . . This is the greatest catastrophe of my life, for which there can be no consolation.

His own last appearance as a conductor in the Munich National Theatre had been on 20 October 1942 when he conducted *Daphne*, forty-six years after his first engagement there. Shortly after the Munich bombing, the Garmisch *Gauleiter*, a Nazi since 1923, went to the Strauss villa to order Strauss to take in evacuees and other homeless people. There was an argument and, because Strauss kept referring to Herr Hitler, he was ordered to 'say "the Führer"'. Strauss replied 'I call people by their names. I say Herr Hitler.' He was told that 'even you must make sacrifices for our people's heroic struggle', to which he replied: 'No soldier needs to fall on my account. I did not want this war, it is nothing to do with me.' The *Gauleiter* shouted: 'Other heads than yours have already rolled, Herr Doktor Strauss.' Strauss's remarks were reported, and he was saved only through the intervention of Dr Hans Frank, a Nazi leader who later butchered thousands of Poles but apparently liked music. Not entirely saved, however, for Hitler's deputy, Martin Bormann, spoke to Hitler about the affair and on 14 January 1944 transmitted Hitler's order that the Garmisch porter's lodge was to be commandeered and that 'leading party personalities who have hitherto had personal contacts with Dr Richard Strauss are to cease to do so in any way'. Strauss was also forbidden to go to Switzerland for his annual 'cure'.

Bombing and wartime privations made life at Garmisch very hard for the ageing Richard and Pauline. They celebrated their golden wedding on 10 September 1944. She was now something of an invalid and had spent months in bed with pneumonia and erysipelas. Their golden wedding day, Strauss wrote to Franz and Alice in Vienna, would be celebrated 'with tears and sorrow' because their loyal servant Anna had left them to go to relatives because she was dying of cancer. (She died two months later.)

Vienna was now being bombed and Strauss, deeply worried, ordered Franz and Alice to return to Garmisch. At this time a warrant for Alice's arrest arrived at Garmisch party headquarters, but a friendly official ensured that it was never served. Alice knew that members of her family had been taken to Theresienstadt (Terezin) and told Kurt Wilhelm[6] that 'we thought there must be a labour camp there where they were collecting Jewish people before resettling them somewhere. We knew nothing of the extermination and wouldn't have believed it. Now and then we received postcards with a few words of greeting . . . During the war Papa [Strauss] travelled from Vienna to Dresden. He stopped in Theresienstadt and wanted to visit my grandmother. He went to the camp gate and said "My name is Richard Strauss, I want to see Frau Neumann". The SS guards thought he was a lunatic and sent him packing. We did not discover what went on in the camps until after the war . . . Twenty-six of my relatives died.'

Strauss moved back for a time to Vienna. There, at least, he was still

---

[6] K. Wilhelm, *Richard Strauss, an Intimate Portrait*, op. cit., pp. 263–4.

regarded highly, and in spite of the Nazi hierarchy's other edicts they did not forbid, though they did nothing to encourage, celebration of his eightieth birthday. The music could be honoured, but not its composer. Strauss Weeks were held in Dresden and Vienna, where he conducted *Till Eulenspiegel* and the *Symphonia Domestica*. At the State Opera, Karl Böhm conducted *Ariadne auf Naxos* with the young Irmgard Seefried as the Composer and Maria Reining and Max Lorenz as Ariadne and Bacchus, a marvellous performance which was broadcast and is available as a recording. Strauss had also coached and conducted a new young soprano, Ljuba Welitsch, in the role of Salome. Such a week must have compensated for the grimness of his life as an octogenarian; he still worried about the financial well-being of his family after his death and began to write out new autograph copies of some of his most successful works. He wrote to his grandson Richard in October 1944 to tell him that he had begun the score of *Till Eulenspiegel*—'it is more sensible than continuing to turn out senile new works. *Don Juan* and *Tod und Verklärung* shall follow and ought to make a valuable Christmas present for you all. The work is giving me a lot of fun and at least it stops me thinking about other things now that I don't even have an occasional game of skat to divert me.' Strauss also recorded on tape several of his orchestral works, conducting the Vienna Philharmonic, but only that of the *Domestica* survived an air raid.

One other major celebration remained. After the success of *Capriccio*, Krauss had at last persuaded Strauss to let him produce *Die Liebe der Danae* and the première was fixed for the Salzburg Festival of 1944. During 1943 Krauss assembled sets and costumes, travelling to Italy if he could not get what he wanted in Germany. Then a fire at the Leipzig printers destroyed the orchestral parts and an air raid on Munich early in 1944 destroyed some of the scenery. Transporting the sets from Munich to Salzburg was a difficult task. Some of the drop-curtains had been painted in Prague, but they arrived in Salzburg on schedule. The tailors in Munich had to stop work on the costumes because there was often no electricity supply, so they took all the material to Salzburg and set up a makeshift workshop. But after the Allied invasion of Europe on 6 June 1944 and the bomb plot against Hitler the following month, Goebbels decreed 'total war' and on 1 August ordered the closure of all theatres and the cessation of all festivals, including Salzburg. But the local *Gauleiter*, on his own responsibility, allowed work on *Danae* to continue, including, as an 'unofficial première', the final dress rehearsal on 16 August before an invited audience mainly comprising wounded and convalescent soldiers.

Strauss arrived in Salzburg on the 9th, knowing this would probably be his last première. He attended Krauss's rehearsals, saying little but listening intently. At one of the last rehearsals, during the second scene of Act III, when the orchestra alone plays the interlude known as

'Jupiter's renunciation', Strauss walked down to the front row of the stalls of what is now known as the Kleinesfestspielhaus and stood listening. He remained there throughout the final scene. After some moments of silence at the end, Krauss spoke a few sentences and Strauss looked over the rail of the orchestra pit, raised his hands in thanks and, choking back tears, said to the players: 'Perhaps we shall meet in a better world'. Rudolf Hartmann, who produced, described what followed: 'He was unable to say any more. Silent and deeply moved, everyone present remained still as he left the auditorium, carefully guided by myself . . . A little while later, leaning on my arm, he walked back through Salzburg in bright sunlight. He pointed out the route he wanted to take: "Let's go that way, past my beloved Mozart!"'

To all intents and purposes that historic, strange and emotional first performance was the end of Strauss's operatic career. When Krauss tried to arrange a *Danae* production after the war Strauss adamantly refused. 'Perhaps in five or ten years the new Vienna Opera can open with it,' he wrote. 'Mercury can then personally deliver my greetings telegram.' When Krauss urged collaboration on a successor to *Capriccio* the refusal was graceful and witty but equally firm: 'Do you really believe that . . . anything better or even as good can follow? Isn't this D flat major the best conclusion to my life's work in the theatre? After all, it's only possible to leave *one* will!'

14

Greeting to the world

Stefan Zweig took poison in exile in Brazil in February 1942, leaving a note hoping that his friends might see the dawn—'being too impatient, I go before them'. Romain Rolland died in December 1944. On 1 August 1944 Goebbels had closed all German opera houses and theatres. 'My life's work is in ruins,' Strauss wrote to Hartmann; 'it would have been best if the great geniuses of Olympus had called me to them on the 17th August [the day after the *Danae* première].'

Around him his beloved Germany lay devastated. On 12 February 1945 Dresden was totally destroyed and with it the theatre where his most famous operas had been born. 'I am in despair,' he wrote to Gregor. 'The Goethehaus [in Frankfurt], the world's greatest sanctuary, destroyed! My lovely Dresden—Weimar—Munich, all gone!' In March, the Vienna State Opera House was destroyed. Sixteen months earlier, when Munich's opera house was bombed, Strauss had sketched a few bars which he inscribed 'Mourning for Munich'. He left them on one side, for they reminded him about a waltz—*Ein Gelegenheitzwalzer*—he had written early in 1939 for a film about Munich which had been banned by Hitler. He looked it out and added a minor-key section headed 'In Memoriam'. This new version—*Ein Gedachtniswalzer*—was finished on 24 February 1945. But six months before he wrote this waltz, he distracted himself from the world around him by re-reading nearly all Goethe. In the late summer of 1944 he set a Goethe poem, *Niemand wird sich selber kennen*, which must have struck home to him as tragically significant: 'No one can know himself . . . Yet, let him put to the test every day that which is objectively finally clear: What he is and what he was, what he can and what he may.'[1] He abandoned the vocal setting when he received a commission for a work for strings from the Swiss musician and philanthropist Paul Sacher. He converted the material into a study for twenty-three strings which he eventually called *Metamorphosen*, a title suggested by Goethe's use of the term. He worked on it in August, September and October 1944, describing it to

---

[1] See Timothy L. Jackson, 'The Metamorphosis of the Metamorphosen', in B. Gilliam (ed.), *Richard Strauss: New Perspectives on the Composer and his Work* (Durham and London, 1992), pp. 193–241.

Karl Böhm only as an *Adagio*, then reached an impasse and turned to the Waltz Sequence from *Der Rosenkavalier* and the Munich waltz. In January 1945 he resumed composition of *Metamorphosen*, completing the short score on 8 March and the full score on 12 April. The connection with the Goethe poem suggests that *Metamorphosen* is not just the elegy for the destruction of German culture that has been supposed, but a deeply personal apologia for having had anything to do with the Nazi regime at any time. He began the work just after his return from the Salzburg *Danae*, when the consequences of the total war in which the Nazis has engaged were forcibly brought home to him. *Metamorphosen* is the music of the confessional.

This interpretation of the 'meaning' of *Metamorphosen* is supported by a curious story about the first performance, given by the Collegium Musicum Zürich conducted by Sacher on 25 January 1946. Strauss had told Sacher he did not want to attend the première but would like to attend the final rehearsal the previous day. In an almost empty hall, he conducted the work magnificently, according to Sacher, thanked the players and left. One cannot help deducing that this music had meant so much to him and had purged his soul with such pity and terror while he was composing it that he could not bear to hear it with an audience present who would expect him to take a bow at the end.

At the end of April 1945 the Third Reich perished in the flames of Berlin. The Americans had occupied Munich and their soldiers went to the villa at Garmisch. Its owner was no more pleased to see them than he had been to see the Nazi officials. 'I am the composer of *Rosenkavalier* and *Salome*', he informed them. 'Leave me alone.' At this time he wrote his 'artistic testament' in a letter to Karl Böhm. This was a plan for the revival of opera in Germany and Austria, reverting to his Vienna idea of two or even three theatres, one devoted to established masterpieces—an 'opera museum', the equivalent of the Prado and the Louvre—and the other(s) to lighter works and new works. He sent Böhm a suggested repertory for each theatre. For the opera museum he selected all Wagner from *Rienzi* to *Götterdämmerung*, five by Gluck, five by Mozart, Bizet's *Carmen*, Beethoven's *Fidelio*, three by Weber, two by Berlioz (*Benvenuto Cellini* and *Les Troyens*), three by Verdi (*Aida, Simon Boccanegra* and *Falstaff*) and nine of his own. For the second house the list is longer. It includes operas by Chabrier, Smetana, Gounod, Korngold, Pfitzner, Auber, Lortzing, Tchaikovsky, Johann Strauss, with seven by himself, but only four by Verdi, excluding *Otello*.

In May 1945 Strauss scribbled in his diary under obvious emotional stress:

Germany 1945. 'So, although the body is indeed dead, the spirit is alive.' Luther. On 12 March the glorious Vienna Opera became the victim of bombs. But on 1 May ended the most terrible period for mankind—12 years of the rule of bestiality, ignorance and illiteracy under the greatest criminals, who brought

107

about the destruction of 2000 years of German civilisation and, through a criminal rabble of soldiers, razed irreplaceable buildings and monuments to art.

This moving statement confirms Strauss's real attitude to the Nazi regime. But those who could not forgive him for remaining in Germany and for having briefly held an official post in the Third Reich—though they never tried to discover the facts about the *Reichsmusikkammer* appointment—received new ammunition from a malicious article which appeared in the American soldiers' newspaper *Stars and Stripes* in 1945. It was written by Thomas Mann's son Klaus, who had gained admission to Garmisch under the pseudonym 'Mr Brown' in the company of a German-speaking journalist, Curt Riess. Mann interviewed Strauss in the garden for over an hour, during which the conversation veered towards the subject of how Alice and her family had fared during the Third Reich. With fairness and rectitude but, in the circumstances, with tactless choice of phraseology, Strauss said that Schirach and Frank had been helpful. Mann's article distorted and misrepresented Strauss's actions and views. It was widely circulated overseas and launched the legend of the 'Nazi' Strauss. The composer wrote a furious letter to Thomas Mann, but did not send it. He could still lose himself in his work and completed a second Sonatina for sixteen wind instruments, inscribing it 'to the spirit of the immortal Mozart at the end of a life full of thankfulness'. When *Die schweigsame Frau* was produced in Dresden, he wrote to the conductor, Joseph Keilberth: 'So now the honourable Sir Morosus [the opera's chief character] has been liberated from the concentration camp of the Reich Theatre Chamber and been brought back to his birthplace where years ago I had great trouble getting the librettist's name on the programme.'

Strauss, however, in 1945 continued to 'amuse himself' at his desk with 'wrist exercises'. One of the American soldiers who were invited over the Garmisch threshold was John de Lancie, who had been oboist in the Pittsburgh Symphony Orchestra before joining the army in 1942. He was shocked by the conditions under which the Strauss family were living, with little to eat, no soap and shortage of fuel. He and other American soldiers helped as much as they could. De Lancie and Strauss talked about many subjects and one evening de Lancie plucked up courage to ask Strauss if he had ever considered writing something for oboe. The answer was a curt 'No', but a seed had been sown and a few weeks later he began to sketch a concerto, completing the short score on 14 September 1945.

Germany was now beginning to discover what losing the war meant. The country was in ruins, travel was restricted, food and fuel were scarce, the black market thrived. The Allies set up tribunals to investigate the activities of certain individuals during the Third Reich, a process known as 'de-Nazification'. Strauss, who had held an office under the regime, was told he would be charged. With the prospect of privations at Garmisch in the coming winter—no coal to heat the house, for one thing—Strauss sought permission to go to Switzerland. After much difficulty and only after guarantees from American and Swiss friends, Strauss and Pauline, but not the rest of the family, were allowed to leave. Taking the newly copied-out autograph scores of four of his tone-poems and other manuscripts, he arrived on 11 October in Baden-bei-Zürich where they stayed at the Hotel Verenahof. In his diary for that day, Strauss wrote:

> For us two sad Germans, who have lived only for art, and have fled from chaos, misery, slavery and the shortage of coal, this is heaven; driven by the destruction of our poor ravaged homeland to leave our dear children and grandchildren and the beautiful things we have owned for decades, to come far away from the ruins of our burnt-out theatres and other seats of the Muses, we can pass the rest of our days in peace and quiet, in the company of good people and friends.[2]

There he completed the full score of the Oboe Concerto on 25 October. The first performance of *Metamorphosen* followed in January and the concerto had its première on 26 February. The soloist was Marcel Saillet with the works' dedicatees, the Tonhalle Orchestra of Zürich conducted by Volkmar Andreae. (Before the concerto was published, in 1948, Strauss revised and extended the coda of the finale.)[3]

Strauss soon discovered that Switzerland was not the heaven he had first imagined. When Zürich Opera staged *Arabella* in January 1946, a Swiss soprano tried to prevent the guest appearance of Maria Cebotari because she had sung in Germany during the war. 'Another glorious achievement of the Nazi régime', Strauss wrote, 'that artists are no longer judged by their abilities but by what Americans think of their political opinions.' His royalties were blocked by a Washington agreement. A Swiss newspaper attacked his presence in the country. He became deeply depressed and morose, profoundly pessimistic about the future of music. To Willi Schuh he lamented the opprobrium he now engendered: 'Because I am a German? Wagner is another German. Lehár is Hungarian. The Hungarians also shot at the Russians and two of his operettas are being performed. The Italians fired on the Allies and they're doing three operas by Verdi. Must all the chauvinistic German-hatred of the entire Swiss nation come down on my head alone?' A gleam of light was a brief visit from Alice, to whom he gave some dollars to smuggle back to Garmisch to buy food for the grandchildren. But she also brought gloomy news: she had been to Vienna to visit the house in the Jacquingasse. It had been used by the Russians before it became

---

[2] K. Wilhelm, *Richard Strauss, an Intimate Portrait*, op. cit., p. 275.
[3] The recording made by Leon Goossens in 1947, and issued in January 1948, includes the original (1945) finale. (Columbia DX 1444–1446, 78 r.p.m.)

a British officers' mess. Furniture had been damaged, some paintings and carpets had gone. She took back archives and correspondence to Garmisch. Strauss was so distressed by this news that he made a detailed inventory, room by room, of everything that had been in the house.

In April 1946 Strauss had an appendix operation in Lausanne, recovering quickly. Four months later he and Pauline left Baden for Vitznau. He had discovered that, without his knowledge, British rights to his works had been acquired in 1942 from Fürstner by Boosey & Hawkes. Boosey's chief executive was an Austrian émigré, Dr Ernest Roth, who admired Strauss and visited him in Baden in December 1945. It was Roth who suggested in May 1947, at the instigation of Beecham, that London should hold a Strauss Festival and invite the composer to attend. There was still some doubt in England about Strauss's role under Hitler, and it was hoped that renewed personal contact would dispel it. Strauss agreed, and made his first flight at the age of eighty-three on 4 October. Pauline refused to accompany him but Willi Schuh went with him.

His visit caused the expected stir. To the Press he was laconic and uncommunicative—asked about his plans for the future, he replied: 'Well, to die'—but he delighted in the Royal Philharmonic Society's reception and dinner in his honour and in visits to art galleries. He attended the rehearsals and performances of Beecham's two concerts with the Royal Philharmonic Orchestra at the Theatre Royal, Drury Lane. The first, on 5 October, was the Suite from *Le Bourgeois Gentilhomme*, the Closing Scene from *Feuersnot*, *Don Quixote*, and the new fantasia from *Die Frau ohne Schatten*. This last work was conducted by one of Beecham's horn-players, who was at the start of his conducting career, Norman Del Mar. During the rehearsal Strauss went to the conductor's desk, 'glumly regarded the score for a few moments, muttered "All my own fault", and went away'.[4] The soloist in *Don Quixote* was Paul Tortelier, whom Richard Capell described in the *Daily Telegraph* next day as 'a marvellously gifted young French cellist'. This was his English début.[5] For the second concert on 12 October the programme was *Macbeth*, an entr'acte from *Intermezzo*, *Ein Heldenleben*, and the Closing Scene from *Ariadne*, with Maria Cebotari as Ariadne.

On 19 October Strauss himself conducted the Philharmonia Orchestra at the Royal Albert Hall in *Don Juan*, the *Burleske* (soloist Alfred Blumen), the *Rosenkavalier* Waltzes, and the *Symphonia Domestica*. Before going on to the platform he said to Roth: 'So the old horse ambles out of the stables once more.' It was at a rehearsal for one of these concerts that he made one of his most frequently quoted self-analyses.

[4] N. Del Mar: *Richard Strauss: a critical commentary on his life and works*, vol. I, p. xi.
[5] He was not quite so young as this suggests, being thirty-three. Ten years earlier he had first played the work under Strauss's direction and Pauline had told him it was the first time she had ever enjoyed it—another of her extraordinary comments on her husband's music.

'No,' he told the orchestra, 'I know what I want, and I know what I meant when I wrote this. After all, I may not be a first-rate composer, but I *am* a first-class second-rate composer.' In the audience at this concert was Elisabeth Schumann. She was persuaded by friends to go to see him afterwards even though there had been an estrangement between them since her divorce from Carl Alwin in 1933 and they had not met for fourteen years. Strauss, exhausted after the long performance, did not recognize her. 'Who are you?' he asked. 'Elisabeth', she replied. They had a short chat and she left, wishing she had stayed away. Another visitor was the librettist's widow, Gerty von Hofmannsthal. When she gave her name, his eyes filled with tears. He also attended the first of two BBC Third Programme performances of *Elektra*, in which on 24 and 26 October Beecham conducted the BBC Chorus and the Royal Philharmonic Orchestra at the Maida Vale studio. Strauss warmly embraced his English champion at the end.[6] What was to be his last public appearance in England was at the Albert Hall on 29 October when he conducted *Till Eulenspiegel* at a BBC Symphony Orchestra concert, the remainder of which was conducted by Sir Adrian Boult. He flew back to Switzerland two days later and Roth told the Press that he took with him all the earnings of his four-week stay. In addition, by the recent treaty with Austria, he recovered royalties due since 16 September 1946. After tax, the sum taken back was slightly under £1,000.[7]

In November came signs of a bladder infection, but this did not prevent Strauss from setting to work at once on some sketches for a Duett-Concertino for clarinet and bassoon, with strings and harp, which he completed on 16 December. This had been in his mind since October 1946, as we know from a letter of that date to Hugo Burghauser, former principal bassoonist of the Vienna Philharmonic, who had emigrated to America: 'I am busy with an idea for a double concerto for clarinet and bassoon, thinking especially of your beautiful tone.' This work was performed for the first time on 4 April 1948 by soloists and orchestra of Radio Lugano.

Lugano and Pontresina had been 'home' for the exiles during 1947. (Strauss became an Austrian citizen on 31 January 1947.) He could settle almost anywhere provided he had work to do, but Pauline was bored and missed her friends. She treated hotel after hotel to her tantrums and complaints, and hotel after hotel asked the distinguished guests to leave. In 1948 they settled at the Palace Hotel, Montreux, and it was there that Strauss composed his last work. Towards the end of 1946 he had read Eichendorff's poem *Im Abendrot* (*In the Sunset*) about an old couple who at the end of a long and eventful life look tiredly at the sunset and ask 'Is that perhaps death?' This so exactly fitted the Strausses' situation that

---

[6] Although Leo Wurmser in his article on Strauss as an opera conductor, op. cit., wrote that 'what went on in the difficult and complicated scenes was nobody's business'.
[7] *Daily Telegraph*, 30 October 1947.

he began to set it and was so emotionally stirred that he decided on accompaniment for large orchestra. He completed it on 6 May 1948. A little while before that, an admirer sent him a volume of poems by Hesse. He selected four to make a cycle of five with *Im Abendrot* but completed only three. They were *Frühling* (*Spring*) on 18 July, *Beim Schlafengehen* (*Falling Asleep*) on 4 August, and *September* on 20 September. This last outburst of song-writing was owed to the prompting of his son Franz. When visiting his parents in Montreux in 1948 and seeing how depressed Strauss was, he said: 'Papa, stop writing letters and brooding, it does no good. Write a few nice songs instead.' On his next visit, a few months later, Strauss put some scores on the table in Franz's room and said to Alice: 'Here are the songs your husband ordered.' One of them, *September*, is dedicated 'to Mr. and Mme. Seery', the latter being Maria Jeritza. She was also the recipient of his last completed work, the song *Malven* (*Mallows*), composed on 23 November 1948 and dedicated 'To beloved Maria this last rose'. Jeritza kept the song under lock and key for the rest of her life (she died on 10 July 1982) and it was not performed until January 1985.

In June 1948 the De-Nazification Board cleared Strauss's name from complicity in the evils of the Third Reich. He was free to return home, but in December, after a year of increasing discomfort, he underwent a major bladder operation in Lausanne. 'I ask myself why I am being called back into an existence in which I have outlived myself,' he wrote to Schuh. But he made sketches for a choral work with a fugue, a setting of Hesse's *Besinnung*, and he studied Beethoven quartets and his beloved *Tristan*. On 10 May 1949 he and Pauline returned to Garmisch. He was not well enough to go to Paris for the French celebration of his eighty-fifth birthday but wrote to Gustave Samazeuilh: 'The fact that the broadcast of *Friedenstag* coincides with the Foreign Ministers' Conference is a sign of fate, and I would like to see it as a happy premonition that my vision as an artist in 1938 . . . could now radiate over all the earth from the enlightened city that is Paris.'[8]

On 10 June, the night before his birthday, Strauss miraculously found the strength to travel to Munich to the dress rehearsal of *Der Rosenkavalier*. What is more, he asked to be allowed to conduct the finales of Acts II and III. This episode was filmed and included in an historic documentary, *A Life for Music*, together with later film of his conducting the Presentation of the Silver Rose. On the day of his birthday there was a celebration in Garmisch town hall. He was made an honorary citizen, Munich University made him an honorary Doctor of Law and the city of Munich established a Strauss Foundation. The Piano Quartet and Violin Sonata were performed and he made a speech. The Bavarian authorities had asked which of his works he would most like

---

[8] G. Samazeuilh, 'Richard Strauss as I knew him', *Tempo*, Summer 1964, pp. 14–17.

to see, and surprisingly he chose *Der Bürger als Edelmann*. On 13 June he saw a new production of it at the Gärtnerplatz Theater and was delighted. 'It's a pity Hofmannsthal couldn't have seen it too', he said. A month later, on 13 July, he returned to Munich to conduct the radio orchestra in the Moonlight Music from *Capriccio*. He never conducted again.

His health now began to fail rapidly. He had written no music since leaving Switzerland but he was mentally active with plans for the reconstruction of the Munich National Opera. During August he had several minor heart attacks. On the 29th the Munich producer, Rudolf Hartmann, went to see him and subsequently wrote a moving account of his visit:

> I hear the deep rather hoarse voice speaking about his ever-recurring anxiety for the continuance of the European Theatre. . . . After a while he goes on quietly, in a different tone of voice: 'Grüss' mir die Welt' ('Greet all the world for me'). He stops, asks 'Where does that come from?' I think of the similar words from *Walküre* and say so, but he shakes his head: 'No, no, it's not that, this occurs somewhere else'. . . .[9] He stays silent for a long time. I see that his face is showing signs of fatigue and that it is time to go. . . . He once more grasps my right hand in both of his and holds me back: 'Perhaps we'll see each other again; if not, you know everything.' A last vehement grip, his hands release me, and I quickly leave the room.[10]

The great master of bringing down the curtain was in superb form on his own death-bed. He said to his daughter-in-law Alice, 'Dying is just as I composed it in *Tod und Verklärung*.' In the afternoon of 8 September 1949 he died while sleeping. At his cremation in Munich three days later, the singers he had conducted three months earlier again sang the Trio from *Der Rosenkavalier*. One by one, they broke down with emotion. As for Pauline, her bereft expression told all. Her daughter-in-law Alice said: 'I never knew a person could weep so much. Her life was over.' For six months she returned to Montreux, but in March 1950 Alice brought her back to Garmisch. On 13 May, she died, nine days before the first performance of the *Four Last Songs*, sung by Kirsten Flagstad and conducted by Furtwängler, in London, the city which in 1922 and again in 1947 had drawn Richard Strauss back into the international fellowship of music where he belongs. 'Grüss' mir die Welt.'

---

[9] It is Isolde's farewell to Brangäne in Act I of *Tristan*.
[10] R. Hartmann, 'Letzte Besuch bei Richard Strauss', *Schweizerische Musikzeitung*, Jg. 90, vol. 8/9.

15

Early works

The 'received opinion' of Strauss's career is of radiant dawn, a glorious noonday, a sleepy afternoon and a glowing sunset. The sleepy afternoon has tended to dominate critical assessment of him, even though its contents are much less well known and therefore perhaps superficially judged. Slings and arrows have been aimed at his achievements from one source or another for the past fifty years, but all attempts seriously to diminish his stature have failed. He has been castigated for what he was not, which is wasteful, negative criticism. He was not a Mahlerian figure, agonizing over mankind's destiny; he was not a spiritual philosopher; he was not a fully-paid-up member of the avant-garde of successive generations; he was not a mystic nor was he a demon. Stravinsky, whose antipathy did not prevent his acknowledging Strauss's greatness, said of him: 'He is not a composer, he is a connoisseur.' But so was Stravinsky! Most composers are eclectics. Provided they have a leavening of genius, it is a fruitful condition.

Strauss was an entertainer, a story-teller, an illustrator, a sensualist. He regarded music as a holy art, Mozart's art, and it is a silly evasion of the problems he presents to misrepresent him as some sort of composing-machine for ever churning it out from Garmisch. The impression is often conveyed that he was lackadaisical and complacent in his approach to composition. In fact, he was meticulous in his complete concentration on the task in hand, whatever it was. He would make any sacrifice for music, which obsessed him to the point where it seemed to represent the only reality, hence his egoism and his apparent insensitivity to the sufferings of the twentieth century. But is not this insensitivity a major flaw in his art? Does it not show him to lack real depth and passion? Only if one judges the extent of music's depth by its involvement with subjects such as threnodies for Hiroshima and memorials for Lidice. Strauss knew himself—and perhaps knew the art of music— better than to trespass in such fields. It is significant that he loved *Così fan tutte* above all other operas—where Mozart probed the human heart through artificial trivialities. Strauss confined himself to the Marschallin's sense of the passing of time, to Till's eternal cocking of snooks at authority, to the Countess's dilemma over words and music, to Mandryka's unsophisticated goodness of heart, to his own identification with the great German artistic tradition symbolized by the Munich and Dresden opera houses. Cold, dead-pan exterior may be a mask to disguise banked-up fires, and in Strauss's case it was also a form of self-protection. The disguise was abetted by Pauline, who ensured that every material comfort should ease the process of composition. Her violent behaviour at home deflected Strauss from concern with the outer world (and was also possibly her own outlet for emotional frustration). There is no more symbolic reflection of the Strausses' relationship than the day of Hofmannsthal's death, when Pauline 'diverted' Strauss from the full shock of the news by a series of explosive rages over domestic trivialities such as mud on the carpet or a mistake by the cook. This was the only antidote Pauline knew; useless for Strauss to try to explain that his grief must find some outlet, and not only in continuing to work on *Arabella*. So he took the libretto and called on Elisabeth Schumann, intending to read it to her and Carl Alwin. But she had a small house party and persuaded Strauss to read it to a select few while she entertained the other guests. Later she was told how Strauss 'had suddenly stopped during the reading and burst into a flood of tears. He had wept long and unrestrainedly, tears forced from the very depths of his soul.'[1]

Equally revealing is Lotte Lehmann's admission (in radio interviews) that when staying at Garmisch she was slightly disappointed by Strauss, because his talk was always of fees and royalties and the house seemed to be dominated by Pauline. 'As a rule,' Lehmann said, 'he appeared utterly aloof and impersonal, so cold in his reaction to people that they would withdraw instantly and give up any misguided attempt at friendliness.' But, she added, when it came to rehearsing, he was supreme, he came alive. He kept his warmth and passion for his music.

Strauss's early works are not widely known today. They explain how, before he was twenty, he could be regarded by Bülow with special interest, for they show no subversive signs of 'progressive' music. These works present an accomplished musician in the Classical-Romantic tradition, well versed in Mendelssohn, Schumann, Beethoven, Weber, and Brahms. He had learned his lessons assiduously for, charming though these works are in many respects, they lack real originality. A bar here and there foretells the mature Strauss; and the obvious discomfort he felt within the rigid confines of sonata-form development points to the enthusiasm with which he later recognized his salvation in the symphonic poem. But the overall impression is of a Mendelssohn disciple, genial and bland, probing hardly at all beneath a polished surface. Pianists who wish to vary their recitals of Romantic keyboard music should look up the *Five Pieces*, Op. 3, the B minor sonata, Op. 5, and

---

[1] A. Mathis, 'Elisabeth Schumann', *Opera*, vol. 25, no. 1, January 1974, pp. 27–8.

the *Stimmungsbilder*, Op. 9. In the last-named, the fifth movement, *Haidebild* (*On the heath*), is a strangely atmospheric piece, the bare fifths in the bass forming an imaginative background to two contrasted thematic figures.

The Violin Concerto, Op. 8,[2] combines neatly tailored virtuosity with a rapturous melodic flow, particularly in the slow movement, and earns the gratitude of listeners, if not of performers, by excluding that curse of the concerto, a cadenza. Cellists ought not to overlook the Cello Sonata, Op. 6, haunted by the spirit of Beethoven and dedicated to and first played by Hanuš Wihan, later to be dedicatee of Dvořák's Concerto. Here the clumsy structural handling may have been the result of a strong urge towards emotional expression. No wonder Joachim praised Strauss for the opening theme (Ex. 1), typical already of his ability to begin a work with a bold gesture.

Ex. 1

p con espress.

Although this momentum is not maintained, the first movement has several surges of heroic endeavour before Strauss reverts to the mood of Mendelssohn's *Songs Without Words* for the lyrical Andante. In the finale he quotes from Mendelssohn's C minor Piano Trio, Op. 66—Strauss was never reluctant to acknowledge his sources—before saluting Wagner with a cadence from Act II of *Parsifal*, which he had heard at Bayreuth while composing the sonata. Despite these obvious models, the finale is impressive in its confident assurance even if it is over-reliant on repetition of sequences.

In some passages of the Cello Sonata may be discerned the Strauss of the tone-poems. His gentler, slippers-by-the-fire aspect, when he became charmer as well as explorer, is shown in the two delightful works for thirteen wind instruments, the one-movement *Serenade in E flat*, Op. 7, and the later *Suite in B flat*, Op. 4. Of these the short, well-constructed *Serenade* is the more immediately beguiling, but the four-movement *Suite*, while Brahmsian in spirit and form, is full of Straussian prophecies, notably of his skill in developing short themes. The duet for horn and clarinet in the Allegretto (first) movement is an inspiration; and no one, hearing the oboe solos in the second and fourth movements, need any longer be surprised by the effectiveness of the oboe in *Don Juan*. Yet the best movement is the Gavotte, a pointer to the wit of *Le Bourgeois Gentilhomme*.

---

[2] The opus numbers of Strauss's early works are a misleading guide to dates of composition and publication.

1. Strauss in London, 1903

2. Photograph given 'to my revered friend E. Elgar'. Strauss conducted a concert of his own works in Birmingham in December 1904.

3. With his wife, Pauline, in 1914

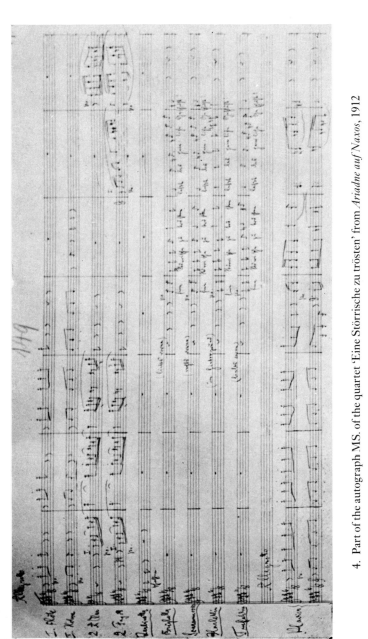

4. Part of the autograph MS. of the quartet 'Eine Störrische zu trösten' from *Ariadne auf Naxos*, 1912

5. A signed photograph of Strauss in 1925

6. Conducting the *Alpine Symphony* in Munich, 1941

7. With Hugo von
Hofmannsthal at
Garmisch, 1911

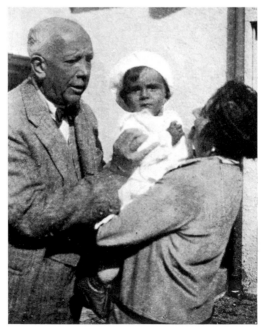

8. With Pauline
and their elder
grandchild,
Richard, 1929

9. Arriving at Northolt Airport, 4 October 1947, after his first flight at the age of eighty-three

10. In Berlin, 1939, with Heinz Tietjen (right), Intendant of the *Staatsoper*, and Herbert von Karajan, the conductor

11. With Clemens Krauss in London, 1947

12. Rehearsing the Philharmonia Orchestra in London, 1947

The Symphony No. 1 in D minor, completed the day after Strauss's sixteenth birthday, is a declaration of how fully the schoolboy had absorbed the music of Mendelssohn, Schumann, and Weber. It is full of echoes of their works, orchestrated with amazing skill in their early-Romantic style. The critic of the *Münchner Neueste Nachrichten* who wrote that 'the work cannot lay any claim to true originality, but it demonstrates throughout a fertile musical imagination, to which composition comes easily' was fair and accurate. If the work is today no more than a curiosity, it is also pleasant listening.

Now that the early symphonies of Dvořák's have been rehabilitated and interest has been re-extended to the symphonies of Raff, Gade and Goldmark, it is surprising that so effective an example of the German Romantic symphony as Strauss's Symphony No. 2 in F minor, Op. 12, should remain neglected, even though it lasts 45 minutes. It establishes beyond doubt that Strauss at twenty was a master of the orchestra. The work is in cyclic form, each movement sharing a theme in fourths first heard on trumpets and horns. The two middle movements, a scherzo and a romantic *Andante cantabile*, are the best. Theodore Bloomfield[3] has pointed out an interesting resemblance between a canon for trumpets and horns in three pairs a quaver apart in the slow movement and the canon for brass in the first movement of Bartók's *Concerto for Orchestra*, perhaps an atavistic reversion by the Hungarian to his youthful enthusiasm for Strauss. The major weakness in the symphony is the finale, where themes from the previous movements are recalled in a gauche manner, no doubt the occasion for Brahms's remark about 'thematic irrelevancies'.

The Piano Quartet in C minor, Op. 13, is a massive act of homage to Brahms, from whom several of the themes are shamelessly plagiarized. Yet it is a step forward from the Symphony because it shows Strauss in control of his design—the developments flow easily, the transitions are less contrived—and its emotional content is stormier. As Arthur Johnstone wrote in 1904, it 'might rank as the mature work of anyone but Strauss'. It was composed in 1883–4. Four years later, in the Violin Sonata, Op. 18, Strauss advanced as far again. This was the last of his classically designed works and his last piece of orthodox chamber music. It is superb. He was already at work on *Don Juan*, and the opening theme and several others have a comparable verve and sweep as if they had been conceived in orchestral terms. The climax of the first movement is almost operatic in its broad proportions, as is much of the impassioned rhetoric of the finale. But Strauss makes the finale structurally interesting by following a sombre introduction with a brilliant episode and by interposing scherzo-like passages among the fervent displays of melody, almost on a scale appropriate to a concerto. The

[3] T. Bloomfield, 'Richard Strauss's Symphony in F minor', *Music and Musicians*, March 1974, pp. 24–8.

central Andante cantabile (*Improvisation*) was written last but shows no sign of hard labour. Its elegant grace has ensured it a separate existence. It pays tribute to Strauss's models: the piano part in the dramatic middle section is so like that of Schubert's *Erlkönig* that the allusion must be deliberate. The return to the main melody is made by way of Chopinesque nocturne references and, in the coda, Strauss links his theme with that of the Adagio of Beethoven's *Pathétique* pianoforte sonata. *Tristan* is quoted in the finale. For Strauss, musical quotation was a legitimate and potent source of inspiration. No composer except Shostakovitch has employed it more effectively, with such point and wit.

High though the Violin Sonata stands among Strauss's early works, two stand higher. The Horn Concerto No. 1 in E flat, Op. 11, is aptly enough his first wholly satisfying composition, since he grew up with the sound of his father's horn as a daily counterpoint to childhood's first impressions. In barely sixteen minutes the work achieves an almost Mozartian grace and humour. Its three movements are played without a break, strict sonata-form is abandoned, and the conversion of the opening flourish into the capricious rondo theme of the finale anticipates other Straussian uses of this method by three or four years. Thematic connections are subtle throughout the concerto and give it a convincing unity. The melodies are memorable, the orchestration is entrancing. It was written for the unvalved horn.

Yet it is the *Burleske* in D minor, for pianoforte and orchestra, which may be described as Strauss's first masterpiece. He never gave it an opus number and seems to have realized its merits only in his last years. It is hard to know which is the more surprising, Bülow's calling it unplayable or its former infrequent inclusion in concert programmes. It is not yet *echt*-Strauss: there are still the influences of Brahms and Schumann. But here are the first authentic glimpses of the urchin humour of *Till Eulenspiegel*, the stirrings of Don Juan's ardour, the wit, fantasy, sparkle and inventiveness of the creator of a gallery of stage characters. Here above all is the fantastic conjuror of the orchestra, juggling with pianist and orchestra as if they were featherweights and producing a rabbit out of the hat for them at the start in the shape of this splendid theme for four timpani:

Ex. 2

which is answered by the orchestra, interrupted by the pianoforte in a burst of merriment, and provokes all that follows thematically. It is not all banter: a lazy waltz episode (an augmentation of the orchestral presentation of the first subject) forms a graceful middle section which is recapitulated in the coda. The nineteen-minute work brims over with ideas, all fertile and concise. It needs a virtuoso performance combining aristocratic reserve with epigrammatic quicksilver, and it is encouraging to find it returning to the repertory in concerts and recordings.

16

The tone-poems

Strauss's fame in the concert-hall rests securely on five of the ten large-scale orchestral works, symphonic poems in one form or another, which he composed between 1886 and 1915. Their composition coincided with the height of the barren controversy about the relative values of 'absolute' music and music which described something, 'programme music'. Barren, because no music can be entirely 'absolute'; equally, can music really describe anything, or does the listener, taking the composer's hint, do most of the work? Would the last scene of *Die Walküre* suggest fire if we did not know what was happening on the stage? Can music sound like fountains, rivers or fireworks? Like Falstaff or moonlight? Realistic 'effects' are one thing, character-studies quite another. Yet such is the suggestive power of music that we 'see' Falstaff as vividly in Elgar's music as in Shakespeare's words—when we know that it is 'about' Falstaff.

Mahler's view was that no music from Beethoven onward was without an inner programme. But, he added, music was worth nothing if the listener had to be told what experience was being re-lived. Strauss's views were equally ambivalent. In 1888 he wrote to Bülow: 'From the F minor Symphony onwards I have found myself in a gradually increasing contradiction between the musical-poetic content which I wish to convey and the ternary sonata-form inherited from the classical composers. . . . I consider it a legitimate artistic method to create an appropriate new form for each new subject.' In 1905 he expressed these views to Rolland: 'To me the poetic programme is no more than the basis of form and the origin of the purely musical development of my feelings—not, as you believe, a *musical description* of certain events of life.' By 1929 he was saying: 'Programme music is a derogatory word in the mouths of those who have no ideas of their own.' He was pulling some nincompoop's leg when he said he wanted to describe things so accurately in music that the listener could tell whether a glass of beer was Pilsener or Kulmbacher. No music will survive unless it has independent life as music: no 'programme' will keep bad music alive. Most of Strauss's programme music can be enjoyed for its purely musical quality. How many listeners, when they have once followed the detailed programme, pay much attention to it again? Very few, I suggest. The music transcends it.

Strauss's first tone-poem was *Aus Italien*, Op. 16, a 'Symphonic fantasy' which is really a four-movement symphony on the lines of Mendelssohn's *Italian Symphony*, showing several signs of influence by Berlioz and Tchaikovsky, with a leavening of Brahms. Yet the real Strauss is beginning to come through, and it is surprising that conductors have not shown more interest in recent years in such a picturesque, melodious and delightfully orchestrated work. The Lisztian first movement, romantic and rhapsodic, is the best and most promising, and in the second ('Ruins of Rome') there is the characteristic sound of Strauss's divided strings which gave such a strong hint to Elgar for *In the South*. The abandonment of sonata-form in pursuit of whatever the 'poetic idea' dictates certainly led in the third movement ('On the beach at Sorrento') to Strauss's first piece of magical tone-painting, with shimmering cascades on violins and flutes suggesting sunlight on the sea, and a broad flowing melody prophetic of the operatic *cantilena* in which he was to excel. It is customary to gibe at Strauss because the 'Neapolitan folk-song' of his finale is Denza's popular song *Funiculì, funiculà*. But it is not a very terrible mistake for him to have made; the catchy tune sounds thoroughly Neapolitan and is treated with wit and restraint. The charge of vulgarity is often levelled against Strauss, but there is no vulgarity if his music is well played and conducted with a respect for the score. This finale is a case in point: it should sound exuberant and bright, not blatant and brash.

A passage in this finale may cause listeners to think of the fight episode in Tchaikovsky's *Romeo and Juliet* (1870). The same reminiscence occurs in *Macbeth*, which really precedes *Don Juan*, although its opus number, 23, and first performance followed it because of extensive revision. Here for the first time Strauss devised a single-movement form based on, but diverging from, Liszt's pattern. It is a sonata-form movement, unified by a motto-theme referring to Macbeth's royal state and with a long, elaborate development section containing two episodes, the first a dialogue between Macbeth and his wife, the second a ceremonial interlude describing Duncan's processional arrival at the castle. It is rich, sombre and well-constructed, interesting to Straussians because of its hints of later masterpieces, but it has understandably been eclipsed by its successors. One has only to hear the exciting, lusty, marvellously scored and imaginatively original opening to *Don Juan*, Op. 20 (Ex. 3), to perceive that real inspiration has taken the place of meritorious workmanship, for out of this composite first statement individual features are to be extended and developed.

The structure of *Don Juan* is the same as that of *Macbeth*, the two independent episodes being a love-scene and a carnival; not that any detailed programme matters, for the music vividly represents 'youth's

Ex. 3

fiery pulses'. The love-scene is dominated by an oboe solo which is the first of many Strauss themes conveying a mingling of hope and regret, of spring and autumn. Strauss's maturity is signalled by the masterly way in which he continues the work after this spell-binding interlude: the music stirs uneasily back to life and to the emergence of a great new theme on four horns, worthy of a hero of any kind of battle, of love or war (Ex. 4).

Strauss makes this magnificent idea the climax of his recapitulation, when it returns a third higher on the horns, to be repeated with even more thrilling effect by unison strings and wind. After this glorious display of orchestral colour, Strauss, with the dramatic instinct for contrast of the born stage composer, swiftly and daringly ends the work with Juan's death—a single dissonant trumpet note—and his last gasps for breath (descending trills). There is not a note too many, not a miscal-

Ex. 4

culated effect, in the whole wonderful score. It should sound erotic. Rehearsing it, Strauss once told an orchestra: 'I would ask those of you who are married to play as if you had just become engaged and then all will be well.'

His next tone-poem, *Tod und Verklärung*, Op. 24, aimed higher and was the first for which Strauss provided a detailed 'plot': of an idealist on his death-bed who, amid physical pain, recalls his childhood, the loves of his youth, and his unfulfilled striving towards his ideals. After death, his soul voyages 'to find gloriously achieved in everlasting space those things which could not be fulfilled here below'. As in *Don Juan*, Strauss's mastery is shown in the skilful deployment of short germinal motifs allied to superb orchestration. The depiction of the sick-room, the dying man's writhings and his memories of childhood and youth are graphic and moving. Strauss was not drawing on personal experience here: his serious illness came later. Strauss again bends his classical training in sonata-form to his own uses: a slow introduction, an allegro section, a love-scene and a finale in which all the themes are woven into a symphonic epilogue. This final 'transfiguration' episode has been much criticized for failing to achieve 'sublimity'. By respecting the directions in the score, the best Strauss conductors achieve a convincing nobility in these final pages which are the forerunner of several of his best operatic finales, using harmonic modulations of ravishing beauty controlled with a sure and steady sense of climactic rise and fall. To achieve the desired effect, Strauss had to invent a memorable melody, as he had in *Don Juan*, and the so-called Ideology theme of *Tod und Verklärung*, with its aspiring octave leap, is *echt*-Strauss, a tune he was to quote several times.

Five years were to elapse before the first performance of Strauss's next tone-poem, *Till Eulenspiegels lustige Streiche*, Op. 28. He had in the meantime written an opera, *Guntram*. Its poor reception by the philistine Munich public perhaps accounts for the cocking of snooks at

authority which gives a sharp and contemptuous, even spiteful, edge to
the impudent humour of *Till*. (Strauss's recorded interpretation is more
barbed than anyone's.) His choice of rondo form for this virtuosic display of musical humour was not the least of the happy touches which
abound. Although Strauss later outlined the events illustrated—Till
causing havoc in the market place, Till in love, arguing with academics,
mocking religion, being hanged—the music is self-sufficient and is illu-
minated by an unchallengeable certainty of orchestral effects, governed
by a light touch which German music had not known for half a century.
It is hardly necessary to go into detail about such a well-loved and firmly
established favourite, except to underline the aptness of the orchestration. This keeps the work pristine and is epitomized by the unforgettable
horn-theme representing Till (see Ex. 5) which is doubly effective for

Ex. 5

coming after the gentle 'once-upon-a-time' opening. Equally memorable
is the use to which the D clarinet is put, its shrill, cheeky sound being
entirely apt for this subject. Yet if Strauss's instrumental expertise in *Till*
is employed with a sophistication which entitled him to be regarded as
the playboy of the symphony orchestra, his skill in composition is no
less awe-inspiring. His trump-card, especially in his operas, was the
metamorphosis of themes. The 'once-upon-a-time' opening assumes
insolent mockery:

Ex. 6

as easily as the principal Till motif (marked *x* in Ex. 5) is transformed
into romance:

Ex. 7

These themes undergo several other changes, for Strauss's ingenuity seems limitless. The wit that was evident in the *Burleske* finds its apogee in *Till*, as Strauss the great actor-manager plays all the roles in his repertory. Few moments in his music are more magical than the swift change from the huge and savage orchestral trill with which Till finally derides the professors to the carefree ditty representing his saucy departure from their company.

Till was to be the last of Strauss's short tone-poems; henceforward they were to last at least thirty-five minutes and to require a huge orchestra. The first of the 'mammoths' was *Also sprach Zarathustra*, his homage to Nietzsche and originally sub-titled 'symphonic optimism in *fin de siècle* form, dedicated to the twentieth century'. This association of music with the poetry and philosophy of that much-discussed author was a brilliant opportunist stroke in 1896, but it means little today. Yet the work grows in popularity with audiences only a fraction of whom are likely to have read a word by or about Nietzsche and even though critics still deride its 'bombast' and 'vulgarity'. It is best enjoyed as a virtuoso example of sumptuous orchestral sound. Its 'sunrise' opening, thematically simple yet massively impressive, was brilliantly commandeered by Stanley Kubrick for a film about space—an acute piece of musical criticism because the passage concerned is film music written before such a commodity was required. Although nothing in the work is as memorable as this in invention, Strauss retains interest by his total mastery of the episodic form in which the tone-poem is cast, welding it into a convincing unity. His sense of humour must have been responsible for the Dance of the Superman being a Viennese waltz—the first occurrence in his music of this dance-form, which assumed for him the same kind of significance as the *Ländler* and the march had for Mahler. On the other hand, in spite of its sense of bourgeois contentment, the waltz also symbolized dynamic energy and that may have been in Strauss's mind here as it was to be over a decade later when he used it for the climactic dances of Salome and Elektra. Norman Del Mar rightly refers to the distinctive flavour of *Also sprach Zarathustra*, its transcendental quality exemplified by the beautiful coda, a nocturne in B major. It will always remain a target for the anti-Straussians, for there is obvious disproportion between the musical achievement and the highfalutin aim of the Nietzschean tribute. But there is something to be admired by all but the most bigoted in Strauss's daring in this work, whether it is the once-novel and still startling polytonal effects or the staggering ease with which he manipulates orchestral tone-colour.

He returned to humans in his next major orchestral work, *Don Quixote*, 'fantastic variations on a theme of knightly character', as he accurately sub-titled it. The first ideas for the work occurred to him in Florence on 10 October 1896. On 16 April 1897 he wrote in his diary: 'Symphonic poem *Held und Welt* begins to take shape; as satyr-play to accompany it—*Don Quichote'. Held und Welt* became *Ein Heldenleben.* Strauss wrote in 1898: '*Don Quixote* and *Heldenleben* are conceived so much as immediate pendants that, in particular, *Don Q.* is only fully and entirely comprehensible at the side of *Heldenleben.*' *Don Quixote* is daring in design: a long contrapuntal introduction, ten variations and an epilogue, an episodic scheme tending towards disjointedness. The use of solo cello and solo viola as the Don and Sancho Panza gives it a concerto element which must be underplayed if it is to succeed completely (but other instruments also represent Quixote, and Sancho is characterized at times by tuba and bass clarinet). As in *Till*, the episodes of Don Quixote's knight errantry are skilfully chosen for musical delineation and contrast. When Strauss so accurately conveys the 'fantastic' element, the insane-sanity of Don Quixote, the borderline between laughter and tears, the poignancy and pathos of the Don's death, he had his mother's mental fragility as painful inspiration. The variations are, in effect, musical character-sketches as pithy and picaresque as the nearly contemporary *Enigma Variations* of Elgar.

Don Quixote is the product of affection and admiration for the literary original. It drew from Strauss some of his happiest melodic inventions, notably the Dulcinea theme (an even lovelier oboe lady than Don Juan's *innamorata*) (Ex. 8) and a dazzling display of thematic transformations of the various Don Quixote motifs. Strauss is at his best in the two-part Variation 3, which begins with a scherzo-like exchange between Quixote and Sancho and ends with the old knight's enraptured vision of the world of chivalry. For this outpouring of high Romanticism, in which Strauss ranges from the tonic of F sharp to the distant keys of G natural and B flat, he provides one of the impassioned, soaring cantilenas for orchestra which he was to use at dramatically critical moments in the operas *Die Frau ohne Schatten* and *Die Liebe der Danae*. Again, in Variation 5, Quixote keeps vigil over his armour in the moonlight: the solo cello meditates on the Dulcinea theme accompanied by the orchestral cellos. The famous pictorial episodes—the sheep, the windmills, the flying horse (with a pedal D to show that it never leaves the ground)—are so vividly done that at first they diverted attention from the work's pervasive poetry of which they are an integral and musical part. Even today some hearers are outraged by the score of *Don Quixote*: it is their grudging way of acknowledging that it is a masterpiece—perhaps his supreme masterpiece.

Its companion-piece, *Ein Heldenleben,* is mainly autobiographical and none the worse for it. 'Only partly true', Strauss said of himself as the hero. 'I didn't engage in battles'; and the final retirement from the world was wishful thinking and always remained so—he used to say he wanted to make enough money to be able to stop conducting and live in Italy doing nothing but compose. The heroine is Pauline, drawn in all her moods, from shrew to coquette, in one of the greatest violin solos in the

Ex. 8

orchestral repertoire. The adversaries (music critics) were identified by Strauss as specific targets. The hero's 'works of peace' are a collage of quotations from his own works. *Ein Heldenleben* is not only a glorious example of a rich orchestral palette used with consummate skill: it is a witty work, never wittier than in the waspish treatment of the critics.

127

The construction is again masterly. Strauss constantly takes the listener by surprise, like a good novelist who prepares unexpected twists in his plot. The six sections are thematically closely linked and a fine performance should leave no doubt of the homogeneity of the work. A curious 'flavour', as distinctive as that of *Zarathustra*, is imparted to the harmonic scheme by the flattened notes which occur first in the seventh bar of the hero's expansive principal theme:

Ex. 9

Throughout the forty minutes the tone-poem lasts, one appreciates Strauss's enjoyment of a sense of risk, of treading a knife-edge between grandeur and grandiloquence. How shocking, his critics say, how exhibitionist, to be the hero of one's own work. He is not alone in this: it was a badge of the Romantic Era. Mahler was the hero of his Second Symphony, Elgar the hero of the *Enigma Variations* and other works, culminating in his choral ode *The Music Makers* in self-quotation on a *Heldenleben* scale and with comparably potent effect.

An astonishing emotional gamut is run in *Ein Heldenleben*, from heroic endeavour to tender erotic passion, from the exuberance of battle to the contentment of pastoral retirement. The Battle Scene was described when it was new as 'an atrocity', but its exhilarating course, involving contrapuntal wizardry on an enormous scale, holds few terrors today. Two of the surprises mentioned above occur within a few pages as the Battle ends. Just as it seems that a normal recapitulation of the hero's themes is under way, Strauss produces a superb new theme ready to provide the basis of the final coda and, as this theme builds to a climax, the moment of crisis is reached with the horns' thrilling statement of the *Don Juan* theme (see Ex. 4). This sets in motion the once-controversial but marvellously contrived assemblage of quotations from other tone-poems, the opera *Guntram* and songs, which paradoxically forms one of the strikingly original passages in *Ein Heldenleben*.[1] This

---

[1] See Appendix E for a full list.

section underlines the emotional links with *Don Quixote*, for it con-
cludes with a turbulent dissonant passage in which the hero is again tor-
mented by the critics' barbs. He seems to succumb but finds escape in a
version of the shepherds' pastoral theme from Variation 11 of *Don
Quixote* while the drums throb like an over-taxed heart just as they did
in Variation 10 when Don Quixote rides home from battle. A great conductor of *Ein Heldenleben* will draw from the concluding section not
only beautiful sounds for strings and horns but a nobility comparable
with the Knight's vigil in Variation 5. And just as the nocturnal peace
of that courtyard is ruffled by disturbing memories, so the hero's idyll is
suddenly shattered by a nightmare which only Pauline's soothing violin
caress can dispel. This hero is no superman, just a Kapellmeister.

With *Till*, *Don Quixote* and *Ein Heldenleben* Strauss achieved a
supremacy as an orchestrator which is still one of the marvels of music.
He used a huge orchestra, as Mahler did, but although harmonically his
music sounds 'fatter' than Mahler's, it is often scored with similar
restraint and delicacy. Both knew the value of contrast and the advan-
tages to be gained from keeping something in hand for the true climactic moment of each work. Both, too, for different reasons suffered in
their lifetime and afterwards from the constant accusations of 'tasteless-
ness'—that imprecise and subjective term. What was said about *Ein
Heldenleben* was mild compared with the abuse hurled at Strauss's next
orchestral work, the *Symphonia Domestica*, one of his most endearing
works.

After one of the first English performances, Ernest Newman wrote
that 'the orchestral colour is grossly overdone; the polyphony is often
coarse and sprawling; the realistic effects in the score are so pitiably
foolish that one listens to them with regret that a composer of genius
should ever have fallen so low'. One reads this with regret that a powerful critic should have shown so little perception. Yet Norman Del Mar
confesses[2] to 'appalling doubts', finds the programme 'intolerable' and
'on that very account' finds the music 'markedly less great than in any
of the previous major works since his maturity'. I do not agree. The
music, while detailedly programmatic, is strong and inventive enough to
stand without the prop of a story. Far from being overdone, the orchestral colours are limned with a humour and deftness analogous to those
of Mahler's Fourth Symphony: allowing for the temperamental differences between the composers, these two works represent their creators,
masters of grandiose effects, in relaxed and childlike mood, although
they highlight the problems each had in ensuring uneasy co-existence
between sophistication and naïveté. As for the subject-matter, Strauss's
rejoinder to criticism was 'What can be more serious than married life?
Marriage is the most serious happening in life . . . Yet life has naturally

[2] N. Del Mar, *Richard Strauss*, op. cit., vol. I, pp. 196–9.

129

got its funny side.' Nothing was of more importance to him than his family, and that fact governed most of his actions in life.

Although *Domestica* is in one continuous movement, the four sections of a symphony may be discerned—an introduction (instead of a regular first movement) on the *Don Quixote* model, followed by scherzo, adagio and fugal finale. The opening is lightly scored, the first theme (Strauss himself) being a collection of short motifs each marked by a change of mood: easy-going (cellos), dreamy (oboe), morose (clarinets), fiery (strings) and merry (trumpet). Pauline's motifs follow, tender, hot-tempered and waspish. The first three notes of her theme are the direct inversion of her husband's. Theme 3, the child, is introduced by solo oboe d'amore, an inspired choice of instrument. In the scherzo ('the child at play, his parents' happiness') the child's theme is treated like a folk-song, with delicate writing for woodwind and violas. The parents' themes (notably the wife's on solo violin) flit in and out; and in this section, as in others, one can detect future Strauss works and procedures in embryo. This is particularly obvious in the serene lullaby (after the notorious bath) where Strauss alludes to a Mendelssohn *Song Without Words* (Op. 19, No. 6) and orchestrates it like the Marschallin's soliloquy in Act I of *Der Rosenkavalier*. Superb writing for flute and oboe distinguishes the reverie which ends this section.

The Adagio has two episodes, the first depicting Strauss at work, inspiration gradually becoming intense. When the wife's themes return, an explicit love scene is followed by the most imaginative part of the work in which the couple's dreams are suggested, their themes being combined, inverted and fragmented ('coarse polyphony' but magical). With the return of day, the household wakes, noisy, bustling, just the occasion for a double fugue. The fierce quarrel here depicted must refer to the divorce threat which occurred while Strauss was writing this work (see pp. 154–5). In the exuberant closing section all the themes are treated with surpassing virtuosity, the horns performing heroic feats in glorification of the child's theme.

The English critic who referred to *Ein Heldenleben* and *Symphonia Domestica* as 'barrage balloons' and deplored the growing enthusiasm for them[3] represents a kind of puritanism which Strauss's music engenders in certain temperaments. Most of us, though, are hedonists who revel in the fine melodies, wonderful orchestration and considerable humour of these works. We can also find pleasure in his penultimate large-scale orchestral work, *Eine Alpensinfonie*. Scored for an orchestra of over 150, this work describes twenty-four hours in the mountains. The twenty-two sections include sunrise, the ascent, a waterfall, flower-meadows, a glacier, the summit, a storm and sunset. The pictorialism is extremely graphic, with Mahlerian cowbells and some approximation to

---

[3] *The Listener*, 16 May 1974, p. 643.

Mahlerian nature-worship, and certain passages are deeply impressive, not only as majestic sound, but in their Brucknerian evocation of the grandeur and remoteness of the Alps which Strauss could see from Garmisch. But the work has been generally underrated. It is far more than the sum of its remarkable effects; repeated hearings reveal its fascination and strength as music pure and simple. This is no eccentric piece of self-indulgence: it is a well-knit, often very moving orchestral creation with a pantheistic spiritual exaltation not found again in Strauss's output until *Daphne*.

Strauss did not help the work by his remark about wishing to compose 'as a cow gives milk' which his enemies seized upon with malicious delight. No doubt he felt justifiable pride in what Samuel Langford, writing in 1923, called the 'long and gorgeous weft of sound' and the effortless mastery of orchestral counterpoint. Yet there is a deeper undertone, a solemnity, which perhaps may be associated with the years of its composition, 1911–15. It is a long farewell to the sumptuousness of the post-Wagnerian orchestra, and its final sunset before the return of night is peculiarly apposite and affecting. Even Strauss must have known that the world after the war would be a leaner, less extravagant place. So he brought down the curtain on his chief orchestral works not with a character-study of a rogue or a hero but with a celebration of elemental and unchanging Nature. In this respect, the work may surely be regarded as Strauss's homage to Mahler. He was working on it when he received the news of his friend's death and he wrote in his notebook words which link him and this music with Mahler: 'Purification through one's own strength, emancipation through work, adoration of eternal glorious nature.'

Some regard *Eine Alpensinfonie* as symptomatic of the onset of Strauss's long decline. That is not my view. It was the end of the beginning. Henceforward Strauss was obsessed by the theatre, having given the world a series of works which will remain indispensable for as long as symphony orchestras continue to exist. But conductors must believe in them. Dispassion or clinical analysis will not do.

17

The operas (1)

Guntram, Feuersnot, Salome, Elektra

Strauss's fifteen operas represent a major attempt by a major composer to extend the boundaries of the form. They reflect his belief in the continuing expansion of repertory opera. This faith was nurtured at Meiningen where, as a young man, he saw drama produced under ideal circumstances. He became and remained stage-struck; and when, as an old disillusioned man in 1945, he wrote his 'artistic testament', it was in the form of proposals for the re-establishment of repertory opera. The view that Strauss stood still after 1912, stuck in the mud and yearly becoming more of an anachronism, is not only superficial but misguided. Earlier chapters have shown with what assiduity he searched for subjects which would extend him further within his capacity.

His first opera, *Guntram*, has never established itself despite the cuts Strauss made in his 'child of sorrow' in 1934. In a sense he had to write it to purge himself of Wagnerianism—'all of *Guntram* is a prelude', he said in old age. It belongs to a world influenced by *Parsifal* and *Tannhäuser*, as the title suggests, but as well as looking back it gives several hints of impending Straussian works, and the broad soaring melodies given to Guntram and the heroine Freihild in Act III have a radiance familiar to us from the later operas. In an ideal operatic world, when Strauss's vision of true repertory-opera has materialized, there will be little justification for continued neglect of a work which, for all its miscalculations and *longueurs*, contains so much good, striking and amazingly mature music. But there is already much less reason for overlooking his second opera, *Feuersnot*, the first of the trio of one-act operas written between 1900 and 1908. This 'poem for singing'—*Singgedicht*—was composed after the great tone-poems and is in the witty and satirical vein of *Till* and *Don Quixote*. Its bawdy plot, scandalous at the time, would hardly flicker an eyebrow today. There is a link with Wagner, of course, through *Die Meistersinger*—both operas are set at midsummer—and there are several Wagner quotations in the score. Dramatically it creaks a bit, and the satire has lost some point, but its musical virtues are so strong that a good producer should easily overcome these handicaps.

The importance of *Feuersnot* is that it is, as Strauss himself emphasized just before he died, the first of the works in which he was to develop his own operatic style, 'dealing with a quasi-personal subject'. After the thick orchestration of *Guntram* the score of *Feuersnot* is brilliantly light and varied, with the warmth and colour of *Der Rosenkavalier* and the transparency of *Ariadne*. The children's choruses are delightful (if a good children's chorus can be found to sing them) as is the cunning use of Munich folksongs; and the childlike exuberance of the score, its unsophisticated yet highly polished geniality and humour, remain unequalled among the later works. It is a good deal more than merely a transitional work, for it is too assured in manner to be regarded as anything but mature. If anything, it attempts too much. Kunrad's oration to the populace, a temptation to Wagnerian moralizing, is treated as the occasion for an early display of Strauss's pot-pourri style and is highly successful. It includes a love-theme from earlier in the work transformed into this waltz, the ancestor of Baron Ochs's favourite tune:

Ex. 10

As has been seen in *Also sprach Zarathustra*, the waltz was of cardinal importance to Strauss. It marks him out as a child of his time in company with Mahler, selecting the elements of his music from many disparate and 'impure' ingredients and blending them into a distinctive style. Both composers were quick to seize on features of popular music to forge their styles. *Feuersnot* is a clear pointer to the Strauss of *Der Rosenkavalier* and a useful essay in the one-act form in which Strauss excelled. It is a veritable compendium of witty allusions and quotations.

A weakness of both *Guntram* and *Feuersnot* is that neither contains a really rewarding principal role, the sort of roles that generations of sopranos, baritones or tenors will want to sing come hell or high water in order to present their credentials. In his next two operas Strauss was to provide such roles, and he continued to do so with enviable prodigality. *Salome* is the first of his immortal individual vocal creations. In Wilde's play he found both a central character whom he could portray operatically as vividly as he had depicted Don Quixote orchestrally and a theme which enabled him to dabble in the fashionable orientalism of the time. Other Eastern operas, he said, 'lacked the colour and the sunlight of the East'. He would provide them. In fact he provided, with astonishing technical resource, the Palestinian night, bathed in moonlight, sultry and fragrant.

Salome is a study in obsession. Gabriel Fauré described it in 1907 as 'a symphonic poem with vocal parts added', an accurate assessment when one contemplates the immense and immensely inventive details of the orchestral score. Using over 100 instrumentalists, Strauss achieves fantastic effects of tone-colour to mirror not only every action on the stage but the thoughts of each character in the drama. Time has not dimmed the startling effects he obtains by means of trills dominated by the E flat clarinet, the exotic percussion, and a whole armoury of sensational string sounds, notably the eerie sound which breaks the silence as Salome leans over the cistern in the execution episode and which is created by four double basses 'pinching' the string with thumb and forefinger and striking it sharply with the bow.

Yet the operatic nature of *Salome* should not be underestimated. Its nightmare intensity, the relentless build-up of horror as Salome's insane sexual desire for Jokanaan's death blots out all other feelings, is achieved by vocal characterization and insight to match the orchestral legerdemain. Perhaps Ernest Newman was right in his belief that the opera grew from the Closing Scene, modelled on Isolde's *Liebestod*, for this is the most fluently organic section of the score, erotic, seductive and genuinely tragic, words and music more closely interlocked than in some earlier parts of the opera. This perverted *Liebestod* includes some of Strauss's most daring harmonic adventures in dual tonality, with cellos in A major clashing with the F sharp major of the violins, the latter being a favourite key for Strauss when expressing consummation of every kind. This startling moment is exceeded by the epoch-making dissonance with which Strauss takes Salome, in C sharp major, to the depth of degradation as she exults 'I have kissed your mouth, Jokanaan' (see Ex. 11).

Arduous and taxing role though it is, Salome attracts sopranos both by reason of its vocal fertility and its opportunities for a striking

Ex. 11

psychological portrayal. It can be filled by a heroic Wagnerian soprano or by a lighter voice. There is an inherent contradiction in the conception of this sixteen-year-old princess singing with the force and maturity of Isolde. Few singers could encompass satisfactorily both the childlike and the sensual elements in the part. Strauss recognized one who could in Elisabeth Schumann and offered to conduct for her and to damp down the orchestra. She did not sing Salome, but for Maria Rajdl at Dresden in 1930, also a light soprano, Strauss reduced the orchestration. Strauss became disturbed, too, by the tendency of singers to overact the role, especially in the Dance of the Seven Veils, where cavortings and capers aroused his ire. 'Salome, being a chaste virgin and an oriental princess, must be played with the simplest and most restrained of gestures,' he wrote. His interpretation of the score was markedly 'deadpan'. He had written all the emotional expression into it and it needs no extra gloss.

If Salome is the first of Strauss's great female roles, Herod is the first great tenor part he wrote. 'It is not a voice, it is a disease' was Bülow's opinion of tenors, and basses and baritones are generally better served by Strauss. But while Jokanaan is more impressive in wrath than in prayer, Herod is a magnificent study in pathological weakness, perversity, feigned dignity and outraged revulsion. In Herodias, too, urging her daughter to murder and depravity, Strauss created another powerful and chilling character. What is perhaps most impressive about *Salome* is its meticulously calculated construction, so typical of Strauss. The music seethes, writhes, glitters, insinuates, yet there is not a stray note. Detachment and control are Strauss's strongest dramatic virtues. Whatever went on in his heart—and in *Salome* he was putting hysteria on to the stage—the brain that guided the hand in the study at Garmisch remained cool. The neat handwriting on all the manuscripts tells its own story.

If, by writing *Salome*, Strauss saw the opportunity to cut into Puccini's box-office profits, it is still understandable that he should have been daunted by the idea of following it with a subject so similar in almost every respect, *Elektra*, the first of his collaborations with Hofmannsthal. Here again was an opera in one act about a demented woman in the grip of an obsession, this time that of revenge. The marvel is that though it is composed almost to the same formula as *Salome*, the resulting music is so different. *Salome* begins with a clarinet glissando followed by Narraboth's apostrophe to Salome's beauty, and his discussion with the Young Page which succinctly sets the scene for the audience before Salome appears; *Elektra* opens with a similar instrumental leitmotif, followed by the discussion between the serving-maids which describes the whole vile atmosphere of Klytämnestra's palace and Elektra's part in it, preparing us for Elektra's first monologue. The opening motif represents Agamemnon, the avenging of whose death has obsessed his daughter Elektra for years (this is another of Strauss's memorable short phrases, similar to the *Naturthema* in *Also sprach Zarathustra*). Both operas are constructed in sections like the episodes of a symphonic poem, with the orchestra taking almost a protagonist's role at an emotional climax; both have a brief and effective moment of light relief in *Till*-like vein, the Jews' theological bickering in *Salome* and the male servants in *Elektra*; both build inexorably towards the heroine's vocal orgasm as she achieves her objective; and in both operas the heroine's consummation is associated with a dance, voluptuous in Salome's case and an epileptic paroxysm in Elektra's.

Yet the opulent glittering score of *Salome* is the more consciously beautiful, even elegant, notwithstanding its marvellous flavour of depravity. *Elektra* is a heavier, thicker score, the colour of blood, with every effect as carefully calculated as in *Salome*. It is a score of amazing richness, the strings divided into several sections, balanced against forty-one wind instruments, including five clarinets (E flat, B flat and A), a heckelphone, two basset-horns and Wagner tubas. This huge array is used with surpassing skill to convey terror, cruelty, frustration, all the darkest secrets of human nature. It produces gigantic dissonance and superb diatonic splendour. In his use of bitonality and of polytonality (especially in combinations of minor triads) Strauss stretched his harmonic vocabulary as far as it was ever to go, to the frontier of atonality, in order to project the nightmare aspects of the drama, as can be heard in the extraordinary passage in Klytämnestra's aria when she describes the nameless nocturnal horror which devours her. Music at this date had never probed so deeply into human psychology and found the right sounds to match. Yet this is the whole point: they were the right sounds for this dramatic situation, they did not represent a change in Strauss's whole attitude to composition. Beginning with the metallic clanking and rattling of the ornaments with which Klytämnestra bedecks her wracked body, the music becomes bitonal and atonal as she recounts her dream that her bone-marrow is melting and that 'something' crawls over her as she tries to sleep. Strauss's genius as an illustrative orchestrator matches every suggestion, every erotic overtone in Hofmannsthal's text. But this music is not merely graphic virtuosity; it comes from the depths of Strauss's own psyche and his torment, so well disguised by outward nonchalance, that his mother was mentally deranged. He saw all that the topically Freudian text of the play offered him and he had the technical and psychological armoury with which to meet its challenge. He opened the way for the Woman of Schoenberg's *Erwartung* two years later, for Berg's wretched Wozzeck, for Shostakovich's Lady Macbeth of Mtsensk and for Britten's Peter Grimes.

However, *Elektra* is not all blood and thunder, not all exhibitionist violence. There is lyricism, some of it among the truest-hearted Strauss composed: for example, Elektra's tender recollection of her childhood (see Ex. 12), which comes all the more impressively after the great motif in octaves that Ernest Newman unforgettably described as 'rising threateningly from the depths to the heights of the orchestra like a great clenched fist'. Again, in Elektra's quasi-Lesbian declaration of love for

Ex. 12

her sister Chrysothemis, the fervent and conventional E flat episode heightens the sudden return to frenzy when Chrysothemis shirks involvement in matricide.

Greatest of all is the Recognition Scene, where Elektra and her brother Orestes are reunited, and Strauss rises to one of the supreme moments in classical drama with a colossal orchestral climax gently subsiding into Elektra's transcendental solo, accompanied by an orchestra in which the strings are much subdivided to produce a bewitching luminous sound, and the soprano sustains a soft high B flat as she sings 'erhabenes Gesicht, O bleib' bei mir' ('Noble countenance, O stay with me'). These and other passages give *Elektra* its balance of contrasts. It is significant that these lyrical passages are comparatively short. Strauss's lyricism was dependent on dramatic situations to which words contributed. In the case of the Recognition Scene he asked Hofmannsthal for some extra lines to enable him to sustain the mood. He was incapable of the broad-spanned lyrical invention needed for symphonic slow movements; he told Mahler that he would have been unable to compose a movement like the Adagio of Mahler's Fourth Symphony. In essence, his was a 'jigsaw-puzzle' mind. His invention was often commonplace, but so skilfully does he piece it together, so subtle are the transformations and so psychologically apposite is the constant re-application of leitmotifs that this jigsaw ability becomes his principal hallmark. (For a fully detailed analysis of this procedure, the interested reader is referred to Del Mar's volumes and their copious music examples.) Strauss once confessed that he 'always spoilt' his music by the use of too much counterpoint, for his mind worked naturally in complex and contrapuntal terms. This was said in a self-doubting moment, but his creative spirit rightly led him into self-indulgence of his gifts where his strength lay.

Hofmannsthal's libretto gave Strauss, for the first time, three major roles for women's voices, two sopranos and a mezzo. In their next opera, *Der Rosenkavalier*, this combination was to encompass the varied moods of love; in *Elektra* it explores psychological obsessions. Elektra herself, Strauss's Brünnhilde, is a classic case of father-fixation. She exists by thinking of 'the deed' she is to do—the murder of her mother and her stepfather Aegisthus—and for which she has buried an axe in readiness. Yet when Orestes comes, he does the deed and she forgets to give him the axe. Her ghastly final dance is an orgy of frustration. Chrysothemis personifies lack of maternal fulfilment. The aria in which she expresses her longing for a normal married life is touching if the character is portrayed as a tragic, wasted, neurotic woman. In Klytämnestra we see the vengeance that guilt can wreak on the body and mind by psychosomatic means. Strauss drew these three wretched hysterical women in sharply defined vocal characterizations; the roles are extremely testing but eminently singable. *Salome* and *Elektra* are 'shockers'—they make the Italian *verismo* composers seem like something from

Children's Corner—but if they sound crude and vulgar the fault lies with singers and conductors, not with Strauss's meticulous scores. When he spoke of *Salome* as 'fairy music by Mendelssohn' and of *Elektra* as like Lortzing, he was of course exaggerating, but he was giving interpreters the strongest possible clue to his intentions. *Elektra* is particularly vulnerable to a too loud and unvaried assault by a badly conducted orchestra; the invariable result is devaluation of the music, which is thus often exposed as no fiercer than Brahms.

Elektra ends with a chord of C major, as if to emphasize that, despite having peered down the harmonic abyss, Strauss had no intention of pursuing a revolutionary course. It is sometimes said that thereby he drew back from reality and took refuge in rococo artificiality. If Strauss had wished to continue along the atonal path, he could easily have done so: few composers have been so formidably equipped technically. But he knew there was room for only one *Salome* and one *Elektra* in his music. He had pioneered that path, let others follow it wherever it might lead. He wanted to do something different and he wanted it to be comedy, but *Der Rosenkavalier* is harmonically as 'tough' as *Elektra*.

Der Rosenkavalier, Ariadne auf Naxos

Strauss was always alert and responsive to the mood of the day, holding a mirror to contemporary life. In *Salome* he reflected the *fin-de-siècle* fashion for decadence and *art nouveau* in the manner of Wilde and Aubrey Beardsley; in *Elektra* there are Freudian overtones, even if they are accidental; and in *Der Rosenkavalier* he wrote the opera *par excellence* which enshrines pre-1914 Europe, its opulence and gaiety, the sense of time running out, the cynicism, the beauty, the abundance of melody, and the refusal to face reality. (Conversion to belief in a *Zeitgeist* is practically ensured by contemplation of the year 1910, with Mahler composing his Tenth Symphony, Elgar his Second and Strauss *Der Rosenkavalier*.) Osbert Sitwell, in his autobiography, recalled that whenever he heard the *Rosenkavalier* waltzes, 'the world is again peopled with a legion of the young, enjoying themselves, who have long since ceased to exist'. In composing his most celebrated opera Strauss created a unique and unmistakable atmosphere, a Vienna, city of everyone's dreams, inhabited by four marvellous characters who rank in the operatic portrait-gallery with the *dramatis personae* of *Le nozze di Figaro* and *Die Meistersinger*. Yet, ironically, the work is a Bavarian parody of Vienna, even to the waltzes, which time has turned into 'the real thing'.

It seems sometimes that everything Strauss wrote before 1909 was sketchwork for *Der Rosenkavalier* and everything he wrote after it took it as a point of reference. It is his quintessence and understandably his most popular work. It has everything that the public loves most: a good plot, sentiment, a mixture of elegant wit and broad farce, waltzes, soar-

ing melodies, a hovering between laughter and tears, and a period setting. (One of Hofmannsthal's many masterstrokes was to place the work
in mid-eighteenth-century Vienna, an era closely parallel to that of the
early twentieth century, when society was on the edge of the precipice;
Strauss added a musical masterstroke by underpinning the whole structure with a glorious anachronism, the waltz.) It is also on the grand
scale, offering opportunities for beautiful sets and costumes, and the
libretto is one of the half-dozen best in existence, truly a 'comedy for
music' but with an independent life as a remarkable piece of dramatic
characterization.

With *Der Rosenkavalier* Strauss moved away for ever from the neo-
Wagnerian saturation of *Elektra* and began the refining process which
was directed towards equating words and music in his brand of music-
drama. True, a large orchestra is still used, but the predominant feature
of the score is the clarity and refinement of the orchestral writing, with
the full forces reserved for passages where their effect will be greatest.
Strauss's craftsmanship in *Der Rosenkavalier* is of a superior order, not
only in intricate and subtle deployment of short and memorable motifs
but in the illustrative quality of the scoring, every detail touched in—a
poignant oboe, a romantic horn, a splash of trumpet tone, a rhythmic
allusion.[1] Not a movement on the stage, not the lift of an eyebrow nor
a meaning glance but is reflected in the orchestra. The erotic horn-calls
in the Prelude tell of the consuming physical nature of Oktavian's relationship with the Marschallin; the flute describes the hairdresser's fingers
in the Levée; the candles at the inn in Act III are lit to woodwind trills.

But the orchestral virtuosity goes deeper than mere illustration. The
justly famous passage of the Presentation of the Rose, one of the great
moments in opera, represented for Hofmannsthal the kernel of the plot,
the moment when two young people meet and are instantly attracted
before they know anything of each other's imperfections, a moment of
dreamlike, idealistic romance. Strauss sets it marvellously, evoking all
the rapture and wonder of the scene, and he produces an unforgettable
sound to fix this moment: shifting harmonies for three flutes, three solo
violins, two harps and celesta.

Yet by these very harmonies the worldly Strauss also conveys the disillusionment to follow, the brittleness of lovers' vows. *Der Rosenkavalier*
is full of such subtleties. Perhaps the most surprising of them, though
the most Straussian in its daring use of thematic transformation, concerns the other climactic passage, the wonderful Act III Trio in which
the soprano voices soar and blend and diverge as the Marschallin,
Oktavian and Sophie express their private thoughts at this crucial junc-

---

[1] It should be added that it remains exceedingly difficult to play well. When Karl Böhm
conducted the 199th Dresden performance he called nineteen orchestral rehearsals, and one
of the senior players told him afterwards: 'It was not one too many. It hasn't got any
easier.'

ture in their lives. The melodic basis has first been heard earlier in the act as the comic waltz to which Oktavian, disguised as a girl, sings 'Nein, nein, I trink kein Wein' when Ochs tries to make her drunk as a prelude to seduction:

Ex. 13

Strauss gloried in the challenge of writing for three sopranos, and he created roles which are as indispensable to women singers as Brünnhilde, Isolde, Leonora and Violetta. The part of Oktavian, the Rosenkavalier, is a *travesti* role, descended from Cherubino, demanding lustrous tone and a gift for comedy from its singer. Perhaps its most arduous requirement is in making the contrast between the impetuous young lover of an older married woman in Act I and the lover of naïve and inexperienced Sophie in Acts II and III. It is fascinating to hear the style Strauss adopted for Elektra's taunting of Aegisthus transformed into Oktavian's mockery of Baron Ochs auf Lerchenau. Sophie, too, is a difficult role, needing a high lyric soprano who can in a sophisticated manner float the ecstatic phrases of the Presentation scene (Ex. 14) and can also suggest without archness an innocence comparable to that required for the last movement of Mahler's Fourth Symphony.

In the bass and baritone roles of Ochs and Faninal, Strauss's music penetrates to the lewd country-cousin boorishness of the former and the

Ex. 14

nouveau-riche snobbery of the latter. Nevertheless the finest role in the opera, the creation which lifts it on to a higher emotional level, is that of the Feldmarschallin. Although she does not appear in Act II and only in a comparatively short episode of Act III, she is the dominant figure. In Strauss's gallery of women the Marschallin (musical cousin of Mozart's Countess) is the most hauntingly and closely observed, a part written by a composer who understood every inflexion of the soprano voice and who also understood women.

Through the Marschallin, Strauss imparted to *Der Rosenkavalier* the poignancy which is a vital ingredient of the finest comedy—'one eye wet, the other dry', as he himself expressed it. There is much to be learned about his skill as a composer of operas from the way he builds the Marschallin's character during the superb first act, so that by its end the audience is at her feet. He does this by means of three subdued monologues which are the parallels of the finest variations in *Don Quixote*. For the first half of the act there is nothing about her specially to engage our sympathy: a thirty-two-year-old wife, bored by her older husband and engaged in the latest of a succession of amorous diversions, holding her morning levée like a Lady Bountiful and becoming irritated because her hairdresser has made her look older. It is only when the levée is over and Ochs and his retinue have left that the woman's deeper feelings begin to emerge—the first time that she is alone. The orchestration, which during the levée[2] has been Strauss the picture-book illustrator at his most graphic—monkeys, parrots, dogs, orphans, all are delineated—is now reduced to the intimacy of chamber-music to accompany the Marschallin's musings. Strauss completely changes the mood of the opera by themes like these:

Ex. 15

[2] This levée scene is an almost exact replica of the fourth drawing in Hogarth's 'Marriage à la Mode'.

Ex. 16

Oktavian returns ready to resume the love-making of the first scene but finds the Marschallin changed and in a mood he cannot understand. The music conveys this emotional change, with Oktavian's impulsive ardour quelled by a new theme in which all the Marschallin's sense of the evanescence of life is expressed:

Ex. 17

In Act III, when she acknowledges that she has yielded Oktavian to Sophie, this theme is recalled with memorable effectiveness. It heralds, in Act I, the tensest music of the opera as Oktavian's youthful pleadings are answered by the Marschallin's philosophizing: 'Bis in mein Herz hinein. . . .' 'In the depths of my heart I sense that one should keep nothing . . . everything dissolves like mist and dreams.' There is no soaring cantilena here, just radiant arioso-like melody culminating in the famous description of Time and of how she sometimes creeps from her room in the night and stops all the clocks. Her simple religious faith permeates the next duet when she explains to Oktavian that she knows he will one day leave her for a younger woman.

If nothing else in the opera, except the final Trio, attains the level of musico-dramatic unity in this act, there is no decline in vitality or outpouring of melody. It is a great confection and for some tastes it is too sweet (the fault of the taste, not the music). The virtuosity of the levée scene, with the Italian Singer's aria in which many a tenor has first caught the public's notice; the Mozartian grace of the young lovers' final duet and of the 'breakfast duet' in Act I; the string of waltz tunes—all these suggest pastiche of a superior kind.[3] Yet there is nothing 'pseudo' about *Der Rosenkavalier*; the Silver Rose is made of sterling silver and the icing on the cake is hard. It is a very long opera (Ochs's part being second only to Susanna's in *Figaro* in length), and there are *longueurs*, intensified in a poor or poorly sung production. It shares some of the

---

[3] The waltz Ochs sings at the end of Act II is identical, even to key, with Josef Strauss's *Dynamiden*, Op. 173—whether by accident or design is not known.

faults, as well as the virtues, of *Die Meistersinger*: the spinning-out of the plot until it threatens to snap, and the cardinal flaw that the discomfiture of Ochs and Beckmesser is not really funny. (Here, also, much depends on how Ochs is acted. Strauss emphasized that he was 'a member of the gentry' if 'at heart a cad'. He modelled him on Falstaff.)

The period element in the opera is simply a dramatic convenience, for it transcends period and becomes timeless, like medieval Nuremberg in *Die Meistersinger* and eighteenth-century Seville in *Figaro*, because the characters are contemporary with every age. *Der Rosenkavalier* may be bracketed with them without offence to the spirits of Mozart and Wagner because it is an opera of inexhaustible fascination, enabling successive singers, conductors, producers and listeners to find something new in it at each revival, to vary the nuances and stress the accents. Although there is much in the rest of Strauss that has been underrated and compared disadvantageously with his greatest success, the unalterable fact remains that he will be known first and foremost as the composer of *Der Rosenkavalier*—and justly so. It may not be his greatest opera, but it has the greatest appeal to the majority of listeners.

Earlier chapters have traced the stormy genesis of *Ariadne auf Naxos*, a crucial work not only in the Strauss–Hofmannsthal collaboration (for it shows them pulling different ways yet arriving at the same destination) but in Strauss's musical development. The original Molière-play–Strauss-opera version is feasible only where and when the Utopian situation exists of first-rate theatrical and operatic companies working in close partnership.[4] Nevertheless, the situation does sometimes exist and when it does, the listener who probably knows the work only from the 1916 revision will be surprised to discover what a different work the original version is. It is not only that there is all the incidental music for *Le Bourgeois Gentilhomme*, the *Ariadne* opera itself has a different atmosphere, is far more insouciant. Moreover, Strauss cut some splendid music, including an extra aria for Zerbinetta which occurs at a crucial moment towards the climax of the opera. The second version, ill-starred at first, has now won a steady place in the repertory and is particularly effective in an opera house like Glyndebourne where exquisite production and singing are *de rigueur*.

No production, however, can disguise the dichotomy of Hofmannsthal's concern for the deep seriousness of his treatment of the Ariadne legend, with its basic theme of fidelity, and Strauss's delight in the *commedia dell'arte* characters, particularly Zerbinetta, who fed his growing appetite for his own lighter *Till* side. The combination of *opera seria* and *opera buffa*, on the lines of Monteverdi's *L'incoronazione di Poppea*, enabled Strauss to show off his versatility and to employ a small

---

[4] It has twice been revived in Britain since the Second World War, very successfully by Beecham at the Edinburgh Festival of 1950 (nine performances) and less well at Glyndebourne in 1962.

orchestra (thirty-six players), as he had done in the Marschallin's monologue in *Der Rosenkavalier.* Even more brilliantly effective is the
Prologue added in 1916 which, in its use of *secco* recitative, *parlando*
dialogue and bursts of melody, is the stylistic forerunner of *Intermezzo,*
Arabella and *Capriccio.* Here, too, Strauss showed himself a 'modern',
a pioneer, by putting on to the operatic stage the realism—albeit within
a 'period' frame—of backstage tantrums and panics, of a composer
undergoing the pangs of inspiration amid the need to make cuts and
alterations, of a tyrannical Maecenas, a philistine impresario, and that
general air of makeshift which is indispensable to the world of the theatre, and it is all done by sophistication mixed with the bran-tub.

By making the Composer an Oktavian-like figure, Strauss created yet
another rewarding and appealing soprano role which, short though it is,
attracts the finest Straussian exponents. Because Strauss understood
these Prologue characters, knew their counterparts in life (none cleverer
than he at placating jealous sopranos), his music for them veers from his
humorous witty vein (Zerbinetta's backchat) to his soaringly lyrical, as
when the Composer composes, when he and Zerbinetta discover that
they are soulmates, and finally in the Composer's ecstatic outpouring to
the holy art of music:

Ex. 18

These moments of rapture for a soprano voice—deriving from his Lieder—were rapidly becoming Strauss's stock-in-trade, but they are all subtly varied to suit the character portrayed. This can easily be seen in *Ariadne* by comparing the Composer's arias with those given to Ariadne herself, which are equally lyrical yet sound as if they were conceived instrumentally in the manner of the final scenes of *Elektra* and *Salome*, whereas the Composer's spring from the text. Strauss certainly understood Ariadne, and in the main part of the opera she achieves musically the importance Hofmannsthal intended. Even so, a listener's memories of *Ariadne auf Naxos* are probably principally of the Nymphs' Rhinemaidenish trio and of Zerbinetta's showpiece aria (cut and transposed down from the first version) rather than of the long Bacchus-Ariadne love-duet which ends the work. Fine though this is, it makes a conventionally rhetorical ending to a delightful if self-consciously 'specialist' entertainment, and one regrets the elimination of the first finale in which Zerbinetta and her followers bring down the curtain on a note of mockery and artificiality. There is no reason why the prologue should not be followed by the original *Ariadne*.

There is good music in the final duet. William Mann went too far in calling it 'a lengthy failure'. Admittedly one has heard performances which justify this stricture, but also ones which, if only temporarily, sweep away any suspicions that this is Strauss below his best, attempting to re-create the Recognition Scene of *Elektra* but without the real impetus to do so. The genuine note of exaltation can seem to be either missing or contrived. Perhaps he felt that Hofmannsthal's text never fully succeeds in conveying the lofty content of the poet's intentions; or perhaps the root of the trouble is that he was always more inspired if there was an element of scepticism in the text. Part of the reason why the end of *Der Rosenkavalier* is so moving is the worldliness of the unanswered questions: will Oktavian and Sophie be happy, has the Marschallin really renounced him? Strauss was a master of this cynical mood. He tried to inject it into the end of *Ariadne* by giving the closing passages of the love-duet echoes of the *Rosenkavalier* Trio and by prefacing Zerbinetta's brief final entry by the celesta, but we do not experience a comparable *frisson*.

For Ariadne, especially when writing in D flat, the key he loved best for passionate exposition, Strauss could do the trick; he was less sure with Bacchus. Strauss could write well for character-tenors—Herod, Aegisthus, Valzacchi—but the tenor as hero was not his element until he came to the Emperor in *Die Frau ohne Schatten*. There is also the visual factor. 'Young, magical, dreamy' is the stage description of this god when he arrives—after a big build-up from Echo, Naiad and Dryad—tactlessly mistaking Ariadne for Circe, with whom he had spent the previous day. Few tenors with the voice for Bacchus have the looks, too, and in that respect the role is more convincing on a recording.

There is the additional point of the vocal style in which the role is sung. The tendency is to turn it into Wagnerian *Heldentenor* territory. There is no denying that the music invites this approach, but the best singers of Bacchus have been those who, remembering that Richard Tauber once sang the role, have applied a lighter, more lyrical palette.

The student of Strauss will find continual delight in the quotations buried in the score—references to *Tristan*, to a Schubert song and to Mendelssohn, among others—and in the felicity of the scoring. An interesting inclusion is the harmonium, already used in *Feuersnot*, *Salome*, and *Der Rosenkavalier* but here given an important function in the *opera seria* sections to supply something of the warm and full sonority of which Strauss had deprived himself by his chamber format. He used it, in his own words, 'simultaneously with, and as a substitute for, whole groups of instruments, such as fifth and sixth horns, trombones, bassoons, flutes, oboes, clarinets, etc.'. In the *buffo* episodes the pianoforte is used as the continuo instrument, entirely happily.

These instrumental forces, excluding the harmonium, are also those required for the music for *Der Bürger als Edelmann*, now usually known under its French title *Le Bourgeois Gentilhomme*. This is more familiar to audiences as a concert suite of nine movements. Indubitably this is the best of Strauss the connoisseur. In his vein of highest-quality pastiche there is nothing to touch it. By comparison the *buffo* music of *Ariadne* is less sparkling. The wit is Haydnesque, the elegance and charm are Mozartian, the whole is Straussian. There is the inevitable waltz, one of the most delicious he wrote, and the melody which the Composer writes on stage in the Prologue to the second version of *Ariadne*—'Du Venus Sohn'—is first heard as the oboe melody of the Sicilienne, as captivating in its lilting grace as are the Minuet and Courante. The Dinner Music is the acme of Straussian parody, Jourdain's menu being carefully devised by Hofmannsthal to give his partner every chance for apt allusions. The waiters enter to a distorted version of Meyerbeer's Coronation March from *Le Prophète*; Rhine salmon evokes the Rhine motif from Wagner's *Ring*; the saddle of mutton evidently came from the flock of sheep Don Quixote encountered, and while it is eaten a solo cello suggests that the Don is not far away; a dish of larks and thrushes provides the opportunity to recall the birds in Act I of *Rosenkavalier*; and the surprise in the *omelette surprise* is provided by the kitchen boy who jumps out of the huge dish and dances— not such a surprise—a Viennese waltz.

In *Music Ho!* Constant Lambert called Stravinsky the 'time-traveller'. The term may be applied to many composers, not least to Strauss. It was the age of time-travelling in music—Ravel to Mozart and Couperin; Webern, Schoenberg, Elgar and others to Bach and Handel; Vaughan Williams to Tallis; Stravinsky to Pergolesi. Strauss time-travelled to Lully, Couperin, Mozart, to the waltz, to the age of Schumann. He borrowed their styles and made them his own so convincingly that they are valuable in their own right, not as imitations. *Le Bourgeois Gentilhomme* stands with Stravinsky's *The Rake's Progress* and Prokofiev's *Classical Symphony* as a supreme example of its genre.

Die Frau ohne Schatten, Intermezzo

Die Frau ohne Schatten (The Woman without a Shadow) is likely to remain the most problematical and tantalizing of Strauss's operas. Some consider it to be his greatest, but although it contains passages which rank as the greatest music he wrote, its satisfactoriness as an opera is questionable, because of the labyrinthine complexity of Hofmannsthal's plot and libretto. It is a hymn to the sanctity of marriage, and deals with the vital need for sexual satisfaction between the partners, allied to the importance of children and the problems arising from childlessness. But these elementals are camouflaged amid such a forest of obscure and pretentious symbolism, prolonged to Wagnerian proportions, that the majority of the audience leaves the theatre baffled by the meaning of it all and even perhaps sniggeringly contemptuous of such scenes as unborn children pleading to be brought into existence while fishes materialize from the air and land in a frying-pan; dream lovers appearing in visions; and *Zauberflöte*-like trials by fire and water. The analogy with Mozart's last opera is further emphasized by the contrasted strata in which the action occurs: the fairy-tale world of Emperor and Empress dominated by the magician Kaikobad and the drab human world of the dyer Barak and his barren wife.

Hofmannsthal enjoyed implying that Strauss was much his intellectual inferior, and his admirers blame Strauss for failing fully to comprehend the genius of the poet's ideas. Strauss was certainly, if not an intellectual, a man of intellect in his own right when one considers his deep knowledge of Goethe and of classical literature, his love of paintings and his encyclopaedic knowledge of a vast range of music, but he was never pretentious. His practicality and his Bavarian bourgeois common sense protected him from the bogus. He appreciated the inner meaning of *Die Frau ohne Schatten* but, as the letters quoted in Chapter 9 show, he feared it would not come through in the opera-house in dramatic terms. He sensed that the characters were symbols, not true human beings, and he felt ill at ease with abstract ideas. It remains a near-miracle, therefore, that he was able to breathe so much operatic life into them.

Operas survive obscure libretti if their music is strong enough, and Strauss saved *Die Frau* by a Herculean display of prowess. Norman Del Mar's application of the term 'mental lethargy' to post-1913 Strauss, and many other writers' too glib assumption that Strauss ceased to progress after *Elektra*, are alike confounded and contradicted by the wonderful score of *Die Frau ohne Schatten*. In every way it is an astonishing advance, technical and emotional, on all that he had hitherto written. As *Also sprach Zarathustra* has a special quality of sound among the tone-poems, so has *Die Frau* among the operas. Writing for a large and exotic orchestra, Strauss achieved a major advance in his striving towards a correct balance and blend between voices and instruments. The translucent quality of the scoring, and the emphasis on a *concertante* instrumental style, suggest the influence of Mahler's *Das Lied von der Erde* (indeed the spirit of Mahler broods over the whole work, for the grandiose finale owes much to the finale of the Eighth Symphony and fails or succeeds in performance for most of the same reasons).

Act I in particular is a *locus classicus* for students of Strauss's orchestration. It is the best act in the opera, for one senses Strauss's initial enthusiasm for the subject and his interest in creating the characters. Its episodic lay-out allowed him to revert to the symphonic-poem style of *Salome*. He worked best when short-winded, or when vignettes were required rather than landscapes, and it is noteworthy that for all its large and opulent scale *Die Frau* might have been called 'fantastic variations on a theme of magical character', with the eight orchestral interludes playing a significant part in conveying by exclusively instrumental means the ideas which Hofmannsthal failed to elucidate. Here, in the first scene, are the ingredients which guaranteed Straussian success: creation of a sinister atmosphere, depiction of hunting, of a falcon (a superb and unforgettable theme, first heard on piccolo, oboes and E flat clarinet), the limning of a beautiful woman (the Empress, bewitchingly introduced and accompanied by solo viola, solo violin, flageolet notes on the second harp, and piquant woodwind), and a sunrise.

More unexpected is Strauss's success in writing convincingly lyrical heroic and passionate music for the tenor who sings the Emperor. Yet fine as his Act I aria is, even finer is that in Act II, Scene 2, a long monologue in the Emperor's hunting-lodge. This is preceded by a masterly orchestral introduction in which the falcon's desolate cry on the woodwind is superimposed on two of the Emperor's principal themes played with melancholy and sombre beauty by a solo cello and elaborated by solo cellos, solo viola and solo double-bass in a notable anticipation of Strauss's late-period writing for strings (see Ex. 19). The aria itself is a desolate outpouring of inner isolation, almost unique in Strauss's music. This, the listener feels, is Strauss without a mask of any kind.

Equally successful is Strauss's treatment of the good-hearted character of Barak the dyer, one of his most rewarding bass-baritone roles. The explanation may be sought in the autobiographical nature of the characterization, since Strauss would easily identify himself with an even-tempered, hard-working, simple man like Barak, whereas he would never have laid claim to the pious godliness of a prophet. Barak's wife is also a vivid character, being yet another manifestation of Pauline. A further chapter of the *Symphonia Domestica* is the orchestral interlude in the first scene between Barak and his wife which epitomizes Barak's compassionate nature and his love for her. The passage is a simple melodizing round the tonic key of D major for full strings with conventional woodwind and brass. It is among the loveliest episodes in any Strauss opera.

Ex. 19

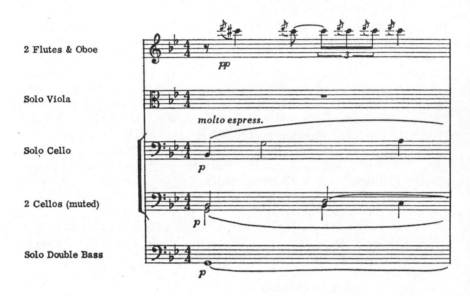

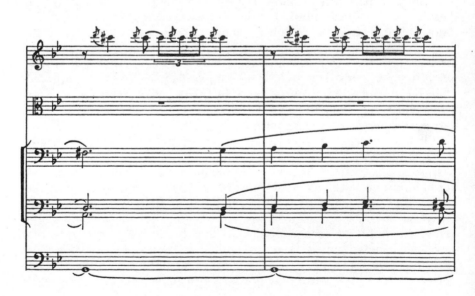

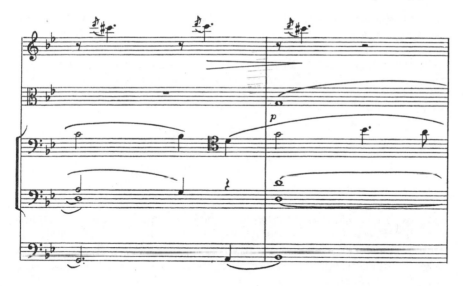

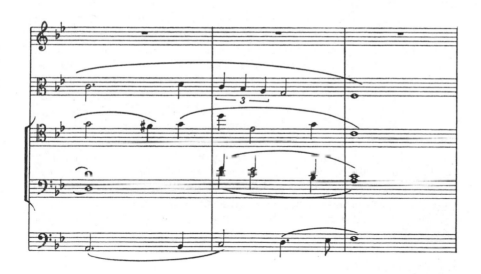

This particular passage is harmonically simple. Yet there are several occasions where the harmonies are as rootless and as near to atonal as any in *Elektra*. The extraordinary scene of the Empress's dream, for example, ends with an orchestral interlude in which the strangeness of the harmonies is responsible for summing up the nightmarish quality of the preceding scene. Another amazing orchestral passage is the description in Act I of the journey of the Empress and the Nurse to earth in which the discordant treatment of the themes is intensified by the transference of the falcon's cry to tubas, a crude but undeniably effective device. In this passage Strauss employs his large array of percussion, including Chinese gongs, castanets, whips and xylophone (possibly giving a hint to Puccini for *Turandot*, which in several curious ways resembles *Die Frau ohne Schatten*, and not only in the obvious similarities of an Oriental setting and overtones of erotic sadism). Another feature of the score is a glass harmonica, used with perfect judgment in the final scene where some apposite but unusual sound was needed to depict the Empress's acquisition of a shadow.

The last act is the least successful, although it opens impressively with a magnificent duet for Barak and his wife, Barak's 'Mir anvertraut' being one of the best tunes in the opera, and contains a great aria for the Empress in which the woodwind's accompanying phrases anticipate *Daphne*. But as the plot thickens—no cliché in this case—so does Strauss's power of invention as he struggles to clear a path through the increasingly tortuous complexities of Hofmannsthal's thought-processes. An uncut performance of the opera—alas, a rare occurrence—enables one to appreciate the magnificent achievement of the role of the Nurse, one of Strauss's most subtle and telling portraits of an evil, obsessed woman, and in this last act there is also the intensely dramatic episode of the Empress's *melodrama*, the climax of the great scene in which she gains her humanity. Having dismissed the Nurse, she hears the anguished voices of the separated Barak and his wife calling to each other. She is awaiting judgment and if she drinks from a golden fountain, she will obtain Barak's wife's shadow and will be able to bear children. But even though she is shown her husband, the Emperor, turned to stone, she refuses to drink, preferring to die rather than harm the other couple. It is at this point that she pours out her self-recrimination in speech, a passage of immense power. If it is cut, as it often is, the opera is deprived of its climactic impact. In the last scene, their trials over, the two couples are reunited, soon-to-be-born (presumably) children sing, the Empress's shadow becomes a golden arch, and the whole extraordinary culmination calls for music of transcendental sublimity. Strauss failed to provide it; although he pulls out every stop in the orchestra to provide a feast of colourful sound, he can no more avoid banality than Mahler did when he strove to universalize religion and eternal womanhood in his Eighth Symphony. In terms of such high-flown operatic endeavour, only Mozart in *Die Zauberflöte*, Beethoven in *Fidelio* and Vaughan Williams in *The Pilgrim's Progress* have matched the sublime mood of their final scene. So Strauss's relative failure may be accounted glorious.

The difficulties of *Die Frau ohne Schatten* lie not only in its symbolism. It is the Strauss–Hofmannsthal 'opera-spectacular' requiring the production skills found more often in Drury Lane musicals of 1935 vintage than in opera houses. Transformation scenes, materializations, scenic effects—only *Das Rheingold* gives the stagehands and electricians a comparably perilous and exacting evening. It is no wonder that Strauss was dissatisfied with most of the productions he saw, for the skills applicable to pantomime were not to be found in Dresden, Munich and Vienna. Also, it is an opera for a cast of great singers under a great conductor. So are all Strauss's operas: nothing but the best will ever do for them, for he was the supreme craftsman turning out very high-class goods. His demands in *Die Frau* are almost superhuman, and he was fortunate that the work was launched by such legendary artists as Lotte Lehmann, Maria Jeritza, Lucie Weidt, Richard Mayr and Karl Aagard-Oestvig. Only when such a cast can be assembled, with a glittering production to support them, can *Die Frau ohne Schatten* be performed with anything approaching justice to its many inspirations of genius, and this usually means that it remains a festival opera.

This is not undesirable. Like *Parsifal*, it needs to be approached in a devoted frame of mind, after due preparation. In such circumstances, as in Karl Böhm's marvellous 1974 performances at Salzburg, its effect can be overwhelming, for the marvels of the orchestral web, the superb writing for superb voices, and the dazzling stage spectacle can induce temporary suspension of any effort to disentangle Hofmannsthal's farrago while one surrenders to the all-important factor, music, and in the process understands the plot. And for nine-tenths of its course *Die Frau ohne Schatten* is music of spellbinding quality.

Yet it is scarcely surprising that, after writing outstanding music for *Josephslegende* and *Die Frau ohne Schatten* against the grain of his nature, Strauss should have turned for relief to a subject in which he knew he excelled—domestic realism. He was not, and knew he was not, a composer like Mahler and Bruckner who attempted to give their work a Beethovenian universality. Hofmannsthal believed himself to be that kind of poet and tried to take Strauss with him to scale metaphysical heights. In three successive works, *Ariadne auf Naxos*, *Josephslegende* and *Die Frau ohne Schatten*, Strauss was required to compose finales which, to borrow Ernest Newman's phrase, would 'give the cosmos its A'. Each time he failed. His way of reaching the hearts of men and women was through the physical attraction of an Oktavian and a Sophie or the worldly renunciation of a Marschallin, not by attempting to follow Hofmannsthal into such philosophical disquisitions as (apropos of the final duet of *Ariadne*): 'Transformation is the life of life itself, the real mystery of Nature as creative force.' It annoyed Hofmannsthal that Strauss was more interested in Zerbinetta than in Ariadne, but Strauss knew that the audience would be more interested in her too. Probably only in *Elektra*, *Arabella*, and Act I of *Der Rosenkavalier* were Strauss and Hofmannsthal composing the same opera.

The finale of *Die Frau ohne Schatten* was composed during 1916, simultaneously with the new Prologue to *Ariadne*; it is obvious which task Strauss enjoyed the more. In creating the Composer and providing the delicate back-stage love-skirmish with Zerbinetta, he was in his element. Moreover, in his avowed desire to intensify natural diction and speed of dialogue in opera, the *Sprechgesang* style he had adopted in the *Ariadne* Prologue fitted his needs perfectly. His alternation of *recitativo secco* with *recitativo accompagnato* was assured and polished. Now, after his success with the Composer, he was ready to start the domestic 'slice of life' on which he had long set his sights. He called it *Marriage Intermezzo*, but shortened this to *Intermezzo*, the title of a Schnitzler play on a similar theme.

Intermezzo is the 'satyr-play' to *Die Frau ohne Schatten*, in the same relationship as *Don Quixote* to *Ein Heldenleben*. In Strauss's sketchbook for *Intermezzo*, the theme of the Unborn Children in the earlier opera becomes the central theme of reconciliation in *Intermezzo*. Baron Lummer, the sponger whom the wife in *Intermezzo* befriends, is wittily given a motif derived from the Shadow theme in *Die Frau ohne Schatten*, and the wife's quarrelsome motif has links with the corresponding theme for Barak's wife. That Lotte Lehmann created the roles of Barak's wife and the wife in *Intermezzo* merely confirms the interrelationships between the two operas.

As mentioned in Chapter 6, *Intermezzo* was based on an episode in the Strausses' life arising from a misunderstanding in a Berlin bar in 1902, when an Italian tenor and an impresario were approached by one Mieze Mücke for two tickets for the opera. They introduced her to their companion, the company's conductor Josef Stransky (who was later to succeed Mahler in New York). The Italian repeatedly mispronounced his name as Strausky. Stransky forgot the tickets, and the persistent Mieze looked up what she thought was his name and address in the telephone directory. But she found Hofkapellmeister *Strauss* and sent this note to Joachimsthalerstrasse:

> Dear Herr Strauss, I expected to see you yesterday in the Union Bar, but in vain, alas. I am writing therefore to ask if you will be so kind as to let me have a few tickets for Monday and Wednesday of this week. With my best thanks in anticipation, yours sincerely, Mieze Mücke. Lüneberg-Strasse 5, ground floor right.

Hardly a declaration of illicit passion. Strauss was staying on the Isle of Wight when this note arrived at his home. Pauline opened it, assumed the worst, telegraphed her intention of seeking a divorce and saw their lawyer, Friedrich Rösch. She returned Strauss's letters unopened and withdrew 2,000 marks in gold from the bank. Strauss's letter to her of 26 May shows how well he understood her:

> This business with the Mücke woman is so stupid! . . . You take a whole week to decide what to do about your monster of a husband, and the first act of your

revenge is to draw my beautiful money out of the bank. I wish I knew what you intend to do with 2,000 marks. There were no bills waiting to be paid, and that one dress from Gerson's can hardly cost 1,500 marks . . . Now: I have never been in the Union Bar, I don't even know where it is, any more than I know who Mücke is . . . Either precious Mme. Mücke has confused me with someone else—after all, Berlin also boasts Edmund von Strauss, Oscar Straus, etc.—or someone has played a stupid and unnecessary joke on us . . . Yesterday I had begun composing something really nice [*Symphonia Domestica*] and had to waste my time on a letter clearing myself. You really could spare me things like this . . . Loving greetings and kisses from the adulterer to yourself and Bubi . . . Still, for the time being, your Richard.[5]

This, with the addition of a mild flirtation Pauline once had, is almost exactly the plot of *Intermezzo*. Most of the dialogue is taken from life: those who knew Richard and Pauline testified to its accuracy. The stage depiction of Pauline is, to quote Lotte Lehmann, 'a monument to her', in her tantrums, snobbishness, chattering, house-proud fussiness and tyrannical attitude to servants. It shows that, maddening though she was, she was also perpetually attractive to Strauss. For a candid biography of Pauline as her husband saw and knew her, one need look no further than *Intermezzo*. Strauss made no secret of the origin of the opera. He thinly disguised himself as Robert Storch, Pauline became Christine, Stransky became Stroh and Mieze Mücke became Mieze Meier. One of the most brilliant scenes shows his favourite card game of skat. The first singer of Storch at Dresden in 1924, the baritone Joseph Correck, wore a mask to make himself look like Strauss, and Strauss coached both Correck and Lehmann in making their performances as authentic as possible.

For some extraordinary reason, and especially in Britain, the plot of *Intermezzo* used to be regarded as embarrassingly tasteless. (This question of 'taste', always a dubious criterion for forming artistic judgments, seems particularly to trouble English critics of Strauss. One still finds *Salome* described as offensive; and I have known people who, having enjoyed *Der Rosenkavalier*, are overcome by guilt and purge themselves with a course of Bach fugues.) Even fifty years after *Intermezzo* was first performed, one found (in the 'permissive' era) such judgments as 'When we know that they [the characters] are taken from real life and that excruciating disagreeable episodes of the Strausses' household are being paraded before our embarrassed eyes, even the most hardy audiences must be taken aback. . . . The question arises whether such a scene from his home life . . . should be witnessed on any operatic stage.'[6] Somehow I think that audiences are unlikely to feel squeamish at the revelation that married couples row, bicker, falsely accuse each other, and then

[5] K. Wilhelm, *Richard Strauss: an Intimate Portrait*, op. cit., pp. 175–7.
[6] T. Bloomfield, 'Opera domestica', *Music and Musicians*, vol. 22, no. 262, June 1974, pp. 34–40.

make up. It is questionable, if Strauss and Pauline (eventually) did not mind, whether *Intermezzo* was tasteless in their lifetime; it certainly is not now that they have been dead for years. What matters is whether it is a successful opera. Schoenberg thought it was a masterpiece.

It is assuredly one of Strauss's most successful and sophisticated works, except to those who find its subject-matter not so much tasteless as trivial and inflated. The libretto, by Strauss, if self-indulgent is also skilfully effective. The cinematic short scenes, if not ahead of their time, were a marked advance on what had gone before (and may be compared with those in *Wozzeck*, which was composed at exactly the same time). Both Schoenberg, in *Von heute auf morgen*, and Hindemith, in *Neues vom Tage*, owed something to *Intermezzo*. Whether Strauss succeeded in making the words audible is more debatable, for even if conductors observe his very detailed dynamic markings, the incessant garrulousness of the orchestra in the first scenes is more than a match for Christine's ceaseless chatter on-stage. Even so, the scoring for an orchestra of just over fifty players is outstandingly deft. Strauss used only three horns; the writing for the strings is soloistic; and there is effective and restrained use of the pianoforte. Only in the interludes is the orchestration sonorous and polyphonic in complexity. The most remarkable vocal achievement is the convincing and unforced way in which spoken dialogue and recitative are alternated.

In *Intermezzo* Strauss's inventive imagination was working on a level comparable with the best of *Le Bourgeois Gentilhomme*. It may be, as William Mann avers, that some themes are 'nondescript', but they have a way of lingering in the mind none the less; and the waltzes in the Grundlsee scene are as melodically enticing as those in *Der Rosenkavalier*, if necessarily less opulent. (Some derive from sketches made for *Der Rosenkavalier*). Those who enjoy the favourite Straussian game of quotation-spotting will find plenty to amuse them in *Intermezzo*: some *Heldenleben* (when Christine mentions a critic), and snatches of Gounod's *Faust*, Verdi's *Otello*, Mozart's *Figaro*, Wagner's *Tristan* and *Parsifal* and Schumann's First Symphony. There is the usual astonishing display of sheer dexterity, the motifs fitting as in a jigsaw and being used with much subtlety. Those for whom musical 'progress' is synonymous with dissonance will find nothing in *Intermezzo*, but it is the first of several works in Strauss's allegedly 'tired' period when his genius was progressing towards the concluding glories of *Capriccio* and the last instrumental works.

Eleven orchestral interludes link the scenes in the two acts. These are designed—and exactly timed by this master theatrical practitioner—to cover scene-changes, but they are an integral part of the opera's psychological unity. Again I must disagree with those who believe that they inflate 'trivial' material out of all proportion—the same criticism that is made with equal injustice about *Symphonia Domestica*. *Intermezzo* is not a trivial work. Hofmannsthal, though repelled by the whole idea, admitted when he heard it that he was surprised by its seriousness. Like the artist he was, he recognized Strauss's skill in concocting such a satisfying mixture of the brittle, the sentimental, the witty, the grotesque and the potentially tragic—for the threat of divorce and the belief of one partner in the other's adultery are not in themselves comic, though legitimate matter for comedy. Strauss admitted that the real-life events took him 'almost to the point of insanity' and wrote to Hofmannsthal in 1927 that 'harmless and insignificant as the incidents which prompted this piece may be, they nevertheless result, when all is said and done, in the most difficult psychological conflicts that can disturb the heart'.[7] This underlying truth-to-life is developed in the interludes—his genuine distress is reflected in the scene in the Prater; the gorgeous fifth interlude in A flat, richly affectionate and tender, is ample testimony to the real meaning of the Richard-and-Pauline marriage, however it may have appeared to others.

Intermezzo is not a 'great' opera in the sense that we apply that adjective to *Tristan* or *Elektra*, but it is a masterpiece of its genre, a highly entertaining evening, and a remarkable early example of what is now known as 'music theatre'. It has no need to rely on the Strauss-Pauline association for its effectiveness: its intrinsic value needs no such meretricious 'publicity'. It has even been shown by a great actress-singer that Christine need not be portrayed as a shrew or harridan, but as a rather beguiling creature. In other words, the work is capable of more than one interpretation. As one comes to study it more deeply, one finds even more that is meritorious in it, enough, indeed, to declare it Strauss's most original opera. As time passes, its importance will be more widely recognized. Rather as has happened with Mozart's *Così fan tutte*, its true character will be belatedly perceived.

Die agyptische Helena, Arabella

It is no coincidence that of the two operas which Strauss completed in the 1920s—*Intermezzo* and *Die ägyptische Helena*—the former, to his own libretto on a subject he wanted to tackle, is in every way more successful. It was not Strauss who was in decline at this period, but Hofmannsthal (the war had left him psychologically depressed, and he had arteriosclerosis).

As earlier chapters have related, the poet was trying hard to accommodate Strauss's post-war desire for a light subject. It is a thousand pities that *Die ägyptische Helena* was not cast in the one-act form Strauss handled so well, so that the satirical mood of Act I could have

---

[7] It remains puzzling why even the fiery Pauline should have rushed to begin divorce proceedings after eight years of marriage, for Strauss was not a philanderer and no extra-marital affairs have ever been authenticated.

been sustained to the final curtain. In it are the ingredients of a good spoof mythological opera, anticipating by more than a decade the stage success of *Amphitryon 38*. The soprano sorceress, Aithra, with her odd appurtenance an Omniscient Sea-Shell through which she learns what is happening elsewhere in the world, is a delightful creation. Her colony of elves, mocking and deluding Menelaus, are also a good dramatic device and drew good music from Strauss. The snags arise in Act II where Hofmannsthal wades up to his neck in the symbolism of mistaken identities caused by an overdose, in all respects, of magic potions and introduces a sheikh and his son, Da-ud, who both fall in love with Helen. Hofmannsthal's favourite themes of love-at-first-sight, recognition and the binding influence of children are all worked into this act.

Strauss was deeply conscious of the dichotomy between the two acts and knew it was bound to be reflected in the music. He took a long time to get into the mood for Sheikh Altair, and after Hofmannsthal's death he persuaded Lothar Wallerstein to revise part of the action in Act II for Krauss's Salzburg Festival production in 1933 in an attempt to elucidate it.

Of all Strauss's operas, *Helena* has been the least successful and remains the least known. It has been harshly criticized, but the music does not deserve most of these strictures. It is Strauss's *bel canto* opera, written for the great singers with whom he had been working in Vienna. Act I in particular is full of vocal plums which deserve to be better known. All the music given to Aithra is attractive and brilliant. Helen herself, immortalizing elements of Maria Jeritza and Elisabeth Schumann, is a fully realized creation, warm, unpredictable and sensuous; her duet with Aithra is an example of Strauss's skill in blending two types of soprano. Menelaus is a *Heldentenor* role of considerably greater interest than Bacchus in *Ariadne*; indeed, Strauss projects Helen and Menelaus as believable human characters far more successfully than he does Bacchus and Ariadne, even when the words they sing are equally portentous. Their duets in both acts are melodically inspired. I cannot agree that Strauss's invention in this opera is tired and tame; time and again he pulls his librettist's chestnuts out of the fire with a burst of fecund imaginative zeal, such as the glowing theme which dominates the beautiful scene of Helen's awakening (Ex. 20).

Throughout, the orchestration is rich and apposite without becoming fulsome, reflecting a leaner harmonic style of sometimes diamond-like hardness. Helen's great outburst in Act II, 'Zweite Brautnacht', is

Ex. 20

another superb example of Straussian cantilena for a great soprano, and her scene with Da-ud has a tenderness which says much for Strauss's sheer determination to win some kind of dividend from the characters with which Hofmannsthal had landed him. In his memoirs Fritz Busch recounts how, when Strauss played *Die ägyptische Helena* to him at Garmisch, he told him he thought Da-ud's song was 'cheap' and that he ought to weigh such inspirations more discreetly. Strauss was not offended and repeated the criticism with relish to Pauline. He then said: 'That's what's wanted for the servant girls. The general public wouldn't go to *Tannhäuser* if it didn't contain "O du mein holder Abendstern" or to *Walküre* without "Winterstürme". Well, well, that's what they want.' There is still a future for this opera, if the right producer and the finest singers can be engaged for it. It is not a repertory piece; it is a twenti-eth-century vocal equivalent of a Bellini opera, strictly reserved for the best.

It would have been sad if the famous collaboration had ended with so seriously flawed an opera as *Die ägyptische Helena*. But in *Arabella* the two men again found a subject with which each was equally at ease. Strauss had kept asking for a second *Der Rosenkavalier*, had kept hint-ing at his Offenbach tendencies. His contempt for Lehár perhaps masked envy of that composer's success with subjects for which he himself yearned. He was temperamentally attuned to the characters of *Arabella*, odd bunch that they are. Here, at last, after the mythological and mys-tical fairy-tales, was a love-story involving fairly ordinary human beings in Vienna, misunderstandings, renunciations and reconciliation. Here was a heroine compounded of elements of the Marschallin and Sophie, in love with one of the oddest 'heroes' in opera but a hero who had to be a baritone. Mandryka, the wealthy, unsophisticaed Croatian landowner, is the major difficulty in casting *Arabella*, for he must not only be a fine singer but of impressive physical size.

Hofmannsthal, too, regained his fluency in writing this unimposing libretto. It is direct, affecting, free from pretentiousness. He acquiesced much more gracefully in Strauss's requests for changes, all of them directed to making the work theatrically effective. In spite of his dislike of its subject, Hofmannsthal had been impressed by *Intermezzo* when he saw it, and in *Arabella* he gave Strauss similar opportunities for *par-lando* dialogue and for further exercise of his gift for naturalism. There is bound to be a permanent question-mark over the finished result, since there would have been many more changes had Hofmannsthal lived. To that extent, *Arabella* is an incomplete work, falling short of what it might have achieved but still achieving much. A second *Der Rosenkavalier*? It was intended to appeal to the same kind of audience for much the same reasons, and there are obvious superficial resem-blances. But the label adversely affected the acceptance of the opera by the public for at least twenty years, until a series of performances with such singers as Lisa Della Casa, Dietrich Fischer-Dieskau and George London revealed its individual virtues.

In *Arabella* Strauss's orchestra makes some of the most erotic and euphonious sounds to be heard in any of his stage-works. The scoring has none of the ornate splendour of *Der Rosenkavalier*, little of its glittering rococo decoration and underlining of every movement on stage. It abounds in lyrical thirds and sixths, but it is, for all its fulsome tendencies, a slimmer, more transparent score than *Der Rosenkavalier*, showing the economic mastery which came with experience. The flavour of Slavonic folk-music in Mandryka's part is both subtle and piquant. This folk element in the Vienna context is another pointer to the close connection of the work with operetta—a genre in which Strauss obviously had a deep interest. Parts of *Die ägyptische Helena* have a similar tendency; and in the second act of *Arabella*, dramatically broken-backed as it is, Strauss aimed for a *Fledermaus*-like variety, with waltzes, with the coloratura polka song by the cabmen's mascot Milli, and with Mandryka's drunken insistence on Moët et Chandon for the whole company. Not to mention that the plot hinges on the fact that Arabella's sister Zdenka has been brought up as a boy and that the exposure of this masquerade brings a happy ending.

But while Strauss could pose as an operetta composer with the minor characters, such as Arabella's feckless parents, he could not maintain it with his heroine, and it is the music he wrote for Arabella and Mandryka that gives this enchanting opera its claim on our affection. Arabella's first aria, in which she examines her attitude to men and proclaims her certainty that she will know the right one—*der Richtige*—when he arrives, is on a similar level of inspiration to the Marschallin's soliloquy and evoked music of comparable grave beauty:

Ex. 21

Her long aria closing Act I is equally fine, and is notable for its use of a solo viola in the accompaniment to highlight significant emotional points. The Act II love-duet with Mandryka is Strauss at his most warm-hearted, responding with horns, strings and radiant writing for the voices to every prompting of some of Hofmannsthal's best lines. With this adorable music Strauss ensures that the audience care deeply about Arabella's future, and he composed a memorable and unusual finale, with his heroine descending a staircase offering to Mandryka a glass of water, in emulation of the Croatian village custom of which he has told her, whereby the village girls offer their chosen bridegrooms a glass of fresh water as a symbol of chastity. Sentimental, yes; dramatically effective, too; and a touching 'curtain' to the last Strauss-Hofmannsthal opera. Viorica Ursuleac, who created Arabella, told a significant story, of when she sang the role in Amsterdam with Strauss conducting. After the last rehearsal she told him: 'If you conduct the last scene at the same pace this evening, I shall have to gallop down the stairs with my glass of water. It's such a pity when the music is so lovely. All he did was growl: "Oh, those six-four chords!"—and then, in the evening, he took the conclusion with a poetic breadth.' He told Stefan Zweig in 1934 that the success of *Arabella* had surprised him:

> Despite all one knows about the art, one knows least what one is really capable of doing. One is in God's hand . . . What suit me best, South German bourgeois that I am, are sentimental jobs; but such bullseyes as the *Arabella* duet and the *Rosenkavalier* trio don't happen every day. Must one become seventy to recognize that one's greatest strength lies in creating kitsch?[8]

Clemens Krauss was always irritated by the character of the Fiakermilli and her yodelling, and persistently nagged Strauss to downgrade her contribution. For a Munich production in 1939, Strauss agreed to the running-together of Acts II and III by means of a cut in the Fiakermilli's part at the end of Act II and the deletion of the orchestral prelude to Act III. Later Krauss tried to obtain new music for the Fiakermilli for a Salzburg production in 1942 but did not succeed. Many conductors make further cuts in Act III, to no good purpose, and it is rare to hear the opera performed complete in either the three-act original or two-act 'Munich' versions.

Arabella is not profound, but it is splendid entertainment, of more than ephemeral value because of the musical craftsmanship with which it is put together and because it contains three singing roles of exceptional attractiveness. Neville Cardus, writing in the 1930s, cited *Arabella* as proof that 'Strauss was still the best composer of a Strauss opera'. It was a witty remark, but wise too. There is no sign of artistic sclerosis in this score. It looks back rather than forward, but that is irrelevant to its artistic merit. It is fresh, inventive and tender. The elegiac note is entirely missing; clearly he still had more to say. He would have to say it without Hofmannsthal. 'He had a simply astounding flair for the sort of material which, in given circumstances, corresponded to my needs,' Strauss said in 1935. It was a noble tribute, but only partly true, as the careful reservation of 'given circumstances' implies. He wanted to believe it himself, but the zest with which he tackled his first non-Hofmannsthal opera since *Intermezzo* belied him.

[8] K. Wilhelm, *Richard Strauss: an Intimate Portrait*, op. cit., pp. 213–14.

18

The operas (2)

Die schweigsame Frau, Friedenstag

The extravagant praise Strauss lavished on Zweig's libretto for *Die schweigsame Frau* is understandable only in the context of Hofmannsthal's death. That Strauss sincerely mourned his partner is not in doubt; but neither is his sigh of relief at release from some of the rigours of working with him. By a fluke, Zweig, in picking on Jonson's *The Silent Woman* and moving the action forward to the eighteenth century, had found the subject which Strauss had been trying for years to coax from Hofmannsthal, a comedy which would enable him again to indulge the farcical aspects of *Der Rosenkavalier* (having re-explored the lyrical aspects in *Arabella*) and to compose in the successful *parlando* style of the Prologue to *Ariadne*. Moreover, the contrived artificialities of Jonson's plot lent themselves to Strauss's innate Bavarian gift for parody and pastiche—and, of course, the subject provided yet another libretto about marriage. Pauline, one feels, is always waiting in the wings.

So in the London of *Die schweigsame Frau* we meet again a company of actors and singers (a chance for anachronistic quotations from Verdi and Strauss himself). The principal soprano, Aminta, is another manifestation of Zerbinetta, a tender heart behind the trills. The plot to trick the rich old sea-dog, Sir Morosus, who abominates noise, into a mock marriage with a silent woman who will turn into a virago and thus teach him how much happier he is by staying single, is another chance to capitalize on the kind of music which illustrated the discomfiture of Baron Ochs. The third act opens with an orchestral fugato, just as in *Der Rosenkavalier*, and the curtain rises, as in the earlier opera, on a scene of intense activity, with workmen knocking nails into the wall and Aminta, like Oktavian, supervising and instructing.

Strauss's gradual reversion to a 'number' opera, detectable in *Die ägyptische Helena* and *Arabella*, took full effect in *Die schweigsame Frau*, which is pastiche Italian *opera buffa* leavened by Strauss's passionate admiration for Verdi's *Falstaff*. A pot-pourri Rossinian overture; plentiful spoken dialogue; a canzona sung by the Figaro-like Barber, Schneidebart; septet, sextet, nonet; a music-lesson (of a Straussified quotation from Monteverdi's *L'Incoronazione di Poppea*)—there is no question of the kind of comparison Strauss is inviting. He scores for a large orchestra (ninety-five players) but rarely uses it at full strength.

The opera is certainly merry and bright, with not a link of Wagnerian chain-mail left. In the Act I duet for Aminta and Henry; in the ensemble after the 'wedding'; in the poetic curtain to Act II when Morosus, off-stage, falls asleep on a low D flat while Aminta, on-stage with her husband Henry, sings a top D flat; and in the 'reconciliation' scene of Act III, Strauss achieves a blend of Mozartian grace, Rossinian sparkle and the style of his own Lieder which rises above mere pastiche. Yet the work fails to deserve a place among the endearing comic operas because too much of the melodic invention is Strauss below his best, not because he was taking it easy but because he was trying too hard. If he had maintained the quality of the examples I have just cited, the contrived twists of the plot would not matter. The last scene of all, a quiet epilogue in which Morosus sings contentedly such Straussian aphorisms as 'How beautiful life is . . . when one is no fool and knows how to live', fails to stir an audience to its depths because the music is predictable, not memorable. (But Strauss thought it 'most successful'.)

Also, Strauss's besetting sin of going on too long, of extracting more than enough from every situation, shows as a worse fault in comedy than in some of the weightier works. Karl Böhm, the first conductor of the opera, showed that it can be cut without too much major damage; and if the stage production has plenty of pace and freedom, then *Die schweigsame Frau* can make a delightful evening. It will never replace its models, but it contains too much that is good and brilliant to vanish completely from the stage. In it Strauss marked time, looking over his shoulder at the past, before he turned to the creation of his four last operatic masterpieces.

His next opera, the eighty-minute one-act *Friedenstag*, is his most austere. It is also the final answer by Richard Strauss the artist to critics of his attitude to the politics of his time. *Friedenstag* is an anti-war opera, and the monolithic emotional strength of the music is testimony to its utter sincerity. In several ways it is unique among Strauss's mature operas: in its atmosphere of bleak hopelessness, in the important role given to the chorus, in the total absence of self-consciously 'beautiful' episodes, and in the predominance of male voices. Gregor's libretto never achieves the unstilted realism Strauss sought, but it is serviceable, despite its major flaw: that the proclamation of peace comes all too pat, robbing the work of a central dramatic climax.

Although Strauss expressed doubts about his suitability for this subject—'too wearisome a task'—the result was one of his most original works, constructed in order to exploit every possibility of contrast— the Piedmontese youth's Italian folk-song following the gloomy and despairing opening choruses, with their funeral-march ground-bass, and preceding the extraordinary, gaunt music of the starving townspeople's wailing cries of 'Hunger' and 'Bread'. Equally remarkable is the stingingly satirical music in which the Commandant recalls the battle of Magdeburg and inquires from a gunner and rifleman if they will share his decision to stay in the fortress when he blows it up. The deliberate use here of a popular style is extremely effective. This scene, for all its ambivalence—are we meant to sympathize or despise?—is a richer musical experience than the subsequent familiar Strauss cantilena of the long aria for the Commandant's wife Maria. It is a noble aria, but its insistence on the sun as the symbol of hope immediately raises the spectre of *Fidelio* which haunts the whole score.

The loyal and loving wife; the besieged townspeople, in effect prisoners; the noble and resolute Commandant; the bugle-call at a climacteric; and the final cantata-like hymn to peace and friendship—can there be any doubt that Strauss had *Fidelio* in mind and was trying to convey its message not in any vain spirit of rivalry but because he believed that a twentieth-century musician should make the same plea? Strauss could not and does not attain the sublimity of Beethoven—his C major finale is rhetoric, not oratory—but if, because *Fidelio* exists, *Friedenstag* is consigned to oblivion, musical injustice will have been done. For though the similarities between the two works are striking, it is the differences which we should study and cherish.

Few passages in Strauss are more impressive than the scene in which the fortress awaits renewed assault but, instead of cannon-shells there comes the sound of bells, silent for years, pealing the news of peace, and this strong theme thrusts upwards repeatedly on the cellos:

Ex. 22

When the enemy (Holsteiner) troops arrive they do so to a brazen military march, brutal and banal, a Mahlerian touch which was obviously intended as further condemnation by Strauss of militaristic tendencies. The bass to the march is the Lutheran choral *Ein' feste Burg*, for Strauss included the cruelties committed in the name of religions, ecclesiastical and ideological, in his general protest (see Ex. 23).

If Strauss had produced music of this intensity for the final section of the work, there would be no need for reservations in discussing this impressive opera. Yet despite the lameness of much of the final paean, there are ferocity and gritty harmonic strength in the writing for the chorus and in the orchestral coda that keep the emotional temperature high.

Ex. 23

Daphne, Die Liebe der Danae

For his next two operas Strauss returned to the world of mythology which Hofmannsthal had considered the most fruitful. It is ironically amusing to find him, during the compilation of the libretto for *Daphne*, prodding and goading Gregor in much the same direction as his dead collaborator had led him. Notwithstanding the troublesome gestation of this one-act opera, the result was the most consistently lyrical and beautiful of all his stage works. It was as if the broad and flashing humour of *Die schweigsame Frau* and the sombre starkness of *Friedenstag* had resolved themselves into this serene but fervent style. One has only to consider that between his seventieth birthday in 1934 and the end of 1937 Strauss wrote three such different operas as his *opera buffa*, his political testament and his celebration of pastoral love and Hellenism, each with a contrasted harmonic and melodic vocabulary, to realize the wrongheadedness of the view that he was either an extinct volcano or, at best, a garrulous old man composing from memory. *Daphne* by itself is sufficient proof that his genius was burning strongly with a new and thermal glow.

Within the framework of the familiar classical legend of humankind identified with the deities and with nature, Strauss received the kind of verbal stimulus which released the best music in him. As he told Zweig when criticizing Gregor's first draft, 'instead of remaining that boring virgin, Daphne should fall in love with them both, the god [Apollo] and the man [Leukippos]'. The love interest was one strong stimulus; others were the descriptive elements, the storm, the birds, butterflies and trees, nightfall, moonlight, the sexual act, ritual dances, death—all might have been designed for a Strauss festival.

The instrumental prelude is a microcosm of the whole seraphic work, a succession of inspired melodic fragments for woodwind, first the oboe, followed by basset-horn, clarinet, flute, cor anglais. The principal theme:

Ex. 24

comes to the ear like an ethereal echo from the *Heldenleben* coda, and the prelude as a whole is a foretaste of the mellow yet refined instrumental style of Strauss's last years. The Oboe Concerto, the Duett-Concertino and similar works are side-shoots from Daphne's laurel. It is this cohesive and organic mastery which gives *Daphne* its high place in Strauss's output; it is at once a consummation and a new beginning. Let those who wish examine the libretto's symbolism and analyse Gregor's adaptation of a favourite myth: the music disarms criticism by its flow of pellucid vocal melody set against an orchestral background of delicacy, strength and kaleidoscopic detail.

In the title-role Strauss created his finest part for soprano voice since the great roles in *Der Rosenkavalier*. The Composer, Zerbinetta, the Empress, Helen, Aminta and Arabella all have wonderful opportunities, but none can compare with the loveliness of Daphne. The brilliance of Zerbinetta, the innocence of Sophie, the radiance of Arabella are combined into a role to which Strauss additionally imparts an air of innocent unreality in keeping with the elusive nature of Daphne's character. With neither a superfluous bar nor a momentary suggestion of monotony, Strauss gives his soprano a seemingly endless stream of melismatic song. It is a long role but rewarding in every way. Her first aria, in which she identifies herself with nature and apostrophizes her laurel tree, contains the first hints of the marvellous final transformation scene. The strings are divided into several parts, a solo violin twining with the voice while solo woodwind and strings create a mosaic of the pastoral themes associated with Daphne. This silvery sound is unequalled in any other Strauss opera.

Strauss took immense care with instrumental and vocal timbres in *Daphne*. The part of Daphne's Erda-like mother Gaea is given to a contralto capable of a low E flat who is accompanied by the dark colours of the orchestra. Peneios, Daphne's father, is a bass but her lovers, Leukippos and Apollo, are both tenors. This was obviously a deliberate risk on Strauss's part to ensure that high vocal tones should predominate—and his experiences with his Vienna singers in the 1920s seemed to have given him more confidence in tenors as a breed. So well did he understand voices that there can be no confusion between the boyish Leukippos and the heroic Apollo. These are well-delineated roles, but all are subservient to the central superb creation, Daphne herself, in whom Strauss found yet another example of his favourite theme of metamorphosis: nymph into woman into tree, the whole opera designed in a great curve, from darkness to light and back to darkness, the leitmotifs woven into a symphonic structure even more subtly than in *Salome* and *Elektra*.

Like *Salome* and *Elektra*, the opera has its big set-pieces: the Dionysiac feast, the superb duet for Apollo and Daphne before their night of love, the lament for Leukippos and the final F sharp major transformation scene, a miracle of orchestral polyphony leading to Daphne's wordless vocalise as the music sinks back into the quietness from which it grew. There are tenderness, eroticism, grandeur and mystery in this opera, but gone is the swaggering, eight-horn hero of another age, gone is the playboy of the orchestra, showing off with arrogant virtuosity. All is pure music, suffused with the Apollonian warmth of the sunlight which Strauss always needed if he was to work at his best. In *Daphne* he combined successfully at last the chamber-music intimacy of the best of *Ariadne* with the poetic eloquence of the best of *Die Frau ohne Schatten*, and he used a large orchestra with as sure a stylistic touch as he had displayed since *Don Quixote*. Krauss thought the work was too short and wanted Strauss to expand it. Such a course would have been disastrous. *Daphne* shares with *Till Eulenspiegel* the rare distinction among Strauss scores of being perfectly proportioned. For that reason, apart from its intrinsic beauty, it has a special and exclusive place in the hearts of many Strauss enthusiasts.

So, for the comparative few who know it, has *Die Liebe der Danae*, the 'cheerful mythology in three acts' in which Strauss returned to the draft of the 'light, witty' comic opera on a subject which Hofmannsthal had written for him in 1920. The completed opera (1940) may be said to have had five librettists—Hofmannsthal, Zweig, Gregor, Krauss and Strauss himself—and the number of fingers in the pie shows in the dramatic weakness and inconsistencies which no producer, however skilful, can disguise.

Strauss had a strong affection for *Danae*. Pointing heavenwards after the 1944 rehearsal he said: 'When I arrive there I hope I'll be forgiven if I take this with me.' He knew there were uneven passages—which he blamed on the text—but some of it, he thought, was as good as anything he had written. When it was performed at Salzburg in 1952 and in London in 1953, the tendency of criticism was to call it 'the mixture as before', and so, like his other *bel canto* opera, *Die ägyptische Helena*, it was neglected for a generation. Recently, however, some revivals have converted even some dyed-in-the-wool doubters to the belief that *Danae* is an attractive and stageworthy opera containing many of the same lyrical qualities which are rightly admired in *Capriccio*.

The thesis is that love is more important than riches. Again, it is an opera about marriage. Strauss's remark to Bahr in 1916 that he was planning a cycle of five operas about his wife was to some extent fulfilled since, after *Intermezzo*, marriage is also the subject of *Die ägyptische Helena*, *Die schweigsame Frau*, *Arabella*, and *Die Liebe der Danae*. Hofmannsthal combined the story of Danae, to whom Jupiter came in the form of golden rain, with that of King Midas, who turned everything he touched to gold. Gregor introduced Jupiter himself as a main character, thus setting himself intractable problems. Those who wish to study the genesis of the libretto will find an excellent account in Del Mar's Volume III, pp. 121–31. What concerns us here is that, notwithstanding its defects, the text gave Strauss what he wanted for an opera which nearly rivals *Die Frau ohne Schatten* in its complexities as a stage-picture. It is perhaps no coincidence that he escaped from the realities of the outbreak of war in 1914 and 1939 into the composition of operas in which myth and metamorphosis play so big a part.

'Note-spinning' is the pejorative term often applied to Strauss (by himself, among others). But there is no harm in note-spinning if what is spun makes a good pattern and has a firmly woven texture. There is endless fascination to be discovered in Strauss's re-exploration of himself in his last great period, in the consistently more subtle approach to his material, in the re-working of all his familiar harmonic devices, in the mining of new and valuable matter from an old but by no means worked-out seam. In *Die Liebe der Danae*, the old hand has lost none of its cunning but has gained a good deal in economical practice. The autumnal melodic beauty which distinguishes *Daphne* is also marked in *Danae*, notably in the handling of the orchestra. Depicting golden rain must obviously have seemed child's-play to Strauss, but he does it as no one else could, with harps, piano, flutes and muted strings. Elsewhere the orchestra is used either with entrancing delicacy or as a gorgeously rich and sonorous, but never mushy or sickly, backcloth. The symphonic interlude in Act III known as Jupiter's Renunciation ranks with the Barak interlude in *Die Frau ohne Schatten* for sheer nobility and pathos, and the orchestra is left, as in *Daphne*, to provide the emotional climax at the end of the opera.

But this is a singers' opera. Jupiter is a marvellous part, giving the baritone a Verdian range of expressiveness, from majestic wrath in Act I *via* the paternal Wotan-like nobility of Act II to the final duet with Danae which Strauss modelled on Hans Sachs—and these Wagnerian references are clues to the richness of much of the vocal writing. There are also excellent lighter scenes for Jupiter and the tenor, Midas, and for Jupiter and his four ex-mistresses to whom, in differing disguises, he has previously come as seducer.

Danae is one of the most attractive of the soprano roles created for Viorica Ursuleac, exploiting soft high *pianissimo* notes and considerable tenderness of expression in addition to the usual broad-spanned and powerful cantilena. Her big opportunities come in Act III—which was effectively created by Strauss and Clemens Krauss in order to give the singers and the composer an opportunity for a more human and elegiac mood—with an impressive solo aria and the closing duet, but she has earlier had memorable duets with her maid Xanthe in Act I and with Midas in Act I and in Act III when, like Helen and Menelaus, they are in the desert.

'My last acknowledgement to Greece, and the final meeting of German music with the Grecian spirit', Strauss said in 1944, not knowing that the future would bring Henze's *The Bassarids* to continue his tradition. He knew how much depended in *Danae* on brilliant staging—which is only to repeat that his operas can never be done on the cheap or by any but the best singers. As Strauss once told Zweig: 'I have never had the talent to write what can be performed easily; that is the special gift of inferior musicians.' The more I listen to *Die Liebe der Danae*, the more beautiful and successful it seems to me to be. I cannot agree with Del Mar that it 'does not rate a very high place' in Strauss's output. Anyone can see that the opera follows the usual Strauss formula for success, but that hardly matters if it succeeds. From the pungent chorus for the creditors with which it opens to its serene and warming closing chords, *Die Liebe der Danae* is music to delight the ear and uplift the spirit.

Capriccio

In his last opera, *Capriccio*, Strauss set out to please himself and ended by pleasing everybody more, perhaps, than by any of his operas except *Rosenkavalier*. The popular success of a work which its composer at first believed—until he saw it on the stage—should be reserved for connoisseurs is an encouraging commentary on the advance in the public's taste for opera, and an enlightening commentary on the vagaries of creativeness, for the opera—designated a 'conversation piece'—might easily be thought to be too undramatic and specialized to have much general appeal.

Ostensibly the work is a debate about the relative importance of words and music in opera, and this rather academic subject—which fascinated Strauss all his life—is given dramatic meaning by the device of introducing a poet (Olivier) and a composer (Flamand) who are both in love with a young widow, the Countess Madeleine. The scene is a château near Paris in 1770. Artists are gathered there to plan an entertainment in honour of her birthday. The impresario La Roche outlines his plans for this festivity, which are derided by Flamand and Olivier.

To reconcile them he suggests they should collaborate in an opera. Various subjects are dismissed and Madeleine's brother suggests that they should set the events they have just been experiencing. (This, in fact, was Strauss's idea.[1]) All leave for Paris, and Madeleine learns that both poet and composer will visit her next day to learn which of them she chooses—and, symbolically, how the opera is to end. Earlier Olivier has read a sonnet he has written about her, and Flamand has improvised a tune for it. Now, in the moonlight, she sings this to herself and finds she cannot separate words and music. The question is unanswered, but the audience are seeing and hearing the opera she has commanded— *moto perpetuo.*

It could have proved disastrous, but Clemens Krauss, much aided by Strauss, provided a libretto which is better than any of those in which Hofmannsthal attempted to mate abstract theories and their symbolized characterizations. Next to *Der Rosenkavalier* and *Intermezzo*, Strauss never had a better libretto. But the miraculous feat was that it provided him with his best opportunity for years to compose what he did best— autobiography. For this opera is really about Richard Strauss's way of writing operas; one feels that its seed had been in him, fertilizing slowly with the long years of experience, since his stage-struck youth at the Meiningen court. Elements of pastiche, quotations, allusive asides, nostalgic tenderness, a beautiful aristocratic soprano role (one-third *Figaro*-Countess, one-third *Rosenkavalier*-Marschallin, one-third Lieder-singer), an impresario with characteristics of Reinhardt and Hofmannsthal, and of Strauss himself, the theatrical ambience of the Prologue to *Ariadne*—one can almost picture the glee with which the seventy-six-year-old wizard of Garmisch shut himself into his study, shut out the distractions of a European war, and lost himself in setting a text which demanded all the lyricism and wit of *Daphne* and *Die Liebe der Danae* but catered for them so much better.

The opera is designed in the arch-like structure which Strauss handled so well—an instrumental introduction and a long final monologue enclosing a series of 'numbers', including three dances (a chance for some Couperin pastiche), a mock Italian love-duet (a chance to emulate a *Rosenkavalier* 'hit'), a fugal Laughing and Quarrelling Octet in which the ensemble-writing sparkles and bubbles as it never quite did in *Die schweigsame Frau*. In all these he can flaunt his time-travelling mastery of styles with spontaneous ease, and he recaptures the wit and grace of *Le Bourgeois Gentilhomme* and the relaxed sophistication of the *Ariadne* prologue. As for quotations, he has a field-day: references, all prompted by the historical allusions in the text, to Gluck's *Iphigénie en Aulide*, to Rameau's *Les Indes galantes*, to *Tristan*, to Rossini's *L'Italiana in Algeri* and to several of his own works including *Danae, Don Quixote, Ariadne*

---

[1] La Roche had asked for an opera about real people instead of mythological heroes, just as Strauss had pleaded with Hofmannsthal for a contemporary subject.

and *Daphne*. (Originally Krauss intended that the opera planned by Flamand and Olivier should be *Daphne*, to be performed as part two of a double bill, but fortunately Strauss had the better idea of making *Capriccio* itself the opera.) The most significant self-quotation, though, is of the pianoforte interlude from his 1920 song-cycle *Krämerspiegel* (Shopkeeper's Mirror), a beautiful melody which becomes the basis in *Capriccio* of the lovely Moonlight Music:

Ex. 25

This stroke of genius at once gave *Capriccio* its unique feature. It became a mirror-image of itself; and the mirror became its symbol. The story goes that Strauss himself had forgotten this melody and that his son Franz reminded him of it, saying that so beautiful a tune should not be buried in a song-cycle which had only been privately printed. (Because its twelve songs satirized the leading German publishers of the day, with whom Strauss was in dispute over performing rights, there was then no chance of Bote & Bock or anyone else publishing it.)

It is hard to believe that Strauss had forgotten the melody, since his memory for music, whether written by other composers or himself, was phenomenal. In this case, too, the melody was singularly apt for its purpose in *Capriccio* in which Strauss, with the lightest of touch, was intent on projecting a detached view of opera as both sublime and ridiculous. The melody first insinuates itself into the texture in the orchestra when the Countess sings that 'the theatre unveils for us the secrets of reality. In its magic mirror (*Zauberspiegel*) we discover ourselves. The theatre moves us because it is the symbol of reality.' At the word 'mirror', the 1918 melody is first heard. Yet it does not flower fully until a few pages later when the Count sings 'An opera is an absurd thing' and goes on to mock operatic conventions—'a murder plot is hatched in song . . . suicide takes place to music'. Strauss uses his melody, therefore, for the dual purpose of underlining opera's magic power to disclose reality and its absurdity. This ambivalence was present, too, in *Krämerspiegel*, where the melody occurs twice. In the eighth song, it forms the long piano prelude and postlude to the words 'Art is threatened by businessmen, that's the trouble. They bring death to music and transfiguration to themselves.' Even more significantly, in the last song, it is reintroduced at the word 'Eulenspiegel' ('Owl-mirror') when the singer asks who will stop these merchants' evil ways and answers 'One man found a jester's way to do it—Till Eulenspiegel'. The melody, we discover, is a sublimated variant of Till's principal motif.

Nothing is more typical of Strauss's genius at its ripest than the combination of jesting and tenderness which makes *Till Eulenspiegel* the most endearing of his tone-poems. *Capriccio* too is suffused with a comparable blend of poetry and humour in perfect, symphonic equipoise. Strauss liked to point out that an unusual feature of his tone-poem *Tod und Verklärung* was that its main theme, its point of culmination, was not stated until the middle of the work. He repeated this stylistic *coup* in *Capriccio* with the *Krämerspiegel* melody.

The superb Sextet for strings which opens the opera (and by a brilliant stroke, when the curtain rises, is found to be the music to which the Countess and her guests are listening) is a lyrical effusion as inspired as that which opens *Daphne*, but where that was the essence of pastoral peace, this seems to be an epitome of the domestic delights of chamber-music. The felicity of the scoring throughout the opera is flawless; not a note too many, not a sound misjudged, not a word which cannot be clearly heard, yet with no loss of richness, warmth and harmonic dexterity. The setting of the Love Sonnet is exquisite, cool rather than impassioned, but as fine a tenor aria as Strauss wrote, accompanied by harpsichord and very quiet strings.

Thirty years earlier Strauss had told Hofmannsthal: 'It is at the conclusion that the musician can achieve his best and supreme effects.' He had not always lived up to this, perhaps operatically only in *Der Rosenkavalier*, *Arabella*, *Daphne* and *Die Liebe der Danae*. Most of all in *Capriccio*, and how marvellously he leads to it. The subsidiary characters leave for Paris, each making a subtly delineated farewell. There follows the short scene for the eight male servants who discuss what has been happening, in a charmingly light, scherzo-like ensemble. As the salon darkens and the major-domo begins to prepare for supper, he hears a voice—this is Monsieur Taupe, the prompter, who has slept throughout the rehearsal in the theatre, as the actress Clairon has already told us. He, too, needs to go back to Paris. The major-domo questions and flatters him, to music that is strange and shadowy. With these two scenes Strauss provides the contrast for his skilfully contrived finale.

As the major-domo leads the prompter away, horns sound distant Cs and the gorgeous interlude begins, with the *Krämerspiegel* melody as its theme. It is moonlight and the Countess appears, dressed for supper. So begins Strauss's operatic *Abschied*, his greatest soprano monologue. She sings the sonnet and looks into the mirror as she tries to solve her dilemma: 'What says your heart? . . . You, mirror, showing me a lovelorn Madeleine—ah, please advise me. Help me to find the ending for our opera. Can I find one that is not trivial?' Strauss, music's incomparable jester-poet, then shows beyond any argument where his sympathies lay. For the last words in the opera could not be more trivial: 'My lady, your supper is served'. But they are set to an unforgettably touching, lyrical phrase, prolonged by the orchestra. A horn sounds twice, echoing Madeleine's question, and two clipped chords bring down the curtain. The magic mirror has given its reply, not in words but in music.

Capriccio is Strauss's most enchanting opera, it is also the nearest he came to unflawed perfection in a work of art. It is an anthology or a synthesis of all that he did best, and it is as if he has put his creative process into a crucible, refining away coarseness, bombast, and excess of vitality. It is a testament of all the strongest elements in its creator's make-up, yet it succeeds in spite of a certain weariness in the invention which becomes a positive advantage. For example, the leitmotifs which represent the four characters symbolic of the argument between words and music, Flamand and Olivier, the Count and the Countess, are fairly nondescript and scrappy, but Strauss, by sleight-of-hand worthy of a champion skat-player, shuffles them into a continuously interesting texture. When they emerge in the full glory of his autumnal orchestra during the instrumental interludes in Madeleine's final aria, we realize that he has shed all traces of Wagnerian use of leitmotif and evolved at long last his own more subtle and delicate allusive method. How apt, too, that his last opera, stylistic prelude to the relaxed transparency of his final instrumental works, should also epitomize in its leading role the vocal and physical beauty of the great sopranos, past, present and future, for whom his operas are a *raison d'être*.

Ironically, too, *Capriccio* is irrelevant to the development of music. It is a mixture of eighteenth- and nineteenth-century styles written in the twentieth century. When La Roche says: 'I guard the old, patiently awaiting the fruitful new, expecting the works of genius of our time! But where are they? I cannot find them,' Strauss himself is addressing us. He knew that genius chooses its time and medium and he must have known that in *Capriccio* it had again chosen him. In a world gone mad, Strauss deliberately showed in *Daphne*, *Danae* and *Capriccio* that he regarded himself as the lone upholder of the true German spirit both in art and in life. It has often been asked how Strauss could have written an opera like *Capriccio* in the midst of a terrible world war, with Dachau only a few miles along the road from Munich. There is the theory that he was emigrating 'inwardly' from the horrors of contemporary life. But there are also subtle allusions in the text to current events. La Roche says: 'Your loud veto will never deter me . . . Although the masks are discarded, grimaces greet you, not human dignity! You despise these lewd doings, yet you suffer them. You share the guilt because of your silence. Don't aim your indignant shouting at me . . . the art of our fathers lies in my trust.' The words of Ernst Jürger may be applied to Strauss and *Capriccio*: 'Art is the hot-house of past times—one wanders as if in a winter garden or in salons where palms bloom. This cannot be criticised, for the horrors of destruction are too powerful, too awful, therefore the will to rescue even a shadow is perfectly understandable.'

So he completed his fifteen operas, a contribution to the lyric theatre which ranks him among the six greatest opera-composers. Yet more than half of them are rarely performed, and most of that half are still undervalued. If, before the end of the twentieth century, *Daphne*, *Friedenstag* and *Die Liebe der Danae* can be rehabilitated as *Die Frau ohne Schatten* has been, then the general appreciation of Strauss will be more proportionate to the magnitude of his achievements. Far from declining since 1918, he steadily and patiently, with varying degrees of success, explored diverse subjects for opera without needing a new musical vocabulary or system of composition. He believed that his operas would retain 'an honourable place in world history in relation to all earlier creations for the theatre (Wagner excepted) at "the end of the rainbow"'. It is a belief that the passage of time is showing to be abundantly justified.

19

Ballets and other orchestral works

Interspersed among Strauss's operas between 1903 and 1940 are several instrumental compositions, of which the largest in scale and conception was the Diaghilev ballet score *Josephslegende*. A major point about Strauss, affecting both his music and his attitude to politics, is that he was, and essentially remained, a German Court composer of the old school. He could turn his hand to anything with the certainty that the result would never be less than competent—and, when his heart was in it, very much more. He undertook *Josephslegende* against his inclination, but was urged on by Hofmannsthal's hectoring, the attraction of a large fee, and the undoubted prestige of composing for Diaghilev. The resulting score is better than is usually suggested. If ever a work was a symptom of its period, this is. The scenario is a pretentious mixture of erotic, sadistic and religious symbolism with none of the distinction of *Salome*; the Biblical story, translated into a sixteenth-century Venetian setting of the most lavish kind, is typical of the extravagance of the Russian Ballet at its zenith; the vast orchestra, with threefold division of the violins as in *Elektra*, a double-bass clarinet in the woodwind, and exotic percussion, belongs to the era of Stravinsky's *Le Sacre du printemps*.

What saves the work is the quality of Strauss's music. After a few initial set dances, he abandoned the traditional ballet design and turned the score into another symphonic poem, with a waltz-tune, several splendid 'effects' and a rapturous episode of two-part polyphony melodizing round the tonic key in the style of the great orchestral passage in *Die Frau ohne Schatten*, to which the work as a whole is closely related. The music for Joseph, which Strauss eventually borrowed from his discarded ballet *Kythere*, is choreographically effective; and indeed much of the score—notably the 'mourning' scene—sounds today like high-quality film music written before its time. Associations with Hollywood inevitably now cling to Strauss's harp-celesta-pianoforte tinklings which depict Joseph's innocence and purity and which lead, in the finale, to a peroration indicative of Strauss's inability to invoke celestial visions of a spiritual kind—one has to go to Vaughan Williams's *Job* to find music to match this kind of theme. Yet long stretches of the score are beautiful and imaginative; to attribute its comparative failure, as Norman Del Mar does, to 'mental lethargy' is too sweeping. Perhaps Strauss would have been wiser to refuse the commission, but he gave the subject more than it deserved.

The scoring entitles him to be regarded as one of the leading trade unionists of orchestral music—providing plenty of jobs for the boys. Not only is the double-bass clarinet employed (when Potiphar's Wife creeps in to find Joseph asleep), but four harps, four pairs of castanets, a wind-machine and much besides are demanded. He was almost as extravagant in his next ballet, *Schlagobers* (*Whipped Cream*) of 1922—his attempt to create a *Casse-Noisette* out of Viennese confectionery (the characters have names like the Coffee Prince, Princess Prâlinée and Marianne Chartreuse) and to write a conventional ballet of set numbers. In 1924 he made the remark—which I have taken as motto for this book—about wanting to write the music he pleased in order 'to create joy'. Unfortunately, in indulging himself so wantonly, he failed to deliver the goods or, in this case, the goodies. Although the music comes nearer to the set pieces of traditional ballet than the scenario of *Josephslegende* allowed, one is conscious that Strauss was trying too hard to recapture a style which was wholly inappropriate to the circumstances of Viennese life at the time, when poverty and inflation were rife and few could afford whipped cream. Not that this would have mattered if the invention had been consistently inspired. There is some witty and delightful music in the score, but there are pedestrian passages too. One is driven to the conclusion that Strauss at his best was not a sugar-and-spice-and-all-things-nice composer. The success of *Der Rosenkavalier* lies in the fact that the icing on that great cake is hard and there is a bitter tang to its filling.

He recovered his form later in 1924 with the left-hand piano concerto written for Paul Wittgenstein to which he gave the cumbersome title *Parergon zur Symphonia Domestica*, a clue to the programmatic basis of the work: his son Franz (Bubi) had nearly died from typhus contracted on honeymoon in Egypt and the music reflects the deep anxiety Richard and Pauline underwent, followed by their relief. The anxiety is expressed at the start of the *Parergon* by a C sharp on muted brass which stabs and nags at the Child theme from *Domestica*, presented in F sharp minor in harmonies that toss and turn like a man in a fever. The atmosphere of gloom is extraordinarily vivid. Even the pianoforte's introductory flourishes are darkened by the spectral C sharp, and despite brilliant and stormy episodes for soloist and orchestra, it is a long time before the crisis is passed and a bassoon converts C sharp into the convalescent key of F major, while the clarinet plays a *gemütlich* theme (see Ex. 26).

The remainder of the work is a joyous *scherzando*, with waltz-like interpolations and something of the sparkle of the *Burleske*. Probably its form is against it, for two-handed pianists do not particularly relish

Ex. 26

playing a one-hand work, but the *Parergon* is such attractive music that it is a pity so few people know it. Wittgenstein, with (he said) the composer's approval, made various additions and alterations and recorded this version in 1959—an historical rarity.[1] In 1926, Strauss wrote a second work for him: symphonic studies in the form of a passacaglia called *Panathenäenzug* (Panathenaea was the ancient Greek festival procession in honour of Athene). This is in four sections—introduction, two interludes and coda—like Liszt's B minor sonata, and in the attractive slow section Strauss uses the lyra (a form of glockenspiel) with harp, celesta and the pianoforte to produce some magical sound-patterns. But the work is less compelling than the *Parergon*, though far from negligible.

In 1922–3 Strauss arranged several Couperin keyboard pieces for a Vienna ballet, later publishing it as an eight-movement *Tanzsuite*. To purists these arrangements, like Elgar's of Bach and Harty's of Handel, are no doubt insufferable. Strauss's small orchestra, with its succulent string tone, is a world away—despite the use of a harpsichord—from the pungent clarity of the originals. Yet his arrangements fail to hold the listener because they fall between two stools: they are neither sufficiently Straussified nor sufficiently pure. Stravinsky's *Pulcinella* is a masterpiece because every note is pure Stravinsky. The *Tanzsuite* has intermittent elegance and wit, but the general impression is of prolonged pious homage. In 1940–1 Strauss returned to Couperin, whose music he

---

[1] The recording was made for Boston Records, B-412.

undoubtedly loved, when he added six pieces to the *Tanzsuite* for a 'dance vision from two centuries', *Verklungene Feste*, produced at Munich. The six additions, with two more, were published in 1943 as a *Divertimento* for small orchestra. Here there is a stronger Straussian flavour, with elaborate new contrapuntal treatment of the inner parts, but forty minutes of this kind of thing is about twenty-five too many. In the remaining fifteen there are appealing moments, but neither work is likely, nor deserves, to supplant the wonderful *Bourgeois Gentilhomme* suite in the public's affections.

No Strauss survey can avert its gaze from the occasional pieces, tedious though they are. He provided four items for the golden-wedding celebrations of the Grand Duke of Saxe-Weimar-Eisenach at Weimar in 1892. One of them described the Battle of Lützen in 1692 and Strauss twice more pressed it into service, for the *Rosenkavalier* film in 1925 and, re-titled *Kampf und Sieg*, for the Vienna Philharmonic Ball in 1931. In 1905–7, as a good obedient court composer, he obliged the Kaiser's growing taste for militarism in all forms by composing several military marches, of which only the *Königsmarsch* has any intrinsic musical value. These marches are sheer 'duty'; they sowed no seeds in his great works as Elgar's vastly more accomplished *Pomp and Circumstance* marches did in his.

The pre-1914 Teutonic propensity for bombast and size is reflected in the scoring of these works—there were plenty of military bandsmen, so Strauss gave them work. His sombre and impressive *Feierlicher Einzug*, written in 1909 for the Order of St John, requires fifteen trumpets, four horns, four trombones and two tubas, and his *Festliches Präludium*, Op. 61, of 1913, composed for the opening of the Vienna Konzerthaus, is scored for ninety-six strings, quadruple woodwind, eight horns, six trumpets and twelve distant trumpets, four trombones, tuba, percussion and organ. This is a remarkable work, not to be thoughtlessly dismissed as flatulent occasional music. On the contrary, it is a carefully constructed homage to the nineteenth-century Viennese musical tradition, with quotations from Beethoven, Weber, and Brahms woven into a rich and dithyrambic texture. The climax is an eloquent paean in praise of music as an art.

After 1914 his output of this type of music diminished to a few fanfares. In 1940 he accepted a commission from the Japanese to contribute a work to celebrate the 2,600th anniversary (fictitious) of the Mikado's dynasty. This was the *Japanische Festmusik*, his last composition for a very large orchestra. It begins promisingly, with themes and orchestration which show traces of *Danae* and *Capriccio*, but inspiration and, one suspects, Strauss's interest soon peter out and the music makes meaningless and empty gestures in extravagant fashion.

Before turning with a sigh of relief to the post-1942 instrumental works, mention should be made of the odds-and-ends of *Der*

Rosenkavalier. Some of these belong to the silent film of 1924–5, about which the then penurious Hofmannsthal was enthusiastic. Strauss had no interest in it. There was no question of singing: a theatre orchestra played music to accompany the action on the screen. Strauss realized a new score was needed. He refused to provide it, leaving adaptation of the opera to Otto Singer and Carl Alwin. But the film interpolated new material. (Ochs was shown at home, the Marschallin's girlhood was depicted, as well as her meeting with her husband, who was seen on the battlefield. There was also a spectacular supper-party in the gardens of the Marschallin's Palace.) For these extra scenes Strauss provided, unaltered, two of his Berlin marches, a movement from his 1892 Weimar *Festmusik* and the *Wirbeltanz* from the first Couperin suite, and for the scene at the Feldmarschall's battle headquarters he wrote a new march in F. The film score was recorded in 1980 by an ensemble of 13 players—the identity of the arranger of this version remains a mystery. Various concert arrangements of the waltzes have been published[2] but only the two sets of *Waltz Sequences* are Strauss's work. The first, of waltzes from Act III, was arranged in 1911; the second, of waltzes from Acts I and II, was completed in Garmisch in November 1944 and first performed in London in August 1946 conducted by Erich Leinsdorf. Strauss undertook the task, he said, because he had long been 'irritated by Otto Singer's terrible work [1911–12], with those dreadful transitions'. Strauss's replacement contains new development of the themes, but is only marginally more satisfactory than the *Suite* (1945), arranged by the conductor Arthur Rodzinski, which he approved. It is difficult to believe that anyone who loves the opera can enjoy these concert-hall versions, which merely emphasize that the music belongs to the theatre and nowhere else. If conductors want a good Strauss waltz for their concerts they should try *München*, which is in the *Rosenkavalier* mould but has the advantage of being a concert piece.

After the 1941 opera *Capriccio*, Strauss's work moved into what is called its 'Indian summer'. This is a true description if it is not interpreted as emergence from a decline that never was. It is easy to see how this impression arose. Strauss's almost total immersion in opera from 1920 to 1940 meant that his concert-hall reputation rested on the pre-1914 tone poems. In opera houses outside Germany there was little inclination to explore beyond *Der Rosenkavalier*, which was box-office gold. In Britain up to 1939 *Der Rosenkavalier* was performed 99 times compared with *Elektra* 28 times, *Salome* 17, *Ariadne auf Naxos* (original version) 8, *Ariadne II* 3, *Feuersnot* 5, and *Arabella* 4. Since 1945 *Der Rosenkavalier* has easily led the field and *Ariadne auf Naxos, Die Frau ohne Schatten, Arabella,* and *Capriccio* have been taken into reasonably

[2] The earliest dates from 1911 and was played at the Promenade Concerts in London on 23 August of that year, seventeen months before the opera was heard in England.

regular repertory. *Die Liebe der Danae* has had four performances (by a visiting company), and *Intermezzo* was taken up by Glyndebourne in 1974, having been introduced to Britain in 1965 at the Edinburgh Festival. Glyndebourne also successfully staged *Die schweigsame Frau*. At the time of writing, *Guntram*, *Die ägyptische Helena* and *Friedenstag* have never been performed in Britain (apart from BBC studio productions of *Guntram* and *Friedenstag*). *Daphne* was first staged in Britain in 1987 by Opera North. It has had only a concert performance in London. In the United States, Strauss opera performances have increased since 1945. At the New York Metropolitan they were infrequent in the 1930s but after the war *Der Rosenkavalier*, *Salome*, *Elektra*, *Ariadne auf Naxos*, and *Arabella* became regular parts of the repertory. San Francisco and, in particular, Santa Fe explored the lesser-known operas. No wonder that, at any rate up to 1945, Strauss was regarded as having 'died' as a composer thirty years earlier; and no wonder that when, in the years immediately after 1945, it was discovered that Strauss had since 1942 been writing a series of accessible small instrumental works of high quality, it was considered that he had miraculously come to life again.

The last-period works are so successful, so filled with a slender elegance of style and manner, that one is bound to ask why Strauss turned back after fifty years to the classical instrumental forms he had abandoned when he composed *Macbeth*. We know from his operas that he was a nostalgist. In 1942 he must have been well aware of his isolated position: a last link with the noblest period of German and Austrian art. Isolated, too, politically, living in fear, watching Germany's cultural heritage perverted and destroyed. He re-created his own past as a defiant gesture against the march of barbarism. Many will remember the astonishment with which they heard these works for the first time in the 1940s—that such music should still be composed in our time!

The first of these compositions is the Second Horn Concerto (1942), compact, witty and skilful. The rhapsodic opening to the first movement is balanced by the tender link with the *Andante* in which the solo horn is used primarily as a member of the wind ensemble that dominates this idyll. The finale, very difficult for the soloist, is joyously Mozartian in its combination of grace and exuberance. Strauss's pleasure at discovering that he could still write music of this kind overspilled into the two Sonatinas for sixteen wind instruments, No. 1 in F (1943) and No. 2 in E flat (1945). These were scored for two each of flutes, oboes and bassoons, four horns, a contra-bassoon, two B flat clarinets, a C clarinet, bass clarinet, and basset horn. It is difficult to know which to admire more, the technical ingenuity of the writing or the bubbling good nature of the music. No. 1 is possibly the better constructed, but No. 2 is stronger thematically; it had been conceived as a one-movement Introduction and Allegro, but this movement is now the finale. Its theme sounds like an allusion to Wagner's Rhinemaidens, and this is probably intentional for there is, despite their lightheartedness, an elegiac streak in all these works which reflects what Strauss wrote in a letter about this time: 'Germany has fulfilled its last and highest cultural mission with the creation of German music, and I shall keep this thought in mind until I am called to my gods in Olympus.'

In fact, this sonatina finale was sketched shortly before Strauss revised his *München* waltz to include a section in memory of the Munich opera house. Before that, however, he had begun the weightiest and greatest of his last works, the study for twenty-three solo strings, *Metamorphosen*. This long adagio, which unfolds and proliferates in a complex texture of astoundingly rich and varied polyphony, is a sublimated tone-poem, its main theme a reminiscence of the Funeral March in Beethoven's *Eroica* Symphony, although Strauss only recognized it as such while he was composing. He maintained that it had escaped from his pen. There seem also to be allusions to motifs from *Tristan*, and these merely intensify the obvious message of the music: an elegy for himself and his country. The music is genuinely tragic and devoid of self-pity because it is governed by a rigorous classical technique. A conductor must have the measure both of its emotional pulse and of its difficult ensemble, for if over-pressed the clear lines of the meticulously adjusted structure become obscured. Any charge that Strauss's protective armour of self-esteem could not be penetrated fails when confronted with *Metamorphosen*, a masterpiece of Romanticism in its death-agony which Mahler would surely have applauded. Its last bars, where the Beethoven theme is quoted in the bass, deserve illustration (Ex. 27).

The Oboe Concerto dates from the autumn of 1945 and has been well described as an essay in rococo chromaticism. This delightful work was eagerly welcomed by solo oboists even though their first entry involves them in fifty-six bars of uninterrupted playing. The short themes flow one from the other rhapsodically and with the familiar harmonic side-slips, while in the slow movement the long cantabile melody breathes the spirit of another age. The music flows so easily and gracefully that one cannot imagine that its composition gave Strauss any trouble. Yet a sketchbook which surfaced in 1980 and belongs chronologically between the first sketchbook of 1945 and the short score is of special interest. Günter Brosche, director of the music collection of the Austrian National Library, has written:

> Although entire passages clearly correspond with the final version, they none the less are not arranged in what would be their ultimate sequence; indeed, by comparison they appear to have been thrown together higgledy-piggledy. This curious layout suggests an intermediate stage of evolution . . . The passages themselves may have been worked out musically to their final stage, but their actual sequence would not be determined until later . . .[3]

[3] G. Brosche, 'The Concerto for Oboe and Small Orchestra' in B. Gilliam (ed.), *Richard Strauss: New Perspectives on the Composer and his Work*, op. cit., pp. 177–92.

Ex. 27

IN MEMORIAM

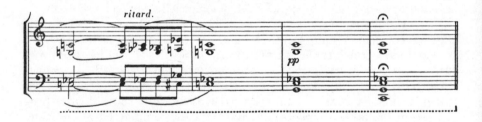

It was followed two years later by the *Duett-Concertino* for clarinet and bassoon, which has been much less frequently heard, perhaps because the long and garrulous finale tends to nullify the effect of the two ravishing short movements, each of which is dominated by one of the solo instruments. The work opens with a superb melody (Ex. 28) for the clarinet following a prelude for strings which belongs to the world of *Capriccio*.

The work has a programmatic basis. Strauss told Burghauser, the bassoonist for whom it was written, that he had in mind a dancing princess (clarinet) alarmed by the grotesque cavortings of a bear (bassoon). But at last she dances with it and it becomes a prince. It is obvious from Ex. 28 that the princess's name must have been Daphne. As in the sonatinas for wind, Strauss's fertile mind led him into the prolixity of the finale.

Ex. 28

He confessed on more than one occasion that he spoilt his works by 'putting far too much in them . . . I write in too complex a way. It's because I have a complicated brain.' But one can forgive this flaw, if such it be, for the sake of the beauty he created in a lifetime as a master of the orchestra.

With this too-rarely heard concerto Strauss ended his instrumental work. 'Mozart', he told Burghauser, 'was the one to have all the most beautiful thoughts, coming straight down from the skies!' Some came down to Richard Strauss, too, in those years of his old age.

20

Songs and choral music

Strauss's choral works are too rarely heard. The first of them, *Wandrers Sturmlied*, to words by Goethe, was composed in 1885 for six-part chorus and orchestra and, as is obvious from almost every bar, was inspired by a hearing of Brahms's *Gesang der Parzen*. Its rich harmonic scheme and elaborate contrapuntal texture are admirable in themselves, the serene coda being especially fine. In 1897 he published his first large-scale work for unaccompanied mixed chorus, two settings of poems by Schiller and Rückert. *Der Abend* is the choral equivalent of the pulsing ardour and perfect proportions of *Don Juan*. Schiller's poem is subtitled 'After a painting', but no one has yet identified which, if any, painting was its inspiration. Strauss paints a glowing picture of sunset and the arrival of 'fragrant night'. The voices are divided into sixteen parts, with the four sections (SATB) subdivided into four lines. Strauss alternates antiphonal block passages with intricate polyphony. The Rückert setting, *Hymne*, is also in sixteen parts but the division is more complex. The voices are divided into two choruses, one twice as big as the other and with three-part sub-divisions of the second chorus. The second chorus carries the burden of the main verses, while the first chorus is reserved for the recurring refrain of *O gräme dich nicht* (Grieve no more) at the end of each verse. The song opens lustily when the prodigal son returns, but becomes more sombre, and at one point fugal, as the text grows more philosophical. These settings are difficult to sing, requiring extremes of range from the chorus and the utmost professional skill in negotiating the chromatic modulations and flowing decorative figures. It is astonishing that such masterpieces should have remained unperformed in London until 1975, for they rank among Strauss's great works.

An astonishing *pièce d'occasion* is *Taillefer*, composed in 1902–3 for the centenary of Heidelberg University, which then conferred an honorary degree on Strauss. The text is a ballad by Uhland about the Battle of Hastings and the courage of Taillefer, minstrel to Duke William of Normandy. Strauss wrote for a colossal orchestra (145 players) and as large a choir as could be mustered. Big effects are therefore the order of the day, including a battle scene which outdoes *Heldenleben* in noise, but some of the music is heroic and frankly enjoyable, with effective solos for soprano, tenor and baritone and clear, lyrical writing for the chorus. On a similar scale is the Klopstock *Bardengesang* of 1906, an offering to Kaiser Wilhelm, of interest only because one can detect in embryo methods more worthily applied in *Elektra*.

Strauss returned to Rückert for the words of his *Deutsche Motette*, for four solo voices and *a cappella* mixed chorus. It was completed at Garmisch in June 1913 and therefore belongs to the period of *Die Frau ohne Schatten*, *Eine Alpensinfonie*, and *Josephslegende*. It is dedicated to the Berlin Court Opera chorus and its great chorusmaster Hugo Rüdel who gave the first performance on 2 December 1913. It has been described as probably the most challenging tonal choral work ever written with a range of four octaves—top D flat for sopranos and bottom B for basses. The voices are divided into twenty-three parts (sixteen chorus lines and seven soloists) and the dynamic range is from *pp* to *ff*. Rückert's text is in the form of a 'Persian Ghasel'. This means there is a rhyme in the first two lines (*gesangen, befangen*) and thereafter in every subsequent even-numbered line (*zugegangen, ausgegangen*, etc.). In addition the refrain *O wach in mir* (Watch in me) occurs at the end of the rhyming lines. This structural discipline in no way inhibited Strauss, rather it seems to have spurred his imagination to ecstatic flights. The ground plan of the *Motette* is an opening section with antiphonal effects followed by a polyphonic middle episode reaching a climax in which the two sections are combined. In a long coda, the chief themes are nostalgically reviewed. The music throughout is Strauss at his most luxuriant, characteristic, and masterful.

He set Rückert again in February 1935, three poems for unaccompanied male chorus and the light-hearted *Die Göttin im Putzzimmer* (The Goddess in the Boudoir). This last he first set for bass voice and piano late in 1934, but abandoned it in favour of an unaccompanied eight-part choral setting in the same key and using the same initial theme. Strauss is here at his most humorous and unbuttoned in his response to a text which is basically an allegory about artistic creation, always a subject to draw the best from him, especially when allied to confusion and bustle and when not treated pompously or too seriously. One remembers in this context the prelude to Act III of *Der Rosenkavalier*, the Prologue to *Ariadne auf Naxos*, and the quarrelling octet in *Capriccio*. Rückert's poem invites similar treatment and inspired Strauss, with its opening lines 'What disorder . . . What a riot of erotica', to a display of intricate counterpoint as he describes 'all those little niches . . . all those little shelves! . . . cupboards full of powder-puffs . . . all sorts of stockings, all sorts of braid . . . What formidable enchantress must this be to order chaos into harmony?' The muse of creativity, of course; and at the word *plötzlich* (suddenly) as the goddess stands dressed 'in colourful frippery' and 'all things around her come to life', the music of chaos lengthens into lyrical lines of block harmony. The magical ending is a clue to

Strauss's essential integrity where artistic matters were concerned as he salutes the muse and Love—'both of you turn . . . into a raiment of celestial light'. This enchanting work was not performed until after Strauss's death: Krauss conducted the Vienna State Opera Chorus on 2 March 1952.

In December 1927 Strauss completed an atmospheric and romantic cycle of four Eichendorff settings for male chorus and orchestra, *Die Tageszeiten*, in which the orchestra is the principal medium for evoking the sights and sounds of the times of day. These unjustly neglected songs were first performed in Vienna in July 1928. A version for mixed chorus and orchestra was arranged later by Richard Rossmayer.

The last of his choral works was *An den Baum Daphne*, an elaborate 'epilogue' to the opera *Daphne* and composed in November 1943 after a request for an *a capella* work for the Vienna State Opera Chorus. Strauss set a new text by Joseph Gregor instead of the librettist's original choral ending to the opera which Strauss had discarded in favour of an orchestral description of metamorphosis. The setting is for nine-part double chorus with an upper part added for boys' chorus (the Vienna Boys' Choir). Themes from the opera are recycled in this exquisite work, which is shaped as an introduction, several sections, and an extended coda in F sharp major in the second part of which the voices are wordless as the metamorphosis of Daphne into laurel occurs and a boy and a solo soprano alternate, as did the voice of Daphne and an oboe in the opera. The ending is not a fade-out, as in the opera, but a full-blooded return to the work's opening theme—*Geliebter Baum* (Beloved Tree)—and a song of love and of eternity. The first performance was not given until January 1947.

Strauss's large output of Lieder is still perhaps generally underrated. It requires a book to itself and two, both excellent, have been written.[1] Purists reject Strauss Lieder because they are not exclusively for voice and pianoforte—a stultifying attitude. Strauss's major contribution to the Lied was in his development of orchestral accompaniments, extending the achievements of Berlioz and Mahler. He orchestrated many of his songs which originally had pianoforte accompaniments, and it is in this form that they are most popular. About one thing there can be no question: his Lieder proclaim Strauss as one of the great melodists. More than half of his total output of over 200 Lieder was written between 1884 and 1906, and one of the most prolific periods was between 1899 and 1901, when he and Pauline were busy giving recitals, with Strauss as accompanist or conductor. Many of these were in Berlin where Strauss was chief conductor of the Court Opera. He orchestrated seven of his songs for their concerts together. Their last recital was in Munich in

[1] B. Petersen, *Ton und Wort: the Lieder of Richard Strauss* (Ann Arbor, 1977) and A. Jefferson, *The Lieder of Richard Strauss* (London, 1971).

January 1908, after which Pauline retired and Strauss wrote no more songs until 1918.

During their tour of America from February until April 1904, the Strausses participated in thirty-five recitals and concerts. Criticism of Pauline's voice by German and American critics suggest that she was a superb interpreter of her husband's music but sometimes had vocal problems. Richard Specht said she was incomparable in the *Drei Mutterlieder*, and others especially praised her performance of *Junghexenlied*, Op. 39, No. 2. A German critic described her 'bell-like silver voice, to which is added an expression, a rapture, which forces everyone momentarily into its power and under its spell'. As she grew older and technically less secure, she became more eccentric, wearing extravagant dresses, making operatic gestures and upstaging her husband by inviting applause when her contribution was over even if the composer was playing a piano postlude. But they had a unique mutual understanding, because Strauss would often vary the accompaniments, possibly because he was bored with the 'old favourites' and also because his active brain could never resist the chance of re-composing them. They became improvisations.

If one includes his *juvenilia*, Strauss's career as a writer of songs stretched over seventy-eight years: a sketch for a song was on his desk the day he died. Only a handful can be mentioned here. His childhood songs amounted to forty-two, many written for his aunt Johanna Pschorr, who greatly encouraged his early ambitions. A good many have been lost. It is interesting to note that at the age of thirteen he wrote two songs with orchestra, the setting of *Der Spielmann und sein Kind* (The Minstrel and his Child) being almost a *scena* in its ambitious length and scope. The 1878 *Ein Alphorn* is noteworthy, too, because it was one of only three songs in which Strauss used an extra obbligato instrument, in this case a horn, for the song was dedicated to his father. The poem, by Justinus Kerner, is nostalgic longing for the sound of the alphorn. Strauss set it with folk-like simplicity in ternary form. He revised the horn part in 1926.

Strauss's song-writing maturity dates from his settings of Gilm published as Op. 10 and previously attributed to 1882–3. It has now been discovered that August to November 1885 is the correct date. The group contains three of his best-loved songs, the impulsive *Zueignung* (Dedication), the restrained yet intense *Allerseelen* (All Souls' Day) and the superbly accomplished *Die Nacht* (Night), its first phrase an anticipation of the oboe solo in *Don Juan*. The song reflects, with mature skill, the lover's fear that night, which takes away the colours and shapes of flowers, rivers and buildings, will also steal his beloved—'sie stehle dich mir auch'—and on the word 'auch' the key changes dramatically from D major to B flat major and the pianoforte postlude struggles with difficulty back to D. Although Robert Heger orchestrated *Zueignung* (a product of Strauss's passion for Dora Wihan) in 1932, Strauss did not make his own version until 1940 as one of several orchestrations for Ursuleac. He varied the text at the end to pay her a compliment—'du wunderbare Helena, habe Dank'.

His Opp. 15 and 17 groups, to words by Schack, contain the tender *Heimkehr* (Homecoming), its consecutive thirds a typical Strauss feature, and the extremely popular *Ständchen* (Serenade). If the latter song has become hackneyed, that should not anaesthetize our response to its delicate *vivace e dolce* accompaniment of the tender and shapely melody. The Op. 19 settings are also of Schack and open with the masterly *Wozu noch, Mädchen?* (Why must you, girl?), its lovers' banter a foretaste of the operas' conversational style. Placed centrally is the energetic *Wie sollten wir geheim sie halten?* (How should we keep it secret?) with vocal portamenti and an exuberant sense of the union of love and Nature in which German songwriters excel—a strong contrast to the closing song, *Mein Herz ist stumm* (My heart is mute), a gloomy but powerful vision of old age. For his Op. 21 Strauss set five poems by Felix Dahn, opening with the jolly and Brahmsian *All' mein Gedanken* (All my thoughts) and the G flat major love-song, *Du meines Herzens Krönelein* (You, the crown of my heart), charming in its conventional simplicity of melody and Schubertian accompaniment.

With the four songs of Op. 27, his wedding present to Pauline, Strauss produced a quartet of winners. Three of the poems are by two Socialist-radicals, Karl Henckell and the Scots-born J. H. Mackay, but Strauss selected examples of their Romantic love-poetry. The first song, *Ruhe, meine Seele!* (Rest, my Soul), is a dark, mysterious, tranquil setting, the voice floating above sustained chords. Fifty-four years later Strauss orchestrated it, making it a gloomier, more tragic, even more beautiful song. *Cäcilie*, composed in a brilliant E major, is the most impassioned and joyous love-song Strauss wrote, rhapsodic and ecstatic. The same intensity of mood, but in a more flowing, transparent sound-texture, is found in *Heimliche Aufforderung* (Secret Invitation) where the voice's rapture is supported by a pianoforte accompaniment which Strauss made no attempt to transpose into orchestral terms. The last of the group is the wondrous *Morgen!* (Morning) which custom can never stale, if the singer is an artist. It opens with a pianoforte statement of the melody, the voice stealing in, as if in mid-sentence, to begin a long arching variation of the melody. The impression is of rapt and timeless wonder, sustained when the voice stops and a long pianoforte coda brings the song to an end that is no end. The voice-and-piano version is the best, but Strauss's orchestration for solo violin, three horns, strings and harp miraculously keeps the delicate atmosphere.

The nostalgic poignancy of *Morgen!* is again present in *Traum durch die Dämmerung* (Dream in the Twilight), the first of three Otto Bierbaum poems which constitute Op. 29. This is the song said to have been composed in twenty minutes, the time allotted to Strauss by Pauline before she insisted that they should go for a walk. Strauss admitted that some poems immediately suggested music to him, and this was obviously one such. Op. 31, composed in 1895–6, contains *Blauer Sommer* (Blue Summer) and is of interest for its chromatic modulations of a five-bar melodic phrase, each statement falling a minor third until the original key (B major) is reached again. The fourth song of this set, *Stiller Gang* (Silent Walk), exists in two versions, one with pianoforte accompaniment, the other with viola or violin obbligato, and was his first setting of verses by Richard Dehmel, author of the poem which inspired Schoenberg's *Verklärte Nacht*. There is, in fact, a Schoenbergian tonal and harmonic waywardness in this melancholy and descriptive song.[2]

Henckell is the poet of three of the five Op. 32 songs, though the best known of them, *Sehnsucht* (Yearning), is a setting of Liliencron. When it was new, this ambitious song led critics to declare that Strauss had abolished rhythm. They were puzzled by the effect, in the accompaniment, of the long minim and the tied crotchet which is sustained by pedal into the next bar. The key-signature of the voice-part is also ambiguous. *Ich trage meine Minne* (I Bear my Love) is in an unequivocal D flat, always a fruitful Strauss key, a straight-to-the-heart love song which has overshadowed the sparkling *Himmelsboten* (Heavenly Messengers), Strauss's first setting of a poem from *Des Knaben Wunderhorn* (Youth's Magic Horn).

His first song-cycle composed with orchestral accompaniment (and no alternative pianoforte) was the *Vier Gesänge*, Op. 33, of 1896–7. These emulations of Mahler's example are rarely heard, perhaps because they require two singers, high baritone and soprano. No. 1, *Verführung* (Seduction), is another passionate Mackay poem and is provided with an elaborate and imaginative instrumental texture. No. 2 is the *Gesang der Apollopriesterin* (Song of the Priestess of Apollo) and belongs to the world of Greek mythology which Strauss loved so much. Opening with a fanfare for three trumpets, its splendid principal melody is not unlike a theme later to be used in *Salome*. It is a rapt, stately song, harmonically rich, such as Ariadne or Daphne might have sung at a sacred rite in a cypress grove. The first song of Op. 36, Klopstock's *Das Rosenband* (The Rose Garland), was also composed for orchestra. Undeterred by Schubert's setting, Strauss here wrote one of his most gorgeous songs, its final cadenza on the word 'Elysium' being an early example of the soprano cantilena that he was to make into a speciality. A magnificent song; and in the same opus is the humorous *Wunderhorn* song, *Hat gesagt*.

Next in this astonishing flood of lyrical invention which followed

[2] This rare, beautiful and unusual song should be restored to singers. The alternative version with viola or violin obbligato was not included in the Complete Edition of the Songs, and the condensed version of the voice-and-piano setting is not accurate because it omits to mention the altered vocal line in the latter part of the song.

Strauss's marriage is Op. 37, six songs which include the most touching of his cradle-songs, the intimate, crooning *Meinem Kinde* (To my child); the most heroic of his love-songs, in a *Heldenleben* E flat, *Ich liebe dich* (I love you); and one of his most enigmatic compositions, *Mein Auge* (My Eye), its mood of devotion made more explicit in the 1933 orchestration. *Ich liebe dich* was not orchestrated until August 1943 when Strauss was acutely conscious of the dangers to his Jewish daughter-in-law and her sons. The text's references to 'our hands may bleed, our feet be sore, four pitiless walls, no dog recognizes us' unmistakably suggested his family's circumstances to Strauss. Four poems by Dehmel and one by Bierbaum make up Op. 39. The Bierbaum song is *Junghexenlied* (The Young Witch's Song), a strange fantasy about a witch's feelings for her children which, Strauss said, was a perfect vehicle for Pauline's wit and imaginative insight as an interpreter. *Leises Lied* (Gentle Song) reminds some writers of Debussy, and *Befreit* (Set free) is among Strauss's highest achievements, its repeated cry of 'O Glück' being deeply stirring, although Dehmel, the author of the poem, later expressed himself as disappointed by the 'weakness' of Strauss's musical interpretation of the text. This group also contains the gritty 'protest song' for a male singer, *Der Arbeitsmann* (The Workman), a dramatic and pessimistic composition inspired by the descriptive nature of the poem rather than by any conversion on Strauss's part to Dehmel's radical opinions. The orchestral version of this song, made in December 1918, was first performed in Berlin in 1919 and was then lost. The score re-surfaced at a Sotheby's sale in 1986 and has since been recorded.

How different is the Dehmel of *Wiegenlied* (Cradle-song), the first of the Op. 41 group of 1899 and perhaps the most frequently sung of Strauss's lullabies—though a lullaby, surely, to the mother rather than the child. Its broad-spanned cantilena over an *arpeggiando* accompaniment makes it a certain winner. The other four songs in this set are almost unknown—a pity in the case of the energetic, E flat *In der Campagna* (Mackay). Of the three Op. 43 songs, too, only the delightful *Muttertändelei* (Mother's trifling) has established itself, not surprisingly, for it rivals in frothy whimsy the best of Mahler's *Wunderhorn* settings.

Opp. 44, 46, and 47 have found little favour. The two songs with orchestra of Op. 44—*Notturno* (Dehmel) and *Nächtlicher Gang* (Night Journey) (Rückert)—require huge forces. In both there are pointers to *Elektra* and, in *Notturno*, further uses of the bitonality found in *Also sprach Zarathustra*, in this case the extreme keys of F sharp minor and G minor. *Notturno* lasts over eighteen minutes and is virtually a *scena*. The long poem, described by Dehmel as a 'romance "apparition"', is about a dream vision of Death who appears, in the guise of a beloved friend, in moonlight and playing the violin. Strauss omitted the first stanza and the last line because he thought the idea of the apparition as a dream weakened the drama. Strauss omitted horns, trumpets and percussion and relied on three trombones to create a nocturnal atmosphere. He wrote it 'for deep voice'. Bare and bleak fifths are heard in the mysterious orchestral introduction. When the singer becomes aware of the dead friend, the solo violin enters on a high F sharp, slowly descending to lead into the song's main theme (at *'wie einst so mild'*). In a series of impassioned climaxes, including a seductive expansion of the main theme, the opposing keys strive for dominance. The bare fifths recur in the long and chilly coda, which ends on a chord of G minor. A bass sang the first performance in Berlin in December 1900, but when the voice-and-piano version (by Otto Singer) was first performed in 1902, the soloist was the contralto Ernestine Schumann-Heink, later to create the role of Klytämnestra in *Elektra*. That opera sounds not too far away in parts of this remarkable song. The Rückert setting is a gothic horror-story of a man running for his life—and dying. Strauss's melodramatic powers are fully employed in this exciting curiosity. Singers could well look out the five Rückert settings of Op. 46, notably *Morgenrot* (Sunrise), lively and impulsive, and *Ich sehe wie in einem Spiegel* (I see as in a mirror), sentimental and old-fashioned but none the worse for that. The Uhland settings of Op. 47 contain the forgotten and radiant *Rückleben* (Living backwards), and the better-known *Einkehr* (Lodging), a captivating piece.

Op. 48 begins with Bierbaum's poem *Freundliche Vision* (Friendly Vision), set by Strauss in his most sensuous manner: ingratiating harmonies, ecstatic soprano voice seemingly detached from the accompaniment, the Strauss most people love. The remaining four Henckell settings include the jovial *Kling!* (Ring out!) and the two winter songs, *Winterweihe* (Winter Consecration) and *Winterliebe* (Winter Love), in which it is possible to detect pre-echoes of themes from *Arabella* and *Die Frau ohne Schatten*. The eight songs of Op. 49 are a varied selection, some of them jaunty folk-songs, but containing two superb Dehmel settings, the lyrical *Waldseligkeit* (Woodland Bliss), worthy of comparison with the last songs of 1948, and the adorable *Wiegenliedchen* (Little Cradle-song). Then follows another Henckell setting, *Lied des Steinklopfers*, an angry, bitter bass song about a starving stone-breaker, the piano accompaniment vividly depicting the clatter of his work. Much of it is non-tonal, the chordal progressions are weird, and the final despairing E minor reflects the poem's sense of the futility of the man's social plight.

With the six songs of Op. 56, composed in 1903–6, we reach the end of Strauss's prolific Lieder period. They open with a Goethe setting, *Gefunden* (Found), written for Pauline and altogether in his 'domestic' vein, as is the Heine setting, *Mit deinen blauen Augen* (With your blue eyes), where the final Sophie-Oktavian duet is not far away. *Im Spätboot* (On the last boat), a setting of Meyer, is perhaps Strauss's finest bass song, significantly in his beloved D flat. On a more elaborate scale is another Heine song, *Frühlingsfeier* (Spring Festival), which demands virtuoso singing—laughing, sobbing, lamenting—if its pagan erotic turbulence, another piece of Strauss's Hellenism, is to be satisfactorily realized. It is followed by one of Strauss's few religious works, *Die heiligen drei Könige aus Morgenland* (The three holy kings from the East), a song of rich beauty conceived with orchestral accompaniment, although Strauss published it in Op. 56 with his own piano accompaniment. The orchestration is as graphic as in *Symphonia Domestica*— brass for the ox's bellowing, woodwind trills and violins for the child's crying. The three kings give rise to thirds, triads, and triplets and they are regally accompanied by trumpets and drums. Two harps and celesta represent the star. The song's vocal line is ecstatic, its long orchestral coda an example of sustained rapture to melt the heart of an atheist.

The gap in Strauss's Lieder output from 1906 to 1918 is explicable by his immersion in his operas, by Pauline's retirement, and by a long wrangle with publishers over copyright and performing rights. One of the firms eventually threatened him with legal action if he did not fulfil a contract for a song-cycle. With the spite which was a part of his character—exemplified in *Heldenleben*, *Feuersnot* and *Intermezzo*—he asked the literary critic Alfred Kerr to write him some scurrilous poems introducing the names of various publishers and their managers. He set these—there are twelve—between March and May 1918 and offered them to the litigating publisher (Bote & Bock) who refused them and thereafter won a court injunction against Strauss. Such is the history of the *Krämerspiegel* (Shopkeeper's Mirror), Op. 66, which was privately published in 1921 in an edition limited to 120. The songs, which began as 'in-jokes' full of Strauss self-quotation, are worth getting to know, and the pianoforte introduction to No. 8, recurring as the coda to the cycle, was rescued by Strauss for magical use in *Capriccio*. The songs, Op. 67, with which Strauss eventually fulfilled his contractual obligation are three of Ophelia's nonsense verses in *Hamlet* and three of Goethe's ill-humoured verses from the *Westöstlicher Divan*. All, especially the austere Shakespeare, are worth revival. The irregular, declamatory vocal line of the first Ophelia song, *Wie erkenn' ich mein Treulieb?* is an astounding portrait of insanity, another disturbing reminder of how deeply his mother's affliction had affected Strauss. In the second of the Goethe settings, *Hab' ich euch denn je geraten?* (Have I ever advised you?), Strauss quotes from *Eine Alpensinfonie* and from the just-completed *Die Frau ohne Schatten*.

His next published group, Op. 68, composed early in 1918 before either Opp. 66 or 67, is a masterpiece, six glorious settings of poems by Clemens Brentano, joint compiler of *Des Knaben Wunderhorn*. They were written for Elisabeth Schumann, but it is extremely doubtful if she ever sang them all (nor were they dedicated to her). It is claimed that she sang them at the 1922 Salzburg Festival, but if she did it was at the 1922 festival of the International Society for Contemporary Music held in Salzburg. No printed programme survives. Five of them were sung in Vienna on 12 October 1918 by the baritone Franz Steiner, accompanied by Strauss. Schumann seems to have sung only one or two of the cycle on her American tour with Strauss in 1921. Strauss orchestrated the sixth song, *Lied der Frauen*, in 1933 and the first five in 1940, all for Viorica Ursuleac. But in this form all six, published in 1941, were first sung in Düsseldorf by Erna Schlüter (a great Elektra). The set is notable for its detail, its intricate and adventurous harmonies and its absolute mastery of word-setting. The chromatic *Ich wollt ein Sträusslein binden* (I wanted to tie a nosegay) and the tender love-song *Säusle, lieb Myrthe* (Whisper, sweet myrtle) are among the gems of Strauss's art, but the concluding (and little-known) *Lied der Frauen wenn die Männer im Kriege sind* (Song of women when the men are at war) is the greatest of all, requiring a strong soprano to dominate the stormy opening and also to give full majesty to the poignant ending. A noble song, which shows that Strauss was very far from impervious to the suffering all around him in May 1918. The five settings of Arnim and Heinrich Heine which comprise Op. 69 are also of superior invention, including the fluent *Der Stern* (The Star) which Strauss told Max Marschalk he wrote 'on the spot' when he read the poem, and the enchanting *Einerlei* (Sameness), pure Strauss sugar, no doubt, but intensely lovable, as is the humorous and witty *Schlechtes Wetter* (Wretched Weather), which ends as a waltz!

In a necessarily brief survey, there is room only to draw the attention of conductors and singers to the three Hölderlin hymns with orchestra, Op. 71. These were composed in Vienna between January and April 1921 and were first sung in November of that year by Barbara Kemp (wife of Max von Schillings) in Berlin. Strauss at his richest and most alluring, they are scored for a very large orchestra and their elaborate style, intensely lyrical, is a forerunner of the *Vier letzte Lieder*. The songs have been interpreted as a declaration by Strauss of musical nationalism. Their titles are *Hymne an die Liebe* (Hymn to Love), *Rückkehr in die Heimat* (Return to the Homeland) and *Die Liebe* (Love). In all three poems love is equated with love of one's country. In the second song Strauss quotes the childhood theme from *Tod und Verklärung* when the poet muses on the passing of youth, and alludes to *Eine Alpensinfonie* in the first song when the 'wild mountains' are mentioned. For many years the songs were completely neglected—they require a strong dramatic soprano and expensive orchestral forces—but have now been recorded, revealing their mastery. The long orchestral peroration to *Die Liebe* looks ahead to the 'Indian Summer' works. It ends with the singer quietly repeating the last verse's prayer that 'the language of lovers be the language of the land, their soul the sound of the people'. But still almost unknown are the Op. 77 Bethge settings of 1928, *Gesänge des Orients* (Songs of the East), dedicated to Schumann and Alwin. These are the last songs to which Strauss gave opus numbers, but of the nine he wrote between 1929 and 1942 two are of particular biographical interest. The 1933 *Das Bächlein* (The Brook) was dedicated to Goebbels to mark Strauss's appointment to the presidency of the *Reichs-musikkammer* (and probably in an effort to protect Zweig), and it ends with the words 'mein Führer' (in 'wird mein Führer sein') repeated thrice. Put Hitler out of your mind, if you can, as you enjoy this Schubertian song; if you were born after 1945 the reference is merely historical curiosity. Strauss provided an orchestral accompaniment in 1935 and dedicated this version to Viorica Ursuleac. Words by Goethe were used two years later in *Zugemessne Rhythmen* (Formal Rhythms), which remained unpublished until 1954. Strauss wrote this song in gratitude to Peter Raabe for defending him in print against a Nazi party-line attack on his 'feminine voluptuousness and torpor of sounds padded with fat'. The Goethe poem refers to the need to create new forms, which Strauss had done in his time, and the music quotes not only Strauss works but Brahms and Wagner too, in support of the victory of new ideas over pedantry.

One would say that the apotheosis of all that is best in Strauss Lieder is to be found in the Countess's last aria in *Capriccio*, were it not for the existence of the *Vier letzte Lieder* (Four Last Songs) of 1948. The genesis of this glorious cycle has been described in Chapter 14. Perhaps I can best sum up its appeal to performers and audiences alike by this informal quotation from a letter to me from that lovely Strauss singer, the late Elizabeth Harwood: 'I went to sing the *Four Last Songs* in Vienna with that superb orchestra. I was just in seventh heaven from beginning to end. I couldn't tell them, but I kept asking to repeat them at the rehearsal just to hear the sound!!' The vocal line, floating, curving, soaring in an ecstasy of cantilena, is given a backcloth of Strauss's most glowing, richly harmonized, detailed and evocative orchestration. Indeed, the voice becomes almost a solo instrument. Arabella, Daphne, the Countess, Sophie—all are reincarnated in these wonderful songs. No one knows whether Strauss intended them to form a cycle. The title was posthumously bestowed by his publisher, Ernest Roth, but is inaccurate because, unknown to him, there was another song, *Malven*, a gift to Maria Jeritza. They are Strauss's last orchestral songs. But there is evidence that he planned their performance and himself chose Kirsten Flagstad as soloist. Her accompanist Edwin McArthur wrote[3] in 1965 that Flagstad's stipulation was that there had to be 'a first-class conductor'—Wilhelm Furtwängler. Flagstad sang in Zürich twice in 1947 and again in 1948, and could have met Strauss then.

---

[3] E. McArthur, *Kirsten Flagstad* (New York, 1965), pp. 289–90.

The American Strauss scholar Timothy L. Jackson has made an extremely convincing case[4] for his belief that the cycle should comprise five songs and that the orchestral version of the 1894 song *Ruhe, meine Seele!* should be the penultimate item, preceding *Im Abendrot* (At Sunset), a setting of Eichendorff which was first sketched as early as April 1946 and completed in May 1948. *Ruhe, meine Seele!* was orchestrated in June 1948. Jackson believes, and so do I, that the poem of *Im Abendrot*, in which two old people contemplate death after their wanderings in 'need and joy'—*Not und Freude*—reminded Strauss of the similar sentiments expressed in the earlier song, especially the reference to 'momentous times' which 'place heart and mind in need'—*Herz und Hirn in Not*. The line 'Rest, rest, my soul and forget what threatens you' would also have struck home in 1948.

In orchestrating *Ruhe, meine Seele!*, which has an almost static piano part, Strauss added two bars to the introduction and four to the postlude. He also brought forward the appearance of an accompanying figure and used it more often than in the piano version. The orchestral song is altogether weightier and more sombre.

The Hesse poems later selected by Strauss—*Beim schlafengehen* (Falling Asleep), *September*, and *Frühling* (Spring)—all share the theme of a wish to die, exactly the mood of depression which descended on Strauss during his Swiss exile while awaiting de-Nazification. All four of the *Letzte Lieder* were significantly dedicated to people who had supported and succoured Strauss at this time: Willi Schuh and Roth and their wives, Adolf Jöhr (Strauss's Swiss banker) and his wife, and Jeritza and her husband, who had given Strauss moral as well as financial support. Yet it cannot be doubted that it is Pauline who haunts every bar of each song. Pauline, death and transfiguration. The old man had turned his back finally on the madness of the world and sent this last message from the mellifluous age of his golden years; of course, they are contrived with superb artifice—the voice in *Beim schlafengehen* entering exactly as in *Morgen!*, the long violin solo epitomizing so much of Strauss in similar vein, the trill of larks in *Im Abendrot* like the birdsong at the start of *Der Rosenkavalier*, the apt quotation from *Tod und Verklärung* at 'Ist dies etwa der Tod?' ('Is this perhaps death?', Strauss having significantly altered 'das' to 'dies'), the horn solo bringing *September* (composed last) to a valedictory rather than elegiac end. No suggestion of religious consolation, even *in extremis*. The beauty of the world and the beauty of the female voice were uppermost in his thoughts to the end. Has there been so conscious a farewell in music, or one so touchingly effective and artistically so good? He was tired, ready like summer in *September* to close his weary eyes, but there is no unevenness in these four benedictions on the world of Romantic music, no faltering,

[4] T. L. Jackson, '*Ruhe, meine Seele!* and the *Letzte Orchesterlieder*' in B. Gilliam (ed.), *Richard Strauss and his World* (Princeton, 1992), pp. 90–137.

not a false or a superfluous note. There was no winter in Strauss's life, only a long and gorgeous-hued autumn.

These songs were the great culmination of a great career. It could be said of Strauss when he died, as Boito said of Verdi: 'He has carried away with him an enormous quantity of light and vital warmth.' Those who refer to 'the tragedy of Richard Strauss' are those who would like him to have been a different kind of composer. If some of his failings stem from an uneasy co-existence of sophistication and naïveté typical of his period, part of his fascination lies in his contradictoriness—the huge orchestra hammering away in *Elektra* should, he said, be like fairy music; the Mozart world of *Rosenkavalier* is presented on the scale of Wagner's *Die Meistersinger*; his operatic heroines are required also to be Lieder-singers. He keeps himself aloof. Perhaps his soul was as scarred and flawed as Elgar's and Mahler's, but if it was, he does not tell us in his music (apart from once or twice) or in his letters. He shows us his family album, not his intimate diaries. The court composer always knew his place, after all. But his achievement remains and, like it or not, it is big, for he was a big artist. That is why his detractors will always find him too much of a good thing, whereas those who cannot have too much of a good thing will continue to relish him, warts and all. It has been thus for nearly a century; yet since his death his stature has steadily grown as more of his work has come into perspective, divorced from sterile theories about its 'relevance' to the time he lived in. He wanted to give pleasure, to create joy, for he understood the human heart. That was his greatest strength and it made him a master musician not for an age but for all the time mankind allows itself.

Appendix A

Calendar

(Figures in brackets denote the age reached by the person mentioned during the year in question.)

Year	Age	Life	Contemporary musicians and events
1864		Richard Georg Strauss born 11 June at Munich, Bavaria, son of Franz Joseph Strauss (42) and Josephine, *née* Pschorr (27).	D'Albert born, 10 Apr; Meyerbeer (72) dies, 2 May. Berlioz aged 61; Bizet 26; Brahms 31; Dvořák 23; Elgar 7; Janáček 10; Mahler 4; J. Strauss (ii) 39; Wagner 51; Verdi 51.
1868	4	Piano lessons from A. Tombo.	Bantock born, 7 Aug; Rossini (76) dies, 13 Nov. Wagner's *Die Meistersinger* first perf. Munich, 21 June.
1870	6	Composes *Schneiderpolka* and *Weihnachtslied*. Begins schooling. Sees first operas, including *Der Freischutz*.	Lehár born, 30 Apr.; Schmitt born, 28 Sept; Pfitzner 1. Franco-Prussian War.
1872	8	Violin lessons from Benno Walter.	Alfvén born, 1 May; Zemlinsky born, 4 Oct; Vaughan Williams born, 12 Oct. Bayreuth Festival Theatre foundation stone laid, 22 May.
1874	10	Enters Ludwigsgymnasium, Munich, where he remains a pupil until 1882.	Hofmannsthal born, 1 Feb; Schoenberg born, 13 Sept; Holst born 21 Sept; Ives born 20 Oct; Rakhmaninov 1; Reger 1.
1875	11	Studies musical theory, etc., with F. W. Meyer.	Ravel born, 7 Mar; Bizet (36) dies, 3 June.

Year	Age	Life	Contemporary musicians and events
1876	12	Composes *Festmarsch* in E flat, 3 overtures, and various songs.	Falla born, 23 Nov.; Bruno Walter born, 15 Sept; Götz (35) dies, 3 Dec. First *Ring* cycle, Bayreuth, 13–17 Aug; Brahms's Symphony No. 1 first perf. Karlsruhe, 6 Nov.
1880	16	Composes String Quartet in A and Symphony No. 1 in D minor.	Bloch born, 24 July; Pizzetti born, 20 Sept; Offenbach (61) dies, 4 Oct. Mahler (20) completed *Das klagende Lied.*
1881	17	String Quartet in A performed in Munich, 14 Mar; *Festmarsch* in E flat performed in Munich, 26 Mar; Symphony No. 1 performed in Munich under H. Levi, 30 Mar. Composes *Five Piano Pieces*, Chorus from *Electra* (perf. Munich Ludwigsgymnasium during this year), Pianoforte Sonata in B minor, Cello Sonata, and *Wind Serenade* in E flat. *Festmarsch* published.	Bartók born, 25 Mar; Mussorgsky (42) dies, 28 Mar. born, 3 Dec;
1882	18	Enters Munich University. Visits Bayreuth, August. *Wind Serenade* in E flat performed in Dresden, 27 Nov; Violin Concerto performed in Vienna (violin and piano), 5 Dec.	Stravinsky born, 17 June; Szymanowski born, 6 Oct; Kodály born, 16 Dec; Raff (60) dies, 24 June. First perf. of *Parsifal*, Bayreuth, 25 July; Berlin Philharmonic Orchestra founded.
1883	19	Completes composition of First Horn Concerto. Composes *Romance in F* for cello and orchestra and Symphony No. 2 in F minor. Cello Sonata performed in Nuremberg, 8 Dec.	Casella born, 25 July; Bax born, 6 Nov; Webern born 3 Dec; Wagner (69) dies, 13 Feb. First perf. of Brahms's Symphony No. 3, Vienna, 2 Dec.
1884	20	Conducts Meiningen Orchestra in first perf. of *Suite* in B flat for wind instruments, Munich, 18 Nov. Composes *Stimmungsbilder* for piano. Symphony No. 2 in F minor has first perf. in New York, 13 Dec.	Smetana (60) dies, 12 May. Bruckner's Symphony No. 7 first perf., Leipzig, 30 Dec.
1885	21	Becomes assistant conductor to Bülow (55) at Meiningen on 1	Berg born, 9 Feb; Varèse born, 22 Dec; Wellesz born, 21 Oct.

Year	Age	Life	Contemporary musicians and events
		Oct, chief conductor on 1 Nov. Meets Brahms (52) at Meiningen. Comes under influence of Wagnerian Alexander Ritter (52). Piano Quartet first perf. 8 Dec. at Weimar and awarded first prize in Berlin competition. Horn Concerto first perf. at Meiningen, 4 Mar (Gustav Leinhos soloist, Bülow conductor). Composes *Wandrers Sturmlied* and *9 Gilm Songs*, Op. 10. Begins *Burleske* for piano and orch. Mother has first mental breakdown.	First perf. of Brahms's Symphony No. 4, Meiningen, 25 Oct.
1886	22	Leaves Meiningen post on 1 Apr. Visits Italy in summer and begins composition of *Aus Italien.* Visits Bayreuth to hear *Tristan* and *Parsifal*. Becomes third conductor at Munich Court Opera, 1 Aug. Conducts first opera, Boieldieu's *Jean de Paris*. Composes song *Ständchen*, 22 Dec.	Liszt (74) dies, 31 July.
1887	23	Conducts first performance of *Aus Italien* at Munich on 2 Mar and of *Wandrers Sturmlied* at Cologne on 8 Mar. Meets Pauline de Ahna (25) at Feldafing in August. Meets Gustav Mahler (27) in Leipzig in October. Composes Violin Sonata and begins tone-poem *Macbeth.*	Villa-Lobos born, 5 Mar; Borodin (52) dies, 28 Feb. First perf. of Verdi's *Otello*, Milan, 5 Feb.
1888	24	Visits Italy again. Violin Sonata performed in Elberfeld on 3 Oct. At work on tone-poem *Don Juan.*	Lotte Lehmann born, 27 Feb; Alkan (74) dies, 29 Mar.
1889	25	Assistant conductor to Hermann Levi (50) at Bayreuth and meets Cosima Wagner. Becomes second conductor at Weimar Court Opera, 1 Oct. *Don Juan* has first perf. on 11 Nov at Weimar. Composes *Schlichte Weisen* songs, Op. 21. Completes *Tod und Verklärung.*	Elgar's *Salut d'Amour* published in London. First perf. of Mahler's Symphony No. 1, Budapest, 20 Nov.
1890	26	Conducts first perfs of *Burleske* (soloist Eugen d'Albert) and *Tod*	Martinů born, 8 Dec; Franck (67) dies, 8 Nov; Gade (73)

Year	Age	Life	Contemporary musicians and events
		und Verklärung at Eisenach on 21 June, and of *Macbeth* at Weimar on 13 Oct. Pauline de Ahna joins Weimar Court Opera as a leading soprano in September.	dies, 21 Dec. First perf. of Elgar's *Froissart*, Worcester, 9 Sept.
1891	27	Severely ill with pneumonia in May and June. Attends Bayreuth Festival while convalescing as guest of Cosima Wagner.	Bliss born, 2 Aug; Prokofiev born, 23 Apr; Delibes (54) dies, 16 Jan. Mahler becomes chief conductor at Hamburg Opera.
1892	28	Conducts uncut *Tristan und Isolde* at Weimar on 17 Jan. Ill again (pleurisy and bronchitis) in June. Visits Greece and Egypt in November and December. Begins work on music of first opera, *Guntram*.	Honegger born, 10 Mar; Milhaud born, 4 Sept. First perf. of Bruckner's Symphony No. 8, Vienna, 18 Dec.
1893	29	In Egypt, Sicily and Corfu until June. Completes *Guntram* at Marquartstein on 5 Sept. Conducts first perf. of Humperdinck's *Hänsel und Gretel* at Weimar on 23 Dec.	C. Krauss born, 31 Mar; Gounod (75) dies, 18 Oct; Tchaikovsky (53) dies, 6 Nov. First perf. of Verdi's *Falstaff*, Milan, 9 Feb.
1894	30	Becomes engaged to Pauline de Ahna at Weimar, 22 Mar, and marries her on 10 Sept. Conducts first perf. of *Guntram* at Weimar on 10 May. First Bayreuth appearance as conductor in *Tannhäuser*, with Pauline as Elisabeth. Composes *Morgen!* and other songs for Pauline and begins *Till Eulenspiegel*. Appointed assistant conductor to Levi at Munich Court Opera from 1 Oct. Conductor of Berlin Philharmonic Orchestra for 1894–5 season.	Warlock born, 30 Oct; Bülow (63) dies, 12 Feb; Chabrier (53) dies, 13 Sept. First perf. of Bruckner's Symphony No. 5, Graz, 8 Apr.
1895	31	*Till Eulenspiegel* first performed at Cologne on 5 Nov. S. conducts *Guntram* in Munich on 16 Nov but it is a failure.	Hindemith born, 16 Nov; Orff born, 10 July. First perf. of Mahler's Symphony No. 2, Berlin, 13 Dec.
1896	32	Completes *Also sprach Zarathustra* between February and August and conducts first	Gerhard born, 25 Sept; Bruckner (72) dies, 11 Oct. Mahler's *Lieder eines fahren-*

Year	Age	Life	Contemporary musicians and events
		perf. at Frankfurt on 27 Nov. Becomes chief conductor at Munich Opera. Visits Russia as conductor.	*den Gesellen* performed in Berlin, 16 Mar.
1897	33	Son, Franz, born on 12 Apr. S. visits Paris, Brussels, Amsterdam, and London for first time. *Enoch Arden* performed in Munich on 24 Mar. S. completes *Don Quixote* on 29 Dec.	Korngold born, 29 May; Brahms (63) dies, 3 Apr. Mahler becomes director, Vienna Court Opera, 8 Oct.
1898	34	First performance of *Don Quixote* given in Cologne on 8 Mar. S. founds society to protect German composers' copyrights. Leaves Munich to become conductor of Royal Court Opera in Berlin from 1 Nov. Completes *Ein Heldenleben* on 27 Dec.	Eisler born, 6 July; Gershwin born, 26 Sept. Elgar's *Caractacus* first perf. at Leeds, 5 Oct.
1899	35	S. conducts first perf. of *Ein Heldenleben* in Frankfurt on 3 Mar. Prolific period for composition of songs.	Poulenc born, 7 Jan; Chausson (44) dies, 10 June; J. Strauss (ii) (73) dies, 3 June. First perf. of Elgar's *Enigma Variations*, London, 19 June.
1900	36	Meets Hugo von Hofmannsthal (26) in Paris in March. Begins to sketch opera *Feuersnot* in autumn.	Copland born, 14 Nov; Křenek born, 23 Aug; Weill born, 2 March. First perfs. of Puccini's *Tosca*, Rome, 14 Jan., Charpentier's *Louise*, Paris, 2 Feb, and Elgar's *Dream of Gerontius*, Birmingham, 3 Oct.
1901	37	Conducts first all-S. concert in Vienna, including *Ein Heldenleben*, on 23 Jan. *Feuersnot* first perf. under Schuch at Dresden on 21 Nov.	Egk born, 17 May; Rubbra born, 23 May; Verdi (87) dies, 27 Jan. First full perf. of Debussy's *Nocturnes*, Paris, 27 Oct; first perf. of Mahler's Symphony No. 4, Munich, 25 Nov.
1902	38	Mahler conducts *Feuersnot* in Vienna on 29 Jan. S. tours extensively as conductor. In May, Pauline threatens divorce over misunderstanding. S. begins to sketch *Symphonia Domestica*. Pays tribute to Elgar at Düsseldorf lunch on 20 May.	Walton born, 29 Mar. First perfs. of Mahler's Symphony No. 3, Krefeld, 9 June, Schoenberg's *Verklärte Nacht*, Vienna, 18 Mar.

Year	Age	Life	Contemporary musicians and events
1903	39	Strauss Festival in London in June. Holiday in Isle of Wight in June and July. Honorary doctorate of philosophy, Heidelberg University, on 26 Oct, after which S. conducts *Taillefer*. Returns to England in December, conducting in London, Glasgow and Birmingham. Moves into new house in Berlin. Completes *Symphonia Domestica*, 31 Dec.	Blacher born, 3 Jan; Khachaturian born, 6 June; Wolf (42) dies, 22 Feb. First perf. of Bruckner's Symphony No. 9, Vienna, 11 Feb.
1904	40	First visit to United States from February to April for concerts and recitals with Pauline. S. conducts first perf. of *Symphonia Domestica* in New York on 21 Mar. Begins to compose *Salome*.	Dallapiccola born, 3 Feb; Skalkottas born, 8 Mar; Kabalevsky born, 30 Dec; Dvořák (62) dies, 1 May. First perfs. of Janáček's *Jenůfa*, Brno, 21 Jan; Puccini's *Madama Butterfly*, Milan, 17 Feb; Mahler's Symphony No. 5, Cologne, 18 Oct.
1905	41	Conducts *Symphonia Domestica* in London in February and in Strasbourg in May. S.'s father Franz Strauss (83) dies on 31 May. Triumphant first performance of *Salome* at Dresden, 9 Dec.	Tippett born, 2 Jan; Lambert born, 23 Aug. First perfs. of Schoenberg's *Pelleas und Melisande*, Vienna, 26 Jan; Debussy's *La Mer*, Paris, 15 Oct, and Lehár's *Merry Widow*, Vienna, 30 Dec.
1906	42	Performances of *Salome* throughout Europe, many of them conducted by S. He conducts Vienna Philharmonic at Salzburg Festival on 17 Aug in Mozart and Bruckner (Symphony 9). Agrees to compose *Elektra* to Hofmannsthal's libretto.	Lutyens born, 9 July; Shostakovich born, 25 Sept. First perfs. of Delius's *Sea-Drift*, Essen, 24 May, and Mahler's Symphony No. 6, Essen, 27 May.
1907	43	Conducts six performances of *Salome* in Paris in March. Guest conductor of Vienna Philharmonic. At work on *Elektra*. Composes military marches.	Fortner born, 12 Oct; Grieg (64) dies 4 Sept. First perfs. of Schoenberg's String Quartet No. 1, Vienna, 15 Feb, and Sibelius's Symphony No. 3, Helsinki, 25 Sept. Mahler leaves Vienna for New York.
1908	44	Succeeds Weingartner in May as conductor of the Berlin Court Orchestra. Moves into villa at	Messiaen born, 15 Dec; Elliott Carter born, 11 Dec; Rimsky-Korsakov (64) dies, 21 June.

Year	Age	Life	Contemporary musicians and events
		Garmisch in September. Completes *Elektra* on 22 Sept. Granted year's leave from Berlin Opera.	First perfs. of Mahler's Symphony No. 7, Prague, 19 Sept; Rakhmaninov's Symphony No. 2, Moscow, 8 Nov; Elgar's Symphony No. 1, Manchester, 3 Dec.
1909	45	First performance of *Elektra* at Dresden on 25 Jan, followed by performances in New York, Munich, Berlin, Hamburg, Vienna and Milan, all before 7 Apr. In May, S. begins to compose *Der Rosenkavalier*.	Albéniz (48) dies, 18 May. First perf. of Rakhmaninov's Piano Concerto No. 3, New York, 28 Nov. Schoenberg completes *Drei Klavierstücke*, Op. 11, on 7 Aug.
1910	46	Conducts two performances of *Elektra* in London on 12 and 15 Mar. S.'s mother dies, aged 73, on 16 May. S. conducts at Vienna Court Opera for first time in June (*Elektra*). Completes *Der Rosenkavalier* at Garmisch on 26 Sept.	Samuel Barber born, 9 Mar; Balakirev (73) dies, 29 May. First perfs. of Stravinsky's *Fire-Bird*, Paris, 25 June; Mahler's Symphony No. 8, Munich, 12 Sept; Vaughan Williams's *Sea Symphony*, Leeds, 12 Oct; Elgar's Violin Concerto, London, 10 Nov.
1911	47	Extremely successful first performance of *Der Rosen-kavalier* at Dresden on 26 Jan, followed by productions in Nuremberg, Munich, Hamburg, Milan, Prague, Berlin and other cities. S. begins to compose *Ariadne auf Naxos* and *Eine Alpensinfonie*.	Menotti born, 7 July; Mahler (50) dies, 18 May. First perfs. of Sibelius's Symphony No. 4, Helsinki, 3 Apr; Elgar's Symphony No. 2, London, 24 May; Mahler's *Das Lied von der Erde*, Munich, 20 Nov. Webern begins *Five Pieces*, Op. 10.
1912	48	Completes *Ariadne auf Naxos* at Garmisch on 25 Apr and conducts first performance at Stuttgart on 25 Oct.	Françaix born, 23 May; Cage born, 15 Sept; Massenet (70) dies, 13 Aug. First perfs. of Mahler's Symphony No. 9, Vienna, 26 June; Schoenberg's *Five Orchestral Pieces*, London, 3 Sept, and his *Pierrot Lunaire*, Berlin, 16 Oct.
1913	49	Conducts *Elektra* in St Petersburg in February. Journey to Italy with Hofmannsthal in April to discuss *Die Frau ohne Schatten* plot. Composes *Deutsche Motette*, 22 June, and *Festliches Präludium* for dedication	Lutosławski born, 5 Jan; Britten born, 22 Nov. First perfs. of Schoenberg's *Gurrelieder*, Vienna, 23 Feb; Stravinsky's *Le Sacre du Printemps*, Paris, 29 May; Elgar's *Falstaff*, Leeds, 1 Oct.

203

Year	Age	Life	Contemporary musicians and events
		of Vienna Konzerthaus, 19 Oct. Begins to compose *Josephslegende*. First London (29 Jan) and New York (9 Dec) performances of *Der Rosenkavalier*.	Webern completes *Five Pieces*, Op. 10.
1914	50	S. conducts first performance of *Josephslegende* in Paris on 14 May. In London for his fiftieth birthday on 11 June and receives honorary degree of Doctor of Music at Oxford on 12 June. Begins composition of *Die Frau ohne Schatten* just before outbreak of First World War on 4 Aug. His money banked in London is sequestered.	Mellers born, 26 Apr; Schuch (67) dies, 10 May; Liadov (59) dies, 28 Aug; Sgambati (73) dies, 14 Dec. First perf. of Vaughan Williams's *London Symphony*, 27 Mar.
1915	51	Completes Acts I and II of *Die Frau ohne Schatten*, begins Act III. *Eine Alpensinfonie*, completed on 8 Feb, receives first performance on 28 Oct in Berlin.	Searle born, 26 Aug; Waldteufel (77) dies, 16 Feb; Skryabin (43) dies, 27 Apr. First perf. of Sibelius's Symphony No. 5, Helsinki, 8 Dec.
1916	52	Revises *Ariadne auf Naxos*, completing new Prologue on 19 June. Meets Hermann Bahr during summer to discuss libretto for domestic comedy which became *Intermezzo*. Second version of *Ariadne* performed in Vienna on 4 Oct, with Lotte Lehmann as the Composer.	Babbitt born, 10 May; Granados (48) dies, 24 Mar; Reger (54) dies, 11 May; Butterworth (31) dies, 5 Aug; Richter (73) dies, 5 Dec.
1917	53	Visits Switzerland to conduct in February. Becomes co-founder of Salzburg Festival Association to establish festival on annual basis. Completes Act III of *Die Frau ohne Schatten*, 24 June. Conducts hundredth Dresden *Rosenkavalier* on 13 Dec. Works on music for *Der Burger als Edelmann (Le Bourgeois Gentil-homme)*. While in hospital in Munich in July writes his own libretto for *Intermezzo*.	First perfs. of Puccini's *La Rondine*, Monte Carlo, 28 Mar; Falla's *Three-Cornered Hat*, Madrid, 7 Apr; Pfitzner's *Palestrina*, Munich, 12 June.

Year	Age	Life	Contemporary musicians and events
1918	54	*Der Burger als Edelmann* performed in Berlin on 9 Apr. S. at work on *Intermezzo*. In conflict with Berlin Opera management and considers move to Vienna. Dispute with Bote and Bock over contract for Lieder leads to composition of *Six Brentano Songs*, Op. 68, in February and May and satirical song-cycle *Krämerspiegel*, Op. 66, in March and May.	L. Bernstein born, 25 Aug; Taneiev (68) dies, 7 Feb; Cui (83) dies, 24 Mar; Debussy (55) dies 25 Mar; Boito (76) dies, 10 June; Parry (70) dies, 7 Oct. First perfs. of Prokofiev's *Classical Symphony*, Petrograd, 21 Apr; Puccini's *Trittico*, New York, 14 Dec.
1919	55	First performance of *Die Frau ohne Schatten* in Vienna on 10 Oct. S. becomes joint director of Vienna State Opera from 1 Dec and moves to Vienna.	Leoncavallo (61) dies, 9 Aug. First perf. of Elgar's Cello Concerto, London, 27 Oct.
1920	56	Visits South America from August to November to conduct his operas and concerts with Vienna Philharmonic.	Maderna born, 21 Apr; Fricker born, 5 Sept; Bruch (82) dies, 2 Oct. Mahler Festival, Amsterdam, 6–21 May; first perf. of Korngold's *Die tote Stadt*, Hamburg, 4 Dec.
1921	57	Begins to compose ballet *Schlagobers*. Composes *3 Hölderlin Hymns*, Op. 71, in January and April. Attends first Donaueschingen Festival in August and meets Hindemith (25). Conducts concerts and operas throughout Europe. Conducts orchestras in North America and accompanies Elisabeth Schumann at Lieder recitals in autumn.	M. Arnold born, 21 Oct; Caruso (48) dies, 2 Aug; Humperdinck (67) dies, 27 Sept; Saint-Saëns (86) dies, 16 Dec. First perf. of Janáček's *Katya Kabanová*, Brno, 23 Oct.
1922	58	Visits London in June for first time since the war. Conducts Mozart operas at Salzburg in August. Completes composition of *Schlagobers* at Garmisch on 16 Sept.	Xenakis born, 29 May; Lukas Foss born, 15 Aug; Nikisch (66) dies, 23 Jan. Broadcasting of music begins in England.
1923	59	*Dance Suite* from Couperin pieces first performed in Vienna on 17 Feb. Visits South America from July to September with	Ligeti born, 28 May. First perf. of Sibelius's Symphony No. 6, Helsinki, 19 Feb.

Richard Strauss

Year	Age	Life	Contemporary musicians and events
		Vienna Opera and completes *Intermezzo* in Buenos Aires on 21 Aug. In October begins composition of *Die ägyptische Helena* to Hofmannsthal libretto.	
1924	60	S.'s son Franz marries in Vienna on 15 Jan and becomes seriously ill on honeymoon in Egypt. S. conducts first performance of *Schlagobers* in Vienna on 9 May. Widespread celebrations of his sixtieth birthday. Conducts his new version (with Hofmannsthal) of Beethoven's *Ruins of Athens* in Vienna on 20 Sept. Moves into house in Belvedere Gardens district of Vienna built on plot of land leased to him by the city. Disagreements with Franz Schalk lead to S.'s 'resignation' from Vienna Opera. Conducts first performance of *Intermezzo* in Dresden on 4 Nov.	Nono born, Jan. 29; Busoni (58) dies, 27 July; Fauré (79) dies, 4 Nov; Puccini (65) dies, 29 Nov. First perfs. of Sibelius's Symphony No. 7, Stockholm, 24 Mar; Schoenberg's *Erwartung*, Prague, 6 June, *Serenade*, Donaueschingen, 20 July, *Quintet*, Vienna, 13 Sept, and *Die glückliche Hand*, Vienna, 14 Oct.
1925	61	Visits France and Spain in February. Completes *Parergon zur Symphonia Domestica* which is performed at Dresden on 16 Oct. Visits Italy in November and December. Selection of correspondence with Hofmannsthal published, edited by Franz Strauss.	Boulez born, 26 Mar; Satie (59) dies, 1 July. First perf. of Berg's *Wozzeck*, Berlin, 14 Dec.
1926	62	Conducts première of *Rosenkavalier* film in Dresden on 10 Jan and in London on 12 Apr. Makes electrical recording of extracts from *Rosenkavalier* in London on 13 Apr. Visits Greece in June. *Ariadne* performed at Dresden Festival in August, conducted by Clemens Krauss. Conducts his own works, with Elena Gerhardt as soloist, in Manchester on 14 Nov. Reconciliation with Vienna Opera, where he conducts *Elektra* in December.	Henze born, 1 July. First perfs. of Puccini's *Turandot*, Milan 25 April; Shostakovich's Symphony No. 1, Leningrad, 12 May; Kodály's *Háry János*, Budapest, 16 Oct; Hindemith's *Cardillac*, Dresden, 9 Nov; Janáček's *Makropoulos Affair*, Brno, 18 Dec.; Sibelius's *Tapiola*, New York, 26 Dec.

206

Year	Age	Life	Contemporary musicians and events
1927	63	Vienna première of *Intermezzo* on 15 Jan. First Paris production of *Der Rosenkavalier* on 8 Feb. S. conducts Beethoven's Ninth Symphony in Dresden on 27 Mar, centenary of Beethoven's death. Composes *Panathenäenzug* for piano and orchestra. Completes *Die ägyptische Helena* on 8 Oct. Grandson Richard born on 1 Nov.	First perfs. of Křenek's *Jonny spielt auf*, Leipzig, 11 Feb; Berg's *Chamber Concerto*, Berlin, 27 Mar; Stravinsky's *Oedipus Rex*, 30 May; Busoni's *Doctor Faustus*, Frankfurt, 29 June; Schoenberg's Third String Quartet, Vienna, 19 Sept.
1928	64	First performance of *Panathenäenzug* in Berlin on 16 Jan, Paul Wittgenstein soloist and Bruno Walter conducting. Fritz Busch conducts première of *Die ägyptische Helena* at Dresden on 6 June and five days later, on his birthday, S. conducts its Vienna première. Performances in Berlin on 5 Oct, Munich on 8 Oct, and New York on 6 Nov. S. receives libretto of Act I of *Arabella*.	Barraqué born, 17 Jan; Musgrave born, 27 May; T. Baird born, 26 July; Stockhausen born, 28 Aug; Janáček (74) dies, 12 Aug. First perfs. of Ravel's *Boléro*, Paris, 22 Nov; Schoenberg's *Variations*, Berlin, 2 Dec.
1929	65	S. ill during early part of year and goes to Italy in April and May to convalesce. Suggests revisions in libretto of *Arabella* Act I. After these are completed, Hofmannsthal dies on 15 July. S. conducts at Munich Festival in August and completes version of Mozart's *Idomeneo* on 28 Sept.	G. Crumb born, 24 Oct; Hofmannsthal (55) dies 15 July; Diaghilev (57) dies, 19 Aug. First perfs. of Prokofiev's Symphony No. 3, Paris, 17 May; Hindemith's *Neues vom Tage*, Berlin, 8 June; Webern's Symphony, New York, 8 Dec.
1931	67	S. conducts *Idomeneo* at Vienna Opera on 16 Apr.	Nielsen (66) dies, 3 Oct; D'Indy (80) dies, 2 Dec.
1932	68	Grandson Christian born on 27 Feb. S. conducts *Fidelio* at Salzburg in August. Completes *Arabella* at Garmisch on 12 Oct. Meets Stefan Zweig on 20 Nov in Munich.	A. Goehr born 10 Aug; Sousa (77) dies, 6 March.
1933	69	S. conducts Berlin concert in place of Bruno Walter on 16 Mar and *Parsifal* at Bayreuth in place of Toscanini in July. Berlin Radio performance of *Guntram* in June. First performance of	Penderecki born, 23 Nov; Duparc (85) dies, 13 Feb; Hitler comes to power in Germany, 30 Jan; Schoenberg arrives in the United States, 31 Oct.

Year	Age	Life	Contemporary musicians and events
		Arabella conducted by Krauss at Dresden on 1 July. First performance of revised version of *Die ägyptische Helena* conducted by Krauss at Salzburg on 14 Aug. Berlin première of *Arabella* conducted by Furtwängler on 12 Oct and Vienna première with Lehmann in title-role on 26 Oct. S. becomes president of German *Reichsmusikkammer* on 15 Nov. Throughout the year S. works on *Die schweigsame Frau*, to Zweig's libretto.	
1934	70	Widespread celebrations of S.'s seventieth birthday on 11 June. Nazis forbid him to conduct at Salzburg and begin campaign against Zweig. S. completes full score of *Die schweigsame Frau* on 20 Oct and composes *Olympic Hymn* for opening of 1936 Games in Berlin. Increasing Nazi pressure on Jewish musicians and, in December, virulent attack on 'moral decay' of Hindemith's music.	Birtwistle born, 15 July; Maxwell Davies born, 8 Sept; Elgar (76) dies, 23 Feb; Schreker (56) dies, 21 Mar; Holst (59) dies, 25 May; Delius (72) dies, 10 June. First perfs. of Shostakovich's *Lady Macbeth of the Mtsensk District*, Moscow, 24 Jan; Hindemith's suite *Mathis der Maler*, Berlin, 12 Mar; Walton's Symphony No. 1 (minus finale), London, 3 Dec.
1935	71	Nazis forbid further collaboration between S. and Zweig, but Zweig agrees to supervise libretti written for S. by Joseph Gregor. S. meets Gregor in April. First performance of *Die schweigsame Frau* at Dresden on 24 June, but opera is banned after fourth performance. S. forced to resign presidency of *Reichsmusikkammer* on 13 July. At Garmisch in autumn, with Gregor, he begins work on *Friedenstag*.	Maw born, 5 Nov; Dukas (69) dies, 17 May; Berg (50) dies, 24 Dec. First perfs. of Vaughan Williams's Symphony No. 4, London, 10 Apr; Gershwin's *Porgy and Bess*, Boston, Mass., 30 Sept; Prokofiev's Violin Concerto No. 2, Madrid, 1 Dec.
1936	72	Conducts *Arabella* in Genoa in March and fulfils other conducting engagements in Italy, Belgium and France during March and April. Completes	R. Rodney Bennett born, 29 Mar; Cardew born, 7 May; Amy born 29 Aug; Stransky (63) (original of 'Stroh' in *Intermezzo*) dies, 6 Mar;

Year	Age	Life	Contemporary musicians and events
		Friedenstag in Garmisch on 16 June. Conducts *Olympic Hymn* at opening of Games in Berlin on 1 Aug. Begins composition of *Daphne* in late summer. Visits London, receives Gold Medal of Royal Philharmonic Society on 5 Nov and conducts *Ariadne* at Covent Garden on 6 Nov. Conducts in Italy during December.	Glazunov (70) dies, 21 Mar; Respighi (56) dies, 18 Apr. First perfs. of Berg's Violin Concerto, Barcelona, 19 Apr; Prokofiev's *Peter and the Wolf*, Moscow, 2 May.
1937	73	Visits Italy in March. Famous Munich operatic era under Krauss opens with *Salome* on 18 May. S. cancels Paris World Fair visit in September because of illness. While convalescing, completes *Daphne* at Taormina on 24 Dec.	Widor (92) dies, 12 Mar; Szymanowski (52) dies, 28 Mar; Gershwin (39) dies, 11 July; Pierné (73) dies, 17 July; Roussel (68) dies, 23 Aug; Ravel (62) dies, 28 Dec. First perfs. of Berg's *Lulu*, Zürich, 2 June; Orff's *Carmina Burana*, Frankfurt, 8 June.
1938	74	In Italy until April. Begins to compose *Die Liebe der Danae* in June. First performance of *Friedenstag* on 14 July at Munich, and of *Daphne* on 15 Oct at Dresden. Returns to Italy in November.	
1939	75	Intensive celebrations of his 75th birthday on 11 June include revised version of *Arabella* conducted by Krauss in Munich on 16 July. In Baden-bei-Zürich taking cure for rheumatism at outbreak of war on 3 Sept.	Holliger born, 21 May. First perf. of Bartók's Violin Concerto No. 2, Amsterdam, 23 Mar.
1940	76	*Daphne* performed in Vienna on 25 Apr. Completes *Japanische Festmusik* in April (first performed in Tokyo on 14 Dec). Completes *Die Liebe der Danae* on 28 June. Begins to compose *Capriccio* to Krauss libretto in July. Revised *Guntram* produced at Weimar on 29 Oct.	First perf. of Stravinsky's Symphony in C, Chicago, 7 Nov; Schoenberg's Violin Concerto, Philadelphia, 6 Dec.
1941	77	Ballet *Verklungene Feste*, with more Couperin-Strauss arrangements, performed in Munich on 5 Apr. S. completes *Capriccio* on	F. Bridge (61) dies, 10 Jan. First perfs. of Rakhmaninov's *Symphonic Dances*, Philadelphia, 3 Jan;

Year	Age	Life	Contemporary musicians and events
		3 Aug. Moves to Vienna, where his version of *Idomeneo* is performed in December.	Hindemith's Cello Concerto, Boston, 7 Feb.
1942	78	Conducts *Daphne* at Munich National Theatre on 20 Oct, his last appearance there as conductor. First performance of *Capriccio* in Munich on 28 Oct. Completes Horn Concerto No. 2 on 28 Nov. Awarded Vienna Beethoven Prize in December.	Zweig (60) dies, 22 Feb; Zemlinsky (69) dies, 16 Mar.
1943	79	Composes Wind Sonatina No. 1. First performance of Second Horn Concerto at Salzburg Festival on 11 Aug. Munich National Theatre bombed on 2 Oct. Composes *An den Baum Daphne* in November.	Rakhmaninov (69) dies, 28 Mar; Schillings (75) dies, 23 July. First perf. of Vaughan Williams's Symphony No. 5, London, 24 June.
1944	80	'Strauss Weeks' in Dresden and Vienna to mark his 80th birthday. First performance of Wind Sonatina in Dresden on 18 June. Dress rehearsal of *Die Liebe der Danae* at Salzburg Festival on 16 Aug were although all theatres closed in view of war situation. Begins *Metamorphosen* in August. Golden wedding on 10 Sept.	Tavener born, 28 Jan; Sinigaglia (75) dies, 16 May; R. Rolland (78) dies, 30 Dec. First perfs. of Hindemith's *Weber Metamorphoses*, New York, 20 Jan; Schoenberg's Piano Concerto, New York, 6 Feb; Bartók's *Concerto for Orchestra*, Boston, 1 Dec.
1945	81	Dresden and Vienna opera houses destroyed in February and March. S. revises *München* on 24 Feb and completes *Metamorphosen* on 12 Apr. Writes artistic testament in letter to Karl Böhm in April. Completes Wind Sonatina No. 2 on 22 June. Moves to Switzerland in October where he completes Oboe Concerto.	Mascagni (81) dies, 2 Aug; Webern (61) dies, 15 Sept; Bartók (64) dies, 26 Sept. First perfs of Prokofiev's Symphony No. 5, Moscow, 13 Jan; Britten's *Peter Grimes*, London, 7 June. Germany surrenders to the Allies, 9 May.
1946	82	In Switzerland. First performances of *Metamorphosen* in Zürich on 25 Jan, of Oboe Concerto in Zürich on 26 Feb, and of Sonatina No. 2 at Winterthur on 25 Mar. Sketches song *Im Abendrot*.	Falla (69) dies, 14 Nov. First perfs. of Stravinsky's *Symphony in Three Movements*, New York, 24 Jan; Bartók's Piano Concerto No. 3, Philadelphia, 8 Feb.

Year	Age	Life	Contemporary musicians and events
1947	83	Still living in Switzerland. Visits London from 4 to 31 Oct for series of concert and opera performances organized by Beecham. S. conducts *Till* at Royal Albert Hall on 29 Oct, his last public appearance in England. Completes Duett-Concertino on 16 Dec.	Casella (63) dies, 5 Mar.
1948	84	First performance of Duett-Concertino in Lugano on 4 Apr. Completes song *Im Abendrot* on 6 May. Cleared by De-Nazification Board in June. Composes *Frühling* (18 July), *Beim Schlafengehen* (4 Aug) and *September* (20 Sept). Composes last song, *Malven*, 23 Nov. Serious operation in Lausanne in December.	Wolf-Ferrari (72) dies, 21 Jan. First perfs. of Vaughan Williams's Symphony No. 6, London, 21 Apr; Schoenberg's *Survivor from Warsaw*, Albuquerque, 4 Nov.
1949	85	Returns to Garmisch on 10 May. Hon. Doctor of Law, Munich University, hon. freeman of Garmisch and Bayreuth to celebrate his 85th birthday on 11 June. Conducts for last time on 13 July. Heart attacks in August. Dies at 2.10 p.m. on 8 Sept in Garmisch. Cremated, 11 Sept. Memorial concerts in Vienna (Krauss) on 18 Sept and Bayreuth (Keilberth) on 9 Oct.	Turina (66) dies, 14 Jan; Pfitzner (80) dies, 22 May; Skalkottas (45) dies, 19 Sept.

Appendix B

List of works

(Dates given are of composition. Dates of major first performances may be found in the text and in Appendix A. Some early unpublished works composed between 1870 and 1880 are omitted.)

OPERAS

1887–93   *Guntram*, Op. 25. Libretto by R. Strauss in three acts. Revised 1934. (Aibl; rev. version, Fürstner, 1934)

1900–1   *Feuersnot*, Op. 50. 'Poem for singing' in one act; libretto by Ernst von Wolzogen. (Fürstner)

1904–5   *Salome*, Op. 54. Drama in one act to libretto by Hedwig Lachmann based on Oscar Wilde's play. (Fürstner)

1906–8   *Elektra*, Op. 58. Tragedy in one act to libretto by Hugo von Hofmannsthal. (Fürstner)

1909–10   *Der Rosenkavalier*, Op. 59. Comedy for music in three acts by Hugo von Hofmannsthal. (Fürstner)

1911–12   *Ariadne auf Naxos*, Op. 60. Original version: play *Le Bourgeois Gentilhomme* by Molière and opera in one act by Hugo von Hofmannsthal; second version (1916), Prologue and opera in one act by Hugo von Hofmannsthal. (Fürstner)

1914–17   *Die Frau ohne Schatten*, Op. 65. Opera in three acts by Hugo von Hofmannsthal. (Fürstner)

1917–23   *Intermezzo*, Op. 72. Bourgeois comedy with symphonic interludes in two acts by R. Strauss. (Fürstner)

1923–7   *Die ägyptische Helena*, Op. 75. Opera in two acts by Hugo von Hofmannsthal. Revised 1933. (Fürstner)

1930–2   *Arabella*, Op. 79. Lyrical comedy in three acts by Hugo von Hofmannsthal. Revised 1939. (Fürstner)

1933–4   *Die schweigsame Frau*, Op. 80. Comic opera in three acts freely adapted from Ben Jonson by Stefan Zweig. (Fürstner)

1935–6   *Friedenstag*, Op. 81. Opera in one act by Joseph Gregor. (Oertel)

1936–7   *Daphne*, Op. 82. Bucolic tragedy in one act by Joseph Gregor. (Oertel)

1938–40   *Die Liebe der Danae*, Op. 83. Cheerful mythology in three acts by Joseph Gregor, using a draft by Hugo von Hofmannsthal. (Oertel)

1940–1   *Capriccio*, Op. 85. Conversation piece for music in one act by Clemens Krauss (and others). (Oertel)

BALLETS AND OTHER STAGE WORKS

1892   *Festmusik, 'Lebende Bilder'* for orchestra. Composed to accompany *tableaux vivants* in celebration of golden wedding of Grand Duke and Duchess of Weimar. Revived as *Kampf und Sieg* in Vienna 1931. (Published Heinrichshofen 1930)

1913–14   *Josephslegende*, Op. 63. Ballet in one act by Count Kessler and H. von Hofmannsthal for full orchestra. (Fürstner)

1917   *Der Bürger als Edelmann* (*Le Bourgeois Gentilhomme*) (incorporating music for original *Ariadne*, 1912), Op. 60. Comedy, with dances, by Molière, freely adapted in three acts by H. von Hofmannsthal. (Fürstner)

1921–2   *Schlagobers*, Op. 70. Viennese ballet in two acts devised by R. Strauss. (Fürstner)

1940–1   *Verklungene Feste*, dance vision from two centuries with music after Couperin.

ARRANGEMENTS OF STAGE WORKS BY OTHER COMPOSERS

1889–90   Gluck, *Iphigénie en Tauride*, arranged with additional trio in finale. (Performed Weimar, 1900.) (Fürstner)

1922–4   Beethoven, *Die Ruinen von Athen*, music, including parts of ballet *Die Geschöpfe des Prometheus*, edited and arranged by Strauss and Hofmannsthal, with newly composed *mélodrame*. (Fürstner)

1929   Mozart, *Idomeneo*. 'Re-working' in association with L. Wallerstein, including altered recitatives, orchestral interlude and new Act III ensemble. (Heinrichshofen)

ORCHESTRAL

?1873   Overture *Hochlands Treue*

1876   *Festmarsch No. 1* in E flat, Op. 1. (Breitkopf, 1881)

1877   *Serenade in G.* (MS)

1880   Symphony No. 1 in D minor. (Schott)

1881   *Serenade in E flat* for 13 wind instruments, Op. 7. (Aibl)

1883   *Concert Overture* in C minor. (Schott)

1883–4   Symphony No. 2 in F minor, Op. 12. (Aibl)

1884   *Suite* in B flat for 13 wind instruments, Op. 4. (Leuckart, 1911)

1886   *Aus Italien*, symphonic fantasy in G, Op. 16. (Aibl)

1887–8   *Macbeth*, tone-poem, Op. 23. Revised 1889–91. (Aibl)

1888   *Don Juan*, tone-poem, Op. 20. (Aibl)
    Festmarsch No. 2 in C. (MS)

1888–9   *Tod und Verklärung*, tone-poem, Op. 24. (Aibl)

1894–5   *Till Eulenspiegels lustige Streiche*, after the old rogue's tune, in rondo form, Op. 28. (Aibl)

1895–6   *Also sprach Zarathustra*, tone-poem, Op. 30. (Aibl)

1896–7   *Don Quixote*, Fantastic variations on a theme of knightly character, Op. 35. (Aibl)

1897–8   Ein Heldenleben, tone-poem, Op. 40. (Leuckart)
1902–3   Symphonia Domestica, Op. 53. (Bote and Bock)
1905   Königsmarsch für Wilhelm II. (Fürstner)
1906   Two Military Marches, Op. 57 (Militärmarsch in E flat; Kriegsmarsch in C minor). (Peters)
1907   De Brandenburgsche Mars. (Fürstner)
          Königsmarsch. (Fürstner)
1909   Feierlicher Einzug der Ritter des Johanniterordens for brass and timpani. (Lienau)
1911   Waltz Sequence from Der Rosenkavalier, Op. 59, Act III. (Fürstner)
1911–15   Eine Alpensinfonie, Op. 64. (Leuckart)
1913   Festliches Präludium for orchestra and organ, Op. 61. (Fürstner)
1915–19   Suite, Le Bourgeois Gentilhomme, Op. 60. (Leuckart)
1922–3   Tanzsuite after keyboard pieces by Couperin. (Fürstner)
1924   Wiener Philharmoniker Fanfare for Vienna Philharmonic ball on 4 March 1924, for brass and timpani. (Boosey and Hawkes, 1960)
          Fanfare for wind instruments, for opening of Vienna Music Week, 14 September 1924. (Boosey and Hawkes, 1960)
1932   Orchestersuite aus dem Ballett Schlagobers, Op. 70. (Fürstner)
1933   4 Sinfonische Zwischenspiele aus Intermezzo, Op. 72. (Fürstner)
1938–9   München, waltz for orchestra, first version. See 1945. (MS)
1940   Japanische Festmusik, Op. 84. (Oertel)
1940–1   Divertimento for small orchestra after keyboard pieces by Couperin, Op. 86. (Two new arrangements added to those made for Verklungene Feste: see under Ballets, 1940–1.) (Oertel)
1943   Festmusik for Vienna city trumpeters, for brass and timpani, two versions. (Boosey and Hawkes, 1978).
          Sonatina No. 1 in F, for 16 wind instruments. ('Aus der Werkstatt eines Invaliden.') (Boosey and Hawkes, 1964)
1944   First Waltz Sequence from Der Rosenkavalier, Op. 59, Acts I and II. (Fürstner)
1944–5   Sonatina No. 2 in E flat, for 16 wind instruments. ('Fröhliche Werkstatt'.) (Boosey and Hawkes, 1952)
          Metamorphosen, study for 23 solo strings, in C minor. (Boosey and Hawkes, 1946)
1945   München, memorial waltz (revised version). (Boosey and Hawkes, 1951)
1946–7   Symphonic Fantasy from Die Frau ohne Schatten, Op. 65. (Fürstner)
          Josephslegende, Op. 63, symphonic fragment. (Fürstner)

SOLO INSTRUMENT(S) AND ORCHESTRA

1879   Romance in E flat for clarinet and orchestra. (Schott)
1880–2   Violin Concerto in D minor, Op. 8. (Aibl)
1882–3   Horn Concerto No. 1 in E flat, Op. 11. (Aibl)
1883   Romance in F for cello and orchestra. (Schott)
1885–6   Burleske in D minor for pianoforte and orchestra. Revised 1890. (Steingräber, 1894)
1924–5   Parergon zur Symphonia Domestica, Op. 73, for pianoforte (left hand) and orchestra. (Boosey and Hawkes, 1964)

1925   *Military March* in F (for film of *Der Rosenkavalier*). (Fürstner)
1927   *Panathenäenzug*, Op. 74, symphonic studies in form of passacaglia for
        pianoforte (left hand) and orchestra. (Vienna 1928, Boosey and
        Hawkes, 1953)
1942   Horn Concerto No. 2 in E flat. (Boosey and Hawkes, 1950)
1945   Oboe Concerto. Finale rev. 1948. (Boosey and Hawkes, 1948)
1947   Duett-Concertino for clarinet and bassoon with strings and harp.
        (Boosey and Hawkes, 1949)

CHAMBER MUSIC

1880   String Quartet in A, Op. 2. (Aibl)
1880–3 Sonata in F for violoncello and pianoforte, Op. 6. (Aibl)
1884   Quartet in C minor for pianoforte, violin, viola and violoncello, Op. 13.
        (Aibl)
1887   Sonata in E flat for violin and pianoforte, Op. 18. (Aibl)
1945   *Daphne-Etude* for solo violin. (Katzbichler, 1969).
1948   *Allegretto* in E for violin and pianoforte. (Katzbichler, 1969).

KEYBOARD WORKS

1870   *Schneiderpolka*
1879   *Aus alter Zeit: Gavotte* (Tutzing, 1985)
1881   *Sonata* in B minor, Op. 5. (Aibl and UE)
        Five Piano Pieces, Op. 3. (Aibl and UE)
1884   *Stimmungsbilder*, Op. 9. 1. Auf stillem Waldespfad; 2. An einsamer
        Quelle; 3. Intermezzo; 4. Träumerei; 5. Haidebild. (Aibl and UE)
        14 Improvisations and Fugue in A minor on an Original Theme. (Fugue
        published by Bruckmann, 1898)
1905   *Parade-Marsch*. (Fürstner)
        De Brandenburgsche Mars. (Fürstner)
1924   *Hochzeitspräludium* for two harmoniums. (Vienna, 1948)
1944   Suite from *Capriccio* for harpsichord. (MS)

MELODRAMAS

1897   *Enoch Arden* (Tennyson), Op. 38, for voice and pianoforte. (Forberg,
        1898)
1899   *Das Schloss am Meere* (Uhland), for voice and pianoforte. (Fürstner,
        1911)

WORKS FOR CHORUS

1881   Third Choral Speech from *Electra* (Sophocles) for male chorus and small
        orchestra. (Breitkopf and Härtel, 1902)
?1884   *Schwäbische Erbschaft* (Loewe), for four-part male chorus. (Leuckart,
        1950)
1885   *Wandrers Sturmlied* (Goethe), Op. 14, for six-part chorus and full
        orchestra. (Aibl)

215

1886   *Bardengesang aus die Hermanns-Schlacht* (Kleist), for male chorus and orchestra. (Lost. See 1906.)

1897   2 *Gesänge*, Op. 34, for unacc. 16-part mixed chorus. 1. Der Abend (Schiller); 2. Hymne (Rückert). (Aibl)

Hymne, for women's chorus and orchestra, 'Licht, du ewiglich eines' (for opening of Secession art exhibition, Munich, 1 June 1897). (MS.)

1899   2 *Choruses*, Op. 42, for unacc. male voices, from Herder's *Stimmen der Völker*. 1. Liebe; 2. Altdeutsches Schlachtlied. (Leuckart)

Soldatenlied (Kopisch) ('Wenn man beim Wein sitzt'), for unacc. male chorus. (Bauer, 1900)

3 *Choruses*, Op. 45, for unacc. male voices, from Herder's *Stimmen der Völker*. 1. Schlachtgesang; 2. Lied der Freundschaft; 3. Der Brauttanz. (Fürstner)

1903   *Taillefer* (Uhland), Op. 52, for soprano, tenor and bass soloists, mixed chorus and orchestra. (Fürstner)

Canon, 'Hans Huber in Vitznau', for four unacc. voices. (Doblinger, 1974)

1905   6 *Folk-songs* arranged for unacc. male voices. 1. Geistlicher Maien; 2. Misslungene Liebesjagd; 3. Tummler; 4. Hüt' du dich; 5. Wächterlied; 6. Kuckuck. (Peters)

1906   *Bardengesang* (Klopstock), Op. 55, from *Hermanns-Schlacht* for three male choruses and orchestra. (Fürstner)

1913   *Deutsche Motette* (Rückert), Op. 62, for soprano, alto, tenor and bass soloists and unacc. 16-part mixed chorus. (Fürstner)

1914   *Cantata* (Hofmannsthal), 'Tüchtigen stellt das schnelle Glück', for unacc. male chorus. (Junker & Dünnhaupt, 1935)

1925   *Hymne auf das Haus Kohorn*, for 2 tenors, 2 basses. (Schneider, 1986)

1927   *Die Tageszeiten* (Eichendorff), Op. 76, for male chorus and orchestra. 1. Der Morgen; 2. Mittagsruh; 3. Der Abend; 4. Die Nacht. (Leuckart)

1929   *Austria* (Wildgans), Op. 78, for male chorus and orchestra. (Bote and Bock)

1934   *Olympische Hymne* (Lubahn), for mixed chorus and orchestra. (Fürstner)

1935   *Die Göttin im Putzzimmer* (Rückert), for unacc. eight-part mixed chorus. (Boosey and Hawkes, 1958)

3 *Choruses* (Rückert), for unacc. male chorus. 1. Vor den Türen; 2. Traumlicht; 3. Fröhlich im Maien. (Boosey and Hawkes, 1958)

1938   *Durch Einsamkeiten* (Wildgans), for unacc. four-part male chorus. (MS)

1943   *An den Baum Daphne* (Gregor), Epilogue to *Daphne*, Op. 82, for unacc. nine-part mixed chorus. (Boosey and Hawkes, 1958)

SONGS

1870–83   *Jugendlieder* for voice and pianoforte. 1. Weihnachtslied (Schubart, Dec. 1870); 2. Einkehr (Uhland, Aug. 1871); 3. Winterreise (Uhland, 1871); 4. Der müde Wanderer (Fallersleben, 1873); 5. Husarenlied (Fallersleben, 1876); 6. Der Fischer (Goethe, 1877); 7. Die Drossel

(Uhland, 1877); 8. Lass ruhn die Toten (Chamisso, 1877); 9. Lust und Qual (Goethe, 1877); 10. Spielmann und Zither (Körner, 1878); 11. Wiegenlied (Fallersleben, 1878); 12. Abend und Morgenrot (Fallersleben, 1878); 13. Im Walde (Geibel, 1878); 14. Nebel (Lenau, 1878); 15. Soldatenlied (Fallersleben, 1878); 16. Ein Röslein zog ich mir im Garten (Fallersleben, 1878); 17. Alphorn, with horn obbligato (Kerner, ?1878); 18. Waldesgesang (Geibel, 1879); 19. In Vaters Garten (Heine, 1879); 20. Die erwächte Rose (Sallet, 1880); 21. Begegnung (Gruppe, 1880); 22. John Anderson, mein Lieb (Burns, 1880); 23. Rote Rosen (Stieler, 1883).

1878   2 *Songs* with orchestra: Arie der Almaide (Goethe); Der Spielmann und sein Kind (Fallersleben). (MS)

1884–6   5 *Lieder*, Op. 15, for medium voice and pianoforte. 1. Madrigal (Michelangelo); 2. Winternacht; 3. Lob des Leidens; 4. Dem Herzen ähnlich; 5. Heimkehr (orch. L. Wenninger, 1920). Nos. 2–5 poems by Schack. (Rahter). No. 5 arr. as pianoforte solo by Gieseking.

1885   9 *Lieder* aus 'Letzte Blätter' (Gilm), Op. 10, for voice and pianoforte. 1. Zueignung (orch. Heger 1932, Strauss 1940); 2. Nichts; 3. Die Nacht; 4. Die Georgine; 5. Geduld; 6. Wer Hat's gethan?; 7. Die Verschwiegenen; 8. Die Zeitlose; 9. Allerseelen (orch. Heger 1932). (Aibl 1885 except No. 6, which remained unpublished until 1974, Schneider, Tutzing). No. 9 arr. as pianoforte solo by Reger, 1904.

1886–7   6 *Lieder* (Schack), Op. 17, for high voice and pianoforte. 1. Seitdem dein Aug' in meines schaute; 2. Ständchen; 3. Das Geheimnis; 4. Von dunklem Schleier umsponnen; 5. Nur Mut!; 6. Barcarole. (Rahter). No. 2 arr. for pianoforte solo by Rath, 1897, and by Gieseking, 1923; orch. F. Mottl, 1912; arr. for orch. (no voice) by L. Wenninger, 1903.

1888   6 *Lieder* (Schack's *Lotosblättern*), Op. 19, for voice and pianoforte. 1. Wozu noch, Mädchen; 2. Breit' über mein Haupt; 3. Schön sind, doch Kalt die Himmelssterne; 4. Wie sollten wir geheim sie halten; 5. Hoffen und wieder verzagen; 6. Mein Herz ist stumm. (Aibl). No. 2 arr. as pianoforte solo by Reger, 1899.

1888–9   4 *Mädchenblumen* (Dahn), Op. 22, for voice and pianoforte. 1. Kornblumen; 2. Mohnblumen; 3. Efeu; 4. Wasserrose. (Fürstner)

1889–90   5 *Schlichte Weisen* (Dahn), Op. 21, for voice and pianoforte. 1. All' mein Gedanken; 2. Du meines Herzens Krönelein; 3. Ach Lieb, ich muss nun scheiden!; 4. Ach weh mir unglückhaftem Mann; 5. Die Frauen. (Aibl)

1891   2 *Lieder* (Lenau), Op. 26, for high voice and pianoforte. 1. Frühlingsgedränge; 2. O wärst du mein. (Aibl)

1894   4 *Lieder*, Op. 27, for high voice and pianoforte. 1. Ruhe, meine Seele! (Henckell) (orch. Strauss, 1948); 2. Cäcilie (H. Hart) (orch. Strauss, 1897); 3. Heimliche Aufforderung (Mackay) (orch. Heger, 1932); 4. Morgen! (Mackay) (orch. Strauss, 1897). (Aibl)

1895   3 *Lieder* (Bierbaum), Op. 29, for high voice and pianoforte. 1. Traum durch die Dämmerung (orch. Heger, 1932); 2. Schlagende Herzen; 3. Nachtgang. (Aibl). Nos. 1 and 3 arr. as pianoforte solos by Reger, 1899 and 1904.

1895–6   4 *Lieder*, Op. 31, for voice and pianoforte. 1. Blauer Sommer; 2. Wenn; 3. Weisser Jasmin (texts of 1, 2 and 3 by Busse); 4. Stiller Gang (Dehmel) with viola or violin obbligato, Stiller Gang (1895). (Fürstner)

1896   5 *Lieder*, Op. 32, for voice and pianoforte. 1. Ich trage meine Minne (Henckell) (orch. Heger, 1932); 2. Sehnsucht (Liliencron); 3. Liebeshymnus (Henckell) (orch. Strauss, 1897); 4. O süsser Mai (Henckell); 5. Himmelsboten (*Des Knaben Wunderhorn*). (Aibl) Wir beide wollen springen (Bierbaum) for voice and pianoforte. (Boosey and Hawkes, 1964)

1896–7   4 *Gesänge*, Op. 33, for voice(s) and orchestra. 1. Verführung (Mackay); 2. Gesang der Apollopriesterin (Bodman); 3. Hymnus (author unknown); 4. Pilgers Morgenlied (Goethe). (Bote and Bock)

1896–8   6 *Lieder*, Op. 37, for voice and pianoforte. 1. Glückes genug (Liliencron); 2. Ich liebe dich (Liliencron) (orch. Strauss, 1943); 3. Meinem Kinde (Falke) (orch. Strauss, ?1900); 4. Mein Auge (Dehmel) (orch. Strauss, 1933); 5. Herr Lenz (Bodman) (composed June 1896); 6. Hochzeitlich Lied (Lindner). (Aibl)

1897–8   4 *Lieder*, Op. 36, for voice and pianoforte. 1. Das Rosenband (Klopstock) (orch. Strauss, 1897); 2. Für funfzehn Pfennige (*Des Knaben Wunderhorn*); 3. Hat gesagt—bleibt's nicht dabei (*Des Knaben Wunderhorn*); 4. Anbetung (Rückert). (Aibl)

1898   5 *Lieder*, Op. 39, for voice and pianoforte. 1. Leises Lied (Dehmel); 2. Junghexenlied (Bierbaum); 3. Der Arbeitsmann (Dehmel) (orch. Strauss, 1918); 4. Befreit (Dehmel) (orch. Strauss, 1933); 5. Lied an meinen Sohn (Dehmel). (Forberg)

1899   5 *Lieder*, Op. 41, for voice and pianoforte. 1. Wiegenlied (Dehmel) (orch. Strauss, 1900); 2. In der Campagna (Mackay); 3. Am Ufer (Dehmel); 4. Bruder Liederlich (Liliencron); 5. Leise Lieder (Morgenstern). (Leuckart)

3 *Gesänge*, Op. 43, for voice and pianoforte. 1. An sie (Klopstock); 2. Muttertändelei (Bürger) (orch. Strauss, 1900); 3. Die Ulme zu Hirsau (Uhland). (Challier)

2 *grössere Gesänge*, Op. 44, for low voice and orchestra. 1. Notturno (Dehmel); 2. Nächtlicher Gang (Rückert). (Forberg)

Weihnachtsgefühl (Greif), for voice and pianoforte. (Boosey and Hawkes, 1964)[1]

1899–1900   5 *Gedichte* (Rückert), Op. 46, for voice and pianoforte. 1. Ein Obdach gegen Sturm und Regen; 2. Gestern war ich Atlas; 3. Die sieben Siegel; 4. Morgenrot; 5. Ich sehe wie in einem Spiegel. (Fürstner)

1900   5 *Lieder* (Uhland), Op. 47, for voice and pianoforte. 1. Auf ein Kind; 2. Des Dichters Abendgang (orig. version in E flat, but orch. Strauss, 1918, in D flat for soprano); 3. Rückleben; 4. Einkehr; 5. Von den sieben Zechbrüdern. (Fürstner)

5 *Lieder*, Op. 48, for voice and pianoforte. 1. Freundliche Vision (Bierbaum) (orch. Strauss, 1918); 2. Ich schwebe; 3. Kling!;

---

[1] Although included among the *Jugendlieder* in the complete edition of Strauss songs, this *Lied* was composed at Charlottenburg on 8 December 1899.

4. Winterweihe (orch. Strauss, 1918); 5. Winterliebe (orch. Strauss, 1918). Texts of 2–5 by Henckell. (Fürstner)

1900–1 8 *Lieder*, Op. 49, for voice and pianoforte. 1. Waldseligkeit (Dehmel) (orch. Strauss, 1918); 2. In goldener Fülle (Remer); 3. Wiegen-liedchen (Dehmel); 4. Das Lied des Steinklopfers (Henckell); 5. Sie wissen's nicht (Panizza); 6. Junggesellenschwur (*Des Knaben Wunderhorn*); 7. Wer lieben will, muss leiden (Elsässische Volks-lieder); 8. Ach, was Kummer, Qual und Schmerzen (ditto). Fürstner)

1902–6 2 *Gesänge*, Op. 51, for bass and orchestra. 1. Das Tal (Uhland); 2. Der Einsame (Heine) (also with pf.). (Fürstner)

1903–6 6 *Lieder*, Op. 56, for voice and pianoforte. 1. Gefunden (Goethe); 2. Blindenklage (Henckell); 3. Im Spätboot (Meyer); 4. Mit deinen blauen Augen; 5. Frühlingsfeier (orch. Strauss, 1933); 6. Die heiligen drei Könige aus Morgenland (composed 1906 for soprano and orchestra, accompaniment being transcribed for pianoforte by Strauss for publication in Op. 56). Texts of 4–6 by Heine. (Bote and Bock)

1904 2 *Lieder* for voice and guitar or harps, from Calderón's play 'Der Richter von Zalamea'. 1. Liebesliedchen; 2. Lied der Chispa. (Boosey and Hawkes, 1954)

1906 Der Graf von Rom, *vocalise* with pianoforte (2 versions).

1918 *Krämerspiegel* (Kerr), Op. 66, for voice and pianoforte. 1. Es war ein-mal ein Bock; 2. Einst kam der Bock als Bote; 3. Es liebte einst ein Hase; 4. Drei Masken sah ich am Himmel stehn; 5. Hast du ein Tongedicht vollbracht; 6. O lieber Künstler sei ermahnt; 7. Unser Feind ist, grosser Gott; 8. Von Händlern wird die Kunst bedroht; 9. Es war mal eine Wanze; 10. Die Künstler sind die Schöpfer; 11. Die Händler und die Macher; 12. O Schöpferschwarm, O Händlerkreis. (Cassirer, 1921, limited edn of 120; Boosey and Hawkes, 1959).

6 *Lieder*, Op. 67, for voice and pianoforte. 1–3, 3 *Lieder* der 'Ophelia' (Shakespeare): Wie erkenn'ich mein Treulieb; Guten Morgen, 's ist Sankt Valentinstag; Sie trugen ihn auf der Bahre bloss; 4–6, 3 *Lieder* from Goethe's 'Büchern des Unmuts' (Westöstlicher Divan): Wer wird von der Welt verlangen; Hab' ich euch denn je geraten; Wandrers Gemütsruhe. (Bote and Bock)

6 *Lieder* (Brentano), Op. 68, for high voice and pianoforte. Nos. 1–5 orch. Strauss, 1940, No. 6 orch. Strauss, 1933. 1. An die Nacht; 2. Ich wollt ein Sträusslein binden; 3. Säusle, liebe Myrthe; 4. Als mir dein Lied erklang; 5. Amor; 6. Lied der Frauen. ((Fürstner, 1918, orch. version, 1941)

5 *kleine Lieder*, Op. 69, for voice and pianoforte. Texts of 1–3 by Arnim, 4–5 by Heine. 1. Der Stern; 2. Der Pokal; 3. Einerlei; 4. Waldesfahrt; 5. Schlechtes Wetter. (Fürstner)

1919 Sinnspruch (Goethe), for voice and pianoforte. (Mosse)

1921 3 *Hymnen* (Hölderlin), Op. 71, for high voice and orchestra. 1. Hymne an die Liebe; 2. Rückkehr in die Heimat; 3. Die Liebe. (Fürstner)

1922 Erschaffen und Beleben ('Hans Adam war ein Erdenkloss') (Goethe), for bass voice and pianoforte. (Oertel, 1951)

1925   Durch allen Schall und Klang (Goethe), for voice and pianoforte. Composed for R. Rolland's 60th birthday on 29 Jan. 1926. (Boosey and Hawkes, 1959)

1928   5 *Gesänge des Orients* (Bethge), Op. 77, for voice and pianoforte. 1. Ihre Augen; 2. Schwung; 3. Liebesgeschenke; 4. Die Allmächtige; 5. Huldigung. (Leuckart)

1929   2 *Gesänge* (Rückert), for bass voice and pianoforte. 1. Vom künftigen Alter; 2. Und dann nicht mehr. (Universal, 1964)

1930   Spruch: 'Wie etwas sei leicht' (Goethe), for voice and pianoforte. (Boosey and Hawkes, 1968)

1933   Das Bächlein (author unknown), for voice and pianoforte (orch. Strauss 1935). (Universal, 1951)

1935   Im Sonnenschein (Rückert), for bass voice and pianoforte. (Universal, 1964)[2]

        Zugemessne Rhythmen (Goethe), for voice and pianoforte. (Boosey and Hawkes, Strauss Yearbook, 1954)

1939   Hab Dank, du gütger Weisheitsspender, for bass voice unacc. (Strauss Yearbook, 1960)

1940   Notschrei aus den Gefilden Lapplands, for soprano or tenor unacc. (MS)

1942   2 *Lieder* (Weinheber), for voice and pianoforte. 1. Sankt Michael (bass); 2. Blick vom oberen Belvedere (soprano). (Universal, 1964)[3]

        Xenion (Goethe), for voice and pianoforte. Composed for Gerhart Hauptmann's 80th birthday on 15 Nov. 1942 (Strauss Yearbook, 1960)

1943   Wer tritt herein, for unacc. soprano or tenor (MS)

1946–8 4 *letzte Lieder*[4] for high voice and orchestra. In order of composition: 1. Im Abendrot (Eichendorff); 2. Frühling; 3. Beim Schlafengehen; 4. September. Texts of 2–4 by Hesse. (Boosey and Hawkes, 1950, in the order 2, 4, 3, 1. Strauss is said to have favoured the order 3, 4, 2, 1.)

1948   Malven (Knobel), for soprano and pianoforte. First perf. New York, 10 January 1985, Kiri te Kanawa acc. by Martin Katz. (Boosey and Hawkes, 1985)

---

[2] This song, with the two 1929 Rückert songs and the 1922 Goethe song, appears in the 1964 collected edition as *4 Gesänge* for bass voice under the spurious opus number 87.

[3] These songs, with *Das Bächlein* (1933), appear in the collected edition under the spurious opus number 88.

[4] The title *Four Last Songs* was given to this set by Strauss's publisher, Ernest Roth, after the composer's death.

Appendix C

Personalia

Alwin, Carl (1891–1945). Operatic conductor who was married to the soprano Elisabeth Schumann from 1919 to 1933. Was on conducting staff of Vienna State Opera from 1921 to 1938. Assisted in arrangement of music for film version of *Der Rosenkavalier*. Conducted first British performance of second version of *Ariadne auf Naxos* (Covent Garden, 27 May 1924).

Bahr, Hermann (1863–1934). Austrian playwright whom Strauss first approached for libretto of *Intermezzo*. Was married to the great Wagnerian soprano Anna von Mildenburg, formerly Mahler's mistress and a notable exponent of Strauss operatic roles.

Beecham, Sir Thomas (1879–1961). English conductor and impresario who was a leading champion of Strauss's works. Conducted first English performances of *Elektra* (19 Feb. 1910), *Feuersnot* (9 July 1910), *Salome* (8 Dec. 1910), *Der Rosenkavalier* (29 Jan. 1913) and *Ariadne auf Naxos* (27 May 1913). Organized 1947 London Strauss Festival.

Bierbaum, Otto Julius (1865–1910). Bavarian novelist and poet some of whose verses Strauss set to music, notably *Traum durch die Dämmerung*.

Blech, Leo (1871–1958). Conductor active especially in Berlin. Was assistant to Strauss when Strauss was chief conductor of the opera there up to 1918. Generally credited with suggestion that the Composer in the Prologue to *Ariadne* should be a *travesti* role.

Böhm, Karl (1894–1981). Austrian conductor who held many important posts in Germany and Austria, notably at Dresden from 1934 to 1942. Conducted first performances of *Die schweigsame Frau* and *Daphne*.

Bülow, Hans von (1830–94). Pianist and conductor of immense eminence, notably at Munich, Meiningen and Hamburg. Conducted first performances of Wagner's *Tristan und Isolde* and *Die Meistersinger*. Appointed Strauss as his assistant at Meiningen.

Busch, Fritz (1890–1951). Conductor of Dresden opera from 1922 to 1933, directing first performances of *Intermezzo* and *Die ägyptische Helena*. Joint dedicatee of *Arabella*. Was first conductor of Glyndebourne Opera.

Dehmel, Richard (1863–1920). German author and poet. Strauss set several of his poems.

Del Mar, Norman (1919–94). English horn-player and conductor and author of three-volume survey of Strauss's music.

Furtwängler, Wilhelm (1886–1954). German conductor, especially of Berlin Philharmonic Orchestra in 1930s. Fell into disfavour with Nazis, but remained in Germany. Conducted first performance of Strauss's *Four Last Songs*, in London in 1950.

Goebbels, Joseph (1897–1945). German Minister of Enlightenment and Propaganda from 1933 to 1945. Appointed Strauss to presidency of *Reichsmusikkammer* in 1933 and dismissed him in 1935.

Gregor, Joseph (1888–1960). Viennese art historian who compiled three librettos for Strauss, *Friedenstag, Daphne* and *Die Liebe der Danae.*

Gutheil-Schoder, Marie (1874–1935). German soprano engaged by Mahler for Vienna Opera in 1900. Exceptional actress. Fine exponent of Elektra. Sang one performance as Oktavian at Covent Garden in 1913.

Hartmann, Rudolf (1900–88). Leading operatic producer, especially at Munich during Clemens Krauss's tenure. Expert on Strauss operas. Author of valuable book on staging of Strauss's operas and ballets.

Hofmannsthal, Hugo von (1874–1929). Austrian dramatist and poet who first contacted Strauss in 1900. They first collaborated on *Elektra*, which was followed by *Rosenkavalier, Ariadne auf Naxos, Die Frau ohne Schatten, Die ägyptische Helena* and *Arabella*. Their published correspondence is of the utmost interest.

Jeritza, Maria (1887–1982). Czech soprano of great vocal and personal beauty. First singer of Ariadne (1912) and of the Empress in *Die Frau ohne Schatten* (1919). Strauss's last song, 'Malven', was a gift to her.

Kerr, Alfred (1867–1948). Berlin theatre critic who left Germany for England in 1933. Wrote the satirical poems for Strauss's song-cycle *Krämerspiegel* in 1918.

Krauss, Clemens (1893–1945). Austrian conductor and director of Vienna State Opera who was great exponent of Strauss and one of his closest friends. Librettist of *Capriccio*. Conducted first performances of *Arabella, Friedenstag, Die Liebe der Danae*, and *Capriccio*. Husband of Viorica Ursuleac. Noted for his work at Munich opera, 1937–44.

Lehmann, Lotte (1888–1976). German soprano who was the most distinguished Marschallin in *Der Rosenkavalier* in inter-war years. First Composer in *Ariadne* and first Christine in *Intermezzo*. Wrote interesting book about working with Strauss.

Levi, Hermann (1839–1900). Conductor of Munich Court Opera during Strauss's boyhood and youth. Conducted first *Parsifal* in 1882 and first performances of several early Strauss works.

Mahler, Gustav (1860–1911). Composer and conductor who befriended Strauss though he regarded him as his complete opposite. Strauss and Mahler frequently conducted each other's works.

Mann, William (1924–89). English music critic. Was a critic of *The Times* of London 1948–60 and its chief critic 1960–82. His classic book on Strauss's operas was published in 1964. Translator of many Lieder.

Mayr, Richard (1877–1935). Austrian bass-baritone whose portrayal of Baron Ochs in *Der Rosenkavalier* is generally regarded as unsurpassable. Was a medical student but became singer on Mahler's advice. Created role of Barak in *Die Frau ohne Schatten* (1919).

Reinhardt, Max (1873–1943). Theatrical producer of genius whose productions in Berlin inspired both Strauss and Hofmannsthal. Supervised first *Der Rosenkavalier* in 1911. First producer of *Ariadne auf Naxos*, which is dedicated to him. One of founders, with Strauss and others, of the modern Salzburg Festival. Emigrated to United States in 1933.

Ritter, Alexander (1833–96). Orchestral violinist and composer. A devotee of Wagner, whose niece he married. Persuaded the young Strauss to follow Lisztian methods of composition.

Rolland, Romain (1866–1944). French writer best known for his novel *Jean-Christophe*. Friend and admirer of Strauss for over forty years. Their correspondence has been published.

Roller, Alfred (1864–1933). Leading theatrical designer at the Vienna Opera under Mahler and later under Strauss. Designed first *Der Rosenkavalier* at Dresden in 1911 and *Die Frau ohne Schatten* at Vienna in 1919.

Rösch, Friedrich (1862–1925). Became friend of Strauss in their student days. *Tod und Verklärung* is dedicated to him. Co-founder with Strauss of *Genossenschaft deutscher Tonsetzer*.

Schalk, Franz (1863–1931). Austrian conductor associated for many years with Vienna Opera which he joined as assistant to Mahler. Joint director with Strauss 1919–24 until they quarrelled. Conducted first performance of *Die Frau ohne Schatten*.

Schoenberg, Arnold (1874–1951). Austrian composer and teacher whose 'system of composing with twelve notes' revolutionized music in 1923.

Schuch, Ernst von (1846–1914). Conductor at Dresden Court Opera from 1872 until his death (musical director from 1882). His interpretations of Strauss were deeply admired by the composer, who awarded him the first performances of *Feuersnot*, *Salome*, *Elektra* and *Der Rosenkavalier*.

Schuh, Willi (1900–86). Swiss music critic and author, chosen by Strauss as his official biographer. Only the first volume of the work, *Richard Strauss: Jugend und frühe Meisterjahre Lebenschronik 1864–1898* was published (1976) before his death. Music critic of the *Neue Zürcher Zeitung* 1928–65. Accompanied Strauss on his 1947 flight to London. Edited Strauss's *Recollections and Reflections* (1949) and Strauss's letters to Hofmannsthal (1952), his parents (1954), Bülow (1954), Zweig (1957), Kippenberg (1960), and to Schuh himself (1969). Dedicatee (with his wife) of *Frühling* in the *Vier letzte Lieder*.

Schumann, Elisabeth (1885–1952). German soprano who was one of the legendary stars of the Vienna Opera between the wars. A marvellous exponent of Strauss; her Sophie in *Der Rosenkavalier* was particularly memorable. Toured North America with Strauss in 1921.

Schwarzkopf, Dame Elisabeth (b. 1915), German soprano whose performances as the Marschallin and as the Countess in *Capriccio* were widely admired. Widow of Walter Legge.

Specht, Richard (1870–1932). Austrian music critic and essayist who wrote biographies of Mahler, Brahms and Puccini. His biography of Strauss was published in two volumes in Leipzig in 1921.

Stransky, Josef (1872–1936). Conductor who, after holding various posts in Germany, succeeded Mahler in New York in 1911. It was he for whom Mieze Mücke's note, which is the basis of the *Intermezzo* misunderstanding, was intended.

Strauss, Franz Joseph (1822–1905). Father of Richard Strauss. Famous horn-player and a member of the Munich Court Orchestra for nearly fifty years. Detested Wagner and his music, which he performed magnificently.

Ursuleac, Viorica (1894–1985). Rumanian soprano and wife of Clemens Krauss.

Created roles of Arabella, Commandant's Wife in *Friedenstag*, Danae and the Countess (*Capriccio*). Was Strauss's favourite soprano in his later years.

Wülzogen, Ernst von (1855–1934). Munich satirist and poet who wrote the libretto of *Feuersnot*.

Wüllner, Franz (1832–1902). German conductor and composer who was appointed a court conductor at Munich in 1864 and after Bülow's departure in 1869 conducted the first performances of Wagner's *Das Rheingold* (1869) and *Die Walküre* (1870). In 1884 he became conductor of the Gürzenich concerts, Cologne, after seven years in Dresden, He conducted first performances of Strauss's *Serenade* (Dresden, 1882), *Till Eulenspiegel* (Cologne, 1896) and *Don Quixote* (Cologne, 1898).

Zweig, Stefan (1881–1942). Austrian novelist and playwright who wrote libretto of *Die schweigsame Frau* and supervised librettos of *Friedenstag* and *Daphne*. His collaboration with Strauss was forbidden by the Nazis because he was Jewish. Committed suicide in South America.

Appendix D

Select bibliography

Abert, Anna Amalie, *Richard Strauss: Die Opern* (Hanover, 1972).

Armstrong, Thomas, *Strauss's Tone-Poems* (Oxford, 1931).

Asow, Mueller von, *Richard Strauss: Thematisches Verzeichnis* (Vienna, 1954–68).

Baum, Gunther, *Richard Strauss und Hugo von Hofmannsthal* (Berlin, 1962).

Beecham, Thomas, *A Mingled Chime* (London, 1944).

Birkin, Kenneth, *Friedenstag and Daphne: an Interpretative study of the literary and dramatic sources of two operas by Richard Strauss* (New York and London, 1989).

—— *Arabella* (Cambridge, 1989).

—— (ed.), *Stefan Zweig-Joseph Gregor Correspondence 1921–1938* (Dunedin, 1991).

Blaukopf, Herta (ed.), *Gustav Mahler-Richard Strauss Briefwechsel 1888–1911* (Munich, 1980). English trans. by Edmund Jephcott (London, 1984).

Böhm, Karl, *Begegnung mit Richard Strauss* (Vienna, 1964).

Brosche, Günter, 'the Concerto for Oboe and Small Orchestra (1945): Remarks about the Origin of the Work' in Gilliam (ed.), *Richard Strauss, New Perspectives on The Composer and his Work* (Durham and London, 1992).

—— *Richard Strauss: Bibliographie* (Vienna, 1973).

Brosche, Günter, and Dachs, Karl, *Richard Strauss: Autographen in München und Wien: Verzeichnis* (Tutzing, 1979).

Busch, Fritz, *Aus dem Leben eines Musikers* (Zürich, 1949).

Cardus, Neville, 'Richard Strauss' in *Ten Composers* (London, 1945).

Del Mar, Norman, *Richard Strauss: a critical commentary on his life and works.* Three volumes (London, 1962, 1969, 1972; rev. 1978).

Deppisch, Walter, *Richard Strauss* (Hamburg, 1968).

English National Opera Guide No. 8, *Der Rosenkavalier*, ed. by N. John (essays by P. Branscombe, M. Kennedy, and D. Puffett) (London, 1981).

English National Opera Guide No. 30, *Arabella*, ed. N. John (essays by K. Forsyth, W. Mann, M. Ratcliffe, and P. J. Smith) (London, 1985).

English National Opera Guide No. 37, *Salome/Elektra*, ed. By N. John (essays by P. Banks, J. Burton, K. Segar, and C. Wintle) (London, 1988).

Erhardt, Otto, *Richard Strauss* (Olten, 1953).

Forsyth, Karen, *Ariadne auf Naxos by Hugo von Hofmannsthal and Richard Strauss, its genesis and meaning* (London, 1982).

Gilliam, Bryan, *Richard Strauss's Elektra* (Oxford, 1991).

—— (ed.), *Richard Strauss and His World* (essays by L. Botstein, B. Gilliam, J. Hepokoski, T. L. Jackson, D. Puffett, M. P. Steinberg, and reprints of various articles) (Princeton, 1992).

Gilliam, Bryan (ed.), *Richard Strauss: New Perspectives on the Composer and his Work* (essays by K. Agawu, G. Brosche, B. Gilliam, S. E. Hefling, J. Hepokoski, T. L. Jackson, L. Lockwood, B. A. Petersen, P. M. Potter, R. Schlötterer, R. L. Todd) (Durham and London, 1992).

Gould, Glenn, 'An Argument for Richard Strauss' and 'Strauss and the Electronic Future' in *The Glenn Gould Reader*, ed. T. Page (London, 1987).

Grasberger, Franz, *Richard Strauss und die Wiener Oper* (Munich, 1969).

—— (ed.) *Eine Welt in Briefen* (Tutzing, 1967).

Gray, Cecil, 'Richard Strauss' in *Survey of Contemporary Music* (London, 1924).

Gregor, Joseph, *Richard Strauss, die Meister der Oper* (Munich, 1939).

Hartmann, Rudolf, *Die Bühnenwerke von der Uraufführung bis heute* (Fribourg, 1980); English version, *Richard Strauss, the Staging of his Operas and Ballets*, trans. Graham Davis (Oxford, 1982).

Hofmannsthal, Hugo von, *Briefe der Freundschaft*, correspondence with Eberhard von Bodenhausen (Frankfurt, 1953).

Jaacks, Gisela, and Jahnke, A. W. (eds.), *Richard Strauss, Musik des Lichts in dunkler Zeit* (essays by K. Böhm, G. Brunner, W. Geierhos, R. Hartmann, G. Jaacks, S. Kohler, E. Krause, W. Schuh, F. Trenner) (Mainz, 1980).

Jackson, Timothy L., 'Ruhe, meine Seele! and the Letzte Orchesterlieder' in Gilliam (ed.), *Richard Strauss and his World* (Princeton, 1992).

—— 'The Metamorphosis of the Metamorphosen: New Analytical and Source-Critical Discoveries' in Gilliam (ed.), *Richard Strauss: New Perspectives on the Composer and his Work* (Durham and London, 1992).

Jameux, Dominique, *Richard Strauss* (Paris, 1986).

Jefferson, Alan, *The Operas of Richard Strauss in Britain, 1910–63* (London, 1963).

—— *The Lieder of Richard Strauss* (London, 1971).

—— *The Life of Richard Strauss* (Newton Abbot, 1973).

—— *Richard Strauss* (London, 1975).

—— *Der Rosenkavalier* (Cambridge, 1985).

Kennedy, Michael, 'Richard Strauss' in *The New Grove Dictionary of Music and Musicians*, vol. 18 (with work-list and bibliography by Robert Bailey) (London, 1980). Reprinted (rev.) in *The New Grove Turn-of-the-Century Masters* (London, 1985).

—— *Strauss Tone Poems* (London, 1984).

—— 'Comedy for Music' in *Der Rosenkavalier*, English National Opera Guide No. 8, ed. N. John (London, 1981).

Krause, Ernst, *Richard Strauss: Gestalt und Werk* (Leipzig, 1955). English version (3rd German edition, 1963) *Richard Strauss: the Man and his Work*, trans. John Coombs (London, 1964).

Lehmann, Lotte, *Singing with Richard Strauss* (London, 1964).

Levi, Erik, *Music in the Third Reich* (London, 1994).

Mahler, Alma, *Gustav Mahler: Memories and Letters*, ed. D. Mitchell (3rd English edition, London, 1973).

Mann, William, *Richard Strauss: a critical study of the operas* (London, 1964).

Marek, George R., *Richard Strauss: the life of a Non-Hero* (London, 1967).

Newman, Ernest, *Richard Strauss* (London, 1908).

Nice, David, *Richard Strauss* (London, 1993).

Osborne, Charles, *The Complete Operas of Richard Strauss* (London, 1988).

Pander, Oscar von, *Clemens Krauss in München* (Munich, 1955).

Petersen, Barbara A., *Ton und Wort: the Lieder of Richard Strauss* (Ann Arbor, 1977).

Prawy, Marcel, *The Vienna Opera* (London, 1969).

Puffett, Derrick (ed.), *Richard Strauss: Salome* (essays by C. Ayrey, T. Carpenter, R. Ellmann, R. Holloway, D. Puffett, M. Praz, R. Tenschert, and J. Williamson) (Cambridge, 1989).

—— (ed.) *Richard Strauss: Elektra* (essays by C. Abbate, T. Carpenter, P. E. Easterling, K. Forsyth, R. Holloway, D. Puffett, and A. Whittall) (Cambridge, 1989).

Puritz, Gerd, *Elisabeth Schumann*, trans. Joy Puritz (London, 1993).

Rolland, Romain, *Richard Strauss: Correspondance et Fragments de Journal* (Paris, 1951); English edition, *Richard Strauss and Romain Rolland: correspondence, diary and essays*, trans. and ed. Rollo H. Myers (London (1968).

Roth, Ernst, *Musik als Kunst und Ware* (Zürich, 1966); in English as *The Business of Music* (1969).

Schlötterer, Reinhold, *Die Texte der Lieder von Richard Strauss* (Munich, 1988).

Schuch, Friedrich von, *Richard Strauss, Ernst von Schuch und Dresdens Oper* (Leipzig, 1953).

Schuh, Willi, *Über Opern von Richard Strauss* (Zürich, 1947).

—— *Hugo von Hofmannsthal und Richard Strauss* (Munich, 1964).

—— *Richard Strauss: Jugend und frühe Meisterjahre Lebenschronik 1864–1898* (Zürich, 1976); English version, *Richard Strauss: a Chronicle of the Early Years, 1864–1898*, trans. Mary Whittall (Cambridge, 1982).

—— *Straussiana aus vier Jahrzehnten* (Tutzing, 1981).

Specht, Richard, *Richard Strauss und sein Werk* (Leipzig, 1921).

Splitt, Gerhard, *Richard Strauss 1933–1935: Aesthetik und Musikpolitik zu Beginn der nationalsozialistischen Herrschaft* (Pfaffenweiler, 1987).

Steinitzer, Max, *Richard Strauss* (Berlin, 1911).

Strauss, Richard, *Briefe an die Eltern*, ed. W. Schuh (Zürich, 1954).

—— *Betrachtungen und Erinnerungen*, ed. W. Schuh (Zürich, 1949); English version, *Recollections and Reflections*, trans. L. J. Lawrence (London, 1953).

—— *Briefwechsel mit Hans von Bülow*, ed. W. Schuh (Bonn, 1954),

—— *Joseph Gregor*, ed. R. Tenschert (Salzburg, 1955),

—— *Hugo von Hofmannsthal*, ed. W. Schuh (Zürich, 1952); English trans. H. Hammelmann and E. Osers (London 1961),

—— *Anton Kippenberg*, ed. W. Schuh (Bonn, 1960),

—— *Clemens Krauss*, ed. W. Schuh and G. K. Kende (Munich, 1964),

—— *Willi Schuh*, (ed.) W. Schuh (Zürich, 1969),

—— *Ludwig Thuille 1877–1907*, ed. A. Ott (Munich, 1969),

—— *Cosima Wagner*, ed. F. Trenner (Tutzing, 1978),

—— *Franz Wüllner*, ed. D. Kämper (Cologne, 1963),

—— *Stefan Zweig*, ed. W. Schuh (Frankfurt, 1957); in English as *A Confidential Matter*, trans. Max Knight (University of California, 1977).

Richard Strauss-Blätter (Journal of the International Richard Strauss Society), published several times a year since 1978. Contains many important contributions.

Tenschert, Roland, *Anekdoten von Richard Strauss* (Vienna, 1945).

—— *Richard Strauss und Wien* (Vienna, 1949).

Trenner, Franz, *Richard Strauss: Dokumente seines Lebens und Schaffens* (Munich, 1954).

—— *Richard Strauss Werkverzeichnis* (Munich, 1993).

Ursuleac, Viorica, and Schlötterer, Roswitha, *Singen für Richard Strauss* (Vienna, 1987).

Wanless, Susan, *Vier letzte Lieder* (Leeds, 1984).

Wellesz, Egon, 'Hofmannsthal and Strauss', in *Music and Letters*, vol. xxxiii, 1952.

Wilhelm, Kurt, *Richard Strauss persönlich* (Munich, 1985); English version, *Richard Strauss: an Intimate Portrait*, trans. Mary Whittall (London, 1989).

—— *Fürs Wort brauche ich Hilfe: die Geburt der Oper Capriccio* (Munich, 1988).

Williamson, John, *Also sprach Zarathustra* (Cambridge, 1993).

Wurmser, Leo, 'Richard Strauss as an Opera Conductor', in *Music and Letters*, vol. lxv, 1964.

Appendix E

The self-quotations in Ein Heldenleben

Here is a list, in order of their appearance, of the self-quotations in the 'Hero's Works of Peace' section of the tone-poem *Ein Heldenleben* which occur between pp. 105 and 117 of the original Leuckart score:

Don Juan (2 extracts, p. 105)
Also sprach Zarathustra (p. 105)
Tod und Verklärung (2 extracts, p. 110)
Don Quixote (3 extracts, p. 110)
Don Juan (2 extracts, p. 111)
Don Quixote (p. 111)
Till Eulenspiegel (p. 111)
Guntram (p. 111)
Guntram (2 extracts, p. 112)
Guntram (p. 113)
Tod und Verklärung (p. 113)
Also sprach Zarathustra (p. 113)
Guntram (p. 113)
Macbeth (p. 113)
'Befreit' (p. 113)
Macbeth (2 extracts, p. 113)
'Traum durch die Dämmerung' (p. 114)
Guntram (2 extracts, p. 114)
Don Quixote (p. 114)
Guntram (p. 115)
Tod und Verklärung (p. 116)
Also sprach Zarathustra (p. 116)
Guntram (p. 117)

Index

Aagard-Oestvig, Karl, 68, 69, 153
Ahna, Maj.-Gen. Adolf de (father-in-law), 16, 26, 27–8
Ahna, Mädi de (sister-in-law), 27–8
Ahna, Pauline de. *See* Strauss, Pauline
Allen, Sir Hugh, 97
Alwin, Carl, 79, 111, 115, 179, 194, 221
Andreae, Volkmar, 109
Andrian-Werburg, Leopold von, 67
Arnim, Achim von, 193
Auber, Daniel, 3, 107

Bahr, Hermann, 45, 64, 65, 76, 102, 168, 221
Bartók, Béla, 66, 117
Bayreuth, 7, 18, 22, 28, 30, 33, 89–90, 92, 93, 116
Beecham, Sir Thomas, 44, 45, 56, 110, 111, 144*n*, 221
Beethoven, Ludwig van, 1, 2, 3, 4, 10, 12, 24, 70, 97, 107, 112, 115, 116, 152, 164, 178, 181, 213
  Die Ruinen von Athen, 75, 78, 213
Berg, Alban, 66, 77, 137
Berlin, 7, 8, 51, 59, 64, 73, 74, 88, 91, 92, 96, 98, 107, 186, 190, 191, 193, 221
  Opera, 9, 31, 32–4, 34–5, 50, 67, 81, 86, 186, 221
  Philharmonic Orchestra, 8, 10, 20, 21, 26, 29, 89, 95, 221
Berlioz, Hector, 12, 17, 24, 35, 107, 121, 186
Bernhardt, Sarah, 41
Bethge, Hans, 194, 220
Bierbaum, Otto, 188, 190, 191, 217, 218, 221
Bilse, Benjamin, 8
Bizet, Georges, 14, 107
Blech, Leo, 60, 73, 221
Böhm, Karl, 46, 93, 97, 104, 107, 140n, 153, 163, 221
Boieldieu, Adrien, 4, 15
Bormann, Martin, 103
Boult, Sir Adrian, 111
Brahms, Johannes, 8, 9, 10–11, 14, 15, 115, 117, 118, 121, 139, 178, 184, 194, 223
Brecher, Gustav, 49

Brentano, Clemens, 192, 219
Britten, Benjamin (Lord Britten of Aldeburgh), 54, 137
Bronsart, Hans von, 18, 20, 22, 24
Brosche, Günter, 181
Bruckner, Anton, 29, 36, 153
Bülow, Hans von, 4, 8–11, 13, 15, 17–18, 20–1, 24, 26, 71, 120, 221, 223, 224
Burghauser, Hugo, 111, 182, 183
Burrian, Karel, 43
Busch, Fritz, 22, 75, 80, 81–2, 87, 88, 159, 221

Cardus, Sir Neville, 161
Cebotari, Maria, 93, 109, 110
Chabrier, Emmanuel, 36, 107
Concertgebouw Orchestra of Amsterdam, 35, 40
Correck, Joseph, 155
Couperin, François, 77, 147, 170, 177, 179, 213

Dahn, Felix, 188, 217
D'Albert, Eugen, 20
Debussy, Achille-Claude, 38, 42, 90
Dehmel, Richard, 189, 190, 218, 219, 221
de Lancie, John, 108
Della Casa, Lisa, 160
Del Mar, Norman, 71, 110, 125, 129, 138, 148, 168, 169, 176, 221
Destinn, Emmy, 43, 53
Diaghilev, Sergei, 55, 56, 175
Dresden, 7, 8, 16, 17, 44, 59, 74, 75, 79, 88, 91, 103, 104, 106, 224
  Opera, 37, 43, 44–5, 49, 68, 80–1, 97, 98, 106, 108, 140n, 153, 221, 223
Dukas, Paul, 36, 96
Dux, Claire, 72

Egk, Werner, 101
Eichendorff, Joseph von, 111, 186, 195, 216, 220
Einstein, Alfred, 86
Elgar, Sir Edward, 36, 65–6, 72, 77, 87, 120, 121, 128, 139, 147, 177, 178, 196
Eysoldt, Gertrud, 42

Index

Fischer, Franz, 14, 18
Flagstad, Kirsten, 113, 194
Fürstner, Adolph, 23, 42, 110
Furtwängler, Wilhelm, 90, 95, 113, 194, 221–2

Garmisch, 44, 47, 48, 58, 66, 67, 76, 79, 83, 91, 96, 101, 102, 103, 107, 108, 109, 110, 112, 113, 179, 185
Gerhardt, Elena, 72
Gilm, Hermann von, 9, 187, 217
Gluck, Christoph Willibald von, 23, 107, 170, 213
Goebbels, Joseph, 90–3, 95, 100, 101, 104, 106, 194, 222
Goethe, Johann Wolfgang von, 9, 23, 106, 148, 184, 191, 192, 194, 215, 217, 219, 220
Goossens, Léon, 109n
Grab, Emanuel von, 73, 74
Gray, Cecil, 77
Greece, 23, 80, 169
Gregor, Hans, 66
Gregor, Joseph, 95–9, 102, 106, 163, 165, 167, 186, 212, 216, 222
Gutheil-Schoder, Marie, 21, 49, 60, 69, 222

Hanslick, Eduard, 7, 21, 29
Hartmann, Rudolf, 76, 96, 97, 100, 105, 106, 113, 222
Hauptmann, Gerhard, 101, 220
Heger, Robert, 187, 217, 218
Heine, Heinrich, 191, 192, 193, 219
Henckell, Karl, 188, 189, 191, 217, 218, 219
Hesse, Hermann, 112, 195, 220
Hindemith, Paul, 66, 95, 156
Hitler, Adolf, 87, 88, 89–90, 91, 93, 97, 103, 104, 106, 110, 194
Hochberg, Bolko von, 31
Hofmannstahl, Gerty von, 58, 111
Hofmannsthal, Hugo von, 39, 44, 47, 51, 56, 57, 58, 59, 64, 65, 67, 68, 70, 75, 77, 80, 81, 83–4, 85, 87, 89, 95–6, 98, 113, 115, 135, 138, 140, 144, 147, 148, 152, 153, 157, 158, 159, 160, 161, 162, 165, 167, 170, 172, 175, 179, 212, 213, 216, 222, 223
Work with R.S. on libretti and scenarios of:
Ägyptische Helena, Die, 78–9
Arabella, 82–3
Ariadne auf Naxos, 51–5
Bourgeois Gentilhomme, Le (Der Bürger als Edelmann), 64–5
Elektra, 44
Frau ohne Schatten, Die, 51–2, 56–7, 58–9, 62–3
Josephslegende, 55–6
Rosenkavalier, Der, 47–8

Hölderlin, Johann Friedrich, 193, 219
Hotter, Hans, 69, 97, 100
Hülsen, Georg von, 43
Humperdinck, Engelbert, 22, 25

Italy, 14, 18, 58, 73

Jackson, Timothy L., 106n, 195
Janáček, Leoš, 78
Jerger, Alfred, 69, 70, 88
Jeritza, Maria, 53–4, 60, 67, 68, 69, 71, 80–1, 112, 153, 158, 194, 195, 222
Joachim Quartet, 8
Johnstone, Arthur, 40, 70, 117
Jöhr, Adolf, 195
Jonson, Ben, 86, 162, 212

Karajan, Herbert von, 98
Karpath, Ludwig, 75
Kemp, Barbara, 193
Kern, Adèle, 97
Kerr, Alfred, 192, 219, 222
Kessler, Count Harry, 47, 55
Khnopff, Georges, 31
Kippenberg, Anton, 86, 223
Klemperer, Otto, 44, 88
Klopstock, Friedrich Gottlieb, 189, 216, 218
Klose, Hermann, 8
Knappertsbusch, Hans, 89
Korngold, Erich, 69, 107
Krauss, Clemens, 80, 85, 88, 91, 97, 98, 99, 100, 101, 104, 105, 158, 161, 167, 169, 170, 171, 186, 212, 222, 223
Křenek, Ernst, 38
Krull, Annie, 44
Kubrick, Stanley, 125
Kurz, Selma, 52, 60, 67, 69

Lachmann, Hedwig, 42, 212
Lassen, Eduard, 18, 20
Lehár, Franz, 78, 87, 101, 109, 159
Lehmann, Lotte, 26, 49, 60, 68, 69, 73, 75, 76, 88, 115, 153, 154, 155, 222
Lenau, Nikolaus, 216
Levi, Hermann, 6, 7, 12, 14, 18, 24, 28, 29, 30, 222
Liliencron, Detlev von, 189, 218
Lindner, Anton, 41
Lindner, Eugen, 218
Liszt, Franz, 12, 15, 17, 24, 35, 70, 177
London, 15, 30, 40, 44, 45–6, 56, 68, 72–3, 80, 97, 110–11, 167, 179, 184, 222
Lorenz, Max, 104
Lortzing, Albert, 21, 37, 44, 107, 139

Mackay, John Henry, 188, 189, 190, 217, 218
Mahler, Alma, 37, 38, 42, 68

Mahler, Gustav, 11, 15–16, 23, 24, 25, 27, 30, 32, 35, 37, 38, 41, 42, 43, 48, 49, 52, 60, 64, 67, 69, 70, 80, 90, 120, 125, 128, 129, 131, 133, 138, 139, 141, 149, 153, 154, 181, 186, 189, 190, 196, 221, 222, 223
Mann, Klaus, 108
Mann, Thomas, 108
Mann, William, 146, 156, 222
Mannstädt, Franz, 8, 10
Marek, George R., 79, 88
Maschalk, Max, 193
Massine, Leonid, 56
Mayr, Richard, 49, 68, 69, 70, 153, 222
Meiningen, 5, 8, 9, 10, 11, 13, 14, 53, 132, 170, 221
Mendelssohn, Felix, 2, 115, 116, 117, 121, 130, 139, 147
Mengelberg, Willem, 35, 40
Meyer, Conrad, 191, 219
Meyer, Friedrich, 2
Mildenburg, Anna von, 64, 69, 221
Molière, 52, 58, 59, 64, 65, 144, 212, 213
Monteverdi, Claudio, 144, 163
Mottl, Felix, 11, 18, 24, 25, 43, 49, 217
Mozart, Wolfgang Amadeus, 1, 3, 5, 10, 90, 92, 94, 105, 107, 114, 147, 148, 156, 183
 Così fan tutte, 14–15, 28, 69, 70, 114, 157
 Don Giovanni, 21, 28, 69, 70
 Idomeneo (Strauss version), 85–6, 213
 Zauberflöte, Die, 2, 21, 56, 68, 148, 152
Mück, Karl, 35
Mücke, Mieze, 154, 155, 223
Munich, 1, 3, 7, 9, 15, 16, 33, 35, 36, 48, 55, 56, 65, 74, 91, 98, 104, 106, 107, 112, 113, 123, 173, 178, 186, 221, 223
 Opera, 14–15, 18, 24–5, 28–9, 30–1, 49, 81, 88, 89, 97, 100, 102–3, 106, 113, 153, 161, 222, 224

Newman, Ernest, 45, 56, 129, 134, 137, 153
New York, 7, 31, 40–1, 43–4, 50, 68, 72, 81, 154, 223
 Philharmonic Orchestra, 7, 71
Niessen, Bruno von, 85, 86
Nietzsche, Friedrich, 24, 29, 33, 125
Nijinsky, Vaclav, 55, 56
Nikisch, Arthur, 26, 29

Offenbach, Jacques, 53, 61, 62, 78
Olympic Games (1936), 92

Paris, 30, 33, 39, 42, 56, 72, 112
Patzak, Julius, 97
Perfall, Karl von, 14, 18, 28, 30, 94
Perron, Carl, 49
Pfitzner, Hans, 69, 107
Philadelphia Orchestra, 71, 72

Pollini, Bernhardt, 27, 30
Possart, Ernest von, 28, 30
Pschorr, Georg, 6n, 14, 23
Pschorr, Johanna, 187
Puccini, Giacomo, 44, 69, 77, 135, 152, 223

Raabe, Peter, 194
Raff, Joseph Joachim, 117
Rathenau, Walther, 90 and n
Ravel, Maurice, 55, 74, 147
Reger, Max, 36, 217
Reichsmusikkammer, 90–3, 108, 222
Reinhardt, Max, 41, 42, 44, 49, 52–3, 59, 64, 69, 88, 99, 170, 222
Reining, Maria, 104
Rethberg, Elisabeth, 70, 80–1
Reucker, Alfred, 87, 88
Richter, Hans, 2, 18, 21
Ritter, Alexander, 11–12, 18, 19, 22, 24, 30, 223
Rodzinski, Arthur, 179
Rolland, Romain, 33–4, 42, 58, 70, 74–5, 77, 79, 88, 106, 120, 220, 223
Roller, Alfred, 48, 67, 68, 70, 223
Rösch, Friedrich, 34, 154, 223
Rossini, Gioachino, 14, 163, 170
Rossmayer, Richard, 186
Roth, Ernest, 110, 111, 194, 195, 220n
Rückert, Friedrich, 52, 184, 185, 190, 191, 216, 218, 220
Rüdel, Hugo, 185
Russell, Ken, 88

Sacher, Paul, 106, 107
Saillet, Marcel, 109
Saint-Saëns, Camille, 3, 17
Salzburg Festival, 65, 69–70, 91, 100, 101, 104–5, 158, 161, 193, 222
Samazeuilh, Gustave, 112
Sardou, Victorien, 8
Schack, Adolf Friedrich von, 188, 217
Schalk, Franz, 49, 60, 66–7, 68–9, 70, 71, 73–5, 80, 94, 223
Schiller, Friedrich von, 184, 216
Schillings, Max von, 38, 193
Schirach, Baldur von, 101, 108
Schlüter, Erna, 193
Schmidt, Franz, 69
Schnitzler, Arthur, 68, 154
Schoenberg, Arnold, 1, 37–8, 66, 88, 137, 147, 156, 189, 223
Schreker, Franz, 69
Schubert, Franz, 10, 118, 147, 189
Schuch, Ernst von, 37, 43, 44, 49, 50, 59, 223
Schuh, Willi, 98, 102, 109, 110, 112, 195, 223

Index

Schumann, Clara, 4
Schumann, Elisabeth, 49, 69, 70, 71, 72, 77, 79, 80, 111, 115, 135, 158, 192–3, 194, 221, 223
Schumann, Robert, 4, 115, 118, 147, 156
Schumann-Heink, Ernestine, 45, 191
Seebach, Count Nikolaus von, 49, 59
Seefried, Irmgard, 104
Seidl, Arthur, 22, 29
Serafin, Tullio, 49
Shakespeare, William, 4, 192
Shaw, Bernard, 45–6, 72
Shostakovich, Dmitri, 88, 118, 137
Sievert, Ludwig, 97
Singer, Otto, 79, 179, 191
Sitwell, Sir Osbert, 139
Slezak, Leo, 69, 71
Sommer, Hans, 34
Specht, Richard, 58, 68, 80, 187, 223
Speyer, Sir Edgar, 58
Speyer, Lotti, 15, 20
Spitzweg, Eugen, 8–9, 21
Steiner, Franz, 193
Stransky, Josef, 154, 155, 223
Strasser, Otto, 69, 98
Strauss, Alice (née Grab) (daughter-in-law), 73, 88, 89–90, 101, 103, 108, 109, 112, 113, 190
Strauss, Christian (grandson), 91, 101
Strauss, Franz Joseph (father), 1, 2, 6, 7, 12, 13, 15, 20, 24, 26, 37, 40, 42, 118, 223
Strauss, Franz ('Bubi') (son), 30, 65, 72, 73, 79, 98, 101, 103, 112, 176
Strauss II, Johann, 11, 107
Strauss, Johanna (sister), 6, 13, 16, 102
Strauss, Josephine (mother), 1, 6, 12–13, 31
Strauss, Pauline (née de Ahna) (wife), 16, 17, 18, 21–2, 23, 25–8, 29, 30, 40, 43, 52, 53, 65, 66, 74, 75–6, 77, 78, 81, 93, 101, 102, 103, 109, 110, 111, 112, 113, 115, 126–7, 129, 130, 149, 154–5, 157, 162, 176, 186–7, 188, 189, 190, 191, 192, 195
Strauss, Richard (grandson), 91, 101, 104
Strauss, Richard Georg,

LIFE
Accompanist, 72, 186–7
Appearance, 19, 33, 45, 70
Attitude to own music, 4–5, 9, 17–18, 20, 37, 43, 46, 61, 81, 120
Childhood, 1–6
Conducting, 9, 10, 11, 14–16, 18, 20–3, 28–31, 40–1, 44–6, 50, 59, 66, 70–1, 73, 81–2, 86
Courtship, marriage, and family, 16–17, 25–8, 29–31, 40, 66, 75–6, 98, 103, 104, 111–12, 129–30, 154–5
Friendship with Thuille, 3–5

Greece, admiration for, 23, 169, 189
Honorary degrees, 56, 112
Illnesses, 22, 23, 65, 102, 110, 111, 112, 113
Librettists, work with, 38–9, 47–8, 51–2, 54–7, 61–2, 68, 77–9, 82–4, 86–7, 91, 92, 95–7, 98–9, 99–100
Mahler, friendship with, 15–16, 37, 42
Money, attitude to, 34, 41, 44, 67, 71–2, 73, 74, 111
Performing rights, work for, 34, 90
Skat, 8, 23, 64, 73, 102, 155
Third Reich, relationship with, 87–94, 96, 101, 102–4, 107–8, 108–9, 112
Vienna, house in, 73–4, 101, 109–10
War, attitude to, 58–9, 66, 103, 193

CLASSIFIED WORKS
Instrumental
Allegretto in E, 215
Aus alter Zeit, 215
Daphne-Etude, 215
Five Piano Pieces, 6, 9, 115, 215
Hochzeitspräludium, 215
Pianoforte Quartet, 9, 13, 112, 215
Pianoforte Sonata in B minor, 6, 115
Schneiderpolka, 2, 215
Stimmungsbilder, 116, 215
String Quartet in A, 6, 215
Suite from Capriccio, 215
Violin Sonata, 17, 112, 117–18, 215
Violoncello Sonata, 7, 8, 9, 16, 116, 215

Melodramas
Das Schloss am Meere, 215
Enoch Arden, 30, 215

Orchestral
Alpensinfonie, Eine, 5, 57, 59, 70, 130–1, 185, 192, 193, 214
Also sprach Zarathustra, 29–30, 35, 70, 97, 125, 128, 133, 136, 149, 213, 229
Aus Italien, 14–15, 40, 121, 213
Burleske, 13, 20–1, 110, 118–19, 176, 214
Divertimento (Couperin), 214
Don Juan, 19, 20, 21, 36, 59, 72, 104, 110, 116, 117, 121–3, 128, 184, 213, 229
Don Quixote, 30, 110, 125–6, 129, 130, 132, 142, 154, 167, 170, 213, 224, 229
Duett-Concertino, 111, 166, 182–3, 215
Fanfare, 214
Feierliche Einzug, 178, 214
Festliches Präludium, 178, 214
Festmarsch No. 1 in E flat, 6, 213
Festmarsch No. 2 in C, 213
Festmusik (Vienna), 214
Festmusik (Weimar), 23, 179, 213
Heldenleben, Ein, 31, 35, 36, 59, 110, 125–9, 154, 156, 166, 184, 192, 214, 229
Hochlands Treue, 213

Horn Concerto No. 1, 9, 10, 118, 214
Horn Concerto No. 2, 102, 180, 215
Japanische Festmusik, 178, 214
Josephslegende Fragment, 214
Kampf und Sieg, 178
Königsmarsch, 178, 214
Macbeth, 17–18, 21, 23, 110, 121, 180, 213, 229
Metamorphosen, 106–7, 109, 181–2, 214
2 Military Marches, 214
München, 106, 107, 179, 181, 214
Oboe Concerto, 108–9, 166, 181, 215
Overture in A minor, 4–5
Overture in C minor, 7, 8, 213
Panathenäenzug, 177, 215
Parergon zur Symphonia Domestica, 79, 176, 214
Romance in E flat for clarinet, 4, 214
Romance in F for cello, 214
Rosenkavalier waltzes, 107, 110, 179, 214
Schlagobers suite, 214
Serenade in E flat, 7, 8, 9, 116, 213, 224
Serenade in G, 213
Sonatina No. 1 in F, 102, 180, 214
Sonatina No. 2 in E flat, 108, 180, 214
Suite in B flat, 9, 116, 213
Suite, *Le bourgeois Gentilhomme (Der Bürger als Edelmann)*. See under Stage Works
Symphonia Domestica, 40–1, 72, 79, 98, 104, 110, 129–30, 149, 155, 156, 176, 192, 214
Symphonic Fantasy, *Die Frau ohne Schatten*, 110, 214
Symphonic Interludes from *Intermezzo*, 214
Symphony No. 1 in D minor, 6, 117, 213
Symphony No. 2 in F minor, 7, 10, 117, 120, 213
Tanzsuite (Couperin), 177–8, 179, 214
Till Eulenspiegels lustige Streiche, 29, 37, 72, 104, 111, 118, 123–5, 129, 132, 167, 172, 213, 224, 229
Tod und Verklärung, 19, 21, 23, 30, 104, 113, 123, 193, 195, 213, 223, 229
Violin Concerto, 7, 116, 214
Wiener Philharmoniker Fanfare, 214

Songs and Choral
Abend, Der, 184, 216
Allerseelen, 9, 187, 217
All'mein Gedanken, 72, 188, 217
Alphorn, Ein, 187, 217
An den Baum Daphne, 102, 186, 216
Arbeitsmann, Der, 190, 218
Bächlein, Das, 194, 220
Bardengesang, 59, 185, 216
Befreit, 190, 218, 229
Beim schlafengehen, 112, 195, 220

Besinnung, 112
3 Bierbaum *Lieder* (Op. 29), 188–9, 217
Blauer Sommer, 189, 218
Blick von oberen Belvedere, 220
6 Brentano *Lieder* (Op. 68), 192–3, 219
Cäcilie, 28, 188, 217
Cantata, 216
2 *Choruses* (Op. 42), 216
3 *Choruses* (Op. 45), 216
5 Dahn *Lieder* (Op. 21), 188, 217
Deutsche Motette, 185, 216
Du meines Herzen Krönelein, 188, 217
Einerlei, 193, 219
Einkehr, 191, 218
Electra, 6, 215
6 *Folk-Songs*, 216
Four Last Songs. See *Vier letzte Lieder*
Freundliche Vision, 191, 218
Frühling, 112, 195, 220, 223
Frühlingsfeier, 192, 219
Gefunden, 191, 219
Gesang der Apollopriesterin, 189, 218
4 *Gesänge* (Op. 33), 189, 218
3 *Gesänge* (Op. 43), 190, 218
5 *Gesänge des Orients* (Op. 77), 194, 220
9 Gilm *Lieder* (Op. 10), 9, 187–8, 217
3 Goethe *Lieder* (Op. 67), 192, 219
Göttin im Putzzimmer, Die, 185–6, 216
Graf vom Rom, Der, 219
2 *grössere Gesänge* (Op. 44), 190–1, 218
Hab' ich euch denn je geraten?, 192, 219
Hat gesagt, 189, 218
Heiligen drei Könige, Die, 192, 219
Heimkehr, 188, 217
Heimliche Aufforderung, 28, 188, 217
Himmelsboten, 189, 218
Hochzeitlich Lied, 41n, 218
3 Hölderlin *Hymnen* (Op. 71), 193–4, 219
Hymne (Rückert), 184, 216
Ich liebe dich, 190, 218
Ich sehe wie in einem Spiegel, 191, 218
Ich trage meine Minne, 189, 218
Ich wollt ein Sträusslein binden, 193, 219
Im Abendrot, 111–12, 195, 220
Im Spätboot, 191–2, 219
In der Campagna, 190, 218
Junghexenlied, 187, 190, 218
5 *kleine Lieder* (Op. 69), 193, 219
Kling!, 191, 218
Krämerspiegel (Op. 66), 171, 172, 192, 219, 222
Leises Lied, 190, 218
Lied der Frauen, 193, 219
Lied des Steinklopfers, 191, 219
5 *Lieder* (Op. 15), 188, 217
4 *Lieder* (Op. 27), 28, 188, 217
4 *Lieder* (Op. 31), 189, 218

Index

Strauss, Richard Georg (*cont.*):
 5 *Lieder* (Op. 32), 189, 218
 4 *Lieder* (Op. 36), 189, 218
 6 *Lieder* (Op. 37), 30, 41n, 190, 218
 5 *Lieder* (Op. 39), 190, 218
 5 *Lieder* (Op. 41), 190, 218
 5 *Lieder* (Op. 48), 191, 218–19
 8 *Lieder* (Op. 49), 191, 219
 6 *Lieder* (Op. 56), 191–2, 219
 Malven, 112, 194, 220, 222
 Mein Auge, 190, 218
 Meinem Kinde, 30, 190, 218
 Mein Herz ist Stumm, 188, 217
 Mit deinen blauen Augen, 191, 219
 Morgen!, 28, 30, 188, 195, 217
 Morgenrot, 191, 218
 3 *Mutterlieder*, 187, 218
 Muttertändelei, 190, 218
 Nacht, Die, 9, 187, 217
 Nächtlicher Gang, 190, 218
 Notturno, 190–1, 218
 Olympic Hymn, 92, 216
 3 'Ophelia' *Lieder* (Op. 67), 192, 219
 Rosenband, Das, 189, 218
 5 Rückert *Gedichte* (Op. 46), 191, 218
 Rückleben, 191, 218
 Ruhe, meine Seele, 28, 188, 195, 217
 Säusle, liebe Myrthe, 193, 219
 6 Schack *Lieder* (Op. 17), 188, 217
 6 Schack *Lieder* (Op. 19), 188, 217
 Schlechtes Wetter, 193, 219
 Schwäbische Erbschaft, 215
 Sehnsucht, 189, 218
 September, 112, 195, 220
 Soldatenlied (1878), 217
 Soldatenlied (1899), 216
 Spielmann und sein Kind, Der, 187, 217
 Ständchen, 17, 188, 217
 Stern, Der, 193, 219
 Stiller Gang, 189, 218
 Tageszeiten, Die, 186, 216
 Taillefer, 38, 184, 216
 Traum durch die Dämmerung, 188–9, 217,
  221, 229
 5 Uhland *Lieder* (Op. 47), 191, 218
 Verführung, 189, 218
 Vier letzte Lieder, 112, 113, 194–6, 220, 222
 Waldseligkeit, 191, 219
 Wandrers Sturmlied, 9, 184, 215
 Wie erkenn' ich mein Treulieb?, 192, 219
 Wiegenlied, 190, 218
 Wiegenliedchen, 191, 219
 Wie sollten wir geheim sie halten?, 188, 217
 Winterliebe, 191, 219
 Winterweihe, 191, 219
 Wozu noch, Mädchen?, 188, 217
 Zueignung, 9, 187–8, 217

Zugemessne Rhythmen, 194, 220

Stage (Operas and Ballets)
Ägyptische Helena, Die, 70, 74, 78–9, 80–1,
  82, 85, 91, 157–9, 160, 162, 167, 168,
  180, 212, 221, 222
Arabella, 70, 82–3, 87, 88–9, 95, 98, 101,
  109, 115, 145, 153, 159–61, 162, 168,
  172, 179, 180, 191, 212, 221, 222, 224
Ariadne auf Naxos (first version), 51–4, 62,
  89, 144, 153, 179, 212, 222 (second
  version), 54–5, 59–60, 62, 63, 64, 65, 66,
  68, 70, 73, 97, 104, 133, 144–7, 154, 162,
  167, 170, 179, 185, 212, 221, 222
*Bourgeois Gentilhomme, Le (Der Bürger als
  Edelmann)*, 52, 64–5, 75, 77, 98, 110, 113,
  116, 144, 147–8, 156, 178, 212, 213, 214
Capriccio, 95, 99–100, 100–1, 102, 104,
  113, 145, 156, 168, 169–73, 178, 179,
  182, 185, 192, 194, 212, 222, 224
Daphne, 96, 97–8, 102, 131, 152, 165–7,
  168, 170, 171, 172, 173, 174, 180, 212,
  221, 222, 224
Elektra, 44–6, 48, 49, 55, 66, 69, 70, 71, 80,
  89, 91, 111, 136–9, 140, 146, 148, 151,
  153, 167, 175, 179, 180, 191, 196, 212,
  221, 222, 223
Feuersnot, 36–7, 39, 110, 132–4, 147, 179,
  192, 212, 221, 223, 224
Frau ohne Schatten, Die, 51–2, 56–7, 58–9,
  61, 62–3, 68, 70, 73, 80, 85, 126, 148–53,
  167, 168, 174, 179, 185, 191, 192, 212,
  222
Friedenstag, 95–7, 112, 163–4, 165, 174,
  180, 212, 222, 224
Guntram, 19, 23–6, 29, 54, 123, 128, 132,
  134, 180, 212, 229
Intermezzo, 38, 40, 65, 71, 75–6, 77, 85,
  145, 154–7, 168, 170, 180, 192, 212, 221,
  223
Josephslegende, 55–6, 73, 153, 175–6, 185,
  213
Kythere (unfinished), 36, 39, 175
Liebe der Danae, Die, 70, 78, 96, 98–9, 100,
  104–5, 106, 126, 167–9, 170, 172, 173,
  174, 178, 180, 212, 222, 224
Rosenkavalier, Der, 17, 47–50, 51, 54, 56,
  57, 61, 66, 68, 70, 73, 74, 77, 79, 82, 83,
  88, 112, 113, 130, 133, 138, 139–44, 145,
  147, 155, 156, 159, 160, 162, 166, 169,
  170, 172, 179, 180, 185, 212, 221, 222,
  223
Rosenkavalier, Der (film), 79–80, 178, 179,
  221
Salome, 36, 41–4, 49, 55, 69, 71, 73, 79, 87,
  98, 134–5, 136, 139, 146, 149, 155, 167,
  175, 179, 180, 189, 212, 221, 223
Salomé (French version), 42–3

Schlagobers, 74, 75, 77, 176, 213, 214
Schweigsame Frau, Die, 86–7, 91, 93, 108,
   162–3, 165, 168, 180, 212, 221, 224
Verklungene Feste, 178, 213
Stravinsky, Igor, 1, 55, 56, 74, 147, 148, 175,
   177
Szell, Georg, 68

Tauber, Richard, 69, 70, 78, 147
Thomas, Theodore, 7
Thuille, Ludwig, 3–5, 8
Toller, Georg, 49
Tombo, August, 2
Tortelier, Paul, 110
Toscanini, Arturo, 43, 88, 89, 93

Uhland, Ludwig, 184, 191, 215, 216, 219
Ursuleac, Viorica, 77, 88, 91, 97, 98, 100,
   101, 161, 169, 188, 193, 194, 222, 223–4

Vaughan Williams, Ralph, 147, 152, 175
Verdi, Giuseppe, 14, 26, 107, 109, 156, 162,
   196
Vienna, 7, 15, 32, 48, 50, 71, 73–4, 83, 91, 97,
   101, 103, 104, 109, 139
   Opera, 32, 37, 38, 43, 45, 46, 49–50, 59, 60,
   66, 67–9, 71, 73–5, 77, 80, 86, 87, 89, 98,
   105, 106, 107, 153, 222, 223
   Philharmonic Orchestra, 8, 21, 67, 69, 71,
   74, 98, 101, 102, 104, 111
Vogl, Heinrich, 29

Wagner, Cosima, 18, 20, 22, 24, 30–1, 33
Wagner, Richard, 1, 2, 9, 10, 12, 15, 24, 35,
   36, 37, 54, 59, 94, 107, 109,112, 116, 180,
   194, 223, 224
   Feen, Die, 18
   Fliegende Holländer, Der, 21, 69
   Lohengrin, 18, 21, 23, 69, 89
   Meistersinger von Nürnberg, Die, 28, 36–7,
   55, 102, 132, 139, 144, 196, 221
   Parsifal, 7, 14, 89, 91, 116, 132, 153, 156,
   222

Rienzi, 21, 35, 107
Ring des Nibelungen, Der, 2, 35, 147
Siegfried, 3
Tannhäuser, 18, 21, 28, 69, 132
Tristan und Isolde, 2, 14, 18, 22–3, 28, 34,
   36, 68, 102, 112, 118, 147, 156, 170, 181,
   221
Walküre, Die, 4, 113, 120, 224
Wagner, Siegfried, 89
Wagner, Winifred, 89, 90
Walker, Edyth, 45, 49
Wallerstein, Lothar, 80, 85, 91, 158, 213
Walter, Benno, 2, 6, 7, 29
Walter, Bruno, 89, 91, 93
Weber, Carl Maria von, 2, 21, 107, 115, 117,
   178
   Freischütz, Der, 2, 34, 51, 69, 102
Weber, Ludwig, 97
Weidt, Lucie, 49, 68, 153
Weimar, 18, 19, 20–3, 24–6, 47, 178, 179,
   213
Weingartner, Felix von, 10, 31, 32, 67, 69, 80,
   94
Welitsch, Ljuba, 104
Wihan, Dora, 16–17, 18, 20, 188
Wihan, Hanuš, 16, 116
Wilde, Oscar, 41, 42, 44, 134, 139, 212
Wilhelm II, Kaiser, 32, 34, 43, 44, 60, 87, 90,
   185
Wilhelm, Kurt, 103
Wittgenstein, Paul, 79 and n, 176, 177
Wittich, Marie, 43
Wolff, Hermann, 9, 26
Wolzogen, Ernst von, 36–7, 212, 224
Wüllner, Franz, 7, 10, 29, 30, 224
Wurmser, Leo, 81, 111n

Zeller, Heinrich, 21, 23, 25
Zemlinsky, Alexander, 69
Zürich, 30, 98, 107, 109, 194
Zweig, Stefan, 68, 81, 82, 86–7, 91–4, 95–7,
   99, 106, 161, 162, 165, 167, 169, 212,
   223, 224